The Walker, Acrylic on canvas by Sonja Kandels

1958 2008

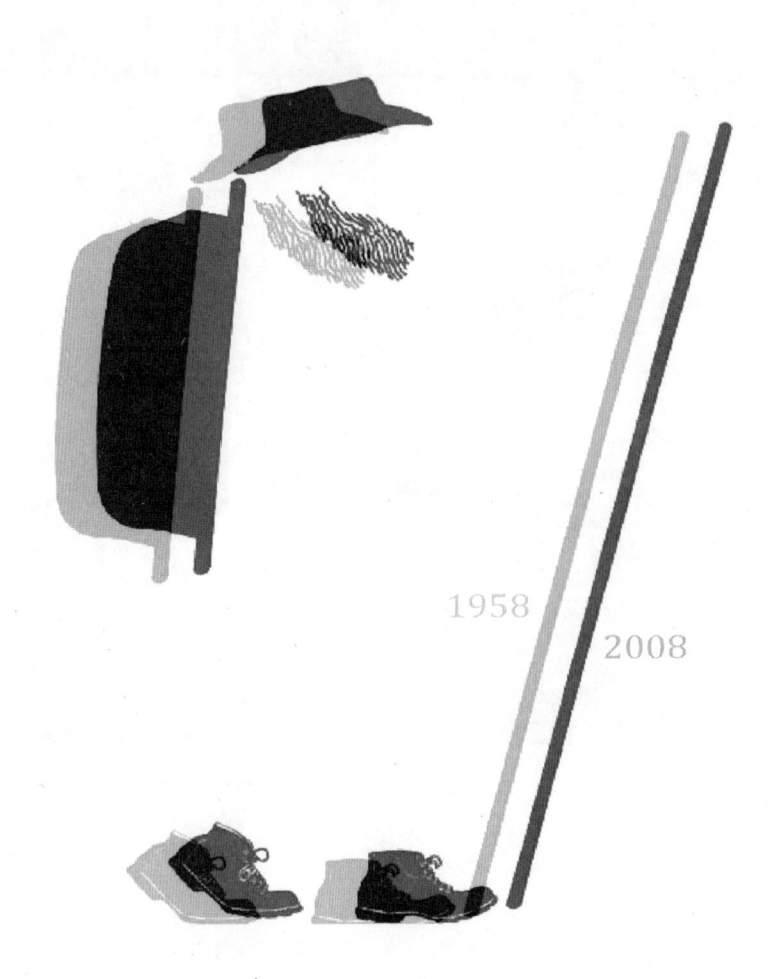

The Thousand-Mile Summer Revisited
by Andreas M. Cohrs

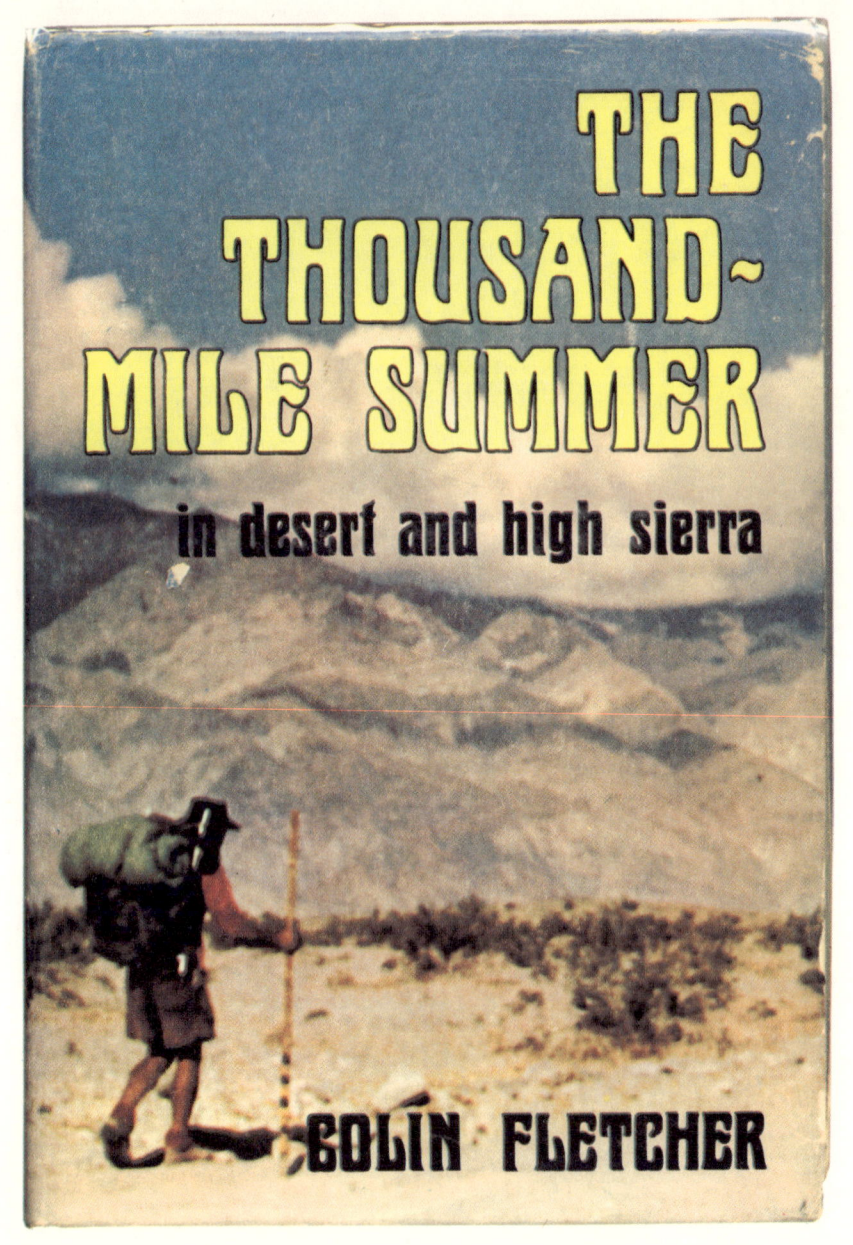

Original hardcover: Howell-North Books, Berkeley, California 1964

ANDREAS M. COHRS

CALIFORNIA SERENDIPITY
IN DESERT AND HIGH SIERRA

Retracing Colin Fletcher's epic walk of 1958
"The Thousand-Mile Summer"

With photographs
by the author

LINDEMANN
TRAVELBOOKS

COLITA PUBLISHING

First Print Edition, 2012
Copyright © 2012 by Andreas M. Cohrs
Maps copyright © by David Lindroth Inc.

All rights reserved under International Pan-American Copyright Conventions.
No part of this book may be reproduced in any form without written permission
from the publisher, except for brief quotations used in critical reviews.

Published in the United States and Germany
by COLITA Publishing and Lindemann Travel Books (Info Verlag GmbH).
Grateful acknowledgement is made to the MDHCA for permission to use
the cultural archives and the Dennis G. Casebier Memorial Library.

Photographs by the author except pages 379/1., 388/3. by Dennis Casebier
and photos on facing pages 8, 9 by Colin Fletcher with friendly permission
by the University of California Santa Cruz.

Book design by Andreas Cohrs

Walked & written in Califrnia
Printed by Creative Print Production, Hungary

The connoisseur of Colin Fletcher's original Thousand-Mile Summer may find various passages
that either quote him or were written in his spirit. However, it is not the author's intention
to simply copy the forerunner but to pick up some of his thoughts.

Library of Congress Control Number: 2012935732

Bibliographic information published by the Deutsche Nationalbibliothek
The Deutsche Nationalbibliothek lists this publication in the Deutsche Nationalbibliografie;
detailed bibliographic data are available in the Internet at http://dnb.dnb.de.

U.S.: ISBN: 978-0-9853803-0-4
E.U.: ISBN: 978-3-88190-680-7

For more information, photos, tours, special sales, please visit:
www.colinfletcher.com
www.1000milesummer.com

Los Angeles, CA
Karlsruhe, Germany

To Nathan

For afterwards a man finds pleasure in his pains,
when he has suffered long and wandered long.
So I will tell you what you ask and seek to know.
HOMER, THE ODYSSEY

1958–2008 In the footsteps of the Walker. Colin Fletcher/Andreas M.Cohrs
1. first steps at the U.S./Mexican Border   2. pausing at a brand new/old car

3. gone fishing in the Northern Sierra   4. arriving at the Oregon border
Photos by Colin Fletcher with friendly permission by the UCSC, Special Collections and Archives.

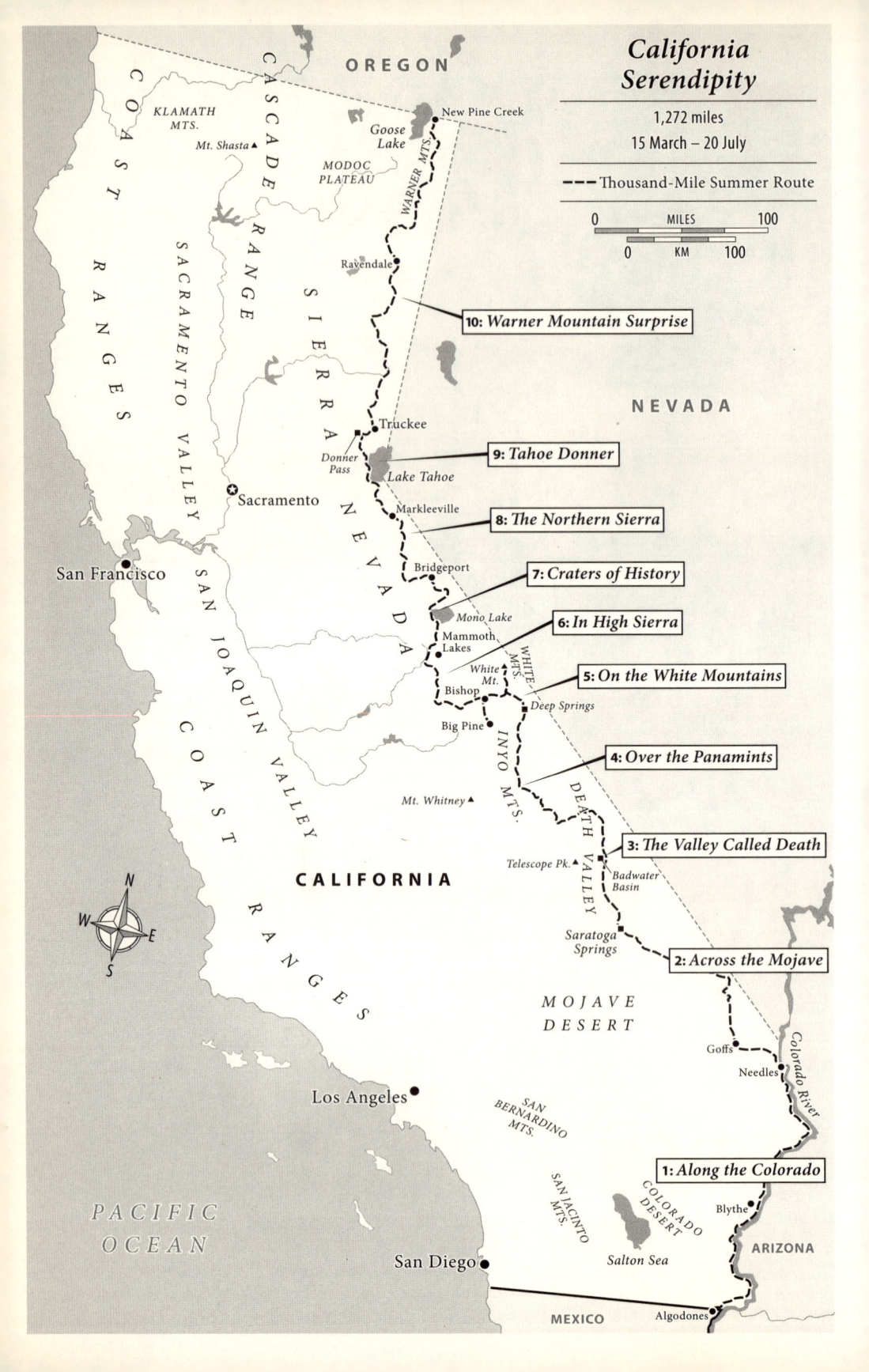

California Serendipity

1,272 miles
15 March – 20 July

- - - - Thousand-Mile Summer Route

1: Along the Colorado
2: Across the Mojave
3: The Valley Called Death
4: Over the Panamints
5: On the White Mountains
6: In High Sierra
7: Craters of History
8: The Northern Sierra
9: Tahoe Donner
10: Warner Mountain Surprise

TABLE OF CONTENT

Prolog 12

Intro   CALIFORNIA & SERENDIPITY 26

One   ALONG THE COLORADO 30

Two   ACROSS THE MOJAVE 92

Three   THE VALLEY CALLED DEATH 124

Four   OVER THE PANAMINTS 144

Five   ON THE WHITE MOUNTAINS 180

Six   IN HIGH SIERRA 208

Seven   CRATERS OF HISTORY 244

Eight   THE NORTHERN SIERRA 270

Nine   TAHOE DONNER 292

Ten   WARNER MOUNTAIN SURPRISE 312

Addenda & accolades 352
DISTANCES, EQUIPMENT, BIBLIOGRAPHY, CREDITS

The longest journey begins with a simple step.

老子 LAO TSE, CHINESE PHILOSOPHER, 6TH CENTURY BC

PROLOG

GOFFS! What sounds like a noise balloon in a Louis L'Amour comic or a *Marvel*-lous 'Phew! I made it!' is in reality a ghost town in the middle of the Mojave Desert. It became the linchpin for a thousand-mile journey through California in the footsteps of backpacking icon and outdoor guru Colin Fletcher.

GOFFS! – I made it! One thousand miles on foot through untamed wilderness and a string of small towns in the east of California, succeeding Alaska and Texas as the third largest state of the united fifty. The first half led me through deserts and rugged canyons, the other half into the snow-covered Sierra, starting with a decent climb on White Mountain, from where I overlooked both desert and Sierra from 14,246 feet.

And – GOFFS! – I didn't reckon what happens to yourself when you set off for a voyage like that. Walking for four months, you end up not just hiking the land; day after day, you journey more into your inner world and learn about yourself, your strengths and weaknesses, your likes and dislikes, your needs and your attitudes. After that you won't be the same anymore.

I knew exactly what Fletcher meant when he wrote about how he got the call of the wild, that ideas bursting at you at three o'clock in the morning "have a despicable habit of losing their luster in daylight," even if they pretended to change your life. I have had quite a few early morning eurekas in my life, sort of providing you with ultimate solutions for all-day life, or things you always wanted to do. However, not very often are you blessed with Bonaparte's three-o'clock-in-the-morning-courage that makes you instantaneously put them into action. As for me, usually, right before I would leave the house for work, they had disappeared or were flushed away with the coffee grounds, giving way to the daily life they were supposed to change.

On a Sunday morning in July 2006, I was hit by such an idea and this time, Bonaparte was with me. The evening before, I had finished the first chapter of an old book I found while perusing a flea market – Fletcher's report about his 1958 *Thousand-Mile Summer*, a six-month walk from the Mexican border to the Oregon state line. Like a sky clearing off, a plan began to develop in my mind overnight, and between dreams and the smell of coffee, I knew what I had to do.

I was in any case ready for a time out and another longer hiking trip. Every some five years, I feel the urge to dissociate from urban life and set out for a wilderness adventure, as Fletcher described it, to choose solitude as my residence and live for a while a more practical life, meaning a challenging and stimulating rather than a safe and comfortable life. When I started dreaming of mountains and canyons nightly, I knew it was about time. After almost six years of struggling with traffic, alleged business partners and a general sensory overload in the heart of Berlin, I longed for the tonic of wildness, and I felt I needed a break and time to think and speak to myself, before making any further steps. American naturalist Henry David Thoreau once explained his two year solitude experience in the woods with: "You hear from everyone else; how long since you heard from yourself?"* In this sense, I was ready to listen.

Late in the evening, I had read Fletcher's last sentences and understood his fear that California would never be the same, that his trip could never be repeated. But by that time, I was also sure that I wanted to do exactly this, repeat his journey fifty years later and see if he was right. It was somehow logical for me to choose this as a hiking idea; not only because I always try to include a historical aspect to my travels, like following a gold rush trail, an emigrants' wagon train route, or the Camino Real, but also because I have spent a lot of free time and vacation in the Golden State since I was allowed to leave home in Germany and travel overseas for the first time. In fact, I had just started tinkering with the idea of relocating, so what would be more natural than to walk the state I was about to call home?

With almost two years time to prepare it, I would try to contact the famed *Walker* and ask for his ideological support. My plan was to accurately follow in his footsteps, and since his book only gave a vague idea of where exactly he walked, I would need his maps, his advice, and maybe some good stories to replicate.

---

* Henry David Thoreau, American author, naturalist, social critic, philosopher, 1817–1862 (For further information, please read footnote at the end of this chapter.)

Time flew by; a year had passed without a letter from Fletcher's publishing company or from the writer himself. It turned summer of 2007; I had just arrived at Los Angeles to visit a good friend and applied myself to my usual welcome-ceremony, having a coffee at the neighborhood coffee shop while browsing through the L.A. Times. Having half-emptied my cup, I was utterly shocked when I turned over the page and found Fletcher's obituary. Just like the validity time of this daily newspaper, my idea began to disappear, the clear sky from last summer darkened with grey clouds.

After complications from head injury, sustained from being hit by a car six years earlier, the Walker had passed away. Although I had not met him personally, it hit me like a hammer. I poured away the coffee grounds, and through the coincidence of my arrival and this news, I felt that my idea had lost its luster too.

When I returned to Germany two weeks later, the pile of California maps was soon snowed under with work. People were readily assuring me that anyway it would not have been possible to leave work and home for such a lengthy journey. Ventures like that are generally most difficult to argue for at home. Since dreams are commonly personal, individual issues, the idea of transmuting them into reality and what it would mean to you can only be understood by yourself. As long as you are just dreaming, people may be lenient, attesting you to be a *visionary*, though with a smile. However, as soon as you begin to plan and suit the action to the word, you find yourself being labeled as a *dreamer*.

Looking for a change would be the last reason you want to mention, since it would exasperate all those who never even thought about the possibility of a change. The more personal importance you attach to it, the more people get anxious you might be on a journey of escapism, or even worse, of self-discovery, the latter amounting to a state where professional attendance would be advised. Quoting Einstein, "You can recognize a really good idea by the fact that its implementation seems impossible in the first place", might help yourself to keep at your idea, whereas others certainly take offense to such *nonsense*.

Fletcher had found an easy answer to it, discovering the state he had just moved to. Another motive for him was that he had been dating a woman in San Francisco, "a very big deal for me," he described it in an interview, and he had to make up his mind whether to marry her or not. Although I was in a comparably precarious situation, I did not expect to solve the problem by being absent. And, of course, no one else at home would have.

Half a year later, my good friend Nathan called me from L.A., asking if I could show up again, he needed to talk to me. When I came back to California around Christmas to see him, I received shocking news again. He broke it to me that he had cancer, and a little more than two weeks, two months, or two years to live. The fact that he mentioned a possible end at all scared me much more than any period of time. Our thoughts only accepted the latter, two years plus, and despite – or perhaps because of – that fact, we were hungrily swallowing the city's variety and frequenting its blues and jazz bars, until I felt that I approached something like a sub-cultural – maybe emotional – overkill. With Nathan feeling as strong as a bear, on the morning of New Year's Eve, I decided that I should allow myself some privacy. I wanted to leave the city lights behind and spend the turn of the year alone in the desert to think about everything, the situation with Nathan, my future plans, and possibly my life. Also I wanted to escape the grueling search for the best party in town, a hopeless quest, since it implicates the certainty that you would miss out on another awesome rave no matter where you go. To me, a certain feeling has always been suggesting that if you retreat to solitude in order to think about something on such an important day, you may gain a better solution.

Early in the morning, I threw a small backpack containing a six-pack, my sleeping bag, and some food in a rental car, left Los Angeles and headed east on I15. On Cajon Summit, where you enter the Mojave Desert, I left the last suburban tentacles of L.A. behind; my mind, all distractions and city amenities. Cruising down the freeway, I thought about that plan I had hatched more than a year ago. I remembered the obituary from the previous summer stating that Fletcher did not leave family. The attempt to google and contact people from his circle, who just might have known a little more about what happened to his belongings, had failed. He had lived an analog life, unlinked from the world of Facebook, Twitter or LinkedIns. My chances of getting access to his material and retrace his route with his maps and diaries now seemed utterly impossible.

Anyway, on this significant day I just wanted to spend one night under a star filled desert sky, provoking my destiny for a *providentia dei*, an intuition whether I should set off for that big adventure all the same or stay home and let the lure of sedentary comfort prevail over my pioneering spirit.

At Barstow, I left the freeway and turned onto old Route 66 for a nostalgic cruise along lost cities and forgotten sites. On my map they had names, but in reality you would at best find a handful of decayed buildings, abandoned gas stations, motels and general stores – modern ghost towns, bearing mute witness to the heyday of Route 66. Today, even the ghosts had left most of these places, probably swept away by the ever-blowing strong desert winds that howl through the streets. Stopping here and there, I could hear windows cracking and roof beams creaking, and a wind pump rhythmically sighing with the wind, all singing the lament of nostalgia.

On a forlorn road junction, there stood a lonely Mexican guy selling beef jerky, honey, and dried fruits to whoever might find his way out here. I asked him about what was going on in this part of California, what people would do here this time of the year. But all he could tell was, go to Laughlin or Vegas, the two gambling towns across the Nevada border. I didn't dare to bother him with my solitude plan for the night, being quite sure he would not understand why anyone would sleep between creosote and sage on New Year's Eve. So I left with some jerky and journeyed into the dusk.

Drifting down on a dark desert highway, I reached a forlorn general store, abandoned and almost collapsed, right at a level crossing of the Burlington Northern Santa Fe main line from L.A. to Albuquerque. Here, I would turn onto a dirt road taking me right into the Mojave Preserve, where I could start a contemplative campfire in a remote desert canyon to think about my friend's situation and muse about vague opportunities.

Being just 200 yards from the railroad crossing, the red signal lights started flashing, along with a high-pitched bell tearing the desert silence. While the crossing gates began to lower, I parked the car and walked closer to the tracks to await the rumbling spectacle. There it came, with greeting headlights, thundering, announcing its already unmistakable presence with four deafening whistles, long-long-short-long. The cool wind in my hair was suddenly blown away by the hot head wind of six diesel engines. Rumbling like an earthquake, they delivered a last extra-long whistle. In passing, its melody changed to a lower sound, as if it was introducing the seemingly unending line of loads; an awe-inspiring parade of engineering power, appealing to all senses. Four minutes later, the last of 140 cars had cleared the crossing, the gates rose back toward the sky, the bells fell silent as if nothing had happened. Only a single red tail light vanishing in the dark gave testimony to the transient commotion.

Behind the gates, the desert seemed to be opened for me and somehow, I felt, I was expected. From my car stereo I heard a familiar tune, the "warm smell of colitas rising up through the air". I jumped back in the car, turned up the volume and hit the cutoff road into the night.

It was a road with no designation – one of these undetermined, interrupted lines on a map, where you can never be sure whether you will reach your destination or get stuck somewhere. These roads are maintained only intermittently, and every so often they give in to natural hazards of biblical proportions, flooded by thunderstorms, buried by sandstorms or blizzards, or just broken up by extreme temperature variation. On the other side, with uncertainties like that, these less traveled back roads suggest a feeling of freedom and adventure, titillating the pioneering spirit, precisely because you might be dependent on yourself. In any case, rather than a highway, they tend to be ways of surprises.

Once more I hit the gas and whizzed past some old houses at 55 mph, obviously another desert ghost town. But wait, one of the houses was brightly lit, and I thought I had seen some 15 or 20 people standing inside as if they were holding a ceremony. I was driving too fast to catch what was really going on. But the farther I veered away the more I was wondering about that scene. What could those people do there, on New Year's Eve, in the middle of the desert? After ten miles my curiosity had grown childlike. What I saw seemed to be somehow unreal and an inner voice told me to turn around and check it out. I remembered that, usually, the more obscure something appeared to me at first sight the more positive the surprise has been once I got to the bottom of it.

Steve McQueen would have been proud as I pulled a 180 in the desert sand and headed back to that ghost town. I thought about what I wanted to do there, just walk in and say, "hello, what are you doing here", or should I sneak up to the house? Way before I arrived at the illuminated building, I slowed down, turned off the radio, and looked for a place to park. I pulled into a driveway at a large ranch-style wooden gate. On the archway above it was written in bold letters: 'STUDY THE PAST'. Some yards down the road there was a town sign, 'Established 1883 – Elevation 2595 – Population 23 – GOFFS, California'.

I backed the car to the curb in order to be able to escape if necessary, just in case, and I tried to avoid any further noise. I looked over to the well-lit house but could not see the windows from here. Unusually high creosote bushes were blocking my view. For a moment, I paused and held my breath to hear if my maneuver had called attention – but it was dead silent.

I slowly pulled the key out of the ignition when suddenly an alarm went off – ding ding ding – hectically I put the key back in; I forgot to turn the lights off first. In such moments I hate modern cars. I preferred to be quiet and remain unnoticed until I would have found out what was going on here. In case I decided to leave and drive back into the desert, I did not want to call attention on me. Taking a deep breath as if to shush the car, I turned off the lights, opened the door and – the bell went off again – diding diding diding – the keys! I pulled them out fiercely and at the same time the lights went on again. I took another deep breath, a light breeze came up, and for a short moment, I heard country music coming from the building. Outside, everything seemed to be quiet and, despite my car's auto-centrism, I still undiscovered.

Sneaking through some pine trees, strange enough for the desert, I could see the house and a tilted window. I moved closer, a heavy desert wind was soughing through the trees, but between the gusts I could now hear a distant laughter. I was just about to check the barbwire fence to find an open spot, when suddenly a tall man appeared out of the dark and planted himself before me. "What are you doin' here? Can I help you?" called he with a flashlight the size of a police baton pointing at my face. "Oh, I am sorry, I was just wondering what was going on here on this particular day," I stammered, "in the middle of nowhere. I am just traveling through the desert. Paused at the crossing for a moment."

I explained myself a little more, that I was on a trip from L.A. into the Mojave and that I lost track of time on Route 66. After examining me carefully, looking me over from head to toe, he replied, "Well, OK, young man, it's dark out there and it is the desert. Think about it. If you're ready for the best New Year's Eve party you ever had, come on in," said the man behind the flashlight, who introduced himself as Mr. Sears, and up to the house we went. I looked back to the car, pushed the remote to close it, and with another honk and two winks of the fog lights we entered the house.

When he opened the door to the main room, I thought I found myself in a Steven Spielberg episode of *The Twilight Zone*, where a group of senior citizens meet in a ghost town, to become – with the help of witchcraft – children again, just waiting to play kick-the-can. There were some twenty people, ladies and gentlemen, sitting around a large table and laughing, and a band of four playing traditional American songs and Country and Western tunes. Out of the kitchen came another gentlemen who could well have been the reincarnated Wild Bill Hickok. However, his hands were loaded with pots and bowls that were filled with fresh cooked vegetables, potatoes and beef; much to my relief, the matching colts were missing. Mr. Sears handed me a plate, silverware, and a glass, and he invited me to help myself and join the festivities.

I cannot leave the dinnerware unmentioned, though. The plate was paper, the knife silver with two swash initials. The fork was plastic and the spoon beyond words and probably found along an old emigrants' trail across the desert. In a former life the glass might have been a mustard or jelly jar. But the home-cooked food was so delicious that the various origins of the utensils served only to underline the quality. There was red wine, cold beer, something sweeter than champagne, ice-cold lemonade and hot tea.

When the band paused to join us for another dinner course, I was introduced to the circle of friends. I completed Sears' story of our barbwire conversation with my idea to walk in the footsteps of that late American author, Colin Fletcher. While I was talking, I felt I was listening to myself and wondering if I just wanted to tell a good story and if in fact I had not already dismissed my plan. "Oh how nice, " everybody applauded, and with a mutual clinking of glasses, cups, and mugs I was accepted and welcomed to the company at table.

I had been seated next to an honorable gentleman, who introduced himself as Dennis Casebier, joined by his wife Jo Ann. I assumed that either he or the other gentleman opposing me must be the chief of this gathering. Red Brooke, a 1924 vintage, could tell the older stories while Dennis Casebier came up with the anecdotes in passing. When I had finished my introduction, Casebier leaned over to me saying that he had met this guy, Colin Fletcher, and that we should have a little talk later. I was getting exited. Would the twilight zone aspect of this meeting cast its spell over me too?

The band lined up for a set of bluegrass, Wild Bill brought the desserts and my gaze was fixed on the cutlery beside my plate, a plastic fork and a Sterling knife with two initials. I tried to make them out, but they were calligraphically deformed to an extent that it could have been anything between JF and CS. John Fisher, Charles Smith – or was it CF? The longer I stared at them, in my imagination the curly letters transformed into more sonorous names; names like Jedediah Smith, Charles Frémont, or – Colin Fletcher.

Meanwhile, I was enjoying a New Year's get-together with this eclectic desert society. Most of them were retired persons, who dedicate a lot of their time to preserving the cultural and historical heritage of this part of the American frontier. Every year, they would spend a month or more in Goffs and work on the premises of the Mojave Desert Heritage and Cultural Association, an institution founded by Casebier in the early 1990s, with the aim to prevent the history of the Mojave Desert from being blown into oblivion. The stories of miners and homesteaders, ranchers and gunslingers, or people who just came through, or never made it through, was a part of the American history that threatened to become lost, pushed aside by surrounding superlatives like the Death Valley, the Grand Canyon, or Las Vegas.

How successful this community is in carrying out its mission has recently been confirmed by a grant from the State of California, giving the association half a million dollars to build a historical replica of the old Goffs Railroad Depot, a two-story climate-controlled home for archives and the new library. The other half was donated by the association's 800 members. The Dennis G. Casebier Memorial Library now is home to more than 100,000 historical photos, 3,000 biographies, 1,000 taped interviews with Mojave veterans, and thousands of books and maps.

A couple of hours later – I had been swapping places to discuss a variety of topics covering World War II, the consequences of German reunification, and those of a visit to the Oktoberfest – Casebier beckoned me over and told me to take his wife's chair. He introduced himself again, this time, just Dennis, but as if the subject would not be appropriate to be discussed that evening, he was constantly watching the round of people while giving me a quick report, like in a military briefing, on how he got to know the famous walker. The following day, if I was still around, I would be invited to learn more. During his explanation, he only took his eyes off the people to stare at the silver fork he played with. In a low but clear voice, he outlined that it was in the late sixties when Fletcher, on one of his travels through nearby desert canyons, had intuitively stumbled over a trunk lying in the canyon sand. Close to it, he had found a mountain cave with many more items and evidence that someone had called this place home for a certain period of time in the 1910s. Fletcher had heard about Dennis' historical expertise and eventually asked him for help and research about this person, whom he called 'The Trunkman'. For many years, it was the working title for a manuscript

PROLOG

until, with the results of Dennis' research, *The Man From The Cave* was published in 1981. In his archive, Dennis still had the correspondence about the investigation and some more personal letters and photos. He also remembered having added a map of the area signed by Fletcher, who had come to visit Goffs and the newly founded association some years later. Since he knew that Fletcher had walked through Goffs during the Thousand-Mile Summer of 1958, the author, too, had somehow become part of the local history. Consequently Dennis kept everything he had about Fletcher in the archives of the East Mojave, Goffs, filed under F. Only then, when he finished, for a short moment his fingers turned the fork upside down and I saw the two initials again, CF, and I wondered if someone had set the silverware like that on purpose, one to my plate and one to his, or if it was just a figment of my imagination.

In any way, I hit the bull's eye. Goffs! And I was eager for spending another day here and go through the Fletcher file on the next significant day, New Year's Day.

In the course of the evening, I learned more about Dennis and his association. The new railroad depot was, as he said, the second major success for the former Marine and Navy scientist Casebier. He told me that it was he, who ended the Korean War in July 1953. He had enlisted in the Marines on July 26, bound for Korea. On the following day, North Korea signed the proposed armistice agreement. He presumed they must have heard of him coming.

Dennis told this story so poker-faced and convincingly as only someone living in a remote place like Goffs could do it. In my experience, this level of dry wit seems to be a special talent of people who spend their lives in harsh areas, where the majority of us couldn't even think of staying longer than a night.

Instead of Korea, he had been sent to the base at Twentynine Palms. There, he gained his desert initiation or, how his wife Jo Ann called it, he fell ill with a special form of desert fever and the only cure would be frequent trips to its remotest parts. Exploring the backcountry in his time off, Dennis lost his heart to the Eastern Mojave Desert. He loved the wide, open spaces and the simplicity, and after his professional career with the Navy, he turned back to his beloved, with his love, Jo Ann. They settled down in this forgotten country, bought some 110 acres of land and founded the association. Ever since, they have been dedicating their lives to one of the most outlying places of American geography. For many before him, the Mojave had been a dangerous and hostile area that had to be crossed or bypassed as quickly as possible. For only a few, it was the place to be.

To my left sat the gentleman who was slinging pots and bowls, Phil Motz, and I wasn't quite sure what kind of fellow he was. Leaning away from us, he seemed aloof, as if he were watching the scene askance from afar. His cowboy hat pulled down low, the cold pipe properly placed beside his wine glass, his eyes were wandering across the room. It took me a while to understand his seeming indifference. It was his responsibility on that night to cater the crowd. Every half hour he got up, adjourned to the kitchen and came back with new meals and drinks. He took his job so seriously that there was no time left for chats and jokes. My stomach appreciated his superior focus on the essentials. Months later I would once again know the true promise of his painstaking commitment.

The band played until five minutes to 9, when Jo Ann leaned over me and said, "I am not sure if we mentioned it before, we use to celebrate the New Year at this early hour, for those who don't want to stay up until midnight." I chuckled to myself; out here people were free to set their own time zone. "We celebrate with the capital and in Washington it is midnight now." Two minutes later, all glasses, mugs, and plastic cups were filled with champagne. Behind me, a 15" TV-screen was turned on, and in New York the ball began its descent as some twenty voices united to count down the final seconds of the year in the East Mojave.

Half an hour later everyone got up and made their way to bed. Phil had already arranged my accommodation and when the last guest had left the ballroom, site managers Hugh and Carol Brown showed me the way to my overnight lodging, a three-bedroom house not far from the restored old schoolhouse, where the party took place. Despite the winter cold, its country house-like veranda was inviting enough for me to await the *real* New Year's Day outside on a rocking chair, wrapped in two army blankets, with a six-pack and some pretzels. At the stroke of midnight, another one of the endless freight trains came crawling up the desert grade, saluting the New Year with its whistle. Somewhere near in the darkness of the desert, a coyote chimed in, trying to strike the same note. With the Milky Way flowing liquidly above us and shooting stars within grasp, the desert began to exert its spell over me, too.

On the first morning of the New Year, I walked down to the association's headquarters, located in a replica of the old courthouse. There was hustle and bustle in the office. Dennis, Hugh, and Phil were discussing some issues with Chris Ervin, the association's president, in order to prepare the quarterly board meeting. Dennis handed me a file from the archives labeled *C. Fletcher* and I delved into their correspondence bursting with curiosity. From these letters I got a first insight into the private Colin Fletcher, how he was, how he wrote and thought, and that he had the same sense of humor, desert-dry, slightly intellectual, and not graspable by everyone. And, most importantly, I found the map. More than thirty years after he had walked through Goffs for the first time, Fletcher had visited this little town again, this time in his sports car. The Craigs he had met in 1958 were long gone and the Casebiers had just moved in founding the new association. Dennis had asked him if he wanted to complete the file about him by putting his signature on a map of the Mojave Desert, for historical purposes of course. So Fletcher drew in his 1958 route along with some annotations. This two by two map of the Mojave Desert with a hand-drawn dashed line, numbers for overnight camps, and arrows pointing at "colorful butterflies here" and a "rattlesnake encounter" there, became the first document that would enable me to walk at least a small part in his footsteps, one twentieth of the whole stretch. In the last letter of their correspondence Dennis had written: "Your Thousand Mile Summer has made you a legend in THE LAND OF LITTLE RAIN." I felt, I was one small step closer to reviving the legend.

When they finished their preparatory meeting, it was my time to consult the chief again. We discussed the problem that my chances for getting access to Fletcher's notes were pretty slim. According to the obituary, he didn't leave family and without further information, just based on his book, it would be impossible to retrace his route. Fortunately, with Dennis, I had met the right person who would not let up on such a plan. He reached back to his research for the trunkman, and he gave me some good pieces of advice about what a historical researcher would do and where he would start detective work to find his belongings. Eventually, it was he who motivated me to continue my New Year's ride to the place where Fletcher used to live, to Carmel Valley.

If you travel to that desert town today, you can be sure to meet some friendly ghosts and a hospitality that is anything but desert-dry. You might expect me telling that on my next visit the town was gone and the only evidence I found was a pair of Sterling cutlery in the desert sand. However, I assure you, you will still find a unique collection of historic memorabilia, buildings, and stories worth listening to, history worth learning. And if you are lucky, site manager Hugh will hold fire and Dennis might give you one of his anecdote-peppered tours while desert aficionado Phil waits at the barbecue pit with a slow-smoked tri-tip rump and the best corn on the cob – from Indiana, of course, where he calls home when not working on the association's grounds. Fifty years ago, Fletcher said about Goffs, "the cluster of buildings that was Goffs did not look the sort of place to be unduly worried by automobiles. Or, for that matter, to be worried by anything very much." That still held true. The only difference to his days may be that now hospitality got company from a great awareness of history.

On January 2, I said good-bye, announced that I might be back, with a pack on my back, to call Goffs my first major break after having left the Mexican border. When I drove through the wooden gate, two vultures were majestically sitting above the STUDY THE PAST sign, spreading their wings in the morning sun and croaking something between warning and welcome. Besides good advice and a lot of recommendations, during my stay at Goffs I also got to hear the inevitable stories about people who lost orientation and vanished in the desert.

Admittedly though, even with that piece of a map and a correspondence about a different book, I was not much closer to the original idea of putting myself in Fletcher's shoes and exactly retrace the one thousand and more miles of his summer. But leaving Goffs, I was highly motivated by that lucky coincidence, and I headed for the coast fueled by early-year energy, which is a quality of the beginning of a year.

Late in the evening, I reached the Coast Mountains and entered Carmel Valley. I checked in at the Blue Sky Lodge and left again to roam the nightly streets of Fletcher's hometown, which he named *Shrubburbia*, describing a spread-out accumulation of villas and farms. It reminded me of Italian villages in dolce Tuscany hills. Somewhere here in these rolling hills, Fletcher had his home and his studio. In the course of his walking career, he wrote *The Thousand-Mile Summer* and six other books, among which *The Man Who Walked Through Time* and *The Complete Walker* became the most famous, making him the backpacking icon and a pioneer of his own.

The first is an artfully worded account of his hike through the Grand Canyon, while the other turned out to be accepted by hundreds and thousands of hikers as the bible for backpacking and outdoor adventure. Simply known as *The Walker*, this exhaustive guide brims with advice, how-to-do's and considerations such as why someone should consider walking through wilderness: "it remains a delectable madness, very good for sanity." Besides his involvement in environmental affairs, his last big trip is told in the book *River: One Man's Journey down the Colorado, Source to Sea*, comparing the course of the Colorado with the stages of life in general and his personal in particular.

Somewhere in these rolling hills, that is, because hardly anyone knew where exactly his writer's residence was. He preferred to live a reclusive life, not being disturbed by uninvited visitors.

Early next morning, I walked to the local Sheriff's office to interview him about possible friends, maybe a shirttail relative, or someone who might have liquidated Fletcher's belongings. A local saw me waiting there and said the Sheriff was out on the highway; a sign at his door stated that he would be 'Back any minute'. Waiting at least thirty-or-so minutes, I realized it was kind of an Ace Ventura-message, "If I'm not back in five minutes, just wait longer." After a while, I got bored and decided to spend my waiting time in the shopping plaza across the street.

Entering a small antique store, I rummaged through a nice collection of pictures, books, clothes, and porcelain. "Can I help you?" asked the lady. "Hi, I am fine thank you, just browsing." She kept at me, "are you just visiting or living here?" So I told her about my research, that I was looking for someone close to the famous author Colin Fletcher, who had lived here, and that I planned to retrace one of his travels and – I halted, looked at her, and noticed a tear in her eye. "Are you OK, ma'am? Did I say something wrong?" "I was his housekeeper," she whispered with a modest smile.

A moment later, a paper sign on her door said, 'Back in 5 minutes.' I found myself on the passenger seat of Holly Henson's car, driving up a winding road into the back hills of Carmel Valley. Calle de la Ventana, Los Ositos, Travesia, Gromaticus, – was that the real world? In front of one of the last mansions she stopped. At the gate there was a wooden sign with a name on it. Surprised I looked at it, then at her, "*Boulton*? I thought …" "Yes," she said, "Colin lived a very reclusive life, didn't like gatecrashers and thought *Boulton* was an inconspicuous decoy name. The other sign saying 'Beware of the Man!' seems to be gone. This is his house."

Holly's sister was his housekeeper for many years, and Holly often joined her to help. So she knew where he wrote and what he liked and disliked. We walked around the wooden house, peeped through the windows and paused on the veranda, overlooking valleys and hills, veritably sparkling one's inspiration.

I spent the evening with Holly and her husband Zen. Through them I got a contact to Fletcher's accountant in Monterey, whom I called the next morning. A very friendly lady with German accent answered the phone, "Angie Luna speaking", listened to my plan, found it "wunderbar", and promised that either she or Mr. Tostevin would call me back soon. That same afternoon I got an invitation for the next day; he wanted to get to know me, then we would see.

J. Breck Tostevin was not only Fletcher's accountant but also his good friend and the executor of his will. He wanted to meet me to see if I was serious about my plan. One hour and a California-map study later, I held a key in my hands and a post-it note with a four-digit PIN that would get me into a storage locker where all of Colin's belongings were stored, his past – and my future. GOFFS! This was my Open Sesame, more than I ever could wish. I was now able to really follow his footsteps, guided by his maps and notes and photos taken during the walk. I even found his old boots, however, I did not plan to be that authentic.

Now I had not much more time for preparation than Colin after he woke up at three in the morning. Two years had shrunk to two months, and soon I found myself, like my forerunner exactly fifty years ago, eat-and-sleep deep in maps and routes, equipment, and clothes.

Because of a little side trip into the Mojave Desert, maybe because my friend Nathan, who knew about my Californian dream, had called for me, maybe because I read the obituary on the day it was published, in any case, in these days I was overwhelmed with a sense of synchronicity, with serendipity, and I realized it would be outrageous, almost sacrilegious, not to do that anniversary voyage anymore.

Perhaps, they all weren't so accidental, maybe I provoked them and they just liked to consort with each other, like an alchemical chain reaction. I had hesitated to fulfill a dream, tempting my fate so hard that destiny couldn't help but open a cornucopia of fortunate events for me. California serendipity.

---

* The Thoreau-footnote: You will run across Thoreau a handful of times in the further course of the book, not only through quotations but also through other historical persons who referred to him or were compared with him.

Henry David Thoreau's (1817–1862) career, which made him the most cited voice for nature, began as a teacher and tutor. Having left Harvard University, he founded an innovative grammar school that introduced alternative courses like practical experiences with local businesses and nature walks. Befriending American author Ralph Waldo Emerson, Thoreau moved to his house for some years where he worked as a private tutor for Emerson's children. Here, he was influenced by the transcendentalism movement, which postulated the authority of the unity of man and nature as opposed to corruptible social institutions like the government, the church, or even the intellectual establishment of Harvard. After a short entrepreneurial sidestep, working in his parents' pencil factory, he was urged by his mentor Emerson and by friends to concentrate on his obvious literary skills. Therefore, he retreated to Walden Woods and built himself a simple cabin in order to cleanse his life from unnecessary things, including the – in his judgment – disproportionate control system of the young state, and to find out about the true essential facts of life. Through reading, nature observation, and basic grassroots activities like gardening, farming, and a lot of do-it-yourself tricks, he found his approach to an analysis of natural and social patterns and he philosophized about their correlations and interdependencies. After two years, two months, and two days alone in the woods, he self-published *Walden, or Life in the Woods* (1854), a reflection upon his own experiences and the insight he gained from simple living and from observations made in natural surroundings.

Though not uncriticized, today *Walden* is regarded as the classic American work of human ecology. Critics have been blaming him mainly for escaping from reality and praising a primitive life instead of facing the challenges of a modern life and for lacking a concept that would work for all.

Bearing his early pedagogic experiences in mind, the main conclusion of *Walden* may be that, in fact, there is no ultimate truth to find or at least that it cannot be taught by a teacher or a tutor, but everyone has to find out about it by him- or herself by regarding the chances of life as questions and respond to them in an according manner.

Yet before the publication of *Walden*, after disputing and concerning himself with government officials, he revised his lectures on *The Rights and Duties of the Individual in Relation to Government* into the essay *Civil Disobedience* (1849), in which he questioned the moral justification of the civil government. Here again, critics aimed at Thoreau's iconoclastic appeal without presenting a clear alternative.

Thoreau continued to write about nature and philosophy, mainly analyzing socio-ecological issues. His mélange of philosophical contemplation and pragmatic how-to-do guidance, along with many references to natural sciences, history, and symbolism, evolved to being one of the main sources for further environmental orientation.

In an introduction to the 150th anniversary edition of *Walden* (Princeton University Press, 2004), American author John Updike has best described Thoreau's status, or also the risk of becoming an icon: "A century and a half after its publication, Walden has become such a totem of the back-to-nature, preservationist, anti-business, civil-disobedience mindset, and Thoreau so vivid a protester, so perfect a crank and hermit saint, that the book risks being as revered and unread as the Bible." And he continues, "Of the American classics densely arisen in the middle of the 19th century ... Walden has contributed most to America's present sense of itself."

CALIFORNIA AND SERENDIPITY

There hardly is a region that has dominated our psyche more than the American West. Writers of fact and fiction, from dime novels to biographies, Hollywood and television have forever been glorifying the stories and fates of the Wild West, exalting some protagonists like Kit Carson, Wild Bill Hickok, Wyatt Earp or just a lonesome prospector to a pantheon of superhuman icons by mixing in myth – but at least grounding it in truth. From the early days until today, the West has been romanticized by fortune-seekers, who spared no efforts, no pains, in order to get there. The frontier was driven by explorers and adventurers, the new land developed by the railroad, settled by the homesteaders, and eventually reclaimed by modern civilization, colonized and cultivated, industrialized and merchandized. Encouraging the new Americans to take advantage of the Homestead Act and develop the vast farmlands in the West, in 1865, New York newspaperman Horace Greeley exhorted "Go West, young man, and grow up with the country!" Millions followed his call and it seems that his echo can still be heard.

On my walk through the length of California, I would find the remnants of many stages of this history and cross the trails of explorers and pioneers, of wagon treks and railroad lines. I would find the remains of transient settlements, of boomtowns and homesteaded valleys that turned into ghost towns and preserves. In order to be prepared for the historic journey, I wanted to know more about the places I would come through. While I spent 24 hours a day leaning over Colin's maps, awake or asleep, studying his notes and photo slides, the little time left I read about the places along my route, the state's history and some historical celebrities whose paths I would cross. With my walk, I wanted not only to retrace Colin's journey but also scratch the history of the West wherever it blazed down on me. Hence I started with this charismatic word describing not only the region I was about to walk through but also the dreams of millions of people, who took off to find out about its promises.

California – it is a land that was shrouded in legend long before the Euro-American colonization began, even before it was discovered by the first conquistadores. For five centuries, it has been inciting people's fantasy all over the world. It is the stronghold of the American Dream, the land of rags-to-riches opportunities or, as you say in Germany, from-dishwasher-to-millionaire.

In fact, *California* is one of the most popular words in the world, neither God nor Michael Jackson, neither Coca-Cola nor Microsoft return as many hits when typed into Google. One of the most played songs of all time bears its name and until today it has been a hotbed of creativity, trends, and quite a few excesses of human life.

When you say, 'I am going to California', you are not just giving directions; there is an implicit meaning that makes the one leaving a little proud and the ones left a little envious. Who or what cooked all that up? By exploring the state's history, I hoped to find some answers to this question.

While the name was imaginary, the land was real, and rarely did a chosen name fit so well for a place as in this case. I started the research in my hometown's library, and I found that, once upon a time in Europe, there was a secret son of an unlawful medieval Spanish-English liaison among royal circles. Raised by noble knights, the marooned Amadís was destined to roam around and embark on many adventures in order to find out who he really was and prove his virtue and respectability. He had to overcome the temptations of riches and power in order to eventually pass through the arch of faithful lovers. Yet, Amadís, too, couldn't avoid repeating history, and so his son Esplandián, the result of yet another illicit meeting, had to undergo over and above his father's fate, including attempted patricide. The indemnification for this archaic sin should be the conquest of paradise for his father Amadís, a mythological land of plenty, a golden state.

In 1510 Spanish author García Ordóñez de Montalvo brought bequeathed and own prose together and published a series of chivalric novels about the adventures of Amadís and his son Esplandián, delivering one of the most influential ideas to Spanish conquistadores. In his books, Montalvo described the son's subject of desire: "Know ye that on the right hand of the Indies there is an island named California, very close to the side of the terrestrial Paradise; and it was peopled by colored women, without any man among them, for they lived in the fashion of Amazons. They were of strong and hardy bodies, of ardent courage and great force. Their island was the strongest in all the World, with its steep cliffs and rocky shores. Their arms were all of gold, and so was the harness of the wild beasts, which they tamed and rode. For in the whole island, there was no metal but gold. In this island called California, there were many griffins, on account of the great ruggedness of the country, and its infinite host of wild beasts, such as never were seen in any other part of the world."[*]

The origin of Amadís' adventures was way before the 1500s, probably in the 13th and 14th century, while the core of this fantasy might well lie in the origins of man.

In the end, the conquest had been succeeded. Triggered by eagerness for power and a gung-ho imagination run riot, the conquerors' mind-picture had already been well established by Montalvo's writing when they arrived in the new world. They had inherited the values and visions of such chivalry stories and saw themselves as the legitimate heirs of legendary Amadís. Facing the natural wonders, they felt affirmed that this was the island of Esplandián.

---

[*] From: *Las Sergas de Esplandián* – García Ordóñez de Montalvo, 1510

PROLOG

Brimming with vigorous manhood and testosterone, numerous conquistadores, including Cortez, Ximenez, and Alarcon, tried to seize the paradisiacal land and from then on they referred to it as California. Unfortunately, when abandoning themselves to their avaricious desires, the real-life conquerors didn't assume the cordiality and thoughtfulness of their fictional ideals.

While they first equated the Baja peninsula with the famous literary paradigm, wishful thinking paired with voraciousness led to applying the term to an area that included not only the future Golden State but also the land as far as Wyoming.

However, here in North America, the Spanish gave up before the riches they sought after were discovered. I was determined to stick to it until the end, until I had unveiled all of the treasures I sought.

For the sake of completeness, while Montalvo's story is widely accepted, theories for the origin of the name of California are numerous, and at least two more turned out to be just as plausible. *The American Heritage Dictionary of Indo-European Roots* by Calvert Watkins mentions what could be a Spanish-English malapropism: *cálida* (Spanish: hot) furnace, or its Latin origin, *calida fornax*. In his *Noticias de la California*, Jesuit historian Miguel Venegas offered an indigenous expression, *kali forno*, meaning high mountains. To me, despite the haziness of the origin, through desert and high Sierra, all of that turned out to be true.

*

Around the same time when Amadís and Esplandián were immortalized, another group of literary figures had set sail to explore the world. Three princes of the island of Serendip were sent out by their father, the king, to become trained in the arts and sciences and gain experience and wisdom. On their journey, they seemed to accidentally run into fortunate situations and make sagacious discoveries, irrespective of whether or not they were looking for them.

This fairy tale, *The Three Princes of Serendip,* was first published by the Venetian Michele Tramezzino in 1557. While the origin of the plot is Persian, Tramezzino located his modernized version on the island of Sri Lanka, Ceylon, in that time also known as Serendip, to render homage to the church's recent proselytizing success. 200 years later, the English art historian Horace Walpole coined the word *serendipity* to describe an aptitude of attracting fortunate events or ideas seemingly by accident.

All serendipitous events, may they be literary or verifiably historical, have one thing in common. They could neither have been gained by sitting around nor by purposefully looking for them. Without a doubt, one of the most momentous events in this vein happened, when Columbus sailed to India, when suddenly the Americas thwarted him and the tide of history.

Explorers or Princes, I believe, it was not so accidental but rather the natural result from the mere fact that they were traveling, that they were open and interested. One has to set off in order to gain experiences and the quality or value of a journey can only be assessed by the experiences one makes en route, corresponding to the Battuta-principle*, "He who does not travel does not know the value of mankind", likewise of nature and also of oneself, which is reflected in both our encounter with others and in the occasional face-off with our lone, inner self.

One cannot force serendipity, one just has to be open, believe and receive. Then, it is in the nature of traveling, then one may make new experiences, meet new people and receive unexpected inspiration for ideas and solutions. However, for many, the most interesting, most unreckoned encounter and the greatest inspiration for one's future self will be to find out more about oneself.

أبو عبد الله محمد ابن عبد الله اللواتي الطنجي بن بطوطة *

Abu Abdullah Muhammad Ibn Abdullah Al Lawati Al Tanji Ibn Battuta, Moroccan Scholar and traveler, 1304–1368

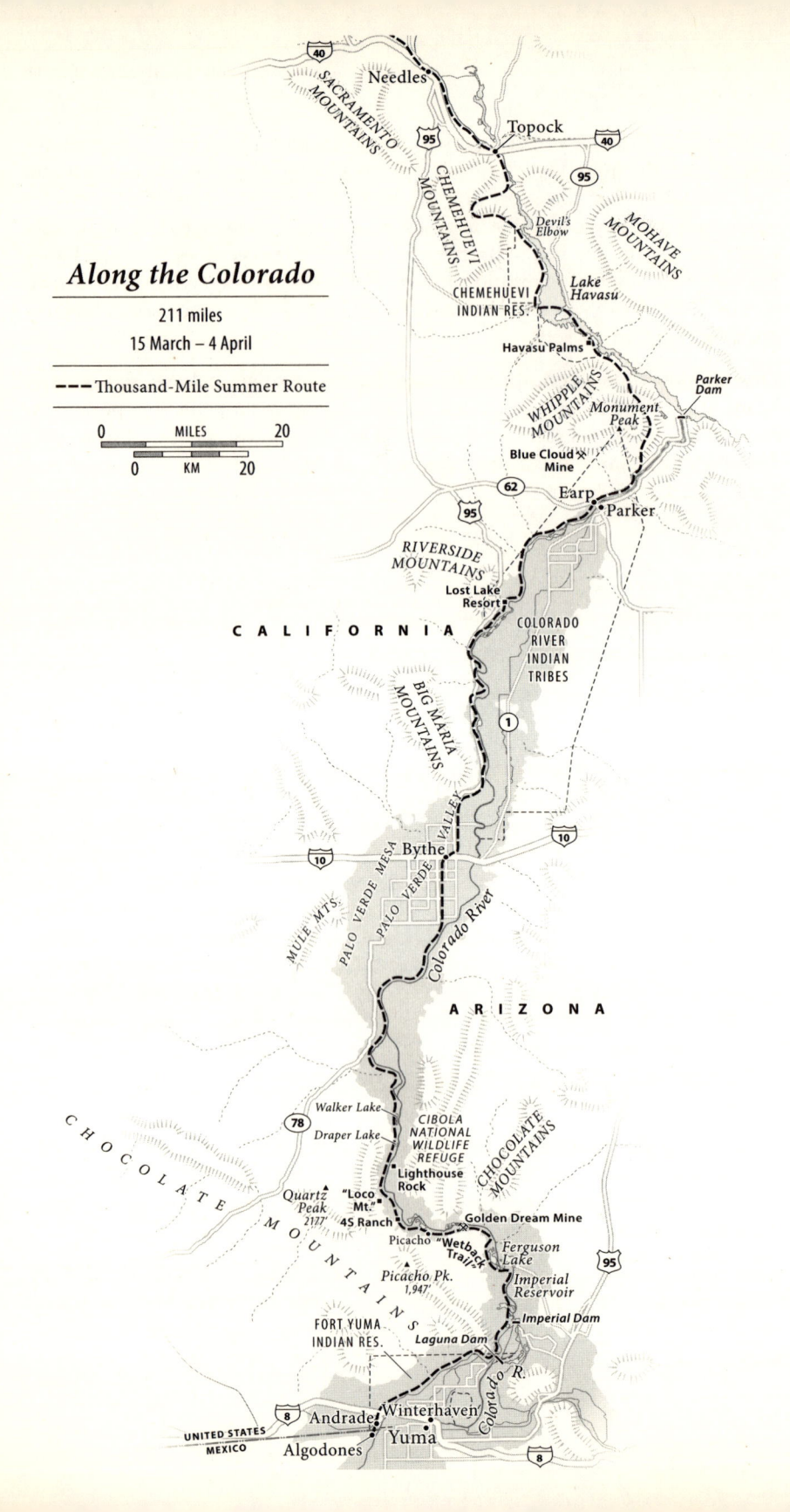

Along the Colorado

211 miles
15 March – 4 April

- - - - Thousand-Mile Summer Route

1. ALONG THE COLORADO

To the desert go prophets and hermits;
Through deserts go pilgrims and exiles;
Here the leaders of the great religions
have sought the therapeutic and spiritual
values of retreat, not to escape but to find reality.

FROM: MAN IN THE LANDSCAPE – PAUL HOWE SHEPARD,
AMERICAN ENVIRONMENTALIST, AUTHOR, 1926–1996

"California? 's crazy! Golden paranoia! No beer after 1.30. And when cops stop you, you're punished. I hate California!" ranted a middle-aged Mexican man sitting next to his wife in front of a million-dollar mansion in Malibu, Los Angeles. I just came from a last stroll down the beach before I would pack my things, when he leaned over the fence to start a conversation, literally assailing me with questions and his own prepared answers. While he buttonholed me a quarter of an hour, his young wife was playing with half a dozen ritzy rings on her fingers. It wasn't hard to guess, her mind was Tiffany-twisted, and that, although she casually looked up to nod her head devotedly, she did not totally agree.

After some more complaints, more or less substantial, I said, "May I ask you a question, Sir? Why are you here then?" He paused and replied, "Because I can say that! And, look at my house! I was nobody, struck it rich here. And, the climate, the nature, muy padre! That's why you're here too, isn't it?"

Somehow, I thought, despite his piecemeal reasoning, he summarized what California is about. "Maybe you're right," I said, and when I turned to say goodbye, he called after me, "It's just not the way it used to be. Watch out guey!"

CHAPTER ONE

One day and 300 miles later, after a breathtaking ride along Southern California's coast and through the Anza Borrego Desert, I arrived at Winterhaven, a small town at the Mexican border. My German business partner and his friend had taken the chance to visit America for the first time and drive me from Los Angeles to where my thousand-mile journey would begin. Indeed, they were stunned in awe, praising climate and the nature, and they envied me for the chance to – somehow – strike it rich here, if only by experiencing for at least four months this state's natural grandeur first-hand or, to be precise, first-foot. After some days, they would meet me at the next possible place, where a road crossed my trail, to see if I was doing fine and still wanted to continue, or if I would rather call it a nice idea.

We checked in one of these forlorn motels for 20$ a room, less to save some bucks, but to get this shabby yet nostalgic desert inn ambience. When I got into my room, I emptied tons of things out of a suitcase, shopping bags, and cartons, placing the virgin backpack right in between and on top of it a small paperback copy of Colin's Thousand-Mile Summer.

As a farewell-to-civilization ceremony, I turned on the TV, as if I could tell the world through it, "Good bye, see you in four months!" Channel 45, *El canal del aviamiento de transformacion*. Oracion, mantra-like prayers, in big letters a phone number faded in on the screen, below in flashing yellow letters, "Donate now!" I pushed the remote, zap! The next channel, *Christian Vision KLAU-LP*, came on with a little more content. A self-proclaimed rock star was droning a song, consisting of eight notes, reprising them forever. It sounded as if the disc had a scratch, but his continuous contortions suggested he was still going on. In his gestures and facial expressions he availed himself of the who-is-who in pop music. An indefinite power, a bizarre fascination, glued me to the program. When finally he was pooped out, a self-proclaimed healer entered the stage, cousin of the first, I guessed. He talked as monotonously as the other guy sang. However, his bosh magically attracted visitors to stand up and walk to him in trance. He tipped them on the forehead and they just fell down like flies, caught by an assistant. "Donate now!" Funny, I thought, the German word *klau* means *steal*. Zap. Channel 47, a Spanish soap with actors, whose skills were so dreadful, any waxworks would have done better. Three more channels, selling Christianity as if it were soap. I remembered having seen a loose collection of notes among Colin's files, where he wrote down quotes he liked. One of them was by American botanist and scientist George Washington Carver, also known as the Black Leonardo, who "loved to think of nature as an unlimited broadcasting station through which God speaks to us every hour, if we will only tune in." I hoped that from tomorrow I would have a better reception.

Channel 50, the *Afternoon Show*, with a Hollywood-blonde presenting her latest book. I got curious, she called it *Hollywood's Diet Secrets*, unveiling the most unbelievable discoveries. So what makes them secrets? What made it even more amazing, she wormed all these secrets out of Heidi Klum, Cameron Diaz, Gwyneth Paltrow and the likes. If you by now get curious too, here are the first three: secret #1: salad has fewer calories than steaks – wow! secret #2: eat salad before steak – amazing! #3: wrap fish in foil and throw it into your dishwasher, that's fat-free cooking – zap!

Here a Mexican and his African-American wife were spreading their marital intimacies for a voyeuristic white-bread audience. Zap. There three cooking shows … zap, zap, zap. Twenty channels with commercials, offering in glowing terms brummagem jewelry, dolls for adults, and a variety of tools and DIY tips fair enough to build the world anew. And then, the NEWS, regarding contents and style not any different from the aforementioned. Two news anchors lapsed into chatting the news, and I thought they would slag someone off, who was guilty of high treason. It turned out to be a respected senator, who made a mistake uttering the wrong words at the wrong time, now being pilloried in the press. A suddenly squalling vermin of political opponents followed by a brainlessly devoted coterie of media, inflated a simple mistake into moral turpitude. A little more entertaining was the following report, a governor's oratorical walk to Canossa after he had been visited by a call girl. And during all that, the real world news were rolling away in the news ticker below, too fast to grasp. Zap.

Back on channel 50, meanwhile, nails were manicured while philosophical dry bread was being ground like broken nails. Zap. There a TV judge was dealing with an enormously delicate case; the plaintiff's collection of karaoke CDs was missing. While they were at it, judge, plaintiff, and suspect regaled viewers with a sampling of their singing voices. Zap. Power-training for your body with the latest professional pull-press-push-step thingamabob, followed by those annoying before-and-after pictures of evidently different people. They did not even try to get close. Are we so dulled and indifferent that it doesn't matter anymore? Zap. Substantial progress on the duke-out-your-marriage channel; the mixed couple came to blows and they were constantly at each other's throats. Their words finally established a certain level, but unfortunately, they beeped everything away. Zap. America, the beautiful. Zap.

I started wondering why I was so upset, and I thought of the Mexican man, "Golden paranoia," he said, "It's just not the way it used to be." I could have just switched off the apparatus, but something like the dark side of the force attracted me to that little box of oddities like a magnet, as if I needed another reason to leave. Tomorrow, in fact, I would leave this wasteland, this mass-produced, pre-packaged sham world, devoid of any meaning. In a single second, putting my left foot on Mexican ground, and my right foot back into the Golden State, the first step of some five million to come, I would enter a different world – being carried by the light side.

CHAPTER ONE

Later in the evening, we went to see the nearby bordering towns of Andrade, CA, and Algodones in Mexico, just to get an idea of how it looked and maybe find a good spot for my first photo in the morning. We passed an officer of the border patrol, who was walking down the highway bank while looking for something with his flashlight. I stopped the car at his side, got out and talked to him. In less than half a minute, three cars surrounded us, skeptically checking what we were doing here. The cars looked like a combination of the best Mad Max race car and a recon vehicle. The border was closed at this time and for sure it was quite unusual to see someone walking toward it now, especially from this side. The officer explained he could not help me now; I would have to address the officer-in-chief next morning about my wish. "What are you doing again? Walk from here to Oregon? Why?"

Having grown up in Germany, my partner on the eastern side and I on the western, we both remembered the GDR wall and its fenced border through the country. Apart from the East German firing order and spring guns, it was a kindergarten compared to the facilities and the collection of watchtowers, barbwire fences, and floodlights we saw here. We left this spooky place and drove back to the motel.

The TV had enough and could not be turned on again, however, instead of calling for replacement, I regarded it as an additional service from the house. Ironically, in one of the drawers, where you normally find two thin-paged books, one with timeless contents, the other comparatively short-lived, I found an old magazine with the last page flipped open. A red circle around a *Calvin and Hobbes* cartoon explained why someone left it right here: "That's the problem with nature. Something's always stinging you or oozing mucus on you. Let's go watch TV."

On the two queen-sized beds, I arranged my gear, my clothes, and my food, the goods and chattels I would load every morning and unload every evening to spread them over the five square yards of California I would from now on call home. I knew for sure that everything neatly displayed here on an area the size of a camping site would fit in that backpack. What looked like the contents of a family's closet should now be squeezed in a cylindrical one-bag pack. If not arranged properly, I would surely find some items only when reaching the Oregon border and wonder, why did I bring it that far.

Besides the main bag, the model I had chosen had only one more on the top; the lower sleeping bag compartment had its own zipper access but was merely separated from the main bag by a drop-down divider. Everyone has to organize things inside the pack his or her own way. Some hikers like to have several small side pockets for faster access to small gadgets, though much of the packing style depends on what you think you will need first or most often, and on whether you carry it just for days or for months. For a long trip into unknown terrain, I preferred an internal-frame model. On steep climbs, the pack and the weight stays as close to the body as possible, making balancing easier, and no protruding side bags or straps get caught in thicket or dense woods. Also the contents were better protected from rain. If nothing else, it was from the same manufacturer Colin favored.

The sleeping bag went into the bottom bag, with spare pants wrapped around to protect it from scratches or sharp rocks. Compressible to the size of a football with an unfurled equivalent of ten woolen blankets, it turned out to be the finest little bed I ever took for hiking.

Above the drop-down divider, all spare clothes went to the bottom of the main bag – that would be my wardrobe. Then the kitchen and the office. The maps and two layers of food bags were placed around everything to prevent pointed items from gouging my back. Basically, I would live on dehydrated food; only fish from the mountain streams in the Sierra would later become a natural addition. Choosing the right variety of meals, I had tried to stay basic and away from the hoopla on the multicolored packaging. On the other side, you wouldn't want to feed solely upon rice and beans. So my collection of meals still sounded more like I did a luxury gourmet tour than a wilderness hike: Jamaican Chicken, Hawaiian Chicken, Chicken Santa Fe, Beef Stroganoff, Southwest Salmon BBQ Inferno, Pasta Primavera, and Chicken & Dumplings already made my mouth water, and when stowing the packs, I thought I would have to control myself not to have seven meals at the same time.

Small items and whatever I needed frequently were stuffed in the top bag, including the small paperback issue of *The Thousand-Mile Summer*, the compass, and the respective local map. Tent, tripod and camera were strapped outside. My house on the back was ready for move-in, cram-full, while all that remained on the two beds was a pair of running shoes, a jacket, a fleece, two books, and about the same amount of food I had already packed.

It is a backpacking phenomenon that, with each further try, your backpack seems to shrink. I could not do without a second pair of shoes; hiking boots and the running shoes were essential, not for running away from something but for easy walking over long level stretches and for quick slip-ins at camp. Fleece and jacket were indispensable since for at least the first six weeks the desert nights would be awful cold. I had calculated two full meals a day until I would reach the first town. That was probably too much, but I could not be sure what my body demanded especially in the first days until I had developed a certain routine and got used to lean cuisine despite the hard work. So my partner and his friend got two books to read until they would meet me along the Colorado. A little squeeze here, reorganizing there, pulling all straps tight, I was ready to go, to take another look at America.

I had separated the maps I would need into four regions, bringing only the first part with me now. The others were sent with replenishment parcels to two places along my walk where I would call in after one and two months, respectively. I chose a mixture of Colin's 7.5-minute and 15-minute maps, current Tom Harrison-maps and torn out pages from the Delorme Atlas & Gazetteer, South and North California, where none of the above was available. Scaling roughly 2.5 inches to the mile, a 7.5 minute would cover an area of 6.5 x 8.5 square miles, if complete; the 15-minute scales one inch to the mile covering approximately 12 by 18 miles. Due to Colin's obsessive removal of everything producing extra and useless weight, he had often cut off the larger vicinity of passed route segments. Just relying on these cut-outs would have been too risky, I thought. I could not be sure that fifty years had not changed the landscape forcing me to find detours. Hence, I completed those with Delorme pages. Having left the Colorado, Colin broke with that habit. Instead and unfortunately, he seemed to have burned some after leaving their boundaries.

In some areas, especially around creeks, rivers, and canyons, I could be sure that Colin's maps would not be the best orientation, since some of them dated back not only fifty years but almost seventy. Naturally, there was no need to frequently update maps that covered areas where Esplandián might have been the last one coming through. At any time, one flash flood could have changed the surface of the planet, at least the course of washes or creeks. There too, expanding my geographical material to Delorme's proved comforting, if only to get a second opinion. Wherever available, I would buy more detailed Tom Harrisons, usually for those places officially declared *wilderness.*

A week ago, I had mailed these replenishment packages from Los Angeles, the first one to the association in Goffs, the second to the local newspaper in Mammoth Lakes. A third one stayed in L.A. until further notice. They contained more dehydrated food, drinking powder, cereal bars, coffee, tea, and my personal mix of spices. Each had a new pair of socks, a shirt, shoelaces, and new maps while the one to Mammoth Lakes, which was a little more than halfway, also had new pairs of shoes. If I were to have carried everything from the start, I would have had to organize a wagon train.

Still, tomorrow I would have some seventy pounds on my back, and that did not include water. It felt OK now, but how would I feel after some miles, let alone on a mountain. The backpack had to hold no less than the necessities of life, and I thought I had necessity balanced against pounds.

I went through my packing list several times, but I did not find any item I could think of leaving behind now. I compared my list with Colin's, and, besides the fact that I was carrying a two-pound solar device, a two-pound MacBook Air for downloading photos and writing articles, and an iPod, there wasn't anything that he did not take. Although many outdoor items today were much lighter than fifty years ago, I was still carrying twenty pounds more than he did. I chalked it up to pre-experienced take-off weight; most likely the definition of 'necessary' or 'dispensable' would be altered with the first miles hiked. In fact, one of the reasons for meeting my partner after four or five days was to get rid of whatever couldn't stand the balancing act between necessary and pounds.

I opened my travel log and looked at the empty pages. From now on, with every day it would gain content until after four months it would be as heavy as a large-print coffee-table book, full of adventures and impressions. Between the last pages, I had put copies of some of Colin's photos with the idea to reenact them. They showed him at various places between Algodones and New Pine Creek, OR. On the first one, he was walking by the border post, behind which was nothing but a brittle fence and open desert land. Right here at the Mexican border the walk began. One month earlier, in February 1958, a newcomer in San Francisco had woken up in the middle of the night, struck by the idea of walking through California from one end to the other. Four weeks later, he was here, shaking hands with the U.S. customs officer. In his journal, Colin had described a scene where a Mexican boy was cleaning the officer's shoes while the latter was lolling in a wicker chair. When the boy had completed his artwork, the officer inspected his shoes, approved, and tossed the boy a coin. Probably the kid went back to his hometown with his fortune, being a king for a day.

That was on March 8, 1958, six days before Colin turned 36. Five years older and fifty years later I stood here, ready for the same long walk, ready for a change. It was March 15, 2008, when I knocked at the door of the commanding officer.

03/15   U.S./MEXICAN BORDER, 20 MILES[*]

"Good morning, Sir, are you in charge here?" – "Who's asking, how can I help you?" the officer replied. It took me half an hour to explain myself and why I would just like to set one foot across the border. I tried to tell him who Colin Fletcher was, that he was here fifty years ago, but the officer was constantly interrupted by incoming phone calls. After the sixth or seventh call, I just kept talking, showed my maps to some of his deputies and described why I would do such a thing again. Finally, between two calls, I was granted permission to walk backwards into Mexico and have someone take a picture of me. "Make sure none of my officers or any of these buildings are on the photo," the chief officer cautioned while putting one hand on the mouthpiece. I refrained from asking him to call his deputies off the compound or if a post picture editing would be OK, otherwise it would not work. Although I felt that, after a while, he began to like the idea or my motives, it was better not to risk his good will with a sloppy question.

---

[*] (Date   Starting point, daily mileage)

CHAPTER ONE

When I left the headquarters, there were voices down the corridor that suddenly fell silent. I pretended to leave the building, but closed the door in front of me and I thought I heard them say, "There is not all right with that lad; through the desert?"

At 6 o'clock, the gate opened, and a long queue of people lined up to get into the U.S. I was among the first, and, although I now had official permission, it seemed as if I was nonetheless eyed with suspicion. However, for a few seconds, I left the jurisdiction of the imperial star wars army in California. Ironically, Imperial County on the California side of the border looked pretty poor and devastated. There were no signs of civilization but the office containers and a long abandoned mobile house lying in the roadside ditch. The town of Andrade consisted of a petrol station and a widely extended but empty parking area, waiting in the desert sand for an increasing want of officers, or just another desert storm. On the other side, Mexico looked rich in colors and buildings. Through a thirty-foot opening in the wall, I peeped into a different world. There were shops, stores, merchants, and marketeers; it was colored, full of lights, loud, and busy, like a huge economic racetrack with thousands of running horses, betters and bookies, and spectators. It looked like a bazaar out of Thousand and One Nights and I felt how it magically attracted me.

I stood there, rooted to the spot, as if I had to imprint this first step and everything I saw indelibly on my mind. Perhaps it was to set something against the emerging expectation of my last steps, when I would reach the Oregon border, an anticipatory yet diffuse emotional state that already began to conquer my mindset. It felt like aeons, though it could not have been more than a couple of minutes until two officers closed in on me. I was afraid the chief officer might forget our little agreement too soon, so I didn't dare to dwell any longer on the other side and turned around to put my first step on California terrain.

While my partner took pictures of me coming from the border, a Mexican American welcomed me. Taking off his sombrero he said "Welcome to California, Sir." and showed me his collection of Mexican souvenirs rolled around his left arm. Or was he an American Mexican? A group of Californian senior citizens waved at me and asked me about my journey. They said, they would frequently visit Algodones for the good food and cheap drugs. With an officer passing us that moment they added, "cheaper medicine, of course."

After saying goodbye to my partner, I did a last call to L.A. Nathan's condition was relatively good, and he promised that from now on he would do his best to keep up and travel with me as long as I kept him informed about mine.

Leaving the frontier fair behind, I walked along a huge irrigation system, stretching some thirty miles from Yuma northeastwards up to Laguna and Imperial Dams. At times, I still felt like taking off for a day trip. What lay ahead of me was yet too amazing to believe it. I was torn between thoughts about my arrival, how I would feel, and a slight uncertainty about my doing, peradventure versus adventure. In any case, I was happy about the possible emergency exit we had arranged for after the first days.

What might have contributed to this state of wobbliness was the surprisingly unspectacular landscape along the first stretch after having left the border. The paralleling All American Canal and its many channels deprived the Colorado River of its lifeblood, making the once powerful river a vanquished almost anemic, mellifluent body. Trailers and fifth-wheels were splattered all over, temporary mobile homes for the seasonal labor. Late in the evening, I passed a large body of water; it might have been the Colorado, it might have been the Canal, or just a cut-off river channel that now formed a lagoon-like lake. An unearthly quiet came from the dark surface, not a place for a night. A little farther a stand of cottonwood trees whispered 'campsite'. There I concluded my first hiking day, too tired to eat, to make a fire, or even to remember. I just lay down and ...

*

The first night outdoors is always something special. As exhausted as I was from the marathon-like walk, I didn't really fall into deep sleep. Too much was going on in my head, the excitement for the days to come had to carve out its place and supersede the trivialities we are always carrying with us. From now on, there would be no more room for those and all my energy had to be available for only one thing, or maybe two, arriving at the destination and living this dream.

Dozing off to the rippling sound of cottonwood leaves, I dreamed I was sneaking out the backdoor of my parents' house to a pockmarked rusty gate. It was Sunday noon right after church. Our parents were expecting visitors, which meant, the time interval until the first calls of "Where are you? What are you doing?" were coming would be prolonged long enough that we dared to tackle an adventure. As soon as the doorbell rang, we tiptoed to that overgrown dark corner of our garden and loosened the chain that kept the old rusty gate closed. Behind lay an abandoned property and behind the property, endless forest, since for our childish eyes, distance was defined by what we could see. Until that day, we had never seen anything but forest back there, never made it beyond its borders, and wherever the end were could as well have been the end of the world. As soon as we were out of earshot, the last resort was to be home for dinner.

The impetus to explore wilderness has always been with me. Lacking grizzlies, gunfighters and Indians, I coerced my sisters or a schoolmate to join me venturing into the unknown land, which opened up beyond the gate. There we pretended to encounter those who lived in the vast lands of the frontier. One of us was the Indians, proud-faced and honorable, one was the outlaws, of evil visage, and one the lion-hearted trapper, friend and protector of all emigrants and Indians – generally that was me.

Usually, we would just disappear into the forest, exploring a small creek for the umpteenth time. After three or four hours, appetite would force us to retreat to base camp. However, I will never forget our parents' faces, when we came back from an all-day adventure. Sticking our heads in the doorway, we saw them sitting in the living room, by the phone, and they were ready to call the police. When we crossed the threshold between the garden and the living room, we left our reality and entered theirs, and we braced ourselves for parental inquisition: "How dare you?" – long interval – "Who do you think you are?" – longer interval – "What were you doing and where were you?" As a matter of fact, at least to the last question we had no answer. To me, or hopefully to us, just being in unknown lands was more than a Toys"R"Us in our garden. Since there had not been any spectacular encounters, I reported innocently that we were in the forest. The only indication I remembered was that exit sign with the name of a town. My parents knew in an instant that this was a freeway sign, and where it was. I don't know what freaked them more, seeing us along the autobahn with cars speeding at 120 mph or the fact that we were able to walk some ten miles without alarming them. Indeed, to my parents it was the end of the world; to me it was the most exciting and adventurous thing I had ever done, so far.

03/16   LAGUNA DAM, 11 MILES

On the first two days, I walked through a patchwork land. The numerous channels fed by the Colorado were cutting through in all directions, creating different-sized parcels of land in a variety of dusty colors. The irrigated land was fighting hard with the desert and it seemed that aridity more or less prevailed.

On every corner, heavy farming machinery roasted in the sun as if it were waiting for mission order. A young Mexican was leaning against one front wheel twice his size. He slightly pulled his straw hat down ostensibly to shade his face from the sun. But he seemed to be peering at me from under his flap. Only when he saw that I would pass, he looked up and took his hat off. I thought he was swaying with it and beckoning to me. Once I was there, we asked the common salutatory questions, however, we realized that our vocabularies were used up soon. He spoke a Latin American dialect, I wasn't even sure if it was Spanish. Offering me a cigarette, we delved into a wordless conversation, nodding, from man to man.

Walking down country roads along the irrigating channels, I finally arrived at Imperial Dam, where I found the trail to old Senator Mine and Senator Wash. Here I left the flat irrigation fields – the desert mounted. Having climbed the first hill, I looked back over a noisy land of geometrically intertwined roads and channels. Ahead lay silent chaos, desert ridges and canyons and a broad river that seemed to abide by no regulations.

I closed the rusty gate behind me and with the first step down it was silent, the hill had swallowed all signs of human civilization, and with it obligated supervision. From now on, my steps, the hours and days, my moments and experiences, would lie in no one else's hands but my own.

This was the moment of initiation, this short moment, not longer than it takes to do one step. Colin celebrated it with words on all of his travels: "I had left behind the man-constructed world. Had already escaped from a world in which the days are consumed by clocks and dollars and traffic and other people. Had crossed over … into a world that was governed by the sun and the wind and the lie of the land." (From: *The Man Who Walked Through Time*)

03/17   IMPERIAL RESERVOIR, 4 MILES

In spite of its ruggedness, the ranges were relatively easy to walk. Every so often I crossed a 4WD road and followed it as long as it kept paralleling the river. Rocky barren slopes took turns with sandy dips, forested with mesquite and palo verde. Whenever I climbed a range, my first look was east to the river. For two hundred miles, it should be my guideline, my natural GPS, an unmistakable sign that I was right, since there was no other water like that between Mexico and Oregon.

Only the occasional purring of a helicopter reminded me of the fact that I was still close to civilization and that I was walking into a dangerous area, where illegal immigrants might dare their own solitary hike, hiding and fighting their way down-and-dirty to the next big city. In this part of California, the border patrol might merciless pony me up and arrest me before they asked questions. Those were the stories told in Winterhaven, and I couldn't help from taking longer strides to make my way out of this area soon. Only when I passed the first major highway, Interstate 10, I should be safe, because there, illegal aliens were usually picked up by their fellows.

Although in the fifties, the U.S. was to all intents and purposes concerned about illegal immigrants, the situation along the border must have been quite relaxed compared to today. The nice little chat Colin had at the border is unthinkable today; that officer also was the Sheriff of Andrade, he was alone at the guard, and he was Mexican. Even then, the passage to the Golden State was a treasure some people paid a lot of money to obtain. Thousands made their way, getting their backs wet by swimming through the Rio Grande or the Colorado and sneaking through sagebrush desert and hidden canyons.

For many, immigration had become not only a question of promises, but also a matter of life and death. In order to be able to travel fast and inconspicuously, they had little water and food and risked dehydration, starvation, or heat stroke in the desert.

Not long before Colin set off, the U.S. government had developed its quasi-military 'Wetback Operation' to search for, seize, and extradite illegals. Hence the momentary mood had not really been relaxed, and to surprise someone bushwhacking through the desert might well have caused unpredictable reactions. Colin was afraid not only of an unintentional encounter on his travel or being surprised in his sleep, but also of finding the decaying remains of those who had failed. I was warned, too, that still, every once in a while, people made it through the fence, following canyons along the old wetback trail until they reached either I-10 or the mercilessness of the desert. If I should meet one, in these times of severe drug and gang wars, my chances for an intercultural campfire discussion about the pros and cons of living in the U.S.A. were rather small. For my own sake, I dismissed these stories to the land of exaggerations; nonetheless, before every curve or hill or entering a canyon, I would sneak around the corner until I was sure that no one and no *body* was there.

Soon I understood that hiking along the Colorado was not as I expected it. Although I saw water whenever I climbed out of a canyon, it was mostly standing water, lakes or lagoons the river had created in more dynamic times. The majesty itself stayed in due distance, as if I had to prove myself before I was accorded an audience. Between me and the river were hills and ranges, obstructing the view to the trough the river had dug for itself. Large fields of reed and scrub had cut off the abandoned waters from the main channel, allowing only casual feed by rain or when the water level was high. The occasions where I saw the actual river were rare, but I knew it was there and that meant walking in peace. Still I was sure, once a day or every ten miles, I would be able to find a spot where I could work my way through to fresh water, have a swim, and refill my water sacks.

It seemed that nothing had changed much along the Colorado but the river itself. As majestic as it was, its flow had now been tamed and quieted, like a monarch that had been deprived of its executive power. Man even took away its red color, what it was once named for, indicating its power and the ferocity with which it forged its way through the desert, cleansing it of loose rocks and soil forever until the dams were built.

Saying that the mountains and canyons framing it had not changed meant they were still wild and altered only by the actions of wind and rain. I learned that hiking with maps older than fifty years could in fact turn into quite an adventure. After river floods and heavy rains, new lagoons had formed, washes had grown wider or filled up with falling rocks; some had turned into lakes, while some lakes did not exist anymore. Only with frequent stops for orientation and deliberation, it was possible to navigate with my old maps, because mountains and deep gorges were reliable and consistent. My safety net was the main route of the Colorado. It would take millions of years and the extinction of mankind for it to find easier ways around massive rock formation. Much more time than I needed to find my way through desert mountains and canyons along its course with compass and maps.

On the first 200 miles along the river, I was not only following Colin' footsteps but roughly the trail that was blazed by two of the earliest pioneers. Fur trappers Peter Skene Ogden and Erwin Young had explored new hunting and trapping grounds throughout the West in the late 1820s. One member of Young's party was the renowned Christopher 'Kit' Carson, whose tracks I would cross many more times during that journey. While Spanish and Mexicans had already been using the mission trail *Camino Real*, which crossed the Colorado where I had started two days ago, Ogden had been the first British-Canadian and Young the first American to come that far south.

Along with Jedediah Smith, who crossed the Colorado in 1827 farther north through the eastern Mojave, these three men were the first pioneers to have traveled thousands of miles across the unknown land beyond the 'Great American Desert'. I felt as if – after Colin – I would make it a handful of people.

Somewhere around Ferguson Lake, I found a small salty pond bounded by mesquite trees. Since I felt my body complaining about the constant work, I looked for a way to the shore and stopped for the night. Supposed you already are basically in good shape, it is an interesting feeling to see your ligaments, muscles, and overall condition adjust to the new situation. Whatever you might have done in fitness preparation, in the first days you feel every single one of them, and somehow, I think, I would have been disappointed if every fiber of my body didn't ache.

At the calming evening fire, the aching muscles would soon be forgotten, and the scratches collected from thorny bushes became nothing less than minor trophies. Only my feet I had to watch, these pampered city feet that at a moment's notice had to carry an additional seventy pounds. They started developing the first blisters. After opening and drying them at the campsite, I walked bare-foot to let them breathe and condition the skin.

Though the lake water was a little too salty for me, there was an abundance of birds. The deeper the sun the louder they were singing, right until nightfall when they all synchronistically stopped. With dusk, two beavers had become active, pushing sticks and branches from one side to the other. My eyes followed them like watching a tennis match until a colorless ball on the water surface in the middle of the lake grabbed my attention. It was too far away

CHAPTER ONE

to see if it was a ball that had lost its owner or the head of another beaver playing possum in order to sneak out of helping his buddies. The thing remained floating on the same spot until the twilight had almost revealed its silhouette. Suddenly it disappeared. I never found out what it was.

Since I had left the border, I saw a small balloon in the air, presumably another border patrol device to monitor all movements on the ground. I would not have been surprised if that ball was an amphibian drone.

Late at night I woke up, in the air high above me, a border patrol helicopter was scanning the ground – just like, to my left, the beaver its little pond. A howling Coyote held vigil, making me fall back to sleep at one with the world.

03/18   FERGUSON LAKE, 6 MILES

The mysterious ball did not bob up with sunrise, but the birds were back at once. Their singing was so intense and of such a great variety, in some moments I thought I heard a cellular phone ringing, or a TV nearby. Still my ears were used to the noisy ocean of civilization and only day-by-day, I was learning to distinguish and pick every single source or sender.

Along the Colorado, lakeshore and lagoons were teeming with wildlife. Now in spring, thousands of waterfowl migrated into the desert to bring it back to life until the summer heat would disrupt their temporary zeal. I found that, whenever I sat down and remained still for a moment, the silence I brought with me as an intruder soon disappeared because all singers came out of their hiding places again. The cowbird came with a large repertoire of songs, whereas the phainopepla will forever be connected with my walk through the Colorado Desert – it was just everywhere. Ducks, geese, great blue herons, egrets, cormorants and ibis appeared, Gila woodpeckers and roadrunners made tracks. White-winged doves and swallows nose-dived down on me as if they wanted to prompt me to play up with them. Joining my breakfast, a bald eagle watched the whole razzmatazz from a distant palo verde tree while gnawing on its own meal.

When I tidied up my kitchen, the buzzing sound of a small motor glider hushed all birds. After having completed two circles above me, it left the scene, but before the lake's choir could raise its voice again, there was another even louder noise coming from the hills around. From the roaring I assumed it were SUVs, climbing hills and diving into canyons. They were getting closer, obviously heading toward my campsite. I threw some hands of sand on the fire, got into my jeans and stood at attention. Slamming on the brakes, two white military vehicles stopped right by my side, one to my left and one to my right. "Border patrol! Good morning!" With their hands on their belts, four dangerous looking guys jumped out of their Hummer-like cars and asked for my purpose of being there. I started telling them about my hike and that I had a conversation with the officer-in-charge at the Andrade station. I didn't need to say more, they remembered some other colleagues talking about a guy walking to Alaska on the radio, or so. They asked me when I scheduled to cross I-10 and wished me a good journey. "Be safe, and don't pick up anybody," they laughed.

It was only 8 in the morning. I rekindled my fire and had two more coffees. Somehow it was bothering, I thought, being watched and disturbed in my retreat to nature, but it also felt reassuring to know that someone knew where I was.

From here, I began an endless climbing into canyons and over hilly tongues of land reaching into the lagoons and side lakes of the Colorado. The river itself was too far away to see it. Around noon it heated up, becoming too hot to continue with some seventy pounds on yet untrained shoulders. I took a long lunch break and thought about the 500 miles of desert lying ahead. If it became too hot to walk in March, how would it be in a month? Like my forerunner, I wanted to be through the desert by the end of April, which meant arriving at Death Valley's Furnace Creek before it lived up to its name.

Without any longer breaks, I had to master roughly twelve miles a day. That shouldn't be a problem as long as my feet were OK with it and as long as I could use most of daylight. If I was forced to skip the midday hours for shadow, I would probably be late and face temperatures in the three digits in Death Valley.

I learned that planning a trip through the desert and studying maps at home only allowed an optimistic theory of how one could cover time and distance; a theory I might have to abandon. Here, things are not always what they seem and estimating distance becomes an art in itself. Both a series of unpredictable canyons or the vastness of barren plains are likely to distort your sense of distance and disjoint time. However, you cannot afford to make too many mistakes here; survival, or at least getting ahead, depends on knowing where you are and where there is water, where you are going, and how long it will take to get there.

As if the river wanted to calm me, in the evening, the Colorado appeared for the first time within reach. I came close enough to find an old gauging site at a one-time river bank, but the river itself had retreated about a hundred yards, making room for a marshy reed shore that separated me from fresh water. After a quick look at my map, seeing that from here I would again walk away from the stream and any marked lakes or lagoons, I decided to give it a try and find a way through a wall of carrizo cane, ten feet high and twenty feet thick.

CHAPTER ONE

Above my head, dark clouds began to form, the reeds swayed in a strong warm breeze. I followed an old rusty cable rope that ran down from a bollard, trailing away somewhere into the cane. There I found a narrow tunnel, an overgrown man-made passage. The marshy standing water was bone idle and stunk to high heaven, but on the other side of the tunnel, I could see a strong current of an alluring blue, the first time I would be at the river, maybe even in it.

When I had packed my gear, I had dithered long about that one and a half pound Bowie knife and whether I would need it. Here, indeed, I was happy I brought it, and, thinking of the old buddy who gave it to me, we cut our way through to the Colorado. Back in Germany, we used to plan common wilderness trips while sitting around a barbecue grill in front of his garage. Unfortunately, due to business reasons and suchlike, most of the times he couldn't join. Yet somehow, with presents like this, he kept the fire burning, and I figured, the extraordinary knife resembled his imaginary participation in a common trip we didn't do. I hoped he would excuse that its initial use was cutting cane and not a wild predator.

Before I would stir whatever the river was carrying on its desert passage, I filled my two one-gallon water sacks, then, I undressed and jumped into the refreshing cold of the Colorado. Now we got to know each other, he was no stranger anymore, no mere landmark in the distance, but my source for water and a fountain of energy. I was overtaken by the power of that dark blue water, flowing unhurriedly but unrelenting. The current was so strong, I had to hold on to the cane not to be flushed away, back to where I started some days ago. When I got out of the water, I sat down and listened while the warm wind dried me in a couple of minutes. I became conscious of the river's sound, a sonorous, sedate mumbling, like an old man; quite different from the childish, vivid chimes of a creek.

With the last shafts of sunlight, I was back at the gauging site. The map recommended a discontinuous dirt road from there leading north. That would be my best choice, I thought, through the coming up and down of hills and canyons. I followed the road into the first wash and lost it. It had been washed away, maybe last winter, maybe fifty years ago.

Washes are natural channels formed by water erosion, which drain the land after rainfall. As irregular and seldom as the rain comes here, the accompanying floods are sometimes so strong that the country would have to be remapped. Where these channels join the river, they collect the little fertile soil that had been washed out of the desert and with the nearby water source they tend to become overgrown with riparian plants.

Trying to walk a straight line to the other side, a thick forest of tamarisk wood forced me to wind my way roughly bearing north to the end of that 500-yard-wide wash. Every once in a while I found myself back on that dirt road for a short stretch until it disappeared in another wash or a forest of tamarisk wood. The maps became useless since my progress depended more on the vegetation than on topographic characteristics. Everything looked pretty much the same; wash succeeded ridge, ridge succeeded wash, and in between some deep canyons forced me to walk back inland to where it was easier to cross them.

Tonight, the rising moon was hiding behind fast moving clouds. When I found an open mining adit, I decided to stay there in case it should rain, and surrender early to darkness. It would have been too easy to lose orientation in that mountainous mess, too risky to climb on steep and disintegrating rock.

03/19   GOLDEN DREAM MINE, 6 MILES

I woke up early at 6, jumped out of my sleeping bag and without coffee or breakfast I was back on no track, trying to cover some miles before the midday heat would again force me to slow down. Today I saw the first wild donkey, one of the wild descendants of burros released into the desert by early prospectors. It kept following me for miles, watching me curiously from a neighboring rim. Sometimes I crossed their paths, surprised one, or a whole group. They looked so cute, even when angrily trying to keep me off their patch and hee-hawing at me, they had this mien that made me wanting to hug them. However, I wasn't so sure if they felt the same and yielded to them the right of way.

Soon I realized that following their trails would be the easiest way to avoid the constant up and down. Indeed, the follow-the-burro-rule worked quite well. In general, the burro or wild donkey is a pretty lazy animal, or clever in a way, not working more than it had to. It would never climb a mountain and waste vital energy if it could go around it. It's just too strenuous, and I guessed that without a notion of time donkeys have time. It didn't matter whether they arrived at a certain point sooner or later. Paradoxically, only we, who have an understanding of time, think we have no time.

Of course burro trails were not shown in a map and I could not see where they were leading to. But I could be sure, they had been pioneering these mountains for so long that they blazed the lesser burdensome ways and that it would never be a cul-de-sac. Following a chain of their paths almost turned into easy trail hiking.

Due to their endurance and being well adapted to that harsh climate, burros were first imported to the West from northern Africa by the Spanish in the 16th century. Prospectors exploring Southern California and Arizona for riches in the 1800s used them as pack animals, and the Frémont campaign accompanied by Kit Carson asked for them more often than for horses when equipping their troops to carry supplies for an upcoming war. During the

CHAPTER ONE

frontier movement and the eventual Americanization of Mexican California, there were so many of them here, it could well have become the heraldic animal of the state.

Instead, in 1846 a gung-ho lad among Frémont's rangers, who had heard rumors that California ought to strike for an independent republic, painted a bear and an imitation of Texas' Lone Star on a white flag when demonstrating the Sonoma capture. The grizzly bear did not only represent the many bears seen in the state those days. The Spanish word *osos* for bears also was the name of a private militia organized by American emigrants to confront the Mexican government. The *Osos* actually took Sonoma from it, and, as in Texas, the star symbolized the victory of the revolt. Ever thought about why a Texan would insult a Californian but never the Californian state flag?

Frémont's unilateralist leanings had successfully transported the Bear Flag into the end of the frontiering century. In the early 1900s, it was in the possession of the Society of California Pioneers. While the original burned during the conflagration of the Great Earthquake in 1906, five years later the state legislature adopted the bear flag as its state flag. A donkey flag would have been a legitimate option. For sure I would not see many grizzly bears on my hike anymore.

Once the lands were rushed, the wars fought, and the land boom was over, most of the burros were set free – if they had not trotted away much earlier. Soon they populated the California deserts, and since there wasn't much to do for them, they developed a remarkable reproduction rate. Today it is not unlikely to become an aural witness to their hee-hawing orgies at night. But with their trailblazing work they were of much more help to me than just for *pornaural* campfire entertainment.

At one point, I tried to shortcut the river's large west turn. My map suggested a jeep road cutting through these mountains; if I found it, I could reach my next stop, the Picacho Ruins, in a couple of hours. So I left the winding burro trail and tried to find a way over the mountains on a road that existed only in my map. I thought I could be smarter than a donkey. That made it two mistakes.

Mapped trails and especially 4WD roads had misled me several times. Murphy must have mapped out some of them. First, they went exactly in the direction lined in my map, then drifting away just a bit, too little to allow for skepticism. With every mile they drifted a little more, but only after an hour or so of hard walking on deep sand, I was sure, enough indications had accumulated to be unsure. Then I looked at my map, checked the compass; there, too, the marked road started in a wash that turned into a canyon, and it did some turns. Maybe after the next bend it would go back into the right direction. But how many bends had I said that before this one? One more? I checked the area for prominent or distinctive features, but couldn't see any.

Uncountable canyons and washes, and all ranges had about the same elevation. The farther I turned west the more I moved away from water, from my lifeline. My supplies were good for that night and another day. But what if I got stuck in these mountains? I decided to leave the backpack – hid it I don't know from whom in a small cave – and climb a range in order to get a better view. From there I could see that the jagged range paralleling this canyon would not allow a road to pass it very soon. So it was more likely that I had missed bypassing that range earlier and that I had been following the wrong wash for a couple of miles.

I walked back to my pack and thought about that misadventure. I had got up early to make up some time and get closer to Picacho. Now I ended up gaming away my lead because I banked on an old map, in an area where maps are only temporarily valid, instead of trusting in trodden trails nature had already prepared for me. Could I have found the right passage? Should I walk back or just cross the mountains in a straight line? I guessed I learned my lesson, the burros would never do that, especially not now, when the sun was about to reach its zenith. When I arrived at the cave, I sat down and paused, made a fire and prepared lunch. Two hours later the canyon rim would afford enough shadow to continue, that is, walk back easily.

In the end, my return was anything but continuous or easy. Of course I had not taken into account that I might have to find my way back, so I hadn't paid attention to specific features. Due to the constant pressure on shoulders and neck, I had formed a habit of walking longer stretches without regarding the area. Thumbs under the shoulder harnesses and head hanging low was the only way to release the stress on the upper part of the body a little bit. Only now, when looking for any features I might remember, I realized how many side canyons there were; or was one of them the main one? Whenever I wasn't sure, I dropped my pack and checked the surroundings or just walked until I found sand on the ground. Either there were my footprints or I was wrong.

Detours like that cost me twice as much energy and time, and I felt that uncertainty was making an already heavy pack even more burdensome. It came out in the wash that, at the meeting with my partner, I would check my pack thoroughly to find more non-essential items. I knew for sure, by then, some would have lost their indispensable pretense. Without water, I still had almost seventy pounds on my back, with one to two gallons, I was at eighty. And that close by a river. What would I do in the Mojave Desert or Death Valley where I needed four gallons from the start?

I finally found that jeep road canyon, a rather narrow side canyon of the one I had already explored. The entrance was hidden behind tamarisk brush and easy to miss. Though I picked up some wheel ruts there, the road was long lost in desert history, constantly interrupted and in places swept away by the last flood. I realized, I would have to make better use of my compass and common sense, or donkey sense, than looking for long abandoned dirt roads and 4WDs, which were – by the way – cut back dramatically since a couple of wilderness protection acts had been signed into law.

I took up the first animal trail to head back closer to the river. There, barren mounds jut out of a mixed forest of tamarisk, mesquite, and palo verde woods. If you stayed on the mounds, you would have to walk up and down; the closer you walked by the river, the lower the mounds were, but there, you could lose sight and end up in impenetrable, thorny brush. Consequently, these smart asses stayed on a constant level above the brush, amply walking around the inlets and mounds, even though they had to put up with large detours – detours long enough that you would never take them into consideration by looking on a map.

Far in the distance, I saw rocky spines protruding from the mountain ranges, and there at their foothill, behind another dozen of canyons, I saw some strange geometrical formations. They seemed to be within a grasp, but it took another two hours to get to the ruins of the Picacho mines. Standing on a hill from where I overlooked the historic remains, I took the last sip of water before I crawled down on my last legs.

Due to the scarcity of water, regular gold panning was not possible in the nearby Picacho Mountains. Early prospectors during the 1860s had to shovel rocks and gravel on a blanket and shake it until only the heavier gold particles remained. Nevertheless, once upon a time in the West, the L.A. Times reported on an "oasis of bustle", where a population of some 2,500 braved the elements and found some $15 million in gold. Closer to the river, they had formed a small self-supporting community of ranchers, cowboys, woodcutters, craftsmen, mechanics, and teachers, not to forget barkeepers and busty Kathies in the town's three saloons, which kept supplying the once "louche Picacho jail". Today, all of that was gone. The remaining ruins consisted of rock basements and the concrete framework of an old stamp mill.

Arriving at the river landing site, I acquitted myself of hat, gear, and shoes and fell dead on a wooden bench. I was too exhausted to go to the fishermen I saw on the other side of a picnic area, holding their rods into the river. Anyway, these fellows seemed not the least interested in me. They didn't even turn their heads for that snorting creature crawling down to the rest area behind their backs. I thought, there could have been two reasons for it, either it was quite common to see hikers around here, or it was so unusual that it wasn't in the realms of possibility, thus I just didn't exist in their reality. I later learned that the most obvious explanation was, they simply were passionate fishermen, which is analog to the latter. A real fishermen, who is concentrated on his potential catch, would disregard the edge of doom and most likely be untroubled by judgment day, just because it didn't happen in his reality.

I mean, I looked terrible, dirty, dusty, scratches all over my legs, my arms, even in my face. On the last several miles, I had to follow a narrow passage through thorny brush, now my body was virtually screaming for a longer pause. When I reached that bench groaning and down on my knees, I filled my two water sacks just to pour one-gallon over me and drink the other, while shaking brush out of my clothes amounting to a small forest. My socks steamed like boiling water, and, by the way, with my dusty clothes and that brown leather hat throwing shadow on my four-day beard, I really looked like a desperado, who had jumped out of a Western movie to escape the louche Picacho jail.

I put up with being a nobody, and after a while I started a fire to cook one of my Jamaican Chicken stews. You can be sure, it did taste like a real Caribbean feast, although it was just a pack of dehydrated food. I would bet my last dollar, if you'd take a food critic on a trip like that, these packs would certainly receive a stellar review.

Eventually, the two kids of one of the fishermen got bored from holding on a rod. They came over to me and asked curiously if I had seen any animals on my way. Of course they were not interested in birds and rabbits, so I told them of a huge lizard with awesome teeth and a mountain lion just like sabertooth. They laughed and screamed and cried for more over-sized monsters, while the fishermen were lost in reverie of suchlike, rapt in their attention.

With dusk they all came over to the picnic site, and, just as if we were introduced long ago, the first one hit me with, "Wanna beer?" The second one took the same line, "You sure look like you've spent some time in those mountains. Have a refreshment," and before I could say thanks for the can, the third one said, "You better come to our campsite, rangers don't like to see you camping down here, they'd wake you up in the middle of the night."

In fact, I had already met ranger Lily while cooking and I remembered a mean look in her face, when she asked me where I wanted to go from here. It wasn't hard to guess that she would not hesitate to kick me out of my sleeping bag should I rest my head on the wrong spot.

So I was happily surprised by the fishermen's new reality and joined them to their campsite. On our way we passed a wooden gate, behind which lay Picacho Road, a dirt road connecting to the outside world. I posted a piece of paper at the gate saying, 'I am here, March 19, Andy'. If all went according to plan, in two days I should meet my partner here. After he had left with his friend, they wanted to explore the desert their way, by 4-wheeling up to Vegas and back. We had arranged to meet either at the Picacho site or further north in Palo Verde, depending on how far I would get in the first days. Now I knew it would have been too risky to proceed without a pause, having to cover another thirty miles in two days. If I weren't up there yet, they would leave and come to Picacho, while I would still be following burros in the wilderness along the river. So I wanted to take the chance for an extended break and wait for them here.

Only a few minutes later, the smell of tamarisk wood was filling the air. The glow of the fire bathed the men's faces in flickering light, their shadows dancing on a one hundred-foot-high stonewall behind them. It was like coming home for Thanksgiving, where everyone was waiting and the open fire was already burning in the living room.

As far as you can own a campsite, this was Dale's fireplace. He obtained the priority of the stonewall claim by coming regularly, and with two trailers he surely brought more than just ordinary camping equipment. Ralph from Arizona had joined the circle and Ronda and Devin closed ranks. Dale was from Salton Sea and he remained a little skeptical about my plans. He was the man who rented Chris McCandless alias 'Alexander Supertramp' the canoe for his dubious trip into Mexico that later ended tragically "Into the Wild". The others were much more interested in my stories from the wilderness and why I would do such a thing. So Dale and I had something like an open competition winning the audience over. Until midnight we had heard all stories about giant blue gill, catfish, bass, and stripers, the most commonly fished in the southern Colorado, and everybody knew how hard it was to walk through the Colorado River desert.

Late in the evening, the ranger came by to see if everything was alright. Again I felt her eyes examining me. In order to charm away her ill humor, I asked her where the name Picacho came from. At least it made her withdraw that piercing look from me. Turning toward the fishermen, she explained that it was named for nearby Picacho Peak and that this was a Spanish-English redundancy, literally meaning *big peak peak*. American settlers felt obliged to rename the peak since the original Spanish name had been *Tetas de cabra* meaning goat tits, referring to the rocky spines I had seen days ago, from another long-gone and faraway reality.

*

While I was cooling off from my first stage, some thirty miles north, a German guy and his friend beckoned a police car asking the officer for help. They gained the officer's attention by reporting that their partner was lost somewhere in these mountains, and that he had probably overestimated his capabilities. He was overdue, had not shown up at the agreed meeting point in Palo Verde, and he was not reachable on his phone. The officer took them to the sheriff's office where immediately the responsible county sheriff in Yuma was informed. They rushed back to Yuma, filed a report, and provided personal details: what he looked like, what he was carrying, colors, sizes, how much water, how much food. The German was browsing through a book from 1958 to give them a vague idea of his buddy's route. The sheriff was quite sure, dehydration! He most likely had not carried enough water, and he handed the nervous German a brochure from the De Anza Rescue Unit about dehydration and consequences. While reading the featured stories of desert victims, the German imagined the worst. The brochure reported: "only eight years ago they had found another guy, who didn't make it. Being injured from a bad fall, he bled to death in the middle of the desert."

Then he called his partner's family at home to let them know how tragically that expedition seemed to have come to an end. There they found the address of the poor hiker's outfitter and made him fax a copy of the boot tread to the sheriff's office. Now the profilers could start working. Half a day later, everybody was informed and a battalion of deputies and rangers set up the first camp to design a plan of action. With the crack of dawn, they would set up a second camp closer to his assumed whereabouts, or his remains.

03/20   PICACHO, 0 MILES

Early in the morning, the sheriff in Yuma and the ranger in charge called everybody together. The action plan was spread; a sound search operation could take place scouring for a body on an eighty-mile stretch along the Colorado River. Backed by a Mexican scout, the K-9 unit of tracking hounds would explore the Chocolate Mountains. The 4WDs would check all dirt roads and washes for traces or abandoned campsites and the helicopters could scan the whole area between the Mexican border and Palo Verde.

*

Waking up with the first sunlight, down in Picacho it was peaceful and quiet; the only thing I heard were the voices of last night's campfire echoing from the stonewall. I tried to move up, but hell no, I felt like I'd been run over by a truck. Every bone and every muscle was hurting. This was the first day off since I started five days ago, and my body used the break to complain about the ongoing burden.

Smelling coffee, I eventually crawled out of the tent. Ralph sat there in the sun, grinning. "You're the talk of the town, walker." "Why, what happened," I asked. "Remember ranger Lily, she's been here to ask about you. If you're OK and so. She'll be back later to see you." Then Devin showed up, a cup of coffee in is hand. "Good morning, I just told the ranger to call off the search." I didn't get a word and asked for some background information. "Well, she told me that a German hiker was missing somewhere here in these mountains and that the search detachment was about to roll this morning. I asked her if she spoke to you, to the gentlemen she gave short shrift to the other day. I said, 'didn't he tell you he was from Germany?' Guess she put two and two together then."

And there she came. Having realized that the German walker they were looking for was indeed the German hiker she had talked to, she called off the search, stating I was found in good shape with no injuries or trauma; maybe just a little hangover, as an aside. To me she said, I would have an interview with the chief ranger later. And as if she needed to reprimand me, she ordered me to stay and not to move from this site until my friends would show up.

An hour later, another fisherman arrived at the campsite with his son. "So you must be the German Andreas walking from Mexico to Oregon," he yelled, "well down here, things go easily around." He proudly waved with his son's catch of the day, six stripers, each at least one foot long, and he chugged to the fireplace.

Slowly but surely I began to put the pieces together. My partners must have forgotten our alternative Picacho. They just stayed in Palo Verde and didn't even wait for the arranged time. The fact that they were unable to get me on the phone caused them to start that mess. It seemed it didn't even cross their minds that mobile phones might not work in the wilderness or that you just wouldn't turn it on unless you were in civilization. I should have considered that, for people who did not have an idea of wilderness, who never heard that call of the wild, I had to have given stricter rules of conduct. They simply apply the same rules to wilderness a life is administered by in the city, and if you try to explain the difference, they become inveterate pessimists. People who are cocksure that such an endeavor just cannot turn out all right would cause a drama even if there was no reason for it. In fact, on and off I learned it is beyond some people's imagination that wilderness still is the last resort untouched by our modern control mania, although, with GPS and satellite phones, we are well on the way to give up that retreat. At least I obtained some amount of infamy, much sooner than I ever expected.

Around noon, my partner and his friend arrived at the Picacho site. I had left my note at the entrance gate, just as if I had to prove that this was part of our plan. The reunion was kind of ambivalent to me. I appreciated his worries and felt being very important to him. With the little English vocabulary he knew, he had started something that could have turned into the biggest search enterprise since Steve Fossett's disappearance from Nevada skies. On the other side, he caused an unnecessary maneuver, produced the biggest phone bill he ever had in his life, and crazed friends and family, just because he forgot our arrangements. The method of the ranger system surprised me no less. I felt quite safe after that, knowing they would move heaven and earth should I really get lost – after the false alarm, though, maybe not so much anymore. However, with a little more deliberateness and methodicalness they would have made sure that someone interviewed all fishermen and campers around Picacho, the only place of civilization where I definitely had to come through, as long as I was alive and kicking. After all, the fact that sheriff and chief ranger turned a blind eye and let us get off cheaply made me happy about the friendship at first and also feel safe and secure for the days to come. And it was a particular concern of my partner and his friend to state that they were always treated friendly and safely in the best of hands, both by the sheriff and the police, and by the rangers.

Late afternoon, chief ranger Marian Brown showed up at our campsite with Lily at her side. Stony-faced she listened to my story, that we arranged a meeting in Palo Verde and that – if I realized I could not make it there in time – I would stay in Picacho and wait for them. Then she told me their version, explaining that my partner had already declared me missing, if not lost. We agreed that I would have to give instructions more clearly and precisely and that the officers may have been a little overeager. Every local who was familiar with the area could have seen with one glance on a map that it was almost impossible to reach Palo Verde in that time, thus checking the only mapped site in between, namely Picacho. I surely had to make my experiences in order to correctly calculate distances and the time needed in unknown terrain, and she was sure that canyons, washes, and banks along the Colorado would teach me my lesson.

By that time, every fisherman between Yuma and Palo Verde knew who I was, the adventurous walker, following in Colin Fletcher's footsteps from Mexico to Oregon, or was it Alaska? Indeed, I felt being hot on his trail; while two U.S. border patrolmen, who tracked him down as a suspect wetback, had told him, after they found out about his legal intent, that they would organize a search if he failed to reach Palo Verde on schedule, sure enough I had finally caused it – almost an irony of history, fifty years later.

Having survived that unintentional little misadventure, I scanned my pack for things I wanted to get rid of. This was the last chance to leave heavy items behind without just dropping them good-bye in the desert. On the list was: the solar panel device I brought for camera and laptop – the two batteries for my camera were good for some 800 pictures and, on average, I should run through a town every other week to reload them. Also, I would use the Macbook only when I stopped in a city to download photos or write a story, and I brought enough gigabytes on memory cards to shoot more than 1,000 photos before I had to download them. Though, as I would soon learn, here I could well reach their limits in a week or two. Other items that flew out of my pack were some clothes – I took too many socks and shirts, and washing those more often would reduce pack weight too; books I would never read on a trip like that – there are just too many other things to do; and, I hoped my buddy would excuse that, too, a one-and-a-half-pound Bowie knife.

All in all, I came out with ten pounds less, totaling sixty without water. I put everything in a bag and handed it over to my partner. A hug and a thumb and they drove away with the last daylight and with them, I thought, all second thoughts.

Yet sometimes when you have to face a difficult task or when you are about to take off for a long journey, on the evening before, there is an uneasy feeling creeping over you, suggesting to sleep through, stay in bed, miss the plane, get sick, or pray for an act of God beyond your control, just to have a reason to cancel everything and hide under the blanket that exonerates you from everything. Months of planning, anticipation, and certainty are suddenly called into question. The *force majeure* clause for adventurers caught me unawares with my pants down right when I wanted to go to bed. It usually hits on the eve of the venture; so it did in the motel in Winterhaven and it came back again that night after they were gone. It may be a natural protective mechanism, or sense, demanding room for a last thought, a last check, 'are you sure you want to do this', testing you with all kinds of clear images of the comforts you are about to give up. The hardships I experienced so far were only a taste of what lay ahead; from here I could still get a ride back to civilization with one of the fishermen. But at the same time, the taste was adventurous and already so heady and auspicious, I knew I could never have resigned.

That feeling would come back in the morning again, being the very first thought right when I woke up, but then it would already be too late, because with the crack of dawn I had to rise to the challenge. Then I couldn't sneak away anymore under the blanket collecting excuses. Once I would leave the bed, the adventure had already begun.

03/21   PICACHO, 8 MILES

I woke up early around 6. Ralph was knocking at my tent after he had packed his traps to say goodbye. As I expected, I was somehow waiting for an offer to ride with him and spend some days at his home in Arizona. Instead he said, "Keep me posted. I really wish I were in your shoes." That was it. He started the engine, waved for a last time, and drove off. His last words should become my motivation for that second first-hiking-day.

Although the campsite started filling with Easter holiday tourists, I somehow felt left alone. On no other destination would anybody wait to see how I was doing. All the fishermen were gone and as much interest they developed in my journey – Ralph compensated Dale's lack – I still had to walk on alone. It's strange how quickly we get used to company. In this rather short time of two days, with his sincere interest in my journey and some rather empathic questions about my motives, Ralph became somehow very familiar. After the unexpected, pleasant company and these two easy days, an uncertain suspense lay ahead of me by hitting the wetback trail.

I felt, I really needed these two days of rest in Picacho to regain my strength. The first blisters could dry before they bothered me and the wadding in my knees turned into steely muscles. While I was repacking my things, I had a nice chat with a Dutch-American senior couple that just arrived and spread their household over the campsite. They belonged to the genus called 'birdies'. After one hour, I knew every bird that inhabited this part of the desert by name. Willemina and Jim planned to stay for two weeks rounding out the photographic collection of black cormorants, snowy egrets, quail, and you-name-it-birds.

I was not a 'birdy', and indeed, of all the fauna it has always been birds I most easily overlooked. Even though they have the most desirable means of travel, unless they reached the size of an eagle, I had never paid much regard to them. This began to change that summer, either because I met the right people to call my attention on them or because the birds sometimes spent their time with me, sitting on a branch and gazing at me provocatively until we established eye contact. While having a farewell cup of coffee with Willemina and Jim, they named every bird we saw, and all of a sudden, when I knew their names, they were interesting. My favorite was a covey of quail, sort of a desert race chicken. Here, we watched two families drifting across the sand on their dawn patrol. Kind of flaunty, with their heads held up high, they were in fact rather drifting on the sand than running or flying. While the whole group was hiding under a creosote, one adult set sail and ran over to the next bush. There, it turned around and called for the others, who immediately formed a line to cross the land of uncertainty. Either these funny birds could count or they proved good visual judgment; while one adult led the group, another one stayed exactly in the middle of the line, and the remaining adults covered the end, constantly looking around.

I was just getting in a good mood, had forgotten my blue feelings, and I was ready for a good start into the afternoon – there came ranger Lily in her SUV. Leaning out of the window, her frown ordered me to come over. A dry "Are you leaving now?" was as nice as she could get and a comparatively friendly introduction to what came next. She felt the need to educate me on the conditions of her territory. "First: there are absolutely no springs or wells for fresh water. Second: north from here, it is impossible to get access to the river for fresh water. Third, fourth, and fifth: absolutely no camping in the wildlife refuge, in the park area, or on BLM land – even though they have their own rules." She knew that you could not reach *permitted* lands in half a day, and she felt that her commandments did not impress me as much as she wanted it. Therefore she topped it off, specifying other important facts, such as a detailed description of snakebite implications. Indeed, that made me feel queasy. "The venom of a rattlesnake is aimed to digest," she paused, "aimed to digest the prey from the inside, meaning as soon as it is paralyzed, the flesh and internal organs begin to disintegrate." I knew when she said *prey* she bit her tongue not to say *you*. However, she couldn't keep from being more precise when she continued, "The same thing would happen to the flesh around a bitten arm, a leg, or even the face if it gets to it while *you*'re sleeping. Well, usually, they're out for extremities. Intense swellings will cut off blood circulation behind the bite, eventually causing the limb to die off." Then, coming closer to me, she lowered her voice, "And by the way, unbearable pains." She meant pains like I'd never experienced before, so bad that I would lose my sense of orientation and probably my consciousness only a little later. I felt as if I had already been bitten and looking in the ranger's eyes suggested I wasn't far from it. Evil flowed out from her grimly gleaming eyes, the same evil I suspected from a belligerent venomous snake. I began to feel faint. Her seeming grip wrapped itself around me while I tried to avoid her gaze. I think I ducked down a little bit, as if I wanted to dodge an attack.

Without taking her eyes off me, she suddenly smiled. It was a kind smile, time to take a breath, and then she said: "At least I have a good advice for you. Best you can do? Don't move and try to get help. That's the best I can tell." I seized this moment of lenity, knocked at the car and wresting myself free I turned around and replied: "I'll do my best, ma'am, thanks for the advice." Walking away from the car, I wondered where I put these copies from the Fletcher file I brought with me. There was one sheet about rattlesnakes and cure, and I wanted to read it at my next campfire. I shouldered my pack and walked away in the shadow of tamarisk, carefully watching every step.

From right after the Picacho site until in the afternoon, I passed several sandy bays along the Colorado, very easy accesses to get water or have a decent bath in knee-deep, little pools. Just before I would have to leave the river in order to get around a string of lakes and marches, I came to a beautiful blue lagoon, protected from the current by large riparian fields of reed. Sitting down for a while to check my map for the further route, I began daydreaming of taking my clothes off for a bath when suddenly someone came swimming from around the reed into my direction. When then an Ursula Andress appearance stepped out of the river, literally emerging from the sea with water drops trickling down her tanned skin like in slow motion, I wouldn't have been surprised if she had the torso and the tail of a fish. Instead, the young lady walked on her feet up the bank toward me, shook her wet hair, and introduced herself as Linda. I was so surprised, and being aware that my own appearance was far from a handsome special agent, I could barely ask her the way. She said, they'd come here for years and that she remembered an off-road trail that should take me around the swampy lagoons. Better I would join her to the campsite and have a look on their maps.

That was it. So much for hiking today. Two hours later we were sitting around a big fire, having steaks, shrimps, crabs, potatoes and salad, wine and beer. Linda invited me to stay and after her husband Benton had eyeballed me for one hour, he not only ruled I was OK, but also that I had to stay. Later on, their son Andrew, his wife Jessica, and their daughter Isa came back from jet skiing the Colorado. The party started and it ended soon after we finished the second *Benton Special*, his own Zombie made of Bacardi White, Bacardi 151, Myers Rum, Malibu Rum, and some pineapple juice – for the color, mind you.

03/22   4S RANCH, 0 MILES

Our breakfast that morning was as superb as the steaks the night before. Benton was an outdoor chef and he knew his onions. The enticing smell that woke me up streamed in from two pans filled with eggs, vegetables, and bacon, placed on his gas stove, which was impressively powered by two twenty-pound propane tanks. Benton took to cooking like a duck to water. As if he had four arms, he swung the two pans, threw toasts on the grill, and filled one plate after the other.

After breakfast he took me on a jet-ski ride. I was lucky, his granddaughter Isa insisted on coming with us. Therefore our excursion down the Colorado was only half breakneck speed. We flew downstream passing Picacho, met ranger Lily there, "You still here?" and flew back upstream to our captain's favorite fishing spot, the Catfish Hole. From there he pointed to a mountain alongside the river and told me its story. "There you will stand tomorrow – you're staying another night, won't you? Okay! – on top of this mountain, and wave down to us. You'll be sitting on a stone and let your eyes wander, and think of a man and his dog."

He reported that, about the time when Colin had come through, there lived a crazy fellow on this mountain. Prospecting the canyons around, he said goodbye to the city and dwelled in an Indian tipi. People often saw him sitting on the edge for hours, his dog next to him, both watching the river below. Sometimes he danced on this mountain, and his dog joined him and jumped and howled to his funny contortions. People got used to him, they believed he was loco, but they did not bother him. One day, his dog died, and *Loco* buried him under a cairn. On top he placed a tombstone, on which he engraved how much he loved him. From that day on, they never saw him dancing again.

When *Loco* died several years later, men went on that mountain and buried him right next to his dog. I couldn't help being moved by his story.

Colin had mentioned an old man living on a hill in an adobe hut near Picacho. A fisherman had told him about that man, stating that here he would walk through California's 'last frontier'. In fact, that mountain was more of a hill, and I felt closer to the Californian frontier than ever before. Still today that seemed to be the reason for fishermen and weekend desert aficionados to come to this part of left-alone wilderness.

We came back to the campsite, a tricky spot to go ashore. Here, the Colorado pushes its waters around a bend, and with a strong sudden breeze from the other side, the jet ski tumbled and we all dived deep. I grabbed Isa and held her above water, with the other hand holding tight to the capsized machine. In only a few seconds we were all out in the middle of the river drifting back toward Picacho. No – I didn't want to give her a chance to state, "Oh, still here!" Not in a situation like that. I did my best to move the jet ski toward Benton, and when he reached us, he climbed the bike, moved it back into position, helped his daughter up, and started the engine. Then I climbed out of the water, sat behind Isa, and we all shook hands. Back ashore, mother and sister were welcoming us. I wasn't quite sure whether their faces were laughing or frightened.

Anyway, enough reason for a Benton Special. With our clothes off, wrapped in towels, the beach party began afresh. Now even Isa, the little girl, who had been harboring her skepticism about that strange fellow with the huge pack on his back, warmed up and came to trust me. I felt flattered when she showed all her charm, "Can I do anything for you, Andy?" while making a curtsy. "Yes, Isa," I said, "call up the captain to please bring me my wine."

Despite being there for only 48 hours, now it felt as if I had known that family for a long time and this would be our farewell dinner after a long camping vacation we had spent together. The captain presented another outdoor gourmet dinner. "Tonight the chef recommends: breaded catfish a la Benton, green vegetables and salad Niçoise. The spare catfish will be wrapped in foil, for you, to go," said the chef and declared the buffet open.

If I kept that speed, averaging eight miles in two days, I could definitely forget about my desert deadline. I was welcome to stay another day, but I felt the urge to move on. Enough of this hanging out, let's get on with it! My mission appealed to my reason, as strange as that sounds for a trip into freedom. For the time being, the end of the desert was my only appointment and I accounted it as a serious one that mustn't be missed.

03/23   4S RANCH, 8 MILES

We got up at six. Benton's home-mixed Quaker's crunch and two cups of coffee were my power fuel for a decent morning hike until I would rest for lunch. I packed my things and looked for the spare catfish. "Did anyone take that fish off the grill last night?" Everybody shrugged his shoulders, everybody but the raccoon, which was probably somewhere kibitzing out of the reed. Benton compensated my loss to the wildlife with two cans of chicken stew. I took only one because of the weight, and having been stuffed like a Thanksgiving turkey for two days, I thought I wouldn't eat much anyway until I reached Palo Verde. Benton led me to the turnoff of the old jeep road, a shortcut that would spare me most of the lagoons and some overgrown wash deltas along the river. "Happy trails, my friend, and say hello to El Loco."

There I was, back alone in the desert, following two paralleling tracks as they wound westwards away from the river, climbed slopes and entered washes again. I should have known better; three canyons later, I had lost the jeep road. In a canyon or wash you could not find the road since the last flash flood that swept down from the mountains had surely covered all tracks with sand, debris, or piles of dead wood. As long as the road continued on the opposing side, you were able to pick it up again, but if it stayed in the wash for a while, chances were low. Here, even on the hills between the washes, it was continuously interrupted. Since the rangers had closed the cutoff, hardly anyone used the jeep road and wilderness accepted the returned ground with alacrity.

I could not be farther than a mile from my guideline, the river, but here, without a trail or tracks, I was lost in a canyon labyrinth surrounded by steep walls and towering rock pinnacles. It is almost impossible to navigate out of a deep gorge since you can hardly see landmarks to calculate your position. My map was useless here. Although most of these canyons had been eroded ten feet and more into the desert ground, this was still no size to withstand flash floods that sweep tons of debris down from the mountains. A sudden rainstorm could have dramatically changed the terrain in no time at all. New ditches might have been washed into existence, older ones blocked, often creating an unclear conjunction of alleys and blinds.

Again I headed back closer to the river. I tried to walk in the shadow of the wall, but the sun was soon scorching the canyon rim, and I could feel that this would become the hottest day so far. I regretted even that one can of stew and poured away one gallon of water since I would soon reach the river anyway. With my head hanging low to avoid the merciless sun, I trotted down the sandy floor surrounded by 10- to 15-foot-high canyon walls. Suddenly, behind the brim of my hat, I sensed a big shadow moving on the rim. When I lifted my head, the shadow became a mountain lion and it jumped right in front of me, no more than twenty feet away. Instinctively I stood upright trying to make myself appear bigger. In a second, all stories I had heard about mountain lions attacking hikers took solid shape. My breath suddenly short, I looked for a stick, or some stones, always keeping one eye on the predator. Only then he turned around and eyed me. Obviously due to the strong adverse wind, he had not smelled me, the sandy canyon floor might have swallowed my steps. And yet his movement was not the kind caused by a surprise but a majestic and lordly look back, demonstrating that there was no being grander than him.

Fascination struggled with fear. Camera, knife, or just stand tall and shout at him? Before I could think it out, he was up on the opposite rim; two jumps that left me alone in the canyon, trembling with suspense. For a single second, I was looking into the eyes of a mountain lion. I guessed, he was as surprised as I was, and maybe in *his* single second he was deliberating "should I, should I not?" Perhaps I was lucky because he had just had a catfish-stuffed raccoon for dinner and he reasoned, "Not worth the trouble."

CHAPTER ONE

It was the scariest moment, remembering that especially hikers run the risk of being attacked mistaken for prey, and it was the most beautiful thing I saw so far. Quite perspicuous, I received a first warning how close danger and adventure are to each other and, at the same time, I realized that the quality of an adventure was closely tied to imminent dangers, at least to their possibility if not their probability.

Those were the moments when places were given names, and accordingly I made an entry on my map. Exiting *Cougar Canyon*, I stood in front of El Loco's mountain, which Benton had shown me on our river cruise. To its right was the river, the cliffs too steep to go around this way, to its left, another overgrown canyon, but in the sand around me, a welcoming clutter of tracks, all ending in one single line, the burro trail winding around that mountain.

Having walked around it by half, all of a sudden, the path turned up to the top. As I tried a few further steps, I understood the burros had quite rational motives for the abrupt change in direction; it was not so much because they felt obliged to pay their last respects to *Loco* but because of the back-braking steep talus slope around the other half. When I got to the summit, I sat down at the shrine, imagined him dancing with his dog, and I understood what made them dance right here from where they overlooked a pattern of colored ranges and peaks, breached by the blue, snaking Colorado. Without a doubt, a very mystic place.

Below that mountain at my feet lay an almost tropically green carpet of brush and trees in a delta created by a broad wash and the bending river. Leaning into a wide turn, the Colorado had forever been washing soil ashore, and with every rain dead wood and roots were washed from the mountains into the delta. From up here it looked like a lush forest, when I got down into it, it turned out to be a chaos of interlocked roots and branches, a meshwork of tamarisk, other plants, and driftwood.

Non omnis arbusta iuvant humilesque myricae. The first time I was confronted with tamarisk was in a Latin verse by poet Vergil. My teacher translated it as: 'Not everybody is delighted by tamarisks and shrubbery.' At that time, I had no imagination of this plant, 25 years later I learned what the poet meant and, before long, that included me.

Commonly known as salt cedar, it is a small shrubby tree with white and pink flowers. However, it loses most of its color the closer you get, eventually showing its grayish-brown branches, while the thorny twigs make sure you do not get too close. Introduced to the U.S. as an ornamental plant in the early 1800s, the tamarisk had taken over large sections of riparian areas in the Colorado Desert, constantly pushing back native legume trees such as palo verde and mesquite, and also cottonwoods and willows.

A huge tree-planting campaign during the Great Depression, which used the plant's resilience to fight soil erosion, had paved the way for its triumphal conquest of the West. Although it called the drier areas of Africa home, the shores of the Colorado offered ideal conditions for it to live off the little fat of this land and feel like being in heaven. Speaking of which, in Vergil's days it was said to be the favorite plant of Apollo, the god of sun and light. I'll bet you. Welcome to California deserts, Mr. Apollo.

Tamarisk is something like the camel of brushes; it survives long arid periods and is on the sauce when there is water. It grows close to riverbeds as well as on saline soils with a marked preference for the washes I needed to cross. Being resistant to almost everything, it is the prime example for 'bad weeds grow tall'. It can tolerate alkali conditions, it is fire-adapted, and it limits competition from other plants. By developing long tap roots that allow them to intercept deep water tables, it takes up salt from there, accumulates and deposits it in the surface soil where it builds up concentrations destructive to most other plants, hence monopolizing the shores. If nothing else, they increase the frequency and intensity of wild fires and floods. Almost a biblical plant.

Why am I telling all these bad things about tamarisk? Because it was mean to me, too. From here up along the Colorado, forests of brush blocked my way several times a day. Its enticing pink and white flowers bloom in dense masses thereby hiding the three-inch-long spikes. I felt invited to touch or smell the bouquets a couple of times, before I learned the thorny lesson. The only good news about tamarisk is that its stem makes a good fire, burning long with a tangy but likable aroma, almost like mesquite wood, which was my most efficient campfire fuel in the desert, burning slowly, enduring, and smokeless.

While I'm at it, the mesquite was the most common native shrub in the desert along the Colorado, growing from small ground-hugging bushes to twenty and thirty-foot-high trees in broad washes and canyons. Their fresh green leaves put an almost unnatural color into the desert, only depreciated by its yellow flowers harboring an own biotope of flying labor for the mesquite honey production. It has always been a useful plant to Native Americans, who make tea, syrup, and a meal called pinole from it. They also use the bark for basketry, fabrics, and medicine, and the flowers of course for honey. Our household use of its wood today is rather fueled by nostalgia, since one clever marketing mind put together cattle industry, cowboy romanticism and, to spice up the TV commercials, some Western-movie scenes. And now, mesquite's fuel value is not only higher than that of pine or juniper, it even has the ability to suggest millions of city dwellers around the world that they are right here in adventure land, frizzling their beef on the smell of the Wild West, real mesquite charcoaled burger. Needless to say that charcoaled mesquite has not much aroma left to flavor anything but the imagination.

On some farmlands in Imperial Valley, I had seen mesquite trees scattered at more or less regular intervals. First I thought they were left there as

CHAPTER ONE

windbreaks or for the field worker to have more or less frequent naps. A farmer instead explained that they collect minerals from deep in the ground and pump them up to leaves and pods, which fertilize the soil when falling off. Remembering this, I looked at it differently, and in fact I often noticed a small harbor of herbs or flowers under the canopies of mesquite.

Later in spring, in the Mojave Desert, I would learn that those washes with mesquite trees had a larger variety of plants and blooming flowers than others, since the fertilizing drop-offs were washed away and dispersed by the floods after rainfall.

The third widespread wash dweller was the palo verde, reaching up to forty feet. Its Spanish name alludes to the plant's greenish bark. One morning, I woke up in one of the few washes where palo verde trees prevailed. I heard a buzzing sound, got up and checked the sky for a border patrol plane. For a minute I walked around with my head in the sky. The noise became louder and louder and when I reached the largest tree, it was all around me. The palo verde was in full yellow bloom, coveted by thousands of bees who were harvesting its clothes of yellow blossoms.

Seeing a wash on a map, commonly marked as a green spot in monochrome desert, you would think that access to or just walking along the river is easier there. But maps don't tell much about the sort of vegetation, and I learned vividly that a green wash was a place to avoid, being either impenetrable brush that consisted of the aforementioned plants or swamp. Here, the burro trail was winding through the thicket of thornbushes, following a thin line where palo verde trees repelled the predominant tamarisk and mesquite. Behind the trail, though, the branches were intertwined into each other as if they were fighting for land rights, aiming for the foundation soil closest to the river.

*

When planning the daily distance you want to cover, you would usually look for a distinctive spot on your map. This evening, I arrived at the place marked as Draper Ranch. However, the two or three mouldering cabins I found there presented but an unconvincing excuse for the entry in my map. Draper Lake, a little farther, was surely not a resource for water but a greenish muddy lake surrounded by tall reed shores. I decided to get water somewhere else on the next day and climbed a rocky mound in order to spend the night above and away from the brush.

Here in the desert, it is always advisable to prevent unwelcome critters from crawling into your sleeping bag, scorpions, black widows, and a strange spider I never heard of before, the brown recluse. One of the fishermen I met had told a story about having been bitten by one, his flesh started decaying and he could do nothing about it. In fact, it had left a big, deep, and ugly scar on his leg. Then there were the snakes; some that would not bother, like the gopher or the king snake, and one that would, the rattlesnake. All these creatures are out for a warm dark nest, and what could be cozier than curling up in a blue sleeping bag at 98° F. Accordingly, I had spent all nights in a tent, so far. However, on that day, I had walked late into the evening, and when I reached the top of the mound, I was too tired to put it up. Up here, I thought, I could do without the tent. There was nothing but plain rock, no plants, no gravel, not even niches or crevices where creepy crawlers could hide.

After having collected some mesquite branches, I came back up and built a small fire on my summit camp, from where I overlooked a peculiar looking formation called Lighthouse Rock and the site of the Draper Ranch.

I thought about the rest of the world, all these people who could not sit at the Lighthouse Rock right now, who lived from Mondays to Fridays, in weekdays and weekends, while I, for the first time, had lost track of time. Was it Monday or Tuesday? Or was it Sunday? I smiled with a slight touch of lordliness, just like when you are awarded a prize and for a short moment in your personal history you feel a little higher than the rest of the world. While the finish still had to be reached, the aim was already achieved.

When the fire was down to a few embers, just a few weak flames struggling against the night cold, I felt the silence of the desert crawling up the rocky mound to its summit. It was a different silence, though, as compared to when you sat in a cave or in a canyon. There, you would accept it, as rocks or walls or just brush seemed to shield any noise. But up here, it was hard to believe that in all this space between Leo and Taurus, between the desert and the sky, there should not be the slightest sound. I looked from star to star, and just when I accepted the positive quality of nothing, a shooting star fell out of the Big Dipper into the darkness on the other side of the river. For a brief moment, the silence was broken. I thought I heard it falling.

03/24   DRAPER LAKE, 15 MILES

I was probably the first man in California to be greeted by the rising sun. There she stood at 6 in the morning against a mountainous Arizona horizon, only a stone's throw away. With her first beam, the night cold evaporated. I turned around and saw the western crestline in morning fire, red-colored rocks and canyons behind me. With a deep the-world-is-beautiful breath, I turned back to indulge myself in another nap. My hands still buried in the sleeping bag, it was just when I laid my head down that I realized a movement on my rocky sheet. I startled; trapped in the sleeping bag I hectically rolled to the side and struggled out of it to have a closer lock. Avidly and fleet-footed, a one-inch long spider was scampering around, not sure about what that big shadow meant above it. That must be it, the brown recluse, long skinny legs, eight – no wait, seven – in number, brownish to yellow body. I saw six eyes,

CHAPTER ONE

arranged in three pairs, just as the fisherman described it. And the black spots on its back, did they form a violin, the distinctive sign for the killer spider, the horrible violin spider, the fiddler of death? I stopped the music. There was no violin on its back, and although it had six eyes, I found them rather arranged in two triads. Anyway, it was a big spider, and God only knew what this one could do. I took the chance for an early start and got up.

The mountain lion the day before and this would-be recluse made me thoughtful. No longer did wilderness merely mean navigating with map and compass or knowing about water resources. Deeper down, of course, I had known that this journey posed very real dangers. As long as you sidestep them, you don't concern yourself very much with them, but now, these two surprise encounters made it plain to me that in a second your plans could be abruptly thwarted and the nostalgic pioneering nonchalance might turn into a matter of survival, even in California, the most populated state in the U.S. Help was far away and, in the case of losing power rapidly or poisoning, it might be unreachable. I decided to be more alert and from now on watch every step I took.

The recluse preoccupied me for a while, and I recalled that fisherman elaborating about the symptoms. The bite itself did not hurt, he said, just a little itchy. The whole program would not start before the next day. When I saw his pit scar, I had no doubt about the effectiveness of the program. Restlessness and weakness would be the start, fever and chills, vomiting and a general pain would mark the first day and get you ready for the not so mild symptoms. I felt something on my left cheek; was that just an itch, a pickle, a bite – or mere hallucination?

Later on I read more about recluses, and I learned that, in fact, they somehow had conquered the Californian world, at least its world of thought. These spiders build their homes in cabins and cottages, sheds or woodpiles, garages, closets, cellars, and storage rooms, generally any place that's dry and undisturbed. They seem to have a marked preference for shoes, inside dressers, wardrobes and in stacks of clothes. They love infrequently used beds, laundry, and bathroom cabinets, but they also settle behind pictures or the philosophers' collection you haven't touched since you put it in the shelves. In a pinch, they are content with baseboards or piles of firewood. Is there any place where they aren't? Yes, California, according to a conversation with an arachnologist. He was absolutely sure, NO BROWN RECLUSE IN CALIFORNIA! He turned out to be sort of a defense counsel for the recluse clan, presenting every thinkable evidence for the lack of brown recluses in this state. He is definitely right in stating that because of the rare occasion of a deleterious venom incident, almost all spiders are lumped into the category of 'squish first and ask questions later'. I did not squish mine. It was scampering so unconcernedly with its missing leg that it also lost its horror-movie stigma for a second. It took the chance and legged it.

As indicated by its name, the recluse is anything but aggressive. Generally, it bites only when pressed against the skin, such as when tangled up within clothes, bath towels, or in bedding – or when laying your head back for a nap.

However, the brown recluse's habitat is exclusively throughout the central Midwest and the South. The only species found in California were probably imported hitchhikers brought by people moving to the West as official records state a mere ten instances in forty years. Nevertheless, there is a great awareness of this spider, not only among fishermen in Picacho but throughout California, mostly through a misguided media barrage, which is stirred by archaic fears of an eight-legged monster menacing the lands and wreaking havoc.

After an occurrence in a small town in California, a local newspaper looking for a sensationalistic sound bite had asked the arachnologist: "What do you think the effect of this brown recluse event will have on southern California?" His answer was, "All the tourists from Missouri, Arkansas and Kansas are laughing themselves off their hotel beds because a story on one alleged brown recluse spider found in Los Angeles makes the evening news." He said that in any barn throughout the Midwest you would need ten minutes to collect more recluses than have been found by the entire California population, ever, and hardly anyone got bitten. Here, he continued, media like to live it up, discussing the vague possibility of one spider that made it into California and welcoming every would-be occurrence as a real gift for the next headline: "Necrotic Wound Blamed on Elusive Spider", "Spider-bite Terror in California", "Likely Bite by Spider Changes Life". He got excited, stated that their stories were speculative and based on the premise that a brown recluse could be found in California. "While this is certainly true, since people move from the Midwest each day, it is also true that because I am a male, I could have an illicit and immoral relationship with a Playboy bunny. This is definitely a possibility. However the chasm between possibility and probability is so wide you couldn't build a bridge between here and there."

I afforded the question, "What if?" to hear if the fisherman had really encountered one. In fact, a small number of bites produce severe lesions of the skin and systemic symptoms, including organ damage and occasionally even death. Where the bite occurred, the tissue would die and the skin would be sloughed off, the wound would grow gangrenous to the size of a palm and last for months, at least leaving deep scars. In any case, you would get a lifelong memory and a conversation-starting souvenir.

Days later, I remembered that I had forgotten to ask about the one that freaked me. I called the institute again and a friendly assistant gave me what I wanted: there's a similar recluse species in the deserts southwest, the desert recluse, and their bites were as bad.

Three pairs or two triads, violin or nonmusical fellow, I made it down that hill into the next wash, and what awaited me there was much more substantial and cleared out the cobwebs. From up on the hill, I had already seen that the overgrown wash basin reached far into a canyon to my left. Behind the canyon, a big lagoon had been cut off from the river, forming a one-mile-long inland swamp. Going around it would have meant at least two miles of struggling up and down, but right in front of me, a tongue of land reached deep down into the tamarisk wash and from the other side another one toward me, thus enclosing the lagoon and separating it from the river. There were only one hundred yards of brush between the two banks. It was midday and hot, and I would have been grateful for every mile I didn't have to walk. So I left my pack behind and tried to find a way to the opposite side. I climbed into the brush, clawed my way through, climbed into some trees and crawled on their branches like a clumsy sloth. I was hardly touching ground anymore; it was like climbing in a frame of rope bridges and monkey bars. After one hour I had to give up. I was totally messed up, dust and sand and branches all over me, and I had not even gotten halfway over to the other side. It took me one hour to do fifty yards; one hour back, one-hour rest, three hours lost. At the end, I walked around it. The burros seemed to steer clear of this area; within a mile around this fiendish meshwork, I didn't see any tracks.

Late afternoon after having digested the wash, I stumbled on a well-trodden trail. To my surprise, it led me to a camp along the river, a small settlement of some twenty riverfront homes, apparently holiday resorts. Very prominent were the huge garages attached to each home, some of them larger than the houses; I could peek into three or four and see why: each one housed at least one pick-up, a boat trailer with motorboat, an SUV, an assortment of jet skis, and a super-sized American refrigerator, all of them preferably in snow-white. Some men were standing at the garages, talking about their amazing sports vehicles while pouring a no less impressive amount of beer cans down their throats. If one of them had invited me to choose anything from this fleet of spotless white luxury vehicles, I would certainly have opted for the refrigerator and its contents. However, here there was no hollering at me, no welcoming nod, not even a cagey wink. Seeing someone like me here seemed to cause suspicion.

I felt it and it cost me quite an effort to ask three brawny, tanned guys for fresh water. They had gathered in front of their fridge, grabbing hold of some beers, and looked at me as if Mars attacked; but muscle-bound as they were, they worked up their courage and gave me a soda and water. I thanked and turned slowly away. I expected more questions – what are you doing, where are you from, where are you heading, but nothing happened; men were quiet and simply waited until I was gone. So I quickened my pace heading for the next boating ramp, undressed, and consigned my weary body to the river.

About a mile along the Colorado, there were more houses, two streets with names but no purpose. It looked as if someone had started to build a new city, believed in its location and a booming future, and after having paved a smaller section of these roads in front of the houses, had given up, for whatever reason. Here, Colin had written about an acre of desert that had been bulldozed into the twentieth century. Fifty years later it was still there, but it made no attempt to follow us into the twenty-first. In all directions, the streets lost their paved pride and turned into sand, two trailed away into the desert, one split up into several 4WD trails and only one could, after some sandy bumps and pits, at least join the major gravel road to the highway. All in all, it was a bleak atmosphere.

Maybe I looked so pitiable, or those gentlemen thought they acted too cool. In any case, just as I was returning from my bath to leave the camp, a red custom-made desert buggy stopped right by my side. Armed with oversized ski goggles, the driver invited me for a ride down the dirt road. He said, this would be the most boring mile out of the next ten thousands, and just as if to make sure I would not feel overwhelmed with hospitality he noted, "Oh, I had to do a test ride anyway."

I was grateful enough, less for the saved walk than for the unexpected invitation. I received a second pair of goggles, no less impressive than his, threw my backpack in the back, and jumped on the passenger seat. Lacking a speedometer, I didn't know how fast we drove, but to me it was supersonic speed, and it felt like riding a desert roller coaster. The test ride ended some minutes later at another dirt road where I started the first really boring hike along graveled or paved roads until I would hit the towns of Palo Verde and Blythe.

03/25   PALO VERDE VALLEY, 16 MILES

Walking some thirty miles through irrigated country along straight roads or farm tracks, I was somehow feeling idle. There was no need to do anything but walk, no need to orientate, to look for a trail, not even for being cautious. In order to get the dullness of thousands of identical steps out of my head, I began whistling and singing various tunes until one melody pushed past the others, and, I noticed, the *horse* had finally gotten a name.

On the first part of the journey
I was looking at all the life
There were plants and birds and rocks and things
There was sand and hills and rings
The first thing I met was a fly with a buzz
And the sky with no clouds
The heat was hot and the ground was dry
But the air was full of sound.[*]

---
[*] From: *Horse with no name* – Dewey Bunnell/America, 1971

CHAPTER ONE

Here for the first time, I had time to think about things that did not have to do with getting ahead. The song reminded me of my youth when I first listened to it and wondered what is was about. I remembered how often I was mind-traveling on maps and how strong my desire had always been to do something like this, and I thought back as far as to our trips beyond the rusty gate. With this journey, I realized, my childhood dream had finally come true. I was exploring real desert canyons and while in general it was exactly what I expected, I was also constantly surprised by details. I think it was the 'plants and birds and rocks and things' in a region where you wouldn't expect them that fascinated me the most. Here indeed, nature had a lot to show, and I discovered more of its surprises every day. Although I did not walk on the carpets of flowers yet that Colin mentioned on his journey – maybe this winter brought less water – it was still amazing to see flowers bloom at all in a brown barren land where you would expect anything but bright colors, let alone tawdriness. The most prevalent cactus was the beavertail with blossoms in flashy magenta, alarming from afar like a siren. Patches of yellow and white flowers speckled the slopes, mostly nestling in crevices or hiding behind rocks from the heat of the sun. Quite different were the ocotillo plant's ultra-red spearheads rising as high as twenty feet while reaching out for the sun. With bees, bugs, and birds, humming, whirring, and buzzing around this blooming variety, the air was indeed full of sound.

Desert ground wildlife was more reticent. Reptiles were just about to emerge from hibernation; lizards took stands on their favorite barbican stones, the snakes slept a little longer. While the mountain lion was most likely a once-in-a-lifetime experience, acoustically the coyote became an occasional guest at night. And a fellow that I had never associated with the desert, was just everywhere, the burro, a frequent companion.

Route planning with maps, even 7.5" or USGS, allowed only a vague sense of what I was getting. The wilderness was alive and it had changed its channels and alleys arbitrarily over the years. Impenetrable brush along the river shore could destroy a day's work and force me back to the roughs of mountains and canyons. Only clear- and foresighted walking helped to orientate in the wilderness and avoid demotivating trial and errors. To step aside and climb a mountain every once in a while was often compensated with a great overlook that would give me an idea of where I was, where I would go, and what to avoid.

Sometimes I felt happy at first to stumble over a jeep- or a 4WD road. Due to frequent off-roaders, these wilderness roads pop up so fast, even a Delorme could not stand the pace. However, usually they took me way off the route, made mysterious fun circles to all points of my compass, and far the worst, they went uphill and downhill – while the burros had already cleared the best possible way for hiking.

Along with orientation, dealing with water supplies was the major issue out there. In this the ranger was right, there were not many places to get access to the river easily. On foot you can rarely get close to the main channel for fresh water or a decent bath. Places that looked easy to go on the map turned out to be the worst and most difficult to pass. Big lagoons or sidearms were enveloped by reed and marshy grasslands, broken only by shallow, standing waters; washes were overgrown by thick tamarisk and mesquite brush restricting access like a standing battalion of well-armed knights. It took me a week and some bad experiences before I understood the real version of my childhood dreamscapes, until I knew how and where to find a way. Slowly but surely, I learned to live with the desert – not fight it, but accept it on its own terms.

03/26   PALO VERDE, 16 MILES

A new aspect in my traveling was the frequent interruptions of my solitude by meeting people. At remote places like Picacho, 4S, or Walter's Camp, I had met messengers from civilization, who were more likely programmed like me in a way, more or less sharing the same purpose. We were all looking for wilderness experiences and closeness to nature, only using different tools; some brought their angling gear, others their binoculars, some were hiking, others resorted to jet sports.

Entering the farming lands of Palo Verde, I was about to hit the first anonymous town. When after another boring stretch I reached the city limits of Blythe, I felt my point of view had changed dramatically in only two weeks. While I had come to Winterhaven as a city boy, fraught with youthful nostalgia and romantic expectations, two weeks later I had become an outdoors person, and I felt my roots were more connected to the desert than I ever thought, more connected to the wilderness than to any house, room, or bed in the world. The city had become but a contemporary phenomenon with some amenities I was happy to receive. However, home was beyond city limits and my house wherever I put it down, unstrapped it, and where I built a campfire.

The personal demands a place like Blythe had to fulfill were a pool-sided motel, a grocery store, and the possibility to get in touch with Nathan to update him on my process and make sure he's still following me. At everything else I looked with a certain amount of wonder, like there were eight to ten gas stations in a mile, as many accommodations, only outnumbered by fast food joints, which would serve a meal way too hastily for someone moving like me. Besides the price, the main criterion for choosing a motel was, naturally, the poolside.

Having walked almost the length of town, I finally found the right one. It had a nice garden area with Colorado-blue pool water, surrounded not by tamarisk but by no less non-native palm trees. I threw my pack in the room, dug for my trunks, and spent the rest of the day in the water.

Since I was still somehow in semi-Mexican territory, I had dinner in one of the many places that chose the sombrero as their logo or mascot. What I like about Mexican menus – besides the food – is, you can't go wrong. No need to study the menu and find the little nuances. Although it comes up with forty different choices, it is generally all the same, a tasty mix of whittled onions, corn, tomatoes, jalapeños and your choice of meat, simply hold together by a corn tortilla. This one actually brings the real variety on the table, being either rolled around the filling (enchilada), wrapped (burrito), folded (taco), or just put under the filling (fajita). Trying to find out the slight little variations in the combinations could easily take up more time than eating it. In the menu here, I saw it was just the order of ingredients that gave a meal a different name. So, I went with the Sombrero Grande, elsewhere better known as the Mariachi Plate, a well-sized combination of one or two enchiladas, tacos, fajitas, and a burrito; a delicious diversity.

03/27   BLYTHE, 12 MILES

Along with breakfast at the poolside, I had the first of several interviews with local papers. While most of them aimed at things I experienced in the wilderness, some dared to ask more personal things. I don't know if it related to the fact that I came from another country, or if it was a matter of mentalities, but while questioners here were more interested in my experiences and potential self-reflecting discoveries, at home I sometimes found myself being confronted with kind of 'Rip-Van-Winkleish' accuses. There, some of the questions were aiming at insouciance or irresponsibility; if I didn't think I would take life a little bit too easy, or if I was escaping from something. Of course, the answer should be a clear YES; yes, I am escaping from daily routine, from habits and conveniences, from dullness and *wasteland*. However, I felt that the question implicated I would be shirking my responsibilities, and that put me in the defensive at first.

There it was again, the wanderer's stigma, escapism; the common assumption for someone who sets out for a journey beyond civilization, for a journey that exceeds an ordinary vacation.

If not so much a hiker, Thoreau seemed to have made similar experiences with his temporary disembarkation to wilderness, as he justified his experiment: "If a man walks in the woods for love of them half of each day, he is in danger of being regarded as a loafer. But if he spends his days as a speculator, shearing off those woods and making the earth bald before her time, he is deemed an industrious and enterprising citizen." So am I, when I am not hiking; industrious and enterprising, working day by day, year after year, just to be able to do another journey. The problem with running a business generally is, when the funds are high, business is going well thus demanding your full attention. But, when the funds are low – it demands no less. So when is the time to do it, where is the time if you don't just take it?

Someone back home, who thought he knew more about my motives than I did, asked me: "Why are you running away from reality?" Much to his astonishment, I replied, "I don't think I am running as fast as you are." In fact, with a journey like this, my intention was to slow down a bit; to me escaping from reality had more to do with living the daily routine and not facing up to changes and challenges that might show us parts of ourselves, about which we would never find out in a society that is so much dominated by hectic pace and stress that it doesn't even allow stepping aside or contemplation anymore. In our daily grind, the time to do so would never be right, there always is a reason why, right now, you just cannot leave. However, when you did it, you cannot imagine how you could have lived without it.

Colin was faced with the same allegations. He felt put on the defensive, too, and he gave a whole load of counter-questions: "Why are people so ready to assume that chilled champagne is more *real* than water drawn from an ice-cold mountain creek? Or a dusty sidewalk than a carpet of desert dandelions? Or a Boeing 747 than a flight of white pelicans soaring in delicious unison against the sunrise? Why, in other words, do people assume that the acts and emotions and values that stem from city life are more *real* than those that arise from the beauty and the silence and the solitude of wilderness?"

In four months hiking, there was only one American who asked me the 'reality-question'. Since he drove up in a buffed and burnished black SUV, he gave me a head start and I said: "Compared to an SUV, which in most cases never gets in contact with the terrain-reality it's built for, my backpack filled with bare essentials had already become very real to me, or rather to my shoulders, as the house on my back." When I asked him about his accent, he said he, too, was originally from Germany.

However, I see that, taking into consideration that Colin was asked almost the same things, it is probably not so much a question of the mentalities but a matter of perspectives. The people of the place you are visiting will always be more relaxed than those you left behind.

And yet, there may be something else that influences the mentality and the thinking, an aspect I was about to understand through this journey; people living in countries, where nature, or at least large parts of it, means wilderness, seem to have a better understanding for the need to escape into it and for the compelling nature of the wild, although, one would think, it should be the other way round.

CHAPTER ONE

So Colin concluded his defense: "Frankly, I fail to see how going for a six-month, thousand-mile walk through deserts and mountains can be judged less real than spending six months working eight hours a day, five days a week, in order to earn enough money to be able to come back to a comfortable home in the evening and sit in front of a TV screen and watch the two-dimensional image of some guy talking about a book he has written on a six-month, thousand-mile walk through deserts and mountains," He said, the last thing he wanted to do was knocking champagne and sidewalks and Boeing 747s; especially champagne. These things distinguished us from the other animals. But he was sure they could also limit our perspectives. He suggested that they – and all the stimulating complexities of modern life – began to make more sense and took on surer meaning, when they were viewed in perspective against the more certain and more lasting reality from which they had evolved – from the underpinning reality, that is, from mountain water and desert flowers and soaring white birds at sunrise.

As modern people we need both, the continuity of 9 to 5 and the possibility to break free. I strongly promote mixing the two. Some people still mistake wilderness trips with alienation from civilization in general. Admitted, my aversion to today's massive unsubstantial affusion by media and industry and the vegging life we are often roped in, is just as big as Colin's, only multiplied by the inflationary increase of fifty years. For sure, this alone is a good reason to escape into nature every once in a while; to me it has always been a sympathetic cure and the best regimen to become friendly with civilization again. Therefore, yes, I am in escapism, not to escape but to find reality. (In fact, more and more modern employers begin to accept nature-oriented excursions or even sabbaticals, if spent meaningful, as an important step in a career, with fountain-of-youth effects both for the individual and the company.)

*

Here my continuity had increased by some hours from 9–5 to 7–7, sometimes until midnight, and it consisted of coming forth and contemplative walking. The afternoon was still young enough for another half-day walk. At least I wanted to get over the first seven dead straight miles out of town, so straight the crow couldn't do it in an inch less. Accordingly, my contemplation turned out to be less philosophical than mathematical and matter-of-fact. This stretch was so dull, I ended up counting my steps and with the help of mile markers compiling interesting, if less important, statistics about hiking.

With zero grade, I needed fifteen minutes to carry seventy pounds over one mile. With increasing grade, the time for the same distance rose exponentially, or the distance I made in the same amount of time fell logarithmically. That didn't mean a negative grade or decline made it easier. Instead, a curve sketching for negative grades would be much more complicated. With a small decline you walk faster than on zero decline until you reach a distinctive point from where the ability to proceed is being reduced, first linearly then exponentially, by the necessity to apply force opposing gravity. Where that point occurred, depended on some crucial parameters – first, the pack weight, second, the base speed, and third, on the number of hours you had spent in the gym to steel your quads. That boring it was.

After exactly seven miles, the road dodged the Big Maria Mountains to lean toward the big river again. I set camp amidst a cluster of farming houses at Palo Verde Dam.

03/28   PALO VERDE DAM, VIA RIVER BEND LODGE, 15 MILES

All along the river I saw large accumulations of RVs and mobile homes, less mobile than homes. These little white communities had exotic names, simulating paradisiacal islands more than the desert, thus concealing the rough terrain that surrounded the silverbirds' homes and their sunset years.

03/29   QUIEN SABE POINT, VIA LOST LAKE RESORT, 14 MILES

Despite the monotony, or maybe just because of it, all the people I met on these roads were frank and interested in what I was doing and why. From a barn on the roadside, a group of kids came running, calling me to wait and overwhelming me with questions. Several trucks stopped to ask if I needed a ride, and one old man decided to join me walking down the road, since his car had broken down four miles from his farm.

Throughout the desert, in no more than five minutes conversations would turn onto risks and dangers, such as rattlesnakes, sidewinders, and Mojave greens, with only one exception that emerges in the vicinity of Death Valley. The closer I got to its geographical location, the more the intense heat made up for better stories, thus killing the snake both literally and figuratively. As is well known, the record high there was 134 F measured in 1913. Nevertheless, this is being disputed by locals generally remembering *up-to-temperatures*, which end in the 140s if not 150s. The old man at least mentioned the 1913 measuring result, his story must have become almost legendary, though, as he began rhyming:

"They say their record high was 134;
they should have come with their instruments
when I got stuck on the valley floor;
had to stay there all day in the shadow of the car,
before I left walking with sunset. Guess 't was up to 150, so far."

CHAPTER ONE

I guessed, as with the wind chill factor, our senses are led not only by measurable facts but personal subjective sensation alike. I knew what he meant. I already had one or two of these days in the canyons along the Colorado, where it was *up to*, too.

But let's go back to the living threats; sure, my short-time travel companion along the highway was not Mr. Tuttle, the old man, who had told Colin a selection of scary stories about snake encounters. However, this fellow kept up with Tuttle, included black widows, omitted the rare-seen Gila monster but added instead a monster-sized catfish that could easily grow to a size where they were dangerous for kids.

In all cases, the rattler remained the king of scary monsters and it remained the predominant theme until I left Southern California to head into the Sierra. I had to admit, the fact that I had not encountered one yet did not add to my composure. A nice gopher snake was all that had shown up on my trail so far. The funny thing was, its pattern looked like the skin of a rattlesnake. It even flattened its head and body when I took a closer look at it, then vibrating the tail end to imitate its notorious role model. Only, it didn't rattle. Less funny was the fact that real rattlers sometimes lose their instrument through breakage or do not develop one yet at an early age.

After all the stories I heard, I had a feeling they were everywhere and it was merely a matter of time when I would step across the first one, unsure how I would react. At the next pause, I finally dug out Colin's article about rattlesnakes from my papers. In order to avoid freaking out and killing the first one I would see, I wanted to add factual information to the legend to understand what I had to look out for, but also how close I could get to watch it.

Most of the seventy snake species and subspecies in California are said to be harmless creatures with a vital purpose in the ecosystem. Only six to twelve, depending on the sub-classification, are venomous kinds. All of them are rattlesnakes, with the sidewinder, the Western diamond back, and the Mojave green awaiting me along my route. Usually, they would sense me way before I got close enough to distinguish the camouflaged body from the ground, and they would try to sneak away. However, the unsettling aspect was the *usually*, especially remembering the Picacho ranger, and for a solitary hiker, this text didn't give much reason for being doubtful about her depiction. While the sidewinder is the most common, its venom is kind of moderate. The diamond back has more to offer and matches the ranger's vivid description, from intense burning, vomiting, breathing difficulties to lowered blood pressure, increased heart rate, and hemorrhaging from vascular breakdown. If my circulatory system didn't fail yet, it would certainly do so from panicking. Their fangs are about half an inch long or more, delivering between nothing and double of what it needs to kill you.

As if that wasn't enough, nature held someone else in store, the Mojave green. I thought, the name alone said everything; I'd rather be bitten by a brown one. But wait for its Latin name: *Crotalus Scutulatus*. To me that sounded like Lovecraft's Great Cthulhu himself, famous for his hideous appearance, its humongous size, and the abject terror it evokes. The green one comes up with two different venoms, a hemolytic and a neurotoxic component, both of high toxicity, thus being something like a cobra and a rattler in one. While the hemolytic toxin is the common rattlesnake venom, the unusually high neurotoxin component is ten times worse than that of any other rattlesnake. It affects the heart, skeletal muscles and neuromuscular junctions. The lethal dose is 10-15 mg, but a grown green might well give you the whole package of more than 100 mg, thus being the most dangerous snake in North America. In my snake papers I read: "It is aggressive! It is responsible for several deaths each year, including in recent years a prominent snake toxin expert. This snake should be avoided."

Now how should I deal with this issue? I was walking through brush and crawling over rocks, their preferred hideouts. Knowing that only a few people die of bites because there are antivenoms was a cold comfort. According to the California Poison Control Center, only one to two out of 800 bites were lethal. But what if those two had been hikers? I knew, I was not supposed to move, let alone run and hurry for help. As the ranger recommended, stay calm and wait for help was the number one rule. Being alone out there, I guessed, I would have to resort to number two.

I tried to protect myself with common sense, watch every step and look under rocks or into crevices before sitting down. Furthermore, I remembered that one third of the bites would be dry, meaning without injecting venom, and that all of them have been frequently reported to warn a passerby by rattling, all but the Mojave green. Although I believed I would be prepared for the first encounter, I was aware that being surprised by that sound for the first time might cause unexpected reactions. It still is a primal fear and has always been one, ever since Adam met Eve.

It may speak for the thinking in Goffs that there I learned a rather funny legend about C. Scutulatus and how it came to produce two different venoms. According to the historic files, during the heyday of homesteading, there was a traveling circus coming to town with all kinds of spectacular species, both human and animals. Unfortunately, the Indian cobra could escape from the cage and legged it into the Mojave Desert. The rest is self-explanatory. After lonesomely winding through the years, it may eventually have glanced at a Western diamondback. That one may have looked flirtatiously at the exotic fellow, and soon they fell in love. Ninety days later, the first Mojave green babies were born.

Among all the danger talks, I remember only one guy saying, "Forget about the snakes, the spiders, and the scorpions!" I was surprised and thought,

CHAPTER ONE

what else might wait out there? "Dehydration is what you have to be aware of, the excessive loss of water from your body. It's not the legendary twenty-foot-long venomous snake that should worry you; it's not the saber-toothed cougar or the fifteen-foot-tall, ferocious bear. Next to unawareness, dehydration and heat-related illness are still the most common cause of mortality in outdoor situations." I told him why the search for me had been started, dehydration was their guess too – and I received a lecture on that issue. He said, the biggest problem would be that I didn't actually recognize the body's loss of water. Especially when hiking or climbing, I would be in danger of entering a fatal cycle. In a stressful situation like extreme effort, heat, and also cold, endorphins would take over. It's a survival strategy of the body to then disregard all physical needs in order to give you as much ability as possible to focus your attention on proceeding, running away, hiding or fighting. Unless you are on a one-day trip and return home after the day-adventure, the body will remain alert and might even spare you its essential needs. Therefore, thirst was not a good indicator for when to drink. Beginning dehydration incrementally decreased the work performance what in return I would try to compensate. Still I would think, I am not thirsty, I better save the water for later. Then he laughed and said: "Not being thirsty in the desert, ha, or after a decent climb? You can be pretty sure you are already dehydrated."

Before I felt anything wrong I might have already lost 2% of my body weight in water. If I had reached 4%, the first symptoms I, or more likely my partner if available, would notice about me, were headaches, dry mouth, decreased urine volume, muscle cramps, tiredness, and impatience. With 6-8%, the blood pressure would decrease, and I became dizzy and might see snow – even at 100 F. At 10% I would eventually lose my appetite, become thirsty but not be able to swallow, and, on the other end, suffer constipation. With more than that, rapid heart rates, irritability, and disorientation, lethargy, seizures, and fainting were the beginning of the end.

Data about the correlation of water loss and symptoms varied. The brochure from the De Anza rescue unit said 6-10% could be fatal, other resources cite 12% as not self-curable and 15-25% as lethal. It all depended on your condition, endurance and what you were accustomed to.

As a matter of fact, I did remember having some of the milder symptoms in my first two weeks. When I had established a good walking routine, I just didn't want to stop or do anything that could trip me up. The stage of dry mouth and beginning headache had been reached once or twice and more often almost no need to pee. The fact that I never really had a serious problem might result from a water budget leveled accurately on the minimum gauge mark.

He furthermore explained, something not commonly taken into consideration was the cumulative effect of dehydration or heat exhaustion. Thinking of the next four weeks, this worried me a little, because when I would leave the stretch along the Colorado, I would enter the *real* desert, the Mojave and Death Valley. I would have to carry much more water there, and a heavier pack would tire me out sooner. On the other hand, I had to pick up my pace to make sure I would be through it before it got too hot. The pack weight was the crucial point. Too much additional water would slow me down, not enough, weaken me. What would be the right amount to make it through Mojave and especially the long stretch from there through Amargosa and Death Valley with no natural water resources?

In the 1950s, I could have called a ranger here and a rancher there and asked them if they would cache a gallon for me at pre-arranged places. I tried what Colin had successfully managed, but unfortunately, I was disappointed. Those ranchers were gone and replaced by ranch industrialists, who would think I was crazy, and the rangers were not allowed to do it anymore because they were afraid of being sued if I was too dumb and blind to find the cache. So I had to bring whatever I needed.

It never occurred to me that I could do it on my own, like driving up to some places along the route before I started walking. To me, that would have been like looking for hidden presents in my parents' closet before Christmas day.

Let me quote the De Anza-brochure again: "It is recommended that at least five gallons of water per person be carried for each day, you plan to spend in the desert." Elsewhere: "Carry plenty of water, preferably cool, good tasting (iced in a cool can) water." Now how am I going to do that, without pulling a cart with a solar panel driven refrigerator and a water filter? It continued stating: "It has been shown that an average 154 lb. person carrying a 20 lb. pack and walking in the sun at 100 degrees Fahrenheit would require 1.3 quarts of water per hour." OK, that's one gallon in three hours, four a day; taking into account that I came with 25 pounds more on my feet and an additional 50 on my shoulders, it somehow added up to the recommended five gallons – per day!

Even though such a brochure would err on the side of caution, I started wondering if I had to consider canceling my endeavor through the Mojave Desert and Death Valley. Or could I dare to do it? At last, the rescue unit brochure filed three deaths of young brave men who had died from dehydration in no more than a day when trying to orientate in the desert without proper clothes or a hat or sufficient water supplies. For now, I postponed the higher maths to later after having gained more desert experience.

With all these vital issues and concrete problems, from hiking statistics to water, I had enough to think as I endured the prolonged stretch from Blythe to Earp.

Along and east of the river lay the Colorado River Indian Reservation, harboring natural wildlife refuges between the fluvial meanders and agricultural lands on the Arizona side. In the west, a chain of rugged mountain ranges,

CHAPTER ONE

reminding me unmistakably of the adventures I had already experienced and the risks I was going to run again after Parker. By now, all abstract problems of a beyond-the-trip life had gone, I was really down-to-earth, rooted to the desert soil. After two weeks walking, my world was nourished from experiences and things I had seen only in this short time, the life before had hardly any meaning. After two weeks, my spirit had caught up with me, and it, too, had finally arrived in the wild.

03/30   OLD PARKER ROAD, VIA EARP, 15 MILES

Earp? – that sounded like another comic word to me, meaning, 'excuse me – what did you say?' Earp, excuse me, wasn't that the gunman from Arizona, the sheriff from Wichita, Dodge City, and Tombstone? Yes he was, and coming to the town of Earp you start wondering why would anybody implicate such a colorful character in a dusty townsite of decaying buildings and crooked billboards.

I checked the 1958-paragraph about it; Colin had seen a huge sign, welcoming highway and Colorado cruisers to 'EARP, CALIFORNIA'. He wrote about a supermarket-sized souvenir store, a gas station, and the obligatory post office handling greeting cards to the East Coast and Europe. Now all of that was gone but the post office. I couldn't even remember having seen the sign, perhaps the trucks parked along the road or the endless line of commercial billboards were disguising it.

So what brought the legendary Wyatt to the factual Earp? Between two billboards, I found the answer. A young traveler stood there leaning at his car and looking kind of lost and pretty disappointed. "Are you as surprised as I am?" I asked, and I made him happy when I continued, if he knew anything about the connection between Wyatt and Earp. "Chuck, Western-movie fan," he introduced himself, and started to throw in his knowledge.

In fact Wyatt Earp had been here, more likely near, spending the presumably only white-bread time of his life on the shores of the Colorado while working claims during the last years of his life.

Throughout his career, his occupations had ranged from farmer, buffalo hunter, running gambling businesses, hotels, and saloons to teamster, boxing referee, lawman, and – miner. Both in his business activities and his law enforcement, he managed to surround himself with an extraordinary group of people, most of whom became notorious historic figures themselves, like his brothers Virgil, Morgan, and Warren, and his friends and companions Doc Holliday, James and Bat Masterson, and Sherman McMasters. Some biographies indicate that he also met Wild Bill Hickok, Jim Bridger, and, during the Alaska gold rush, Jack London. His integrity and respectability was both renowned and disputed, depending on where he was and how many enemies he had there. He was arrested as often as committed as sheriff or deputy marshal. His friend Bat Masterson might have summarized it most aptly: "No man can have a more loyal friend than Wyatt Earp, nor a more dangerous enemy."

After returning from a vendetta ride where he and a bunch of deputy lawmen had been tracking down his brother's murderers and killing most of them, his reputation was tarnished. He understood it would be better to disappear from the scene for a while, so he entered the mining business. For a short time he had, among other places, settled in the nearby desert town of Vidal where he staked gold and copper mining claims in the Whipple Mountains. However, the deposits here did not seem to absorb him much. After ten years roaming around almost every state west of the Mississippi, time had already made him a legend, and he felt ready to come to Hollywood and take care of rehabilitating his tattered reputation for posterity. Shortly after he had arrived in *tinseltown*, he met a young man, whom he impressed so much that this one based his image of the Western lawman on his conversations with Wyatt. The young man eventually became John Wayne, and the stories he told were those of one of the most colorful figures of the West.

It was only in his last years that Wyatt left fairyland and came back to his claims along the Colorado. Earp, California, or to be more precise, the place where I received a lesson in Western-movie history, is located close to his mines, but named after him only for touristy purposes. Now, however, Earp was dead.

I walked past it and headed into the Whipple Mountains, the last obstacle before I would take a rest and a leisure break on the shores of Lake Havasu. Following an old mining road, I set up camp near the Blue Cloud Mine, where Earp's claims must have been close by.

03/31   BLUE CLOUD MINE, VIA MONUMENT PEAK, 9 MILES

When Colin traveled the Colorado Desert he described it as the *Last Wild West* in California. The townsite of Earp was definitely not an indication. With the family he met at the Triple Slash ranch, the last frontiersmen making a living in these desert mountains were gone, and with them, the straying steers. If you will, the burros were the last protagonists of a fading frontier, constantly pioneering the wilderness, which, here, was still untamed and as wild as west.

Often associated with or seen as a survivor of this *Last Wild West* is the by now endangered species of the *desert rat*, commonly understood as a cranky old man, whose character is as sun-dried as his skin. He is said to have a preference for lingering at places with an audience, like roadhouses and roadside cafés, where he would hold fourth about a series of issues, not necessarily in any specific order. However, apart from a sporadical propensity to speak out, desert rats would live a solitary life somewhere beyond civilization's outskirts, like in a remote mountain cabin. Often, their names alone are self-explanatory, Chickenhouse Smith, Frenchy Buchanan, Itchy, Stinky, or Snake-Eye Charley. You wouldn't need to know much more about to envisage them. In general, they were just loners and seekers, people who had enough of big cities, people who tried their luck free-spirited, or people who just loved the desert for its solitude, its quietness, and its untamed beauty. In this sense, I could become one, too. Although hikers seem to match their prey pattern best – I do not know of any hiker who did not meet one – I had not encountered one yet where Colin had already met three. People said, they were still there; every other local purported to know of one, of an old lone prospector somewhere in those hills or a solitary walking staff maker somewhere down the river, though no one could exactly say where one lived.

It seemed that by now they were hard to find, yet, as I stopped at the store in Earp, I noticed a suspect gentlemen sitting in front of the mart. I took seat next to the odd looking appearance, long-bearded, with sun-tanned skin and a yellowed notch in his upper lip from a smoldering cheroot in his mouth. He called my attention because of his eccentric facial expressions, as if he was talking to someone. I cannot remember who started the desert-rat thing, but after a while he uttered with a twitching eye that even if I walked through the wilderness and knocked at the most remote cabins, chances for meeting a Gila monster were greater than meeting one of their vanishing kind, especially if *he* didn't want to. *He* would surely avoid city slickers like me and their quest for nostalgic encounters with grumpy old men. When I looked in his hawklike eyes while he was instructing me, I thought he would match the description best, and I wasn't so sure if he was talking about *them* or about himself. Obviously, he was not in the right mood. The trick must be to make yourself found. From everything one heard so far, if he picked you, you were about to get a conversation you would never forget, and some stories along. For the time being, I was unpicked.

I stayed on mining roads bypassing Monument Peak until I saw an old power line. Surrounded by ranges and mountains, I could not see a sign of the river, although it was here where the Colorado would turn into a lake, retained by the colossal Parker Dam, the deepest in the world. Here, a series of dams had calmed him down to a still powerful but less capricious force. Further up the river, he would also lose his freedom, for when I got closer to the leisure park of Lake Havasu, noisy speed boats and jet-skis would infuse nature with a form of artificial life.

04/01   COPPER BASIN, 10 MILES

The next morning, I stepped on the power line service road, which is congruent with the Trails End Camp Road. Two miles later, it forked into two, the left would trail off and get lost somewhere in the Sonoran Desert, the right way would lead me into the Chemehuevi Indian Reservation and to Havasu Palms, a landing site right across the booming water-sports-city of Lake Havasu. Here I would meet Roland, the first of two friends, who wanted to join me for two weeks of shared hiking.

When I arrived at a forlorn boat landing inside the reservation, two Indians working on their boat threw a piercing look at me. Every now and then, I realized that Native Americans were much more surprised by my sight, if not confused, than others. Did this mean that the American Indian, whom we credit with the closest affinity to nature, was by now more distant from it than our big city fellow Americans? Or was it merely that this kind of outdoors entertainment did not exist in their thinking? Was it a meaningful, pitiful glance because we were using our little, hard-earned leisure time to look for closeness to something we were about to destroy? Maybe I was just reading too much into it.

Sometimes, I am afraid, it was the nonchalance as to how I trespassed their boundaries, and that it was only the pack on my back that might have saved me from being subject to closer scrutiny. However, what can you do as a modern wilderness traveler but be friendly and respect privacy as soon as you see houses or people? I did not ask the Governor, nor BLM, nor Park Service for permission to walk the state, nor did I contact tribal councils. I respected private lands and was always happy to share my rationale and motives should I unknowingly have trespassed those. But at first, there always was a gut feeling when entering Indian lands, and I started wondering if it really was their reservation (in this other sense) or just my own pondering conscience as a *white man* that gave me pause.

Slowly moving, I approached the landing pier. The two Chemehuevi men kept working on the boat, but one could see that they faltered, unsteadily fumbling with tools and talking about me. I asked them if I could sit down for a while, and after having explained myself and the impressive size of my pack, they stood up and said something in a foreign language. One of them leaned into the boat, grabbed for a paper bag and put two stripers in it from a water bucket on the pier. All of a sudden, all doubts were dispelled, flowed away with the river. We didn't talk much, but the gesture was a wordless conversation, and it meant more to me than 1,000 words. Without asking, they invited me for a ride to the other side, to Lake Havasu City. When we crossed the river, I felt like I was drifting through a time tunnel, leaving the *Wild-West* past behind and floating into the modern world. Torn between their ingrained traditions and modern amenities, the Indians allegorized my ferrymen through this tunnel. There could not have been a sharper contrast between their land on the California side and the tourism circus on the other, Arizona side. Here sun-dried trailers and old wooden houses, there hotels, malls, restaurants, and a collection of speedboats that would make any other marina along the West Coast green with envy. It was spring break in California and youngsters from all over the state were flaunting decadency on the water.

My two ferrymen dropped me under the famous London Bridge, wished me good luck on my journey and waved good-bye. This landmark bridge was now the icon of the Lake Havasu leisure park, and I couldn't think of a more-out-of-place and, at the same time, appropriate one.

While Colin described the occasional sound of a jet aircraft as unremarkable, somehow unreal, today it was anything but that. Permanent and surreal, an armada of hyper-powered, aerodynamic speedboats was lingering around the lake, their roaring engines as unrestrained and communicative as a convoy of muscle cars on the Great Salt Lake.

The floating circus could only be topped by that even more-decadent and superfluous project I just walked upon. What could be more preposterous than buying a bridge from *old Europe*, taking it apart and re-assembling it in the middle of the desert, some 10,000 miles away. Was this the *new world*?

The reason for this operation was to establish a tourist attraction, as if there wasn't enough to see and explore already. The fact that the London city council placed the historic bridge, which had fallen into disrepair, on the market in 1967 might excuse the crazy idea. Still, one begins to wonder whether or not there are any limits to the craziness of our species. I am not starting the 'what good could you have done with that money', Mr. Big Oil McCulloch', yet, what else could he have done with that money!

At least, he did it at the right spot. As a matter of fact, the location is perfect because the three main desert schemes – the Great Basin, the Sonoran, and the Mojave – meet right here. The lake offers possibilities to relax and refresh, and other attractions like Vegas, the Grand Canyon, and the Mojave Preserve are close by. Altogether, perfect conditions to see and learn about the desert, its geological and cultural history, its flora and fauna. Here in these desert mountains, one had a chance to experience extreme changes of weather during a single day. The blooming season in spring is a happening one never forgets, and its rock formations were as interesting as the variety of animals, from Mr. Tuttle's zoo to burros and quail. Now since the bridge and succeeding operations created a new market that would not be there without the bridge, one may consider to add something more useful and sustainable than just a marina for tank-like horse-powered monsters on a river section close to some of the last bio water reserves in the Californian desert.

It does not lack a certain irony that, even before the first out of 10,276 granite blocks were put together at the banks of the Colorado River, McCulloch said to himself: "My God, what have I done?"

After a stroll into the artificial town and through an absurdly out of place English-style theme park adjoining the bridge, I got an ice-cold beer and sat down on the sandy beach to wait for my two-week travel companion.

The boat parade went on until dusk. What made it funny to watch was that hardly any boat left the small lake under the bridge. Only here you could be seen from the spectating crowd on the bridge or from other closely passing boats. However, as the speed limit was 5 mph, there was no way to show what you had under the hood. The only alternative for every wanna-be captain was to let his engine roar at regular intervals. They did this so precisely that you thought they were all connected via radio to choreograph who would be next. Never were there two at the same time. And of course, the opportunity to display what they had on the hood was much better here, and safer. It seemed that the louder the engine, the more model-like the bikini-girl hood-ornament was.

Somehow the whole scene reminded me of visiting my uncle in the countryside. After dinner, all kids were allowed to go to the neighbors' farm, and we had a ball watching the roosters fighting for the chicken's attention. Crowing a loud cock-a-doodle-doo taught the opponent how strong he was, and all chickens heard it and acknowledged it.

Late afternoon, Roland came walking down London Bridge, waving with two ice-cold beers. He had arrived via Las Vegas and a bus shuttle to Havasu. We sat there watching the circus until dusk and exchanged news from Germany and from desert canyons. Before long, he felt acclimated and confirmed that we wouldn't miss anything when leaving this place in the morning. He was hungry for a short adventure into the wild.

During the three hours sitting there, only a handful of boats found their way out of the little bay. If more had gone out to cruise up and down the river, the whole scene probably wouldn't even have caught my attention. Knuckling under an excess of testosterones, the rare, little trips were announced by a different set of kick-downs. Cock-a-doodle-doo! Look at me! I am going to dump one hundred bucks into the river in no time. And my chick's all right with that. That spring was when gas prices skyrocketed, probably the explanation for why on my hike along the upper Colorado I could still hear the donkeys hee-haw, birds sing, and snakes rattle.

On the other, Californian side, the Chemehuevi, too, had found their link to the needs of modern civilization. They controlled the ferry business across the river, carrying Lake Havasu tourists into a small casino behind another landing site. Our link for that one night was the menu in one of the restaurants

CHAPTER ONE

overlooking the lake, a motel with swimming pool, and some good beers while watching a group of students how they danced in the courtyard on a spontaneous spring break party.

04/02   LAKE HAVASU, VIA CLEAR BAY, 12 MILES

When we left the motel early in the morning, the usual WELCOME-HBO-POOL-signs were exchanged on the motel billboard and we read in bold black letters: GOOD LUCK ANDREAS, ON YOUR 1,000-MILE JOURNEY, a warm farewell from a friendly, crazy town.

The ferrymen took us back to California. While all of their passengers surged into the casino, only we turned north into the desert to other pleasures, with no payouts, though sure win. About a mile from the landing, we stopped at a picnic site for recreation vehicles, somehow the well-meant link between casino and wilderness. We tied our boots and all straps and checked each other like two astronauts before leaving the capsule. Then we disembarked on desert sand.

I still had the whirring noise of the city in my head. By hindsight, it seemed to me as if I had entered a loud disco to look for a friend, found him, left and shut the door behind us, yet still carrying the reverberations in my head. Being back in the quiet, I had taken the boom-boom of Lake Havasu with me for some time. From where the small trail disappeared in the barren terrain along the Colorado, we saw a span of burros standing on a hill. They were looking to the other side of the river and, for a short moment, I thought they were shaking their heads.

Soon wilderness called upon our senses. We were now approaching the more difficult part of the Colorado River Desert. From here on, the terrain would become more rugged with even less access to water. Even the burros had to take longer detours to avoid climbing the steeper mountains and deeper canyons. Since it was Roland's first day, we would not walk too long, just far enough to be away from city lights and to enjoy a decent campfire musing and fish on the grill.

Dusk was already falling, the short time span when some things just elude one in the twilight. I was walking some ten steps ahead, when suddenly we heard it rattle, right between us. I took two quick steps and looked back at Roland. He pointed down to the bush I had just passed, his eyes wide open, his mouth agape. A look I never forgot since I broke it to him sixteen years ago that we would paddle down the Yukon River, showing him a photo of a roaring grizzly bear. Grizzly or sidewinder, it was the same expression, appalled and curious at the same time, meaning 'wow, that's an adventure!'

We could not detect it anymore. The brush was too thick and after its warning and our surprise, the snake took its chance to disappear. Only then I realized that it just happened; for the first time, I had heard the alleged monster rattling. I was neither scared nor frightened, I just instinctively moved away from it. The snake was probably warming on the trail and felt us coming, eventually doing what we failed to do because we had not seen it, that is, to yield the right of way.

Roland's expression was no less excited when two miles later we saw the second snake, this time a four-foot-long harmless red racer. It seemed that it was getting warm enough now for them to come out and scare hikers, or delight them.

On a narrow hook reaching into a Colorado lagoon, we found the perfect spot for the night. Minutes later, a large campfire was burning with our shadows dancing around us in the light of the flames. From our quiet faces staring into the fire, one could tell that here the landscape didn't give much chance for an easy start.

04/03   BLANKENSHIP BEND, 8 MILES

Just by looking on the map, it dawned to us that this day would be challenging. We were getting closer to a place called Devil's Elbow, where the Colorado cut a deep gorge into a rising plateau. Frequent side canyons would force us into an endless up and down. The smaller canyons and washes joining the river were overgrown with tamarisk and mesquite. And before we reached the Elbow, the hot sun had already made us drink half of our water reserves.

We had missed out on a relatively easy spot because it was only early afternoon and too many miles to walk. You wouldn't want to carry much more than you actually needed for a day over these mountains. Then evening came and we couldn't find another possibility to get water. One wash after the other was full of impassable thorny brush. Now it was getting late, the last sunlight touched the spines of Devil's Elbow, and we found ourselves amid an assortment of hard-shaped pinnacled mountains.

We needed water to cook and for the coming day, which would probably take us some miles away from the river in order to get around the high plateau and its deep chasms. For a better view of the area, we climbed the Elbow, and right below at the river, we descried a narrow green wash reaching down to the shore. We climbed back down and put our packs under the biggest palo verde. There, we lit up a candlelight and hung it into the tree, our lighthouse tree, should the journey take longer than the last crepuscular light to fade. Shouldering the water sacks, we were ready to run the gauntlet

CHAPTER ONE

through a jungle of spears. However, when we entered the thick spiny scrub on the northern flank of the wash, we did not reckon on encountering virtual tamarisk mercenaries.

Did I say, after the first week, I would get along with the desert and I wouldn't have to fight it? That would have been right if I had looked for water early enough. However, on that day we were talking too much and the snakes had kept us preoccupied. Under normal circumstances, we would have called it off, but now it was too late, we had to get water here or walk back some miles the coming day, which would always be the last option.

Looking into the brush, I heard me talking to myself. It seemed to be impassable, impossible to get through to the river. But when you think there is no way to get through, it is often the first impression the eyes and the brain are telling you, wanting to protect their carrier from itches and scratches and too dangerous undertakings. Convincing them that there will be a way and that it would be worth getting hurt because water was crucial now, they eventually agreed. Then, the body assisted by lifting the pain barrier; I didn't even feel some angry thorns, only later we saw the marks they inflicted on our bodies. As I crashed through the brush, it became thicker and thicker and we decided it was no use moving on together. One of us could carry four sacks, and anyway the second one would be preoccupied with warding off the branches striking back from the one ahead. I shouldered the other two sacks and went on, but the closer I came to the river, the steeper the cliffs mounted. After fighting the brush for half an hour, I gave up; there was definitely no way to get through. I would have needed a bulldozer to drive down that forest, so thick that you could just see through to the next tree. My shirt and pants were full of dry everything, sand, mud, little branches, and pollen and thorns. I worked my way back to try the other side of the wash.

Passing the palo verde tree, the candlelight was burning in delight inviting for a dinner that we had to boil with – water. When Roland saw me, he looked a little worried and asked if he should take over. But by now I was driven by ambition. With soaring spirits I left our campsite and climbed the rocks at the other side about six feet high. By staying at that level just above brush line, I made it as close as thirty feet to the river. Here the plants were sprawling ecstatically. They were grabbing for me, eventually forcing me to climb higher. But the higher I got, the worse my chances for lowering the sacks into the fast moving water. I pushed the branches aside; their grasps became vivid, tenaciously trying to block my way as if they owned that water exclusively. I bent them away with all my energy, sometimes using my whole body weight. I did not worry about coming back. If I got through this way, I would make the return too. After every tree I mastered, I had to loosen the most besetting branches that tried to celebrate an insoluble compound with my clothes. A couple of minutes per tree and twenty more feet to struggle. I climbed back down to a point where I saw a small alleyway right between the rockwards turned branches and the rock face. Strong winds blowing through the narrow river gorge at the Elbow had been excoriating the bushes along the rocks, and there they lost their thickness and weapons over time. Then the wash floor became muddy and my boots sank three inches into sucking mud. Then, four inches deep and five, and suddenly, still some ten feet from the water, the jungle of tamarisk and mesquite opened up. A large boulder looking like an oversized tortoise shell reached into the river. I sat down on it, took off my shirt and sank it into the fresh cold. With my face into the wet delight, a great satisfying feeling rose from my head over my shoulders and into my legs. Only then I shouted back to the palo verde tree: "I made it! Water! We won!"

I sat there for ten minutes, watched the river flowing by, and I thought about how much easier it would be to paddle upstream, close to the riverbank, while looking up at these mountains and into all these canyons. But I knew, I would never have seen the desert abloom, nor the burros and rabbits, the lizards and snakes. I would not have heard the coyote at the campfire nor felt the inviting freshness of a shady canyon. I had never overlooked these rugged mountains along the southern Colorado.

With the last light of day, I filled our four one-gallon sacks and dressed my wet shirt to face the brush from the other side, standing tall like a knight, who already won the first two of a three-round tournament. The way back was almost the same, the branches stood there weaponed with new lances reaching out for me where I had broken others before. But the uneasy feeling *what if* was gone, what if I actually can't make it, the angst that all the effort could be for nothing and that we only lost important time.

More than one hour after I struck the match, I arrived back at the candlelight, which was illuminating our late-dinner setting on a pristine palo verde patio. I shook off tons of twigs and branches. Roland collected them to start the fire and put the water pot aside.

It might sound exaggerated, like a trivial, mannish survival story. But coping with a task like that was a real adventure. If there is anything in the wild, where one can prove oneself, it is in finding ways to where you need to get, over a mountain, along a river, or through the boondocks. There is no such thing as coming forth, to give the plantlet of pioneering spirit in you credit, much more than hunting lions, beating rattlesnakes, or smashing spiders.

It is no coincidence that you often have to stand a test at places where the name alone suggests it. Many places have their history and generally they were named for a reason. While the water was cooking, we climbed a crag from where we could measure the Devil's Elbow. It seemed that His scarred body lay ahead of us, where a land like Mordor subjugated even the big river, forcing its waters into a narrow gorge. All ranges had jagged crowns, blazing in red as if they were cast into purgatory. I was thinking to myself, how wondrous that we ascribe the worst possible, the most painful images to some of nature's most stunning occurrences. This could be Heaven or this could be Hell; if it resembled the latter, I was sure, had anybody ever been there, he must have been awed by what he saw, and I doubted that he ever came back.

With the setting sun behind us, we had to climb down before it would get too dark, and I felt an excitement at finding a passage on the coming day across this forbidden land. To commemorate the occasion, we cooked an infernal chili stew before we nestled into the crook of His arm.

Late at night, we were wakened by a group of obviously endorphined burros that burst into tremendous brays over and over again. They were enhancing their hee-haws into an orgasmic libretto that brought all other sounds to a halt. Nature seemed to strain its ears to listen to a brute orgy; even a nightbird that had been constantly calling from one of the palo verde trees fell silent. It definitely reminded us of the most intimate moments of a couple head-over-heels in love. They must be having fun.

04/04   DEVIL'S ELBOW, 6 MILES

Having left the Elbow, hiking soon came to an end. While fifty years ago, Colin had still been able to stay close to the riverbank and cross some washes, we had to give up after several tries. The tamarisk was standing too thick. As I experienced farther down the Colorado, it looked promising from afar, but every try had cost too much time. Here, all we could do was climb, pushing and pulling our packs up 40%-grades of loose gravel, only to carry them down into a canyon on the other side. In order to stay on the mountains and to avoid the constant up and down, we had to leave the river and walk inland at least two miles to where the canyons did not cut as deep. This worked out fine for a while, until that one mountain that was higher than all the others. We tried to circumvent it to avoid climbing its rocky spines but got trapped again. To the north lay a canyon so steep and deep we could never climb down, to the west, two hundred feet vertical, and to the east, a dry fall with loose rocks. The only way out was going back again and taking an even longer way around farther inland.

We zigzagged another mile west away from the water, looking for a Mojave Wash that would lead us first north and then northeast back to the river. Then we would have overcome the worst. The problem was, if we shouldn't find that wash or if we couldn't get down to it, half of the day and half of our water resources would be used up again. After straying around until late afternoon, I realized that one wrong turn could really get us into a critical situation.

Eventually we found a wide wash, turned in and followed it down to the river. Only there we recognized it was the wrong one. Probably we should have gone west another mile and choose the next one. But we got nervous and turned in too early. We paid with another exhausting tamarisk crossing; however, we both thought it was the safer thing to do.

Being worn out mentally and physically, the remaining hike felt endless, although the ruggedest terrain lay behind. Just before we got to Needles, the Havasu Wildlife Refuge added a little Edenic touch to the Colorado River desert, with knobs of waterfowl, pelicans, ducks, and herons, and other animals coming for a drink. Big lakes and lagoons formed the refuge, but unfortunately, without a boat we could not explore this area.

A patio dinner at a small settlement called Topock Marina was the chance to say good-bye to the river. Here, we would leave the Colorado at a moment when I was just about to establish a relationship with him, not that of a friend but that of a yet different-minded but respectful and honorable person, someone you could trust at the end of the day, or when the chips were down.

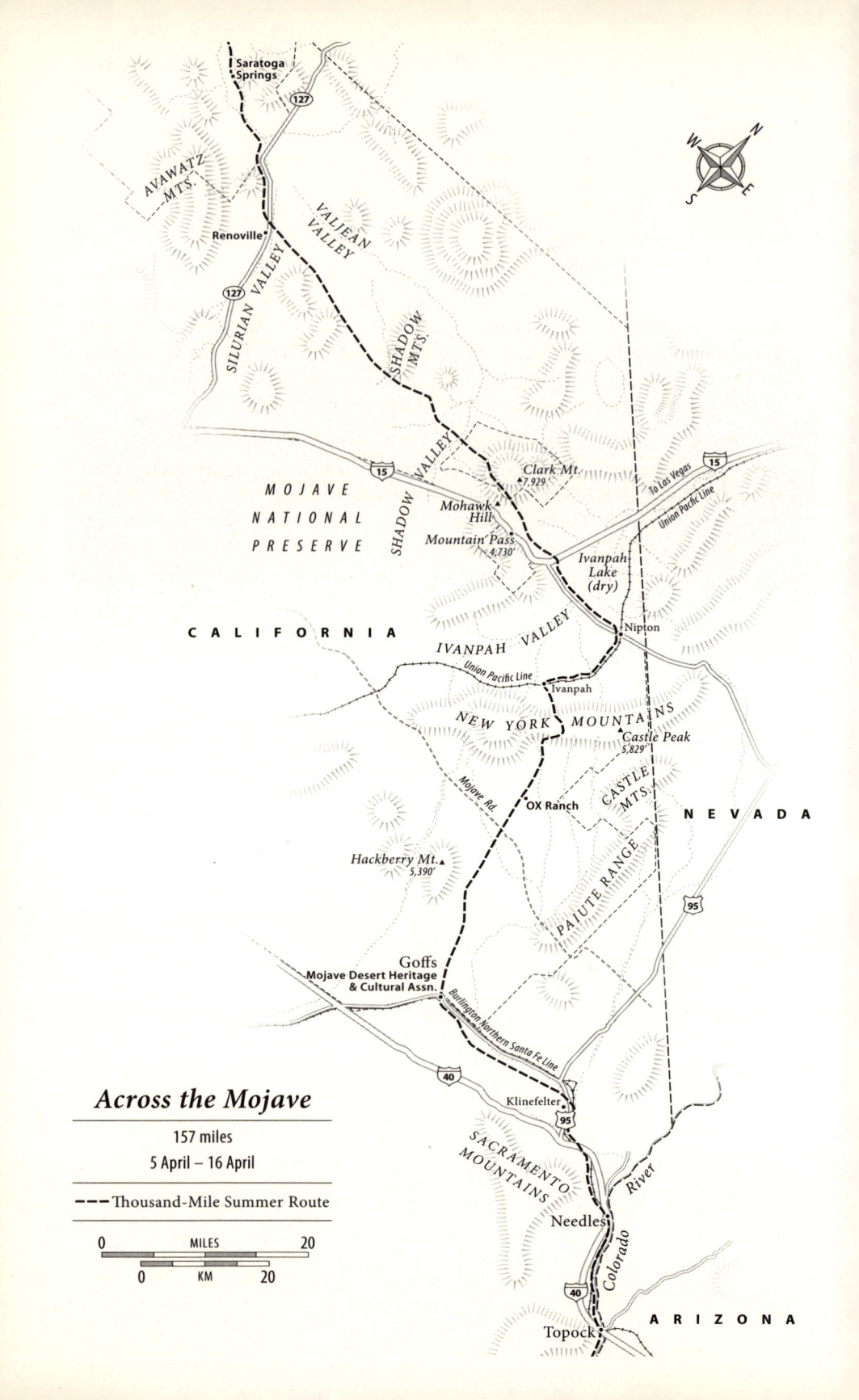

Across the Mojave

157 miles
5 April – 16 April

– – – Thousand-Mile Summer Route

2. ACROSS THE MOJAVE

April is the cruelest month, breeding
Lilacs out of the dead land, mixing
Memory and desire, stirring
Dull roots with spring rain.

FROM: *THE WASTE LAND* – THOMAS STEARNS ELIOT,
POET, PLAYWRIGHT, LITERARY CRITIC, 1888–1965

04/05   TOPOCK/PARK MOABI, 16 MILES

The long gradient along the railroad line to Needles was just enough to whip us into shape for the crossing of the high plains of the Mojave. Although the Colorado's influence on its desert mountains is largely restricted to the riparian areas, lagoons, and washes, for many the *real* desert begins only here, entering the Mojave, which generally describes an area much larger than what it is commonly referred to. In the south and the east, it is bordered by the Sonoran Desert, of which the Colorado River Desert is only a small part. The San Bernardino Mountains and the Sierra in the west are not only geographical borders but also shield it from precipitation. In the north, the Mojave reaches as far as the end of Death Valley and to the Great Basin Desert of Nevada.

In a narrow sense, it is also referred to as the High Desert, which is literally true for its southern plateau-like part as compared to the Low Desert, the Southern Californian portion of the Sonoran. However, in conjunction with my own experiences and considerable and visible differences regarding geology as much as flora and fauna, I am separating this chapter – like Colin did – from the adjacent geological extremes in the north, where broad valleys around and below sea level are being cut by long and comparatively narrow ranges.

CHAPTER TWO

More than any other climate zone, the desert comes up with superlatives and surprises, and it doesn't take long to understand that its common meaning, dryness or aridity, is a kind of false modesty and a clear understatement. The word desert and its Romance cognates (sp.: *desierto*, fr.: *desert*, it.: *deserto*) all lead back to the Latin *desertum*. This word did not relate to an arid area, but to an unpopulated place in general, which explains why we use desert figuratively so often, meaning there is nobody or absolutely nothing.

My geography teacher would have brought it down to a simple 'area with low precipitation', or more precisely, 'with a moisture deficit', meaning the potential loss of water through drain and evaporation is bigger than afflux and precipitation. Due to the dryness, physical alteration becomes a dominating force, supported by immense temperature variation of up to fifty degrees between day and night. Soil development is minimal and vegetation cover becomes sparse. Occasional rain with flash floods could take away all that is loose. Bedrock outcrops, rocks, cobbles, and pebbles is what you walk upon, seldom sand. The climate conditions make living not easy in this area, or hiking, but that's exactly what formed the barren lands with its naked rock formations, which in turn cause the most amazing views when staged by the morning sun, during crimson dusk, or in a full-moon night.

Precisely because you wouldn't expect much, you are overwhelmed by what you get and as soon as you experienced some of its extravaganza, prosaic definitions begin to sound alien to you. Some say that God's last work was the deserts, and when he created those he ran out of ideas, failing creativity. After these weeks along the Colorado River and our walk into the Mojave, I would say that, after finishing the easy and convenient stuff like paradisiacal tropics, pleasant temperate zones, and endless tundra and taiga forests, He must have felt challenged and defiant when shaping these desert mountains, canyons, and mesas, populating them with some of the most unusual or eccentric creatures of this planet, which applies to plants, animals, and people alike. The Californian deserts have little in common with most people's idea of the desert as badlands. Despite their reputation for supporting very little life, I found a rich flora and fauna, which had adapted to these harsh conditions. As an excuse for other arid regions in the world, from all deserts on our planet, the Californian is in fact one of the lushest, most scenic, most populated and biologically most diverse.

After a while you become accepted by the desert dwellers, as much as you learn to establish a certain desert view. The rusher will always remember nobody and nothing. But when you take your time and sit down here and there, stop for a coffee to talk to the people or watch the animal world, you'll be surprised by what you get to hear and see.

There also is a complex correlation between the desert and the characters inhabiting it. As much as one has to adapt oneself to the climate extremes, one has to be prepared for eccentric species, both among plants and animals. The desert is a protective landlord, outfitting its inhabitants with an array of defense mechanisms. It seemed that, due to their alluring creativity, most species were displaying that they want to be treated with the appropriate respect. Almost everything pricks and prickles and stings and bites, and some injuries can leave very bad marks or even be terminal. You just had to learn how to approach, what to avoid, or how to get along with everything. Soon you know where the dangers lurk, what rocks might break off and where to look twice. Sitting down anywhere before checking the ground or putting one's hands in dark crevices would most likely hurt, climbing without exercising extreme caution could be the end of a journey sooner than later, if not due to an attack out of the dark, then due to loose rocks. With a heavy load on your back, add your own weight, even rocks the size of a sofa might break off and give in to gravitation after having waited one thousand years for you to tip the scales.

Nature retains some of the most incredible animals and plants for this environment. Likewise it was a very special brand of people I met out there and I felt I had to experience the desert's extravaganza to understand what binds them to it. There were wilderness campers from San Diego, Los Angeles, or Arizona cities, fishermen, off-roaders and snowbirds, who enjoyed relaxing and venturing in a challenging land. They were nature-loving people who preferred the expansive silence of the desert to forest's stillness. They gathered at outlying campgrounds or just set up their own. Sometimes, when I walked into such a place, my mind played games with me, letting me expect the worst: crazy city people, who play on the remoteness to do things they cannot do at home, loose-cannon survivalists, extremists, and psychos, who let loose their freaky agenda. But I was just as spoiled by movies and media as our whole generation. Chances are, you will meet the best of our species out there. Good and friendly people, open-minded and always equipped with a spare steak or fish and a beer for you. It seemed that these human beings were the only species that frequented the desert without developing spines, poison, or jagged manners.

I made friends in an instant. Sitting together at a campfire, you opened up faster than through ten appointments in a bar or dates at the sports club. We were always grounded and no one had much to show off, apart from an occasional catch of the day, mind you. Staring into the flames somehow made people honest, superficial qualities ended in smoke and human ones came to the fore. Here, you are likely to get to know each other pretty fast.

We were not talking about business, money or cars, not even the political and social agenda. Somehow the environment, the stars. or just the sound of crackling firewood seemed to be inspiring enough to discuss life, the sense of it all, and who created it. Life stories and seldom told private experiences and thoughts were often released by the pure fact that we were sitting face

CHAPTER TWO

to face with not much more than our forefathers had in their caves (except the pick-up truck or the beers).

By the way: the Latin *desertum* is derived from the Egyptian *dsr t*, which literally means 'red land'. This works out better, at least for some places – had the Egyptians actually come to the Californian desert, as a small group of esoteric historians suggests, their description of this 'dry and unpopulated area' might have been *clr d*, or *fl f srprss*.

04/06   NEEDLES, 14 MILES

One full day along the railroad line of the Burlington Northern Santa Fe had taken us sixteen straight miles from Topock into Needles, a former railroad hub. Its history is mainly limited to two developments, the railroad and the highway system. Some of its buildings still reflect the city's temporary crushes, from serving as an icing station for California fruits and vegetables shipped east to being the gateway to the last leg on Route 66, the Golden State.

The city claims to be located on California's 'East Coast', whereas the citizens we asked about it left it open whether their ocean would be the Colorado or the Arizona desert. In any case, Needles has always been a place to refuel. So for dinner, we pulled in the legendary Route 66 relict 'Wagon Wheel Restaurant', and for a couple of drinks we graced the 'Hungry Bear' saloon. After one night in a motel including a washing spree in the pool, we left a city that seemed to be at a crossroads to either becoming a ghost town or an oversized truck stop with not much more than restaurants, motels, and gas stations.

Having left the historical southern gateway into California behind, the Mojave Desert mounted. Looking on our map, we read foreboding names reminding us of our experiences at Devil's Elbow, and we felt the coming weeks promised to be anything but boring. Ahead lay His master's chambers, comprising the Devil's Playground, His Golf Course, and His Cornfield, and, finally, overlooking the valley called death, a viewpoint where Dante relived all steps from hell to purgatory to paradise, with the latter, it is said, here being fictional.

1950s tabloid headlines such as "The Mojave claims another victim" and "Death lurks in the desert" seemed more likely a thing of the past, though they shaped our view of this *real* desert. Without further entertaining the absurdity of these headlines, events and casualties around them have contributed to building and sustaining a daunting reputation for both the plateau of the East Mojave and Death Valley, thus keeping the ghosts from the past alive.

Nevertheless, today especially visitors from more moderate climates feel attracted by such scenarios and the climatic and geological extremes that caused them. While Californians usually content themselves with making a short side trip via an old segment of Mother Road, other Americans might well visit one of the parks for a stroll or a picnic. However, when you detect someone with a backpack, chances are good it is someone from middle Europe, where monthly precipitation exceeds the local yearly figures here considerably.

Every once in a while, travelers, Californian or backpackers, get in serious trouble, which could indeed result in death, if the network of highways and service stations were not as dense as it is today. However, about ten years ago, four German tourists had disappeared in Death Valley, their remains probably found now (forensic specialists were still trying to identify the remains). "Foolhardy tourists vs. the Desert" unfortunately is an ageless headline that will remain good for articles until those traveling understand the risks involved in traversing the desert.

Although it is mostly just ignorance that causes these problems, like walking without a hat or not bringing enough water or gas, as a hiker leaving civilization far behind for days or weeks, you had to assure yourself repeatedly that you could not be trapped or surprised by the extreme degree all four elements can assume in the desert; the sun, constantly firing from above; the air, building up sandstorms, hot during days or chilly at night; the earth, fooling you with distances hard to guess; and water, just by absence or, no less perilous, in form of a sudden flash flood. And still, no matter how well you are prepared, trepidation will travel with you, thus guaranteeing the adventure. Should several elements decide to perform an orchestrated action, even a simple day hike may suddenly get out of control. If something happened on a fifty-mile stretch far away from help, one's soul might well evaporate shortly after one drank the last sip of water – if not the ubiquitous Devil had gotten it first.

Besides such terrible stories, here in the Mojave, we also found relics from all periods and rushes through the Southwest, from the gold-seeking 49ers to the dust-bowl fleeing families from Texas and Oklahoma to the cans and beer bottles from modern weekenders who are coming from the ocean metropolises to leave their not-yet historical traces in the wilderness, which started right where the highway pavement ended. I have always been wondering, who would throw garbage on the roadside, especially where road sign warnings post tangible penalties up to $1,000, not to mention the intellectual performance of the brain initiating the throw. In a park area in the Rocky Mountains, I once saw $5,000-signs, but even there I spotted beer and soda cans, fast food garbage and plastic bags. What causes so much ignorance? What could bring those people to terms? Maybe taking them for a hike into *real* desert?

Behind these roadside artifacts, historical or modern, the new desert system brought out different flowers and more cacti. A strong smelling bush became the predominant plant and often enough a dubious, yet the only sun shade in a shrub-dominated desert. The creosote's smell was so omnipresent that, after a while, the brain put it on a level with the scent of air, eliminating its special aroma in order to be receptive for other odors.

The creosote bush, when used as herbs also called chaparral, reminded me of that Western-movie standard, a man buried in desert sand up to his neck. That bush looked just like a tree with the trunk buried and only the crown poking out. Along with sage it is an extraordinarily adaptable shrub, ranging from the lowest elevations up to 5,000 feet. They are among the oldest plant systems, recloning themselves continuously. The oldest known plant grows here in the Mojave Desert, carbon dated to 11,700 years. Covered with bright yellow flowers in spring, its branches often grow in wiggly lines. Older branches that fell off and lay under the shrub fooled me several times by looking like a snake. But actually, Creosotes are hiker-friendly, preparing a perfect walking desert. Every plant creates a dead zone around itself, where no other plant can grow, thus having cleared the way of other brush and hideaways for snakes and critters. Their root system is so efficient at tapping soil moisture that hardly any other plant would find enough water to start a living in their immediate vicinity.

It has long been the Indians' friend as well. Like the pine tree, creosote is a resin reservoir, generating aromatic oils that not only attract the pollinator and defend against enemies, but have long been used medicinally for numerous diseases; it was, so to speak, the Indian penicillin. In fact the almost 400 components from its oils and leaves are still being studied.

But the most interesting fact to me was that in some Indian peoples' myths of creation, the creosote is shrouded in legend and has often been referred to as the primary plant, from which God or Earth Maker formed everything else, from insects to men. How could they know, without having a radiocarbon dating method, that it is in fact the oldest existing plant system? As biochemically provable, all plants growing in a certain circumference might well arise from one and the same, genetically identical root system. Isn't this is an awe-inspiring example of the meaning of storytelling and how history has been passed down from genesis to generations?

Entering the Mojave, I also had to rethink the water concept. There was no river anymore to refill the sacks. Before we started this new stage, I had to have a close look at my maps for natural springs or wells and ask people about potential water supplies. In Needles I had again called the ranger stations in the Mojave Preserve, Death Valley, and Inyo Mountains. I only briefly touched if it would be within the realms of possibility that someone who might happen to come by my route could drop some water here or there. But I kept collecting denials, so I focused on information about natural springs. By burying water and with the help of a ranger, Colin had at least six additional caches along a 300-mile stretch until the end of the desert. I had good hope and a back that would still need some workout.

As if someone wanted to take away our worries, Roland and I became surprised by getting water from a source we had definitely not taken into consideration. Walking straight through the desert, we came to cross the BNSF line again and just when we appeared from a larger depression overgrown with creosote, one of these mile-long trains came creeping up the slope. The engineer saw us with our colorful packs, blew his horn, and out of the driver's cab flew a twelve-pack of ice-cold water. With a loud bang, the bundle landed right in front of our feet, rousting a sunbathing iguana on a stone nearby. After all, 9 bottles survived, we waved a big thank you at him and drank and drank, refilled our sacks and drank, and showered lavishly with the rest. Taking cover behind a creosote bush, the little saurian kept watching our immoderateness, visibly becoming green with envy. So with the last remaining drops we fed the trusting lizard, who returned our gesture of friendship by posing for our cameras as a stark-naked model against the desert backdrop. As much as I have been worrying about water, for the moment it was no big deal to spare some drops for the thirsty fellow. Our sacks were still full and Goffs was only two days away.

Leaving the tracks to shortcut through desert shrub, we crossed U.S. 95 between two spots that were marked on the map as Klinefelter and Arrowhead Junction. On the roadside sat a Mexican man and his son, selling jerky and mesquite honey out of a trailer. Behind the trailer lay the remains of a settlement, a collapsed shanty town and a graveyard of automobiles, tires, and non-identifiable bulky waste. 'Yes, we're still open', said a sign at one of the decaying doors, when Colin paused here and listened to a lonely, addlepated old man. As we later found out, according to a note in Dennis' archive, the man had adopted – among others – a bad habit of never bathing. It was said that he never took his shirt off. Instead, once or twice a year, he walked into Claypools' department store in Needles, bought a new one and put it on over the remnants of earlier shirts. When he came in, they could smell him all over the store, and therefore the ladies called him 'Itchy'. Other habits are well described in Colin's book, also why at last he had to dash away after sharing a pot of tepid beans with him.

We directed our attention to the Mexican man and were wondering what he might have in his cooler box. I felt he was somehow overstrained by the situation; he was not sure who we were or what kind of authority we might represent. He gave us that sheepish grin like someone who knew he was lost, hoping to appease his accuser with a bashful smile.

I repeated my question in a lower, more friendly voice, explained that we were hiking through the desert and that we were much more interested in his cooler box, sodas and water, than in his regional delicatessen, or anything else. He pressed a smile onto his face and it wasn't hard to see that he didn't believe me. The first sodas were on him.

CHAPTER TWO

He sat there day by day from sunrise to sunset, as if he was left over and forgotten from a time when Route 66 was more traveled. We accepted he had been placed there for us, gave him a couple of dollars for two more, and took our time to explain to him and his son why men would do what we were doing. I couldn't tell if it came across, I hardly think so. But when we left, he took his sombrero off to us and showed us a hidden trail from behind the dump into the desert.

Through Piute Valley we had to take a little detour around large stands of teddy bear chollas. These cute looking but mean cacti grow pretty dense on some rocky slopes, almost forming an impenetrable forest. Suited in a white gown of the finest spines, its stems look fleecy from a distance, hence the cute name version. But you don't have to hug it to find one of its loose branches on your clothes, or worse, on your skin. You pass a cholla only once without keeping the appropriate distance. The Indians had good reason calling it 'jumping cholla'. If you get close enough, they say, it will jump right at you.

Due to its barbed spines, getting rid of one might easily turn into an unintended, time-consuming break one spends with tweezers and clenched teeth. During my last visit to the desert, I had to free a dog from such a branch, not larger than the size of an egg. While hunting rabbits with his best pal, the dog stepped on the dropped cholla egg with his hind leg. He tried to bite it off and had it in his mouth, then tried to remove it with his paws, and, lashing about, he soon had spines all over his body. Holding him down, it took almost an hour to pull some one hundred barbed spines out of his paws, legs, lids, lips, tongue, and palate. A rather demonstrative event showing how a cactus would stop at nothing in order to spread his seeds. An animal falling prey to its reproductive urge would have no chance of survival, being unable to move or eat or drink. A real killer teddy.

The desert tortoise we encountered on a narrow passage through the cacti field seemed unperturbed. It slowly crawled over several cholla eggs until it crouched down on a large gravel field with no vegetation but a small barrel cactus courting the tortoise's favor.

What an amazing animal, I thought, adapting to three totally different natural environments, fresh water, salt water, and hardly-any-water – the desert. When the tortoise realized that the barrel would not reciprocate its feelings, it maundered down into a sandy wash. We followed and found a soft place for the night below the Sacramento Mountains, sheltered from an upcoming storm.

04/07   SACRAMENTO CREEK, 14 MILES

A sight to behold. Coming from the dry washes draining to Sacramento Creek, we climbed a plateau overlooking the East Mojave. It was our first view into the endless vastness of the desert, geographical infinity. On the western horizon we saw the Providence Mountains enthroned like kings and queens above the creosote floor. Some smaller buttes coated in black were scattered around the desert like guardian sentries to the kingdom. Ahead lay the euphonious names of the Mojave and Death Valley, full of history, packed with hazardous stories of threat and survival, a dubious recommendation for the days to come. From the north blew chilly gusts of wind, announcing something, just like that sudden breeze and a sough in a scary movie. I looked at Roland and recited a quote from one of the early emigrants: "Expect to find the worst desert you ever saw and then find it worse than you expected." (John Wood, 1850)

Down below we saw the railroad tracks again, paralleled by Route 66; at the junction of the two, a small settlement, my personal *El Dorado* called Goffs. From up here it seemed undecided, whether it wanted to be a ghost town or still living. Only with my report about the events four months earlier, I convinced Roland that it would in fact be inhabited.

As in most small towns in the West, straying dogs are the first to show up. They come running and barking like the hounds of Baskerville, but the closer they get the more chary their barking, until they duck their heads under your stretched arm. As soon as we patted their necks, they became fast friends. OK, there are others too, but here it worked. They escorted us proudly to the property, where we were already announced. "Come on, come on," called Phil, "I already heard you were on your way." A service guy from the BNSF had announced us a day ago. I could see in Roland's eyes that he, too, was thrilled being welcomed by the reincarnated Wild Bill Hickok, who gave us a quick tour around ground facilities. Then Phil asked for our shopping list since he would drive to Vegas the following day to pick up his daughter Kristy. "I can help out immediately with some basic food," said he, and a minute later he came back with a twelve-pack of cold beer and Hershey's chocolate.

After my early year visit, the township awaited us. Founder Dennis Casebier and his wife Jo Ann showed up and in less than five minutes, the rest of the current town population had gathered around us, Hugh and Carol. There weren't any more people here than fifty years ago, when Colin had entered the general store and, after a little chat, had been invited to the Craigs birthday party of five. One of the guests in 1958, a man called Jim Taylor, stated that Mrs. Craig was Goffs. Now Dennis and Jo Ann were Goffs, and behind them, a number of more or less frequent visitors and helpers to the association.

Barbecuing at the outdoor Flywheel Café, the spot for social meetings, we discussed further routes through the Mojave Desert and Death Valley. I explained my worries about pack weight and water caches and my unavailing calls to the rangers just to hear them say in a roundabout way, I might be too stupid to find the caches. It didn't take long until Phil offered a solution, at

CHAPTER TWO

least for the Mojave part. When picking up his daughter in Vegas next morning, he would take the dirt road through the preserve and cache water bottles close to our trail. With regards to Colin's original route through the Mojave Desert, we had to do a little detour and reach a small settlement on the northern end of the preserve, from where Roland would hitchhike back to Vegas. All the more, we cheerfully appreciated the comfort of a carefree walk through at least the first long dry stretch. And it was totally in line with my idea of experiencing wilderness with the people I would meet. Thus walking through the Mojave would become quite relaxing with never more than one and a half gallons of additional weight on our backs. We promised, scout's honor, not to sue him, should we not find one of the caches.

Leaning to an old telegraph pole, I read the Mojave chapter in Colin's book and compared his map with mine. Roland explored the landscaped garden, following a nature and history trail, which was laid out across the association's property displaying relics and desert plants. Jim Taylor was talking to Colin, told him to sleep in his trailer, "Can't have you sleeping outside when there's a spare bed in Goffs." Incredibly, I just finished that sentence, when Phil came around the corner jolting me into reality by saying: "There's a spare trailer with two beds, or if you want separates, there's two spare trailers. Don't need to sleep on the ground here in Goffs."

Later on, Dennis came by and invited me to have another look into the archive if I wanted. On our way to the library, he told me about a visitor, a professional historian of the National Trails Road, who said to him after touring the property, "Dennis, you know there's no place like Goffs on 66, between Santa Monica and Chicago, I think there's no place like yours in the world." While the historian related more to the association's scientific aspect, its work and the collection, we savored the social aspect and basked for two days in its hospitality.

As we ensconced ourselves in the unusually narrow bunks of our trailer, we emptied the pocket flask of whiskey that Roland had brought to Lake Havasu. I picked up my book again and flipped back to the page where Jim Taylor was sharing his bourbon with Colin, and I read to Roland: "You won't find another Goffs in a hurry, not another place like Goffs, not even in the desert."

We were in complete agreement with him, both regarding the hospitality he had in mind and regarding that *je-ne-sais-quoi* of the desert in general that Jim expressed only parenthetically with the word 'even'. What he meant was the magic correlation between the desert and the people living with it, special characters indulging in the luxury of the ever-shining sun.

After the last nip and the last word spoken, the night belonged to the trains. Every half hour, my companion's nocturnal sounds were mixing with the thundering of an approaching freight train. Creeping up to the higher plateau around Goffs, it reached the former watering station with all engines at full power, drowning out every other noise. There it asserted itself with four whistles, long-long-short-long, before it left me alone again with those of my companion.

04/08   GOFFS, 0 MILES

Early in the morning, Phil left with his truck to cross the Mojave. We took it easy and spent a day hanging in the shadow, repacking our packs, and walking the nature trails across the property.

Goffs was the first place to where I had sent a replenishment package from Los Angeles, containing more dehydrated food, bars, nuts, chocolate, spices, and drinking powder. As to gear and clothes, there were new socks, a shirt, and shoelaces, and, most important, all maps from here to the next major stop in Mammoth Lakes. Here and now, it was like opening a birthday present. I remembered most of the items, but there were also little surprises like a new sort of fruit bars, drinking powder with another taste, or two cans of noodles with vegetables and beef. All of this made my mouth water, and it felt like birthday and Christmas altogether. I put my used maps and some clothes in the box and deposited it in an office trailer for pickup in fall.

While I continued reading Colin's notes about this town and the Mojave, the Goffians busily bustled around the property in golf cars, here naturally called Goffs cars. One cart was armed with shovels, rakes, and a pickax, destined to investigate the site for landscaping tasks like planting trees and cacti, building watering ditches around them, digging a drainage trench to divert flash floods, or pulling out mustard weed and burro bush, which becomes a dangerous fire accelerator when dried up in summer. Another cart transported chairs and tables and a fan to one of the trailers, where new guests were expected for the weekend; on its way back, it brought a load of memorabilia to the museum, donated by a stranger whose grandparents used to live in the area. Once or twice, a car stopped by on Route 66 to ask for Dennis. I picked up one conversation where Phil was welcoming two guys, quite well-padded, from Ludlow, Arizona. They were asking, "Is Dennis 'round", and they received Phil's quick-witted charm, "well, he's not as round as you, but he's *a*round".

For a little settlement like that, there was a lot of activity going on. However, the real treasure of the association wasn't its nature gardens or the historic buildings. It was neither the heritage trail with more than one hundred stations displaying old stamp mills, railroad cars and equipment, water towers, wind pumps, crushers, engines, or ranching utilities, nor the conservation of the Old Mojave Road including a series of published guides. The core heart of the association's collection lay inconspicuously in an archive that was constantly worked on by the same bustling people in either the office building,

CHAPTER TWO

the library, or the schoolhouse – the unique collection of by now more than 1,300 oral recordings and more than 100,000 original photos relating to life in the Mojave Desert.

In that case, Colin was refuted, the Mojave was indeed full of history, and even though frontiersmen at first tried to avoid the southwest deserts, there followed many successive stages that left an astounding number of relics, parts of which were brought together and displayed here while others still lay out in the blue, waiting to reveal their stories.

In the afternoon, Phil came back from his logistics tour, with a smile on his face saying, "Mission accomplished." An hour later we were all sitting around the barbecue grill to enjoy our last supper at Goffs, or, how they call it here, the last-night-in-the-woods dinner. In these two days we spent with a handful of wonderful people who shared their time, their place in the sun, and – it has to be mentioned – the contents of their refrigerators with us, we began to understand why they called it 'paradise'.

During my first visit, when someone said, "Welcome to *paradise*," one did it tongue-in-cheek, assuming that a stranger could not understand it, hence excusing the assumed exaggeration with an ironic smile. On that evening, when the Goffians said goodbye to us, it wasn't said any different from words like *desert* or *sage*, and I knew we were accepted as their peers. We too had become desert lovers. "See you again in paradise, anytime you want."

04/09   GOFFS, 17 MILES

From Goffs, we walked a gradual ascent into the spacious scheme of mountain slopes shaping the East Mojave Desert. Thanks to Phil's spadework, we had time to explore the rich flora consisting not only of flowers and cacti but also of juniper, yucca, and the biggest habitat of Joshua trees in the world.

Phil's caches always were a highlight of a nonetheless exhausting hiking day. Somehow I thought that he was smirking a little when he came back from his support trip. He had this certain look in his eyes. At the first depot we found out why. In the little bag, hidden behind a barrel cactus flagged with a yellow ribbon, there was not only the promised water, but also two cokes. Although anything but cold, they were a welcoming refreshment after the first ten constantly ascending miles, and they brought the spirit of Goffs into the wild. In the evening we reached the second depot where we found two beers as add-ons. Reason enough to set camp and start a fire with creosote branches and roots for lack of wood. After having found the first little surprise, in my wildest daydreams, I saw him waiting at the evening cache, waving with BBQ tools amid thick smoke from sizzling steaks. Unfortunately, that was left to my dreams. Vegetable stew with chopped beef Texas-style was as close as we could get to a barbecue.

With gusts of 40 mph it was hard to maintain a steady flame. This night on the Mojave plateau at 4,000 feet was the coldest I had so far. We kept the fire burning until late when we finally crawled into our sleeping bags.

04/10   MOJAVE ROAD, 19 MILES

One cannot travel through California without coming across a historical marker all along, an old cabin or just a rotten piece of wood nailed to a pine tree, leaving its intent to your imagination. Many of those were echoing the passing of pioneers, prospectors, and settlers, and an emerging state. Whenever I had a chance, I looked up people and places in local libraries. Just hiking geography, without knowing where I walked upon historically, would have been only half the fun, half the excitement or adventure. The more I learned about the local history the more exciting I found it to stumble over these testaments. Thus I was more able to understand, draw conclusions, or even relate to these people and the events, most of which I passed between 100 and 150 years later. Being able to relate to my forerunners often made me feel like a wanderer between the worlds, or rather between the times, their past and my present, like when I discovered wagon traces in a shoreless ocean of sand and sage and I knew that this was not a 4WD road but a wagon trail or an old trade route. Then, still, those voices were calling from far away, and at the next library I would sit down and browse some history books to listen more carefully.

With the rising sun, we found ourselves camped close to the Mojave Road, the oldest trail to cross Southern California. Most early settlements throughout the desert are dated 10,000 to 15,000 years ago, when the ice age provided for a cooler climate with lakes and streams. The Mojave trail had been established as a trade route between coastal and Colorado River tribes and was still in use when in 1776 the first Spanish missionary, Francisco Garcés, was led by Piute guides as far as the Kelso Dunes and the New York Mountains of the East Mojave. Paleo-Indian rock-art can still be seen today along the original route.

Fifty years later, in 1827, renowned trapper Jedediah Smith explored the area twice, in winter continuing into San Joaquin Valley and half a year later to the Pacific coast. Yet everything remained quiet down here; for the immigrating masses, the travel conditions were just too harsh. The Old Spanish Trail that led from New Mexico up north to Salt Lake and back down along the Sierra seemed to be the only reasonable route for newcomers into the Southwest. Although it was quite a detour, it had long been used by Indians, traders, and explorers, and it was the safer route. In the 1840s, a few bold adventures, supposed to find shortcuts farther north, had turned into disasters. Only, when gold was found, reason became secondary. In just ten years, many new trails were trodden by an ongoing stampede of prospectors and settlers. No

CHAPTER TWO

mountain was high enough, no desert dry enough to stop the surge of fortune seekers. Most emigrant treks had gathered in St. Louis to follow one of the bigger rivers as far west as possible. Reaching the Great Salt Lake, from there several routes had been explored through the Great Basin of Nevada and across the Sierra ranges into California. The majority of wagon trails came in north of the Californian desert. Little was known about the south other than rumors that both the desert and the Indians were said to be more hostile than the mountains.

In an effort to connect the Californian boomtowns and the growing cities along the coast with the East, the Mojave Road found itself in the spotlight again. In 1857, Edward Fitzgerald Beale, a Naval officer of the U.S. Army Topographical Corps, laid out a wagon road along the trail, using camels as pack stock. The story goes that the local horses and mules were so frightened by the sight of these humped newcomers that they took off to the hills with wagons and trailers. (see illustration*)

The new road attracted prospectors and surveyors, ranchers and farmers, the first settlers and a lot of would-be miners. Thus it became the major passageway crossing the hostile deserts, which separated the colonized East and Midwest from the promising land full of natural and geological resources in the far West. With more settlers pouring into the region, problems arose and conflicts of interests about the usage of land between Natives and immigrants. The U.S. Army built a line of forts and outposts along that road to secure the passage for travelers. Until the railroad came, the Mojave Road remained the most popular route for travel and trade between Los Angeles and Arizona, somehow becoming the grandfather of Old Route 66.

---

* The comic illustration by Carl Faver (#3 p.378) in fact bears some truth. Through several experiments between Texas and California, expedition teamsters and the U.S. Army counted on the powerful ships of the desert because they could carry heavier loads, walk longer distances, and get by with less water than any other pack animal. Furthermore, they thrived on almost anything growing in the desert. They were not really liked, though, by both packers and fellow animals. Used to the sweet musky smell of horses and mules, everyone traveling with them despised their odor. Their stubborn manner, which let the most stiff-necked ass appear as a compliant companion, made work with them a frustrating, at times dangerous, labor. With their strong jaws and sharp teeth they could well cut an arm to the bone.
  One who must have had some bad experiences described mules' neighs as fine music compared to the camels' noise. In his detailed description of the history of pack animals in the West, Emmett Essin reported, "when full of water, camels tended to spit without provocation," and "after partially digesting whatever they had eaten, they regurgitated their food into their mouths for further chewing or spitting. The cud was a foul-smellin, sticky mass that soldiers were sure caused terrible sores." Studying various reports, Essin found that "the appearance of camels on roads and trails stampeded wagon- and packtrains, cavalry detachments, and civilian riders. Mules and horses literally ran away from camels."
  Due to their outlandish odor, the more native animals sensed their presence way before they actually saw them. When they were forced to work with them, they were said to avoid eye contact and stay in due distance. (*Shavetails & Bell Sharps*, Emmett M. Essin, 1997)

However, the railroad had to follow other geographical criteria, so the Santa Fe Railroad Company built its new line some twenty miles south of the old wagon trail in less mountainous terrain.

In 1833, the town of Goffs was founded as a service station for the new railroad line. By the turn of the century, there were rich mining activities for gold, silver, copper, and zinc in the New York Mountains, which lay ahead of us. Eventually, ranching was established on the unlimited lands around them. With another desert shortline connecting Goffs at the Santa Fe mainline with the high-grade district in the Mountains, the old trail had finally been replaced for good. On the other side of the mountains, the Union Pacific connected through the desert from Salt Lake in the northeast to Los Angeles.

In the 1920s, along the Santa Fe mainline, a newer wagon road was laid out paralleling the tracks, which eventually became the National Old Trails Road and the major east-west connection for automobiles. In 1926 the national highway system was established and the apparently insignificant number 66 was assigned to America's new main street.

With the railroad, mining, and ranching activities, Goffs had turned into the major entry point for the East Mojave. From 1912 for a short period of wetter than normal years, homesteaders followed other businesses and settled throughout the Mojave. The Goffs schoolhouse was built, which became not only a place for education but also served as a community center for town meetings, church services, and dancing. Probably because of its many uses, one did not use the ordinary wood frame and tar paper construction commonly found in remote communities but a unique mission-style architecture with a heavy wood frame, steel mesh, and stucco.[*]

With the homesteaders came an extension of the last Wild West, conflicts that had always been fought over since ranchers, farmers, and settlers drove the frontier, each with a different agenda, each with different views on what was needed. One serious case between the ranchers and the new settlers culminated in a shootout at the cowboy line camp not far from our campsite. It was not really a 'gunfight at the OK corral', but serious enough to become a legend throughout the Mojave itself, as you can learn at the museum in Goffs.

Twenty years later, the drought was back and the first homesteaders gave up. Many mines were exhausted, the desert shortline was put out of service, and when Route 66 was realigned some six miles farther south, Goffs was off the beaten track. While most of the settlers left, only the grazers stayed after they established several water sources sufficient for variously sized herds of cattle.

---

[*] The association we visited eventually rebuilt it in its original style and made it their headquarters, open for public visitation since 1999.

CHAPTER TWO

Throughout Lanfair Valley we discovered historical remnants, cabins, building fundaments, corrals, adit mouths and shafts, water tanks and wind pumps from each of these historical periods. Given that fires had destroyed many more, one could imagine a pretty populated desert at certain times. Its highest population, however, came another ten years later. After all businesses were gone, for a short period during WW II, General George S. Patton set up the Desert Training Center in the Mojave Desert. While he left for North Africa the same year, many more divisions were trained on a ninety-day cycle at several camps until 1944. The division stationed here in Goffs was the 7th infantry division (mechanized), trained for desert warfare and eventually sent to the Aleutians to drive the Japanese out of Alaska. After they had left, only a handful of desert-loving people lived in Goffs, from the Craigs in the fifties to the Casebiers today.

*

Approaching the New York Mountains, the highest range in the preserve, we entered the Joshua forest with trees up to forty feet high. Some of them would grow foot-long panicles of white flowers between their uplifted branches. Mormon settlers felt reminded of the biblical prophet Joshua, who lifted his hands up to the sky to stop the sun by God's command. Here they populated the gravel slopes as if they were masses of pilgrims waiting for the Sermon on the Mount. To the same family belong the Mojave yucca and smaller versions like the Banana yucca with its lance-like leaves, also, and for a good reason, called the Spanish bayonet.

The higher we got the more ranching relics we saw. At a junction where a dirt road cut off to several mining sites in the New York Mountains, we found the derelict buildings of the long-abandoned OX Ranch. With origins tracing back to the 1880s, the OX and other cattle companies had set the pattern throughout the Mojave on a dozen grazing allotments until late into the 20th century. Grazing in a desert may seem marginal and dodgy, nevertheless with unlimited space available, the Rock Springs Land and Cattle Company headquartered at this site counted up to 15,000 cattle grazing the slopes between Mid Hills, Providence, and New York Mountains. Again this proves that there grows much more than we commonly assume.

Today, all but one small ranch were gone since the implementation of the California Desert Protection Act, another wilderness act signed into law in 1994 to preserve the public and natural values of wildlands such as the Death Valley and Joshua Tree National Parks and the Mojave National Preserve. In easy words that means, if you walked for miles through the wild and suddenly see an overgrown sign saying 'No parking from 6 to 9 a.m.', that is a wilderness act.

Per definition, these acts protect environmental, ecological and wildlife, scenic, recreational and educational, and also historical, archeological, and cultural values. As the first wilderness act of 1964 puts it, these areas shall remain unaffected by humans: "A wilderness, in contrast with those areas where man and his own works dominate the landscape, is hereby recognized as an area where the earth and community of life are untrammeled by man, where man himself is a visitor who does not remain."*

Colin complained about the hitherto current habit to disregard the non-human world. Fifty years and several pro-nature enactments later, but also 120 million more people, basically the complaints are still the same. However, I met quite a few – no less environmentally concerned – people who are in rage about a current inclination to exclude our species from parts of nature by precisely these enactments. In areas where people have been making a living amidst and – at least from their point of view – in harmony with nature since the first treks came through the desert, the absoluteness of the protecting acts' statutes placing nature's inviolacy above man-made history led to angry disputes and quite a few dustups in the desert.

Here where we find both, pristine wilderness and human life and history, to many people this subordination of man meant dramatic individual problems, if not a threat to lose their livelihood. Being driven from their lands, which were suddenly declared as protectable wilderness, or being forced to give up historically grown businesses like farming, ranching, or mining, amounted to them as neglecting history and they called the measures 'unnatural' as well. A volley of reproaches has been aiming at political abuse of good and honest concerns, which were picked as popular flagship projects for campaigning politicians in the big cities, that is, far away from the respective subject. In some areas, nature even suffered from these measures, as the sudden change to being set *free* caused instabilities in a new-found balance between human utilization and the immediate environment, like accelerating huge wildfires or boosting overpopulation of certain species unbalancing the food chain.

Consequently, conflicting opinions often differ widely about how to preserve and if historical privileges shall be overrun by nature protectionism. What is natural? And to what point is man-made history worth to be maintained? The East Mojave is a good example of the broad spectrum and the complexity of preserving nature. Although grandfathered uses like mining preexisting claims, hunting, and cattle grazing were excluded by the act, pro nature

---

* Signed into law by President Lyndon B. Johnson on September 3, 1964, the Wilderness Act created the legal definition of wilderness and protected 9.1 million acres of National Forest. In the course of the last fifty years, congress has been including new areas designated for preservation in their natural condition. Today, the National Wilderness Preservation System comprises approximately 5% of the U.S. surface, 110 million acres that are administered by four federal agencies, National Park Service, U.S. Forest Service, U.S. Fish & Wildlife Service, and the Bureau of Land Management. Outside Alaska, the largest wilderness area is the Death Valley Wilderness.

lobbyists made clear that continuing businesses would from now on amount to an administrative hurdle race. Eventually, most of the remaining ranches and mines accepted offers they could not refuse, and they sold their properties to the Park Service. Cattle ranchers left with their stock, and where a somehow stable symbiosis had developed between nature and men, the sudden absence of cattle grazing and thereby removing understory caused one of the biggest fires in the Mojave since human history began here, burning not only 70,000 acres of vegetation but also historical sites throughout the area, sites that cannot regrow, understandably. One side dismissed the loss as acceptable since it was artificial, man-made, and anyway not native to the area. Others replied cynically, so let capitols burn down in Sacramento, Washington, and Rome, since none of them was native to its environs.

After quite a few discussions with both locals and generally not-so-local environmentalists, along with my own experiences at some places, where even a hiker was treated as an intruder into the park guardians' territory, I understood that it is quite a challenge to define, what is *natural* and what is not. Where is the timeline that separates conditions worth preserving from disturbing? If it is the impact of mankind, indeed we are having a problem.

It's not easy to explain that even people or societies who lived in tune with nature are suddenly unwelcome and their work a source of consternation, while all green movements tell us to live in harmony with nature. *Naturally*, that would not mean we had to be separated from it. In the long run, the job will not be done by establishing parks and reserves and kicking out long-established usage. And for sure, over-regulated areas declared wilderness will not save our planet.

We mustn't forget that the status of protection, although granted by congress, can just as well be taken by a future one, according to temporary needs. What we need is an educational approach for our coming generations that helps forming a basic attitude, a common understanding and a change in behavior in how we treat the lands, how we understand nature.

Population keeps growing and we will need more resources and more space, both to live in and to recreate. Despite all modern means available, I am afraid, the only way to gain such an understanding will be through experience, through outdoor-education, and quite easy, by taking our kids out there, camping, fishing, hiking; it's as simple as that. As Saint-Exupéry said: "If you want to build a ship, don't herd people together to collect wood and don't assign them tasks and work, but rather teach them to long for the endless immensity of the sea."

Increasingly, we will all have to be concerned with this in the future, making sure that factual and rational considerations rather than current political campaigning lead to decisions, compromises, and, where protection is needed, to reasonable transition periods. Maybe, one day, we understand the meaning of nature, maybe, one day, mankind treats her with respect, maybe then there's no need to gate it.

*

Hidden behind a fence post of an old corral, we found another cache with water and soda and felt like school kids being rewarded with treats for good behavior or achievements. We put the refreshments in our pack until we reached the pass. There we paused, amazed by the view, overlooking the other side of the Mojave as far as Primm, Nevada, to the east and countless barren ranges to the north and west. Some of them were the southern foothills of the mountains that framed Death Valley.

We looked over vast expanses, a geology lesson was spread out at our feet. Ever-blowing strong winds and a rich volcanic activity until some 800 years ago have been forming a land that had been continuously folded and uplifted in earth's past. Volcanic cinder cones and lava beds alternated with sand dunes, serpentine canyons and steep rising ranges, all anchored in an ocean of desert scrub.

The valleys and mountains appeared in a range of desert colors from all tinges of brown to shades of grey; the dust-dirty greens of sage, creosote, and yucca engaged in an unwinnable campaign to bring color and life to the slopes in between. Life only came to the fore on rocks and gravel within a small radius around us. Here was spring, an eccentric play of colors about to burst forth, there the desert colors were blurring into a monochrome. Here we saw what Colin depicted so colorful, and we found those strange flowers that would come with you: "All around me, bare brown rock stretched toward a horizon of blunt peaks and stiletto pinnacles. In all that immense sweep of brown rock and brown stones I could see no sign of life. Nowhere except at my feet. There, flowers pushed up between the stones and through cracks in the rocks. But their yellows and whites and purples spread only a few yards. Beyond the brownness began." He slipped off his backpack and continued: "I walked forward again to an ocotillo plant that reached up with red-tipped tentacles like a sun-worshipping octopus. Then I looked down – and found my feet still surrounded by flowers. I looked back at my pack. It stood on bare brown rock. And all at once I understood that the barren mountains were not really barren. I knew – though I found it difficult to believe – that in whichever direction I walked over the brown rock, toward whichever peak along that jagged horizon, the flowers would come with me."

Every year in spring, the desert floor starts its short-termed, secret revolution. Tiny little blossoms with ground-hugging green cushion break through the gravel, some stalks standing tall, a foot high, here casting a golden yellow, there a lime-colored flower. There were blankets of yellow daisies and

CHAPTER TWO

dandelions on the ground, pink, yellow, and red cacti protruding, and opulent yucca and Joshua tree with clusters of thick white flowers towering above.

Although blooming cacti had been rare so far, their season was just about to start, whenever I saw one it was a highlight among the flowers. Just the contrast between its hostile garb and its blossoms that surpass every normal flower in creativity and color is amazing. Some cacti flowers reach the high level of orchids or lilies, and in my discretion their effort for this in an arid environment earns 10 points, leaving 9 for the most extravagant tropical flower.

I wondered why Colin remained untouched by cacti. To him, "they had not been a source of wonder like the flowers." One may dismiss his unemotional conclusion, "They had hardly touched my life," as a personal view, but the fact that "they became an almost unnoticed item in the desert landscape" virtually proves that there simply weren't many. You just cannot walk past ignoring them and not being surprised by their voluptuous and flaming chalices. Although he stated in a footnote that he "was lucky to have chosen a wet year", that would not mean it had rained enough or all over California, and I think I was just luckier. However, true for both of us, the desert's extravaganza succeeded in releasing us with the memory of flower gardens.

When traveling through the desert, of course one has to consider that springtime is the much better time for wildlife viewing, for both fauna and flora. Most plants are unable to grow in the cold of winter when the largest amount of rain falls, and summers are too hot and dry. As a result, most annuals have adapted by producing a flush of growth in spring as the weather warms and before the soil moisture is depleted, thus causing spontaneous but spectacular wildflower displays. Many flowers seem to just wait for a decent rainfall and pop off the ground instantly. Especially cacti are accurately timing their short blooming season, like, today is barrel cactus day, and all barrels start blooming on the same day. Three days later the fiesta is over, and it may take a week or two until another cactus species erupts.

Coming down from the mountain slopes, we arrived at Ivanpah, an abandoned ranch site and former station for the other railway system, the Union Pacific. Our night camp close to the ranch house brought ghosts from the past alive, probably because we were roaming the lost place before dinner. Old newspapers and a magazine collection comprising many years told the story of someone who must have lived here for a long time. It appeared to us that, whatever the reason may have been, one had to leave on the spur of the moment somewhen late 2004. This was the issue date of the magazine fairly arranged on the living room table with a pencil and a note pad. In fact, all the rooms looked pretty much as if someone had merely packed the most important items, not wasting time with carefulness or putting left things away in order. There was kitchenware, clothes, and toys scattered on the floor. Pictures still decorated the walls, and the whole living room scene was as if someone had just left to do some groceries. Everything seemed to be more or less intact but a few damages in the rooftop, which looked, with the bright sunlight shining through, like magical mirrors on the ceiling.

Back at the campfire, we let the ghosts tell their story and fantasized about what might have happened here. Only later I learned from the archives of Goffs that it was an elder lady, who fell victim to the Desert Protection Act. Her parents had lived and worked here for long, and as long as they were alive, the place at the northern end of the preserve fell under the grandfathered-activities rule. However, when they died, the daughter was soon prompted to leave. Eventually, after refusing several relocation offers, she was evicted from her family's land.

04/11   IVANPAH, 10 MILES

Another day hike along the Union Pacific line took us back into civilization, somehow, or to Nipton Station, which consisted of a bed and breakfast, a store, and a campground.

Founded in 1905 as a railroad stop, Nipton Station served the nearby ranches and mines and became a social center for a small population on this northern side of East Mojave's mountain ranges. The school and other community facilities were shut down for long, but Roxanne and Jerry, who were running the general store and the little hotel, managed to keep a nostalgic ambiance alive.

Another point of attraction, especially for a hiker, was a handful of outdoor Jacuzzis, scattered over the desert floor behind the hotel. They were cleaned, filled, and heated by the maintenance gentlemen Jim, the good soul of the station, twenty-four hours a day equipped with his coffee cup; never saw him without it.

During the days in Goffs and here again in Nipton, I spent a good amount of time at the railroad tracks, and I started wondering what interested me in these trains and what made up this certain nostalgia and the romanticized role assigned to them. Why would you be rudely awakened by a honking car in front of your door whereas frequent train signals and a rumbling hundred thousands of tons gently rock you to sleep? However, I know I am not alone out there, I saw other people, mostly men, who had that same childish and longing view in their eyes, when one of these up to 9,000-foot-long monsters came climbing up the creosote slope, demanding its attention. By looking in these eyes, I could see the railroad running right through American history, as a symbol for physical vastness, industrial prowess, and unstoppable expansion.

CHAPTER TWO

Besides that, there isn't much to say about Nipton. It lies in a dry basin between Primm, Nevada, and Baker, and it is a major coffee stop for Vegas Vettes, bikers, and other fun-loving motorists. But it would amount to a crime not to mention Bill, the cook at the Nipton Café. Damned maverick, but a nice guy – provided he liked you – surprising the patient visitor with the best steak, the best pork chop, and some extravagant burgeritos in town, I mean in the Mojave, or let's say between Vegas and Los Angeles. Honestly.

Roland had to leave the following day and catch a ride back to Vegas. Reviewing the two weeks we had together, I felt a little unsure about moving on alone. It was OK in the first two weeks, where I actually enjoyed being alone after a hard day. Now I got used to a partner, to exchanging thoughts and feelings. Most of the time we did not walk close to each other, though. Usually, everyone established his trot, and only for breaks, snacks or snakes, or any other sightseeing, we came together and had a chat. Above all, it would be the campfire musing that I missed. And with all contingencies it still is the best safety net to walk with somebody. If one got hurt or cracked or bitten, the other one could hold his nerves and keep cool, go for help or, worst case, hold his partner's hand and inform the family.

Late at night, sitting on the porch of the Nipton Hotel, we saw the shimmering lights of Las Vegas on the northeastern night sky. Roland listed the casinos and bars he wanted to check out there, and for a moment, thinking of miles and days and pounds and feet, I was quite sure I would be ready to cheat and leave with him, at least for a couple of days. Then I thought of my desert schedule, and I remembered the night camps and when, after a strenuous day, I came to a rest sitting at the fire, being in harmony with the nature around me. No matter how hard a day's work had been, the evenings would always reconcile me in a moment, in a flame. And before Roland could finish his sentence: "Come on buddy, just a couple of … ", all temptations luring from across the state border ended up in smoke.

04/12   NIPTON, 0 MILES

Breakfast at Bill's. It seemed that in the morning he was not quite at his most courteous. Before we had a chance to ask for a menu he coughed at us "French toast or eggs?" which made it clear that those were the choices. We didn't dare to ask for extras. With checking in the room you received a yellow slip for 'Free coffee at Bill's'. When we asked for coffee he snared, "if you have a yellow slip, give it to me. If not, it's free anyway."

During breakfast, Roland was offered a ride to Vegas. After a series of extra-long farewell hugs, we waved to each other as he got in the car. It wasn't easy to tell for whom it was harder, but, as he said, his biggest concern was to let me walk into the wild alone while mine was to imagine all the coming adventures he won't be able to experience. I had already turned around to focus on the sun-dried Jacuzzis behind the hotel, when I heard the car bumping over the railroad crossing and the driver honking the horn, long-long-short-long.

I thought I would try one of the outdoor bathtubs and hoped Bill was not the guy to ask for. The thought alone was refreshing, but most of them seemed to be out of order. Then I saw good soul Jim working on one of the tubs, trying to fix something with his left hand, in his right one holding his coffee cup. I asked if he would fill it up for me. Guess how I got him?

No longer than the coffee machine took to prepare the payola and I was sitting in bubbling hot water, and I couldn't tell if it was hotter in the pool or outside. Jim took a chair, sipped his fresh coffee and told about his life. Before he came to the desert, he had a job as a caretaker up north in Yellowstone Park. Every March and April he drove there to free the cabins from ice and clear the trails for early visitors. He had this glint in his eyes, almost teary, when he told me about the animal world there waking up from hibernation, how they played in head-high snow aglow with happiness that spring was coming. I could truly see the good soul in his eyes. He said that now he couldn't make the long drive anymore, and anyway gas prices rose too high. On his last drive north, he had his own serendipitous encounter here, when he stopped at the store in Nipton and met Jerry, who offered him the job he was doing now.

He said he was happy here too, watching the lizards and other critters and listening to the birds visiting his little oasis. However, seeing the longing in his eyes, I wasn't too sure. I think to him the only sense for watering the pools lay in attracting the birds, sitting down with a cup of coffee and watching them how they were beside themselves with joy. True *vita coffeeplativa*.

When I got out of the tub, Jim was up in an instant, using the pool water to spray the garden and some trees on the property. As if he was communicating with them, flocks of birds dived down from all directions, huddling around the runlet coming out of that green hose. For a short while they were drinking, washing, diving, and hopping ecstatically until the last puddle ran dry and another dry eternity was dawning.

After my bath, I pored over Colin's maps and notes, trying to find a solution for the coming 120 miles with just one known natural water source, the Saratoga Springs. It did not take long to find out that it would be quite impossible to make, if not negligent, with the thermometer now hitting three digits.

According to the aforementioned Rescue Unit, I would have to carry at least an additional four gallons to the springs. To be on the safe side, five, in case I needed another day or if the springs didn't spring anymore. In that case, from Saratoga it would be at least another day hike before I hit a highway, either to Death Valley or back down to Hwy. 127 and Baker. More than one hundred pounds total take-off weight, that just would have been too much. And then after the springs, there were another three days through Amargosa and Death Valley until I would get to Furnace Creek, my next sort of civilized stop at the northern end of the Valley. If I stayed on Colin's route all the way into the Panamint Range, I wouldn't even stop at Furnace Creek, but climb the range somewhere between Telescope Peak and Aguereberry Point 10 miles earlier, which meant another day or two and no possibility to refill the water sacks. Without resorting to help from the outside world, it seemed to be infeasible.

About how I would get over the main section of those Panamint Mountains, I didn't dare to think now. Rereading Colin's notes about the Park Ranger, who tried to bar Colin from crossing these ranges at all, stating it would be impossible and that no one had ever done it, was not the lecture I needed to get now. A book of poems I found in the motel reading room was meager-sweet comforting:

*"In the cobalt dome the vulture hovers
scanning with sombre.
Eye the little furry things that scurry to cover.
And you that watch over the delicate wild
things of the heart, remember
Death is an angry lover."* [*]

He made it, though, with water deposits on either side of the range, but how would I?

Sometimes procrastinating pays off, although it does not necessarily characterize the foresighted planner. There is something beyond that, an intuition, a keen sense for things to come. Or it is just serendipity. Either way, later in the afternoon the solution came by itself. I had made some phone calls to friends and family soon after we had arrived at Nipton. Now it turned out that friends from North Carolina were on their way back from Los Angeles. They wouldn't mind taking a little detour and drop a gallon or two about a day-hike from the springs. I closed my maps, was grateful for my patience, and followed an invitation by Jerry's son to join their campfire.

04/13   NIPTON, 16 MILES

The store was the place to get the news. Weather, local road conditions, and tour information, or the latest from D.C., everything was traded here. Before I left the station, I had a couple of coffees and joined a group of pausing

---

[*] From: *An Hourglass in the Mojave* – Ruth Forbes Sherry, 1941

travelers. The subject was, of course, Bill's cuisine. It seemed that every traveler who ever came through and consigned his primary needs to chef Bill would not hesitate to do a 200 miles detour to indulge oneself with his cooking again. One couple said, they would always make sure Nipton was on their itinerary, no matter where they were going. Another guest was Harold, quite a respectable man of 91 years and a life spent on America's highways. As a result of his travlin' bone, Harold had more stories to tell than two ears could absorb, let alone a brain could remember. Suddenly it was too much talking for me. I felt I had to leave or I would get used to company and conversation too much. My next days would be anything but social, maybe the loneliest part of my journey. Leaving the station, some fifty miles of unnamed hills lay ahead of me until I would reach the gate to Death Valley. The only name I found on my maps seemed to explain the lack: 'Shadow Valley', as if the majesty of Death Valley cast a cloud over the area forbidding prominent names in its adjacencies.

After having traveled in twos for some time, with the first solitary steps you inescapably find yourself in an emotional hole – supposed your partner had not constantly wrecked your nerves. Even though we did not talk very much while walking, it was just the sound of accompanying steps you got accustomed to; an occasional harrumph or a stumble and a curse, which make you anticipate the fun of a social campfire, of exchanging thoughts and old stories we experienced together.

Though, in general I liked to walk alone and I would not have accepted more than the two or three intermissions. Being with somebody will always distract you from your environment. You will just miss something, that's all. In company your senses are primarily focused on the other and, depending on whom you are traveling with, also on yourself or your vanities. Chances to pick up even the smallest movements, a sudden odor, or just the phenomenon of prolonged silence are much bigger when walking alone.

Security is an aspect. Period. But, why not go out on a limb, wasn't that where the fruit is?

Having traversed Ivanpah Valley, a moderate barrier had to be crossed. The terrain was relatively easy with an ascent of 2,400 feet on the first day, until Mountain Pass divided the southern Ivanpah Mountains from the northern Clark Mountain Range, both of them pockmarked with mines and shafts. To me, disregarding all the mines and relics was the real big barrier. But I mustn't lose time here since my water cache was still three days away. Allowing myself only one stop for further investigation, I settled down for the night at Mohawk Mine.

Among some less identifiable rusty objects I found an old chair. The wood and the cushions were gone and only a rusty iron skeleton remained. Though,

CHAPTER TWO

I thought, still good enough for that night. I bent down to pick it up, but out of reflex, I pulled my hand back. Belly upward, in a hastily woven web lacking any form or geometry, there was the man-eater, the black widow. The shiny black body was easy to identify. Its distinguishing feature, the orange-red hourglass on the female's belly, sent its warning, 'your time is running out'. However, although it is the most venomous spider in North America, it did not really look frightening. After all the scary stories, one would have expected a scary monster with teeth, claws, and antennas with eyes on them. Instead they look like a small one-inch black jewel. Their bite would be quite painful but not lethal, if treated. Yet, her reputation of killing and eating the harmless male partners, after she got what she wanted, will always be used against her, especially by men. The poor males are harmless and also lack the hourglass.

As inviting as it was to just hit the ground and sleep anywhere, seeing a widow under every other relic I passed, on fence posts and at a cholla cactus, I made sure I would not startle one when I woke up from something crawling on me. With all the leggy movements around my nightly campfires, a tent has always been a safe harbor.

During days and especially around ghosted sites, scattered buildings, or left mining equipment, I saw an abundance of critters, whereas when walking on the desert floor through sage and brush, they were often faster than the eye could see, vanishing in one of a million burrows and holes. In open desert, there seemed to be an inter-species agreement among all desert dwellers for the usage of holes and underground tunnels in case of emergency, which included the approach of oversized, two-legged giants. Everyone used anyone's hole. I never saw one carefully checking whose den it was about to enter. Giant? – Jump! – Hole! Between detecting me and having fully disappeared were often only one or two seconds. For sure, I would not have seen many animals if not for these historical sites or abandoned cabins. Here, the animals seemed to be less shy, and quite contrary to those in open land, some were almost trusting.

As in every society, there were a few rogue species that didn't abide by any rules. They might sit in their – or presumably in someone else's – den and just wait for an asylum-seeker. Once I saw a leopard lizard with his head in an earth hole, while his body lay outside, being kind of tossed and turned around. When I bent down to look into it, I looked into the scorpion's eyes, tiny black dots in a fearsome creature's face. Its body, three inches long, its pincers laid around the lizard's neck as if it felt sorry for its prey, apologizing with a hug of death. A scorpio pattern that may cause hobby astrologers a familiar ring.

Before I came to the desert, like most people, I thought desert flora and fauna were rather poor. Flowers and cacti had already disabused me of that preconception. And here around the mine, in a short while there was more crawling and running around me than in most other regions I had been in North America, except a city zoo or picnic areas in National Parks.

The desert is not only teeming with wildlife, it is also a classroom for observing species' communities, how they live and how they develop survival techniques, displaying fascinating adaption mechanisms to survive these harsh conditions. And sometimes, it is just fun. I escorted the black widow to a pile of railroad ties. Then, equipped with a cup of coffee, I took a seat on the old miner's chair, and sat as still as a relic myself to see what else might show up. In the tranquility of an afternoon hour, the desert awakened to the night, alive with all kinds of prowlers in search of food. A time to hunt, for some. A time to be wary for others.

The first guys dropping by were a couple of round tail squirrels, obviously checking their territory for something nutrimental to nibble. A little farther, an antelope ground squirrel was rolling something to its hole, but before it could hide its booty, the two round tails were at it, pirating the food. There, a desert night lizard seemed to come home from the graveyard shift, threw a nosy look at me and disappeared into the next hole. On a nearby creosote, a group of finks was playing musical chairs (or musical twigs), while a brown bird seemed to be conducting from a skeletonized cholla. Behind a bush of sage, I thought I saw a pair of ears, or was it just funny-looking sage? Then the ears hopped from behind the sage, under the ears was a black-tailed jackrabbit. He appeared for an instant, just to hide behind the next bush, and I began to understand why they had these extraordinary ears, almost the size of their body; it was defense by laughter. A coyote would most likely roll on the floor, howling with laughter, when he saw the long-eared rabbit trying to hide behind sage; then he might forget about his original motives.

With the setting sun, a variety of beetles was walking around me and they all had one thing in mind. The blister beetles were mating back-to-back, walking in the female's direction, a couple of inflated beetles clung to a dandelion stem, shaking their tree, and a romantic long-horned beetle was all over his love, bedding her on a blooming pencil cholla flower. The antelope squirrel was back at the scene, now climbing a two-foot-tall barrel cactus. What did it have in mind? When it got to the top it was balancing itself in an amazing choreography of smooth and mechanical movements. Had it worn white gloves, I would have been sure to meet the animal counterpart of the King of Pop. Eventually, its tiny claws were wrapped around one of the stout barrel spines, its upright body in a 45-degree forward-leaning-maneuver reaching for the forbidden fruits of a neighboring beavertail cactus. What a *smooth criminal*.

Here, Jurassic park lived, every few minutes there was a lizard crossing. After staring at me for a few seconds, it realized that I was the bigger dino and ran

CHAPTER TWO

away upright on its hind legs. In fact some of them reminded me of a miniature version of t-rex. And above us all, in the blue desert sky, patrolled two turkey vultures watching for the slightest inattention from any of us down here.

Before the hour was full, a battalion of black ants had conquered another cohort that was camouflaged in brown. Now they were squarely facing my rock. I stepped aside to have a closer look at their marching order. Then I saw there were three species walking in different directions, long and black, medium and brown, and three feet away a third one, tiny and red, which seemed to take advantage of the others' engagement, busily clearing one of their dens. The white eggs they carried were twice their size and surely not their own offspring. I could have watched them for another hour, especially the interchanges, where they sniffed at each other to find out where the other party was heading.

Given that most desert animals remain hidden during daylight hours to control body temperature and limit moisture needs, I wished I could do the same experiment after dark. When nighttime fell, all critters would leave their holes and hideouts, and the predators concluded their siesta. Again, using a tent was a very good idea in the desert.

Besides the variety of animal life, I also recognized that many seemed to be really curious and interested in me. Maybe in deserted – I mean unpopulated – areas, animals aren't used to people, therefore having no bad experiences with us. Or maybe it was just an exaggerated sense of my own importance. My favorite fellow was this iguana that watched me for a while, turning its head as if it was looking me over from head to toe. Taking pictures, I could get as close as one foot while the saurian was posing its head from profile to close-up. You would hardly find a better place for a documentary about the living desert.

04/14   CLARK MOUNTAIN, MOHAWK HILL, 15 MILES

An early morning storm had covered all tracks of last night's wildlife powwow. I found my coffee cup blown over to the pile of railroad ties. Even the black widows had not gone to work yet. All cobwebs were vacant, although they badly needed some restoration after the storm. It seemed that all animals were asleep, all but the night lizard that steeled itself for early morning shift on the tip of a pointed rock.

Due to the rich mining history in these hills, there were many dirt roads crossing the most barren land I had walked through so far, a vast plain desert, broken only by round hills that lay on the desert floor like giants' graves.

From their tops, other trails or roads could be seen from miles away, and where my trail was discontinuous, I just walked to the next one in a straight line. The slope was so stark and naked at some places, I thought, here, I could walk straighter as the crow flies.

Valley after valley, I flew down to Saratoga Springs. Shadow Valley, Valjean Valley, Silurian Valley. The only remarkable detour I had to take was around a stubborn Gila monster in my way. Its stout body was a foot in length, with orange-yellow blotches on a shining black skin. I felt prompted to touch the beautifully colored lizard, but nature didn't mean so, vesting it with a venomous bite and – probably worse than the injection – a tenacious grip with bulldog-mentality, which has become legendary among tales from the desert. One piece of lizard lore was sort of romantic, though, saying that you had to wait for full moon until it would loosen its grip. Or was it new moon?

Being less spectacular geologically and even hotter and drier than the higher elevations of the East Mojave, the isolated part between the Clark Mountains and Death Valley came closest to our conventional idea of a desert. But as monotone as the landscape was, as amazing were the dramatic theatrical plays that sunset and moon performed on the desert screen. Here in Mojave sunset, I was startled by my own shadow following me on an eastward mountain wall, too far to accept it as mine. Between endless ranges and valleys, the crepuscular light of the moon made me feel like walking through a negative pattern of our world.

It was here in the Mojave when I understood Colin saying, "God is light, we are told, and Hell is outer darkness. But look at a desert mountain stripped bare by the sun, and you learn only geography. Watch darkness claim it, and for a moment you may grasp why God had to create Satan – or man to create both." On that evening at the Shadow Mountains, I was sure, I saw them both.

I realized that, here, flowers and trees would only distract from what you see on a naked land, when the setting sun, the moon, and the stars approach peak form playing on the desert stage against a geo-pornographic backdrop of naked formations and sculptures. And I knew I had to come that far, I had to walk endless miles through a day's boring hot monotony to be receptive for that play of color and geometry.

04/15   SHADOW MOUNTAINS, 19 MILES

For the third night before I would get to the springs, I had to reach a place named Renoville on my map, however, I couldn't see anything unusual but a bend in the road. Nevertheless, it was reason enough for a man named Charlie Reno to build a gas and beer station for local workers and tourists in the 1930s.

CHAPTER TWO

Today, the only hint to civilization was my cache with hot water and a short, reminiscent note from my friends saying: 'If you find this cache, please leave it. A gentleman is passing through on foot in April or May, and he's depending on it.'

It was so forlorn here that a coyote felt obliged to offer me company. While they are usually so shy that you rarely see them, only hear their distant howling, this one took a seat twenty yards from my fire. I wasn't sure if he was just waiting for food or a discussion about life in the desert. His assertive mien suggested the latter. He was definitely listening to me. But then, without any warning, he stood up and went his way, as if I had said something wrong.

04/16   Renoville, 17 miles

With not much left in my last canteen, I reached the Saratoga Springs on the next evening. The little oasis, consisting of three adjoining ponds, was hidden behind a mountain. You had to know exactly where it was or you would just pass it, missing it within only half a mile. Even here, access to water was not easy. I had to wade through knee-deep mud until I could refill my sacks with clear water in the middle of the larger pond.

After four long hiking days, I was too exhausted to start a real campfire with just sage and roots in order to prepare a sumptuous meal. Also, somehow I had too much respect for this little oasis with singing birds and apparently romantic duck couples. So I just made a little fire in a half-foot hole to cook some beans. After supper I put my trimmings in one of the water sacks and leaned back to enjoy a purified lemon-powdered pond cocktail while attending a phenomenal concert by the Saratoga Philharmonic Orchestra, composed for four ducks and one hundred frogs. In these dunes around the pond, I sat in the front row until at midnight the symphony ended all of a sudden. The desert turned to its general quiet dynamic, as if nothing had happened, a coyote here and eons later another one there, or maybe the same.

One of them woke me up late at night, the Milky Way being so brightly lit that I couldn't close my eyes again. I explored the infinite depth above me, and the longer I stared the more stars and galaxies I could see. It was amazing and disillusioning at the same time, because you could never grasp the whole. I wished I could capture the entire firmament with one look, but under the full canopy of the world, you become aware of the narrowness of our field of vision and much more of our mental apprehension, our ability to understand the whole.

From far away I heard a single bird twittering at regular intervals, like a lookout confirming that everything was quiet, no danger. Eventually, his monotone regularity lulled me back to sleep. I dreamed I got stuck in the swamp, sinking deep into the mud until I saw the frogs face to face. They all had violins and cellos and contrabasses, and with a sudden drumbeat, at a single stroke, the pond was dry, the frogs were gone, and I didn't know where I was.

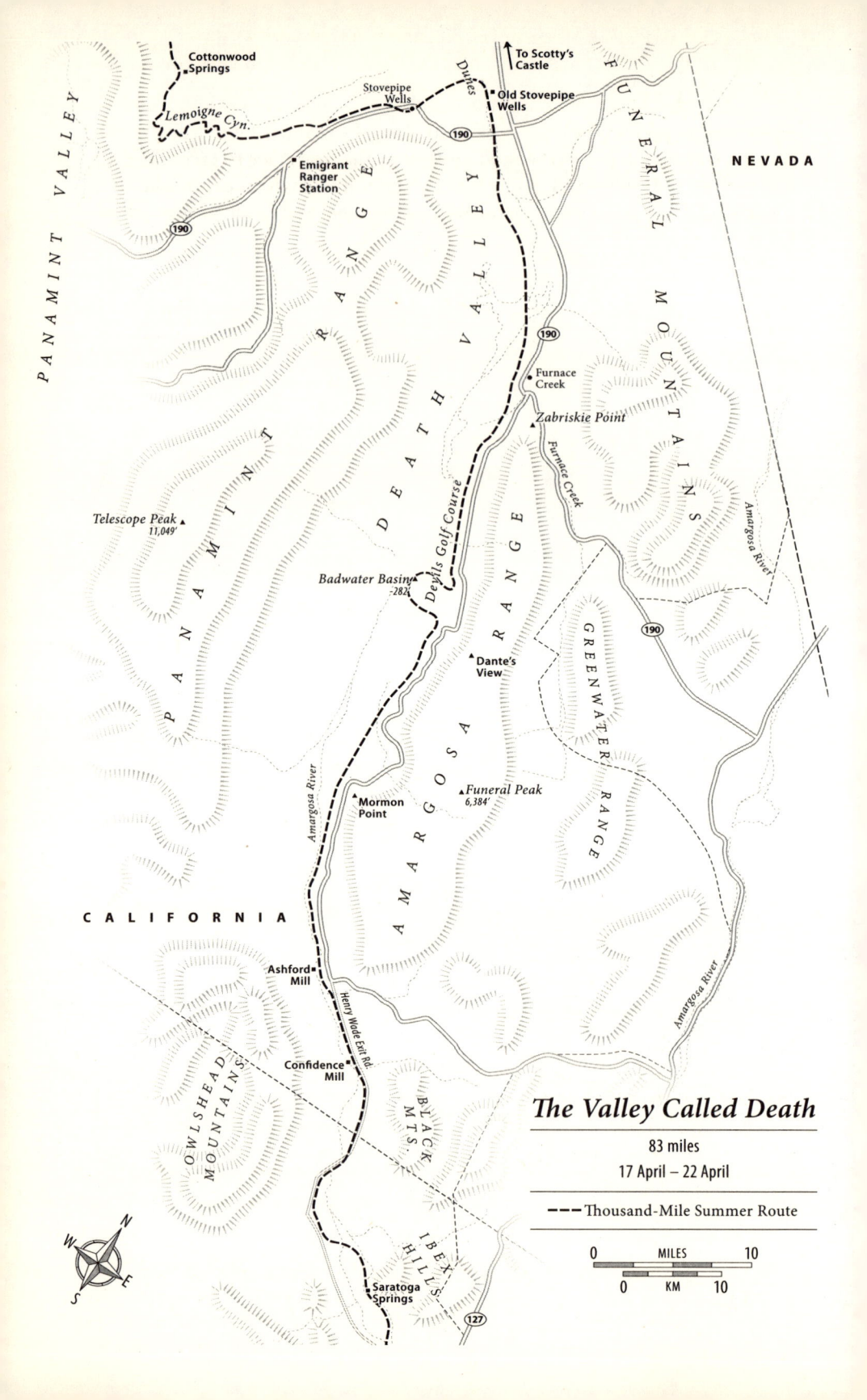

The Valley Called Death

83 miles
17 April – 22 April

- - - - Thousand-Mile Summer Route

3. THE VALLEY CALLED DEATH

*There is shadow under this red rock
(Come in under the shadow of this red rock),
And I will show you something different from either
Your shadow at morning striding behind you
Or your shadow at evening rising to meet you;
I will show you fear in a handful of dust.*

FROM: *THE WASTE LAND, THE BURIAL OF THE DEAD*, T.S. ELIOT 1922

04/17   SARATOGA SPRINGS, 26 MILES

I sat up with a jerk; it took me a while to realize what happened. Two drakes were fighting just a stone's throw away. One of them kept ditching on the water thus causing the flam. The other birds didn't seem to be intimidated by the two ruffians. As I crawled out of my sleeping bag to watch the scene, an ensemble of fowl was striking up, followed by blackbirds and sparrows that hopped through the reed from stalk to stalk while voicing their excitement over the chorus of quacking ducks. Occasionally jumping small fish completed the rhythm into a minimalistic composition of natural sounds.

Somehow this enchanting stay at the Saratoga Springs had not only refilled my water tanks, but also replenished my soul with ecstasy and enthusiasm about what I was doing. I refueled positive energy to weather the coming challenge toward Ashford Mill where I would enter the menacing cauldron of Death Valley.

According to a map of historic pioneer trails, John Charles Frémont must have come through here somewhere to join the Old Spanish Trail and to cross the Mojave Desert after having bypassed the Sierra through San Joaquin Valley. This was the first time of a few that I crossed the paths of his numerous campaigns throughout the state, on most of which he was accompanied by Kit Carson.

At the age of 24, Frémont had received a commission in the U.S. Corps of Topographical Engineers. Four years later, in 1842, he set out for the first of three consecutive expeditions to California. On the last one in 1845, he got involved in the California Bear Flag Revolution, eventually taking an active part in securing interests for the United States. After leading another expedition to the West in 1848, he embarked upon a political career, becoming a U.S. senator and in 1856 the first Republican candidate for president. However, he lost to Buchanan (not to be mistaken for Frenchy Buchanan).

Later on I would again cross the trails of Frémont and Carson south and north of Lake Tahoe.

Although it was the only natural oasis for at least a day's march, two to three days if you walked north, I was sure Frémont had missed the Saratoga Springs. Otherwise they would have been named Frémont Springs if not become a frequented wagon station soon thereafter. Instead a 1870s survey team named the place after the well-known resort of the same name in New York. The word Saratoga presumably derived from the Iroquois *Se-rach-to-que*, meaning 'floating scum on water'. For another decade the scum could float undisturbed until in the 1880s, the twenty-mule-teams hauling borax out of Death Valley used the springs as their primary watering hole. Fifty years later, the last miner had left the camp at the springs; the desert pupfish was alone again, with waterfowls and frogs.

These rare mini fish with several site-specific subspecies are a striking example of evolutionary change. They are reminders that there once was a desert lake system covering large parts of the valley and the Mojave. After the last major ice age, when the lake began to evaporate, different groups were isolated in the separated leftovers like here at the springs, in the Amargosa River, or in the Devil's Hole. Imprisoned in these secluded waters, the pupfish have survived by adapting themselves to water temperatures that exceed 110 degrees and a salinity six times that of the ocean, which is comparable to the Dead Sea. But their struggle against extinction continues; as the water evaporates in summer, they must retreat into even smaller pools. Every year, their population decreases from several thousand to a critical few hundred, hence they feed on algae and on their buddies' bodies.

I took the chance for an early start. Again, I refrained from starting a campfire. I just emptied the rest of my last night's cocktail and popped some cold beans. Then I filled all of my four water sacks, dropped in a couple of purifying drops, and left the lake full of beans with this journey's maximum load of close to ninety pounds, right before the first sunbeam hit the valley floor. I could have gone back some miles and follow Harry Wade Exit Road, a dirt road connecting Hwy. 127 with 178 through Amargosa Valley. Yet crossing the salt flats from here seemed inviting since it would save me some ten miles.

However, my shortcut turned out to be an experience I mustn't take with a grain of salt. What looked like solid salt was rather salty mud. In early spring the flats get enough water from snow melt in the mountains or through precipitation to make walking on salt quite an unearthly affair. So far my plan for the long stretch through Death Valley had been to stay on the western side and cross the flats to the road only in case I ran out of water. Here I realized, with much larger salt lakes there, that would be almost impossible.

The farther I went the deeper I sank into a morass of salt and mud. Tussock and small bushes of sage were the islands of rest. It was like walking on tundra in spring, where thick grass tufts form the only solid soil when the permafrost thaws. After all, my shortcut turned into a fairish delay. Three hours and three miles later I finally reached Harry Wade Exit Road.

Wade had been among the luckier of several 49er teams that tried to cross the deserts between Salt Lake and California in order to escape the grueling winter of northern Nevada. Once they got to Death Valley, they weren't too sure anymore about what was more cruel.

It was the October of 1849, too late in the year to cross the Sierra, and anyway, up there the ill-fated Donner Party had just failed. Several teams were trying to cut through an unknown valley to reach the established Spanish Trail south from here. Drafting a day behind with his team, Wade turned south into Amargosa Valley after three other parties had bogged down in Death Valley. While he made his way out of it here, I was about to meet the other parties' trails.

Since I now walked in the middle of the valley, I had left the morning shadow provided by the eastern range. Here, the sun hit me with full force, and for the next three or four days, my route would be flanked by high and steep mountain ranges, increasingly creating a boiling pot. During the course of a day, the heated air rises, but being trapped by the ranges it cools down only marginally. As it descends again, it is compressed by the low elevation air pressure and heated even more, an ongoing process from dawn 'til dusk. The threshold between Amargosa and Death Valley then becomes a bottleneck for the moving air masses thus causing extreme, hot winds.

As if the heat and the load to carry wouldn't be enough, a heavy sandstorm blew in through this Devil's gate, just as if His exhalation should send me back to where I came from. When blowing too fervidly, He choked, thereby evoking little dust devils. One of these sand twisters got me when I stopped for a drink. With my head up, sucking the last sips off the first gallon, I did not recognize it in time. When I saw it coming, stirring sand and twigs and rising a hat and a piece of paper in the air, it was already too late. I jumped to the side, though, it was exactly where it veered off to. But with closed eyes and mouth, holding my breath for a while, it was a funny feeling getting sandblasted. In five seconds it was over and I think it was me, who took His breath away. The hat was mine, in a cloud of dust it landed two creosotes farther away. I had to take my shirt off and shake off dust and sand, though, due to a constant coat of sweat, most of it stuck with me and from now on I crunched. When I bent down to pick up my hat, I saw that piece of paper again. I reached for it, a yellowed piece of thick, almost leathery paper, weathered by sand and storm and bleached by the sun. Pouring a few drops of water on it to cleanse it, I thought I could see something like a map, with symbols for mountains or hachures for ranges and a dashed line, like for a route. I looked at the piece more closely, there were more symbols for trees and numbers, could have been distances. On one side it was torn off, only part of a name was left, reading like Montesa, Montez, or Montezu ... Ma! A treasure map! When I turned it around, the spark of hope was gone. It was a coupon for a casino in Las Vegas, either blown one hundred miles or thrown away by an unlucky gambler. The picture on it showed a Treasure-Island map rather than a secret desert mine.

While the desert lands of the Mojave were open land, here I felt squeezed from all sides; merciless sun from above, hot gravel below, and an ominous silence between the ranges. For the first time I started asking myself, why am I doing this. A prima facie evidence I was close to Death Valley. Gusts of wind funneled past and a sudden dust devil was only a small excitation on a nerve-wrecking walk along the dry bed of Amargosa River. I started wondering what Amargosa would mean; I thought it didn't really sound like the name of an angel, more like a messenger from hell, the diabolic servant to the horned grandmaster, whom I would meet further up. If it was Spanish, the word *amargo* means bitter. That's close.

Succeeding mountain ranges were forming the end of everything. Their shape was all the same, but they came in various tones of brown and grey or colored in reddish or yellowish. In the Mojave, buttes and mountains poked out of the desert ocean, welcoming landmarks that indicated where I was, how far I went or how much I had already accomplished. Psychologically, these marks and legs were as important as a good condition and endurance physically. From now on the planet was devoid of any such markers. I had no clue how far I got. There were endless ranges to my left and to my right, without any prominent features one could compare with a map.

The other possibility to estimate how many miles I had covered was time. Having spent four weeks outdoors by now, I was pretty good at telling the daytime according to the position of the sun. But with increasingly longer breaks here, I could only do a very rough calculation about my mileage. My aim for today should be the ruins of Ashford Mill, a 26-mile struggle through the valley. The only leg to orientate was the fact that the stretch was almost exactly divided into two halves, the first being almost flat until I reached sea level in the middle of the valley. The second consisted of numerous gradients up and back down to around zero, none of them really steep, but enough to take the view of what lay ahead. Seeing the end of an ascent, you think it can't be very far anymore and you begin to look forward to that plain stretch thereafter. But the closer you think you get, the farther the end moves away and the closer you get to despair.

Talking about the psychological aspect, even worse than having no clue is, if your map gives you one that isn't there, or one that cannot be found. Somewhere along the second half, I was looking for a marked site named Confidence Mill, knowing that in reaching it I would have done two thirds of this day's program. However, I could not see anything that looked like a mill. I began to hope that I missed it, meaning, I passed it and I must be much farther than expected; nevertheless, constant disbelief made me scan the landscape for a sign. Eventually, I accepted it as one of those abandoned sites where weathering time had covered all tracks. For lack of any promising hint, I forgot about Confidence and sat down under a creosote bush to get, though disputable, shadow. Because of the heat, I extended the pause to lunch break and prepared a meal. The water must have been already close to boiling – my stew cooked in a couple of minutes. Above the ground, the air was 110 F. Doubtfully, I checked my water supply; regarding the distance I still had to go, I drank much more than I had calculated. The first sack was almost empty by late afternoon. I had three gallons left.

When the sun left the zenith, I moved on and, hardly surprising, two hundred yards farther I must have reached the point where the mill was. An old timber panel tried to explain but couldn't, someone had taken the sign that was nailed to it. Maybe he got mad too, however, there wasn't anything left to see. Thrown back again, but with the sun at a more gentle height, I slogged slowly into the evening to cover the last third.

With the setting sun, I felt challenged to run a competition with her. Approaching the last ascent before the end of Amargosa Valley, I bet her I would be looking into Death Valley before she was completely down. Far away to the north, I saw the higher ranges with blazing red crowns, in their middle the white top of Telescope Peak. Before darkness would disempower them, I wanted to peer out of the cauldron – even though it was just to see the other, bigger one.

As exhausted as I was, I quickened my pace. The shadows were crawling up the ranges, creating a sharp contrast between the lower parts loosing color and the upper parts, where the sun seemed to intensify the color, in some places even adding new shades that haven't been there before. Behind me, darkness prevailed. The lower peaks could not crane their necks much longer and the first were already surrendering. Before long, I knew I had already lost this game. I slowed down, stolidly putting one foot after the other. I refrained from looking ahead, didn't want to see the higher ranges losing their crowns, too, to prevailing blackness. I just looked down to my feet, to the left and to the right, but neither straight nor ahead.

All of a sudden, without any warning, sunlight was gone, as if someone had drawn the curtain. Instinctively I lifted my head and there, in an undefinable distance, I saw the outlines of the ruins of Ashford Mill towering above the slope that declined well below sea level. Death Valley lay at my feet. Elusive vastness stretched across the planet, made perceptible by an endless chain of mountain ranges – infinity was arranged successively like a store window display of gemstone necklaces. And when I turned around, I thought I saw a reflection of what lay ahead.

The silence had been with me all day; but if there is a comparative for *silent*, it could be heard right here in desert twilight, when the rest of the world started singing and dancing, buzzing and chirping – because here everyone and everything would be quiet and devoutly stunned in awe. The longer I stood there, the more it could also be felt, like gravity. A diffuse gravity, though, that ties you down to where you stand and at the same time pulls you forward to disclose its undiscoverable source.

The scenery literally ambushed me, demonstrating geological history in such a sudden, penetrating, and overwhelming way that I felt a tear in my eyes. Standing on the threshold of the two valleys, I felt reminded of Colin's walk through the Grand Canyon and how he put it in a nutshell by titling his book "The man who walked through time". Up here, with respect to Colin's putative source of inspiration, Sir Francis Bacon, I felt like "the man who saw through time".*

Having walked an endlessly seeming valley, climbing its rim to look into another one twice as endless, suggested a feeling of eternity. From here, I expected to see God at the end, where infinity concludes and eternity begins.

"What is man in nature," the French mathematician and philosopher Blaise Pascal once asked, "nothing in relation to the infinite, all in relation to nothing." Indeed, I felt being something between all and nothing.

After I had recollected, I walked another half hour until I arrived at Ashford Junction, that is where Harry Wade had turned south – exiting Death Valley along the Amargosa River. He had foreseen the errors of the other groups who got stuck in the valley and understood that there would not be a fast route across the western ranges.

---

* In 1973, American writer, philosopher, and scholar Loren Eiseley (1907–1977) published a revised edition of his 1962 book on the Renaissance philosopher and pioneer of sciences, *Francis Bacon and the modern dilemma*. Eiseley renamed his original as *The Man Who Saw through Time*. The professor of anthropology and natural sciences was known as a poetic scientist or a modern Thoreau.

I stood still again, trying to capture the foreboding stories from the past. I was about to betake myself into the valley called death and cross the range that was said to be impassable from the earliest pioneers to the rangers of Colin's days. However, while the first were lost and clueless and, for sure, in no mood to exclaim upon the amazing nature play, I hoped I could trust in my forerunner's maps and abandon myself again to wondrousness.

By now, all light was gone, leaving the formations stripped naked and in a monochromatic tone. The contours became sharper revealing new ranges and peaks that had blended with others in glaring sunlight. Even more so, there were just too many features to grab them all. Somehow I felt lost, I didn't know where to look first. Every single outline was demanding my attention, seemed to be willing me, until a moment later darkness took them all.

I sat down in a narrow side canyon close to the ruins, feeling powerless, small, and unimportant. The spectacle had somehow exhausted me. While I started cooking a pot of ordinary beans, a certain fear took hold of me, a fear that I might never see this theater again, a disconcerting certainty that, one day, I never will.

I dragged out my maps and looked back on a 26-mile marathon, remembering Colin's lines about this tract and more down-to-earth worries. For fear of the valley's reputation, for fear of running out of water, we were hurrying through this part of the desert as if the Devil were behind us. After dinner I wanted to check my maps to see if I could dare the route on the western side of the valley. From here there were two possibilities, the western route on a less traveled dirt road, where Colin had cached water at two places before he started the walk, or the eastern route paralleling the desert highway. At the end of this first day after the springs, I had little more than two and a half gallons left. The amount of water I had consumed on that first leg actually dictated what I should do. I decided to sleep it over.

With the candlelight in my tent, I started reading a text about the '49ers' fate that I had put in Colin's book for later study. There, the Donner Party's tragedy had just left the news, when the first strikes leading to the California gold rush became public. In the fall of 1849, a loose group of emigrants and would-be gold miners from all over the country gathered in Salt Lake City with over a hundred wagons. Organized under the guidance of Captain Jefferson Hunt, they were bound for an unknown land to find riches where hardships would pave their trail. The only known alternative to the Donner route, which had tragically proved impossible to make in winter, was the Old Spanish Trail to the southern end of the Sierra.

Being anxious for an uncertain luck, parts of the group soon fell for another guide's plan, who happened to cross their way. A Captain Smith along with his partner Barney Ward suggested a short cut; they had a copy of Frémont's map showing a land of plenty with rivers and lakes, west of what was known only as 'The Great American Desert'. On their map, this was marked as a blank space labeled by one word in bold letters: 'UNEXPLORED'. However, they were assured there would be a shortcutting Indian trail saving them some 500 miles and leading to lush lands and water for all. What they meant was Owens Valley and Owens Lake, which at that times still was a lake, untouched by Los Angeles' thirst for water.

Being between a rock and a hard spot, opinions varied, and as hardships increased, the groups split and reorganized several times, changing theories of escape and their courage every other day. In the end only those who stayed on the Old Spanish trail arrived safely, celebrating Christmas at their new home. Those following Smith's map were prophesied they would "get into the jaws of hell", and no doubt, they came close to it. When they got stuck in the salty flats of the valley, they were harassed by discouragement. The purported shortcut turned out to be a terrible mistake. While Smith's map merely showed a roughly sketched mountain range, assumably a promontory of the Sierra Nevada separating the desert from the promised land, the party found itself confronted with several higher ranges and the Panamints forming an impassable barrier.

With hardly any drinkable water and their food almost exhausted, they ended up slaughtering the already half-starved oxen and burning the wagons to smoke the meat. The fact that only one 49er seemed to have died in the valley is due to smaller groups that kept trying to find a way out on foot. Gripped with foreboding, a party that called themselves the Jayhawkers, left the desolate camp to hike across the Panamint Range; also the main group, later known as the Bennett-Arcane party, determined that their only chance would be to nominate two tough persons who should scout an evacuation route on foot and procure food and pack animals from the first civilized spot to be found. After a 200-mile walk over the desert ranges of the Mojave, equipped with only a few pounds of dried meat and a makeshift canteen made of gunpowder cans, William Manley and John Rogers had finally found a way out. Arriving at a small settlement near today's Los Angeles, they got food and horses and returned to camp almost four weeks later to lead the party out of the valley. When the party had climbed the last higher range on its exodus, one of the members was said to have paused, looked back eastwards and baptized the place by saying "Goodbye, Death Valley".

All of their lives were hanging by a thread. They had just enough water to wait for help, but they ran out of food and wood and the nights were getting freezing cold. For sure, had they started in summer, with the immense heat they probably wouldn't have made it.

All the while, the Indians had been watching them cautiously. However, as passed down by his granddaughter, at that time Piute Chief Winnemucca was already convinced they were bad people acting in bad faith. He let them walk blindly toward their road to ruin. The Piute assumed that if they abandoned them to their fate, they would all head into oblivion.

With a blink of an eye, history could have turned the expedition into another Donner fatality, but it was merciful, claiming only one life of all the groups trapped in the valley and two more beyond the Panamints. However, the valley's reputation was sealed.

04/18   ASHFORD MILL, 24 MILES

I woke up early, hearing steps around my tent. The sun wasn't up yet; the chocolate-colored mountains on the eastern side of the valley still refused her the view. With perked ears I moved around trying to see anything and find out what was going on. I cursed the zippers of both my sleeping bag and the tent. Whenever you have to get out quickly, the best fabrication turns out to be the stupidest thing in the world, ornery jammed, entangled and the more you curse, it will lock solid in both directions. I thought, whatever it is, it would either have taken to its heels or laughed itself to death, until I would be able to get out of my cocoon and open the tent. When I was finally peeking around, there was nothing, not even tracks in the sand, just the creosote flapping with the wind at my tent.

I was hesitant to start a fire and have coffee. Holding the opened water sack in my hands to measure how much was left, I knew better. Including the other two sacks, after breakfast I would have less than two and a half gallons and I had 44 more miles to go in merciless heat, twice the distance I coped through Amargosa Valley. I realized I must have an early start, walk until noon and pause until the worst heat would be over. With the full moon I could possibly walk until late into the night. Having picked the last cold beans from my pot for breakfast, I checked the ruins of Ashford Mill briefly. They catch your eye due to their unusually massy cement constructions. One hundred years ago, the Ashford brothers found specks of gold in nearby mountains. Although they called it Golden Treasure Mine, there wasn't really much to extract. The name helped more in leasing it out to other fortune seekers. One of them ordered cement for an ore-processing mill, but received twice the amount they had ordered. Since returning it from a remote place like that would have been more expensive than its actual value, they just left it here and the fundaments of the site were built twice as thick as normal. The mine employed almost thirty men; all in all they extracted just $100,000 worth of gold, and since mine expenses exceeded the profit by far, in the 1940s the last miner understood, too, and took the exit road.

Death Valley's true treasure was not in gold but its borax. In the 1880s, a poor fellow, Civil War veteran Aaron Winters, accidentally found out about a strange looking white mineral and its value. He sold his discovery rights to William Coleman for a fraction of what they ended up being worth. Coleman founded the Harmony Borax Company to begin operation. He soon became famous for his twenty-mule team trains, which hauled the mineral out of the boiling pot, and with a sophisticated marketing strategy to promote borax, he changed the image of the valley dramatically. Although in the 1890s, there were new deposits found that were much more conveniently located, the Death Valley Borax works somehow survived by providing for the brand logo for several borax-related products like cleansing agents and cosmetic products. The Twenty-Mule-Team came along well as an exotic logo glamorizing a most labor-intensive work in the cruelest environment. In order to market the brand, art figure 'Borax Bill' had been traveling through the country with a mule team. The popularity of the team endured wars and crises. Borax Bill even made it to Broadway and the Rose Bowl Parade in Pasadena. In the 1930s, a Borax sponsored Death Valley Radio came into life, followed by the 1950s-Western anthology TV series, 'Death Valley Days', hosted by Ronald Reagan among others.

It was only 7 in the morning, the scorching sun breathing down my neck; no point in waiting for a mule team, it was time to leave the ruins. I put on my pack, drew a deep breath, and began the descent to the lowest point in America, being quite aware it could become my lowest point as well.

With every minute the sun colored more ranges and slopes around me, revealing the earth's crust. None looked like the other, the whole scene appeared as if Mother Nature had thrown them together in a capricious moment. While the western ranges looked more like regular mountains, to my right a chaotic mix of badly weathered edges and rims was building up. It looked as unique as outlandish, and for sure that added to retaining the valley's reputation even through the times of Borax Bill until when wagons and trails were upgraded to air-conditioned cars and asphalted roads.

Today, the valley is less a question of survival, as long as you know what you are doing, but more of a playground for visitors and natural historians and geologists. All these landforms and puzzling rock phenomena are virtually hurling their history to the observant visitor. In the 1930's, geologist Levi Noble established that these mountains at the southern end of Death Valley have been faulted and folded in a much more complex way and under more extreme forces than any others. He referred to this characteristic as *chaos*. Other geologists assumed that at some point in earth's history, due to a chaotic event, several layers of rocks and mountains were flipped over, thus bringing older formations on top of younger ones.

Only in the 1980's two geologists, Bennie Troxel and Lauren Wright, found out that, due to the extreme and versatile geological forces, some layers were squeezed to one tenth of their original thickness. As these processes took place, masses of up to 2,000 feet were pressed into 200 feet and sections got mixed with others from different layers.

At the same speed darkness had conquered these ranges the night before, it was now repelled by the sun's paintbrush. The strokes only went the other way, from the peaks down to the bottom, until eventually the glaring light of the midday sun dissipated all colors in luxury. In any case, it seemed to be the sun rather than the Devil holding the paintbrush.

In moments like these, whether one believes in God or not, it was just hard not to feel the Godly around oneself. Likewise, this may happen in wandering through a cornfield in Iowa, only, it might be more difficult there, because the monotony pulls thoughts out of us whereas the geological supernovas here seem to expel all thoughts, baring a supernatural principle with a sledgehammer and creating a vacuum that hungrily fills with thoughts of God.

I had two miles to make up my mind, east or west, close to the highway or two days alone on a forlorn dirt road. Why two days, I thought, it could become three or more. I did not know the terrain, only that crossing the large salt flats would be too dangerous if not impossible at all. If I really ran out of water, it would be along the last third, where I would have to cross the salt lake itself or an even less inviting place called Devil's Golf Course. There, a rough surface of wind- and rain-eroded salt structures would turn a hike with a heavy load into a penitential pilgrimage. I remembered reading that on a hot day with air temperature around 120 F, the ground temperature may rise to almost 200 F. Then you become desert yourself, with an evaporation you can't beat with drinking.

For sure I mustn't count on sporadic cars; I had not seen a single one on Wade's Road through Amargosa Valley, nor did I hear one passing on the highway during the night at the mill. Then I thought, I could still leave my pack if something happened and walk back easy to the highway. But what then? Come back with two sodas only to find myself trapped again?

I was torn between the two ways until I reached the junction. Getting there, I didn't even have to take my pack off to think it out. I felt the sun on my neck, merciless, I looked down the valley, endless; and since I was constantly weighing my sacks, I knew I had only two gallons and one hearty draught left. It would be careless, if not grossly negligent; without the caches, the western route was too risky. I decided to tie myself down to heading for Furnace Creek as my next stop. There, I would refill my sacks before climbing out of the valley over the Panamints.

So I kept trudging down near the highway and started another boring statistical play by counting the cars. It was about 9 a.m. and I had 4 heading north and 4 heading south. All of them were local service cars, probably working either at one of the touristic sites in the National Park or in the town of Shoshone east of the valley. At 11 a.m., the score was 21:13 with the northbound taking the lead. Japanese-made rental cars outnumbered the service trucks now. While the service guys always took notice of me, throwing an affirmative greeting, tipping their hat or just honking the horn, watching the tourists became something like a behavioral scientific study. There was the ignoramus, mostly a family man, who did not want to or actually could not see me because I was not signed on a tourist map. There was the embarrassed, who spotted me and instantly looked away avoiding eye contact. And there were a couple of indignant drivers, don't ask me over what. They saw me, passed me, and shook their heads.

Others were real saluters, I called them my supporter club. When approaching me, they slowed down and cheered me up by honking a staccato fusillade, showing at least one thumb up and taking the imaginary hat off to me. Sometimes, when they had passengers, the driver would turn to them and say something that caused a nodding agreement. In my mind I heard them say: "remember darling, I always wanted to do that".

Interesting was the gender issue. With regards to who was greeting, you would guess that the passengers had more time to watch what was going on left and right of the road than the driver. However, most of the greetings came from the drivers. Those were usually men – for any reason, driving a car still seems to be a man's domain. I developed the theory that it's always the driver because holding the steering wheel you are, somehow, the boss, therefore executing all externally-focused actions on behalf of the whole group, something like the public relations executive of a *carporation*. However, I am sorry to say, my theory had to be abandoned. It didn't matter who was who or sitting where or being what, it was simply only men, not a single woman greeted, waved or sent a sign of recognition, even if she was driving, not even for pity.

Anyway, from this supporter club I drew hope. Left alone in walking trance, I started fantasizing, had visions of an ice-cold can fondly fallen out of a passing car. I thought, one of them had to get the same idea sooner or later and surprise me by putting a soda in my way. In the face of these unfulfilled desires, walking the paths of civilization through wilderness was much harder than beating your own trail on nature's surface, where the only promise lies in you and not in frequently passing cars.

At high noon, the score was 28:19 and no can had left any of these cars. I was ready for a three-hour break and stopped at Coyote Hole, a little salt pond surrounded by mesquite bushes. I wondered if the coyotes gathered here at night, complaining it was only salt water; then the correct spelling would be 'Coyote Howl'.

Resting under a creosote bush, I spotted a desert-five-spot and noticed that I had hardly seen any flowers in the last two days. The salt, which was everywhere, and the abundant creosote seemed to keep other wildflowers from gaining ground here. For one hour, I did nothing but sit, I mean it, I solely sat; I did not read or check maps, I did not take off my shoes, throw stones or poke with a stick in the ground, all these things you usually do when you rest. I did not even think, I just sat. Had it not been so hot I would have fallen asleep. Pushing away thought-images of those gaunt, chapped-lipped Western-movie characters straying through the desert, I kept calculating my chances, balancing water supplies and the condition of my feet and my back against the heat, against many more miles to go, and against these messengers from an outer world that seemed to be accessible only in case of an emergency. The only way would be running down the valley, doing a forced march. Start late and don't stop until I would kiss the grass, if there were any, or bite the dust. I crept under the creosote like a lizard and awaited dusk. Only then I would get up like a nocturnal animal running to reach the next milestone, Badwater.

When I arrived at this largest expansion of the valley's salt pan, I was knocked out. I was so exhausted, my pack literally flew off my back when I dropped down on the shores of that white solid lake called Badwater. Without a doubt, a spooky place to settle in around midnight.

At -282 feet I had reached the lowest point in North America and I had hit rock bottom looking on one of the world's most imposing and contrasting landscapes. When I stood up again, without the load, I felt like I was walking on the moon. I followed the grey path into the salt lake, which had been trotted down by visitors over the years. It was an almost unreal situation. The ocean of salt reflected the only indication that I had not landed on moon's surface, the bright light of the full moon itself. It became surreal when suddenly I noticed this Dolby-surround *cadong* you hear when you walk on a frozen lake and the ice starts cracking in long gashes.

I knew it couldn't be so, but I also did not feel like taking the risk of being taught otherwise. In a land with such outlandish formations, everything seemed to be possible, if not likely. I tiptoed back and found a bed on solid rocks well below a sign nailed to the mountain saying SEA LEVEL.

04/19   BADWATER, 18 MILES

With the first daylight I was up, quickly reading the educative plates at the visitors parking space. Today's salt lakes are the most visible relics of the huge lake system that retreated from being lifted and eventually being cut off from precipitation through high rising mountain ranges.

Until the end of the last ice age, Lake Manly was the remaining body of water, which dominated a valley that was anything but dead. It stretched a hundred miles along the mountain ranges with a depth of 600 feet. Then, the increasing arid climate had transformed a lush Mediterranean basin into what I was passing now. Looking at the surrounding mountains, you can still see horizontal

CHAPTER THREE

lines of exposed former lake bottom sediments. The geometrical mix of these linear forms and older lines that had been tossed and turned by an, even geologically seen, slow folding process formed an almost cubistic pattern.

Across the lake stood the snowcapped 11,049' Telescope Peak, looking down on me dwarf. As so many other sites and places in the valley, it seemed enticing. But being forced to move on and not loose time, they all were out of reach for me. I was just allowed being in transit, following a more or less straight line to the end of the valley, which in fact was full of geological highlights well worth seeing. None of the side roads were open for me, though; one gallon left.

As amazing as the valley's scenery was, yet for a walker it turned out to become relatively monotone with the only highlights being dawn and dusk, when the desert's paint-box was opened and closed, respectively. Down in the valley, I could walk for 20 or 30 miles with the landscape not changing very much. The views at the springs were as imposing as at the mill or here at Badwater. But it was still the same scheme. My walking turned into hastening in order to outpace the monotony and to forget the worries about water. Just like Colin, I did my longest day hike with 26 miles through Amargosa Valley, and I was about to complete some fifty miles in two days through Death Valley. Fifty years ago, he had accomplished the stretch from Saratoga Springs through Death Valley in 51 hours. At the springs he had given his sleeping bag to a ranger, who would leave it at another station at the end of Death Valley. While I was driven by heat, Colin had been taken by surprise by a drastic temperature drop, and he ended up walking through most of the night to avoid trembling sleep. In any case, only with additional walking time into the night, we could make sure that we would make it through.

With temperatures between 90 and 100 degrees, again midday became too hot to walk. In exchange for last night's moonwalk, I rested from 11 to 3, fighting boredom and defending my lunch against a strong blowing wind, which was constantly adding salt and sand to it.

When I continued, I left the scalded blacktop, where the mirage of heat waves had become as grueling as the immense heat it reflected, and I walked on the lighter desert floor. Mile after mile, the earth's gravity seemed to increase, only the western ranges already craning their peaks for sunlight spurred me on.

Creosote milepost 44, it was late afternoon, Furnace within reach. I huddled under a larger bush to take one of my paralyzed, almost unconscious sit-ins, when suddenly, up ahead in the distance, I saw a shimmering light. It seemed that a car had stopped; the setting sun was reflected in one of the mirrors, causing this effect as if someone was sending signals. I leaned back to the creosote, it was too far away – and too unrealistic to wrestle my tired body and all of my logistics in motion. The seed of hope for getting a coke has long been parched. I had stopped counting cars, had not even noticed this one passing, yet the sudden, unusual sound of reversing gear roused me from my lethargy. The car came back, and, to my surprise, a good-looking, nice lady got out of it – no, she literally rose from it. Then she walked straight to my place under the creosote. "You want cool water?" she called with a French accent. I wondered what led her to that idea and at the same time, I was virtually certain that I had not left the comatose state yet.

The lady introduced herself as Cécile, and during a little conversation exchanging the odds and ends of walking through the desert, I had finished a bottle of cold water. I was quite sure nothing better could have happened to me. Yet, I wasn't so sure if I was suffering from dehydration, having reached the 8% level where you start fantasizing. We said goodbye and she went back to her car where she stopped again, turning around: "Want to check out some sites here with me, I have two days off and a motel room over there. It's already paid, expensive enough for two. You can stay with me if you don't mind." Now I knew it, at least 15%. Furnace was only a mile ahead, but what if I lost orientation? The voice continued, "Well, not in the same bed, but we'll find a solution", what brought me down to 10%, and a chance of survival.

Reality or fantasy, I just couldn't resist. I was invited to check out the points of interest here, a one and only chance to see the Death Valley I would never have hiked to and why all today's visitors were coming to one of the most hostile places in the world. Holy prince of Serendip! My route would take me from Furnace Creek to the Emigrant ranger station and out of the valley. I would have missed almost every site that is marked as historical or worth seeing but Badwater. Now, emigration had to wait.

04/20–21 DEATH VALLEY, 8 MILES

In two days we completed the Death Valley sightseeing tour. Zabriskie Point was one of the best spots to see the colorful sharp-formed badlands, uplifted eroded sediments from former lake bottoms. The Artist's Palette displayed a chaotic array of rainbow-colored rock caused by a variety of minerals. From Dante's View we overlooked most of central Death Valley, and I think it was here on this most famous viewpoint, when I noticed that the greatest views of all had yet been the ones I walked to, and above all, there to my left fifty miles in the past, those views into dusk and dawn on the threshold of the valleys, between bitter and dead.

Among the drive-by sights, Devil's Golf Course was my favorite spot, if only, a fortiori, to take a few jaunty steps on His dubious green. In fact this part of the main lake would have been impassable, a deposit of rock salt that seemed to have been sculptured by supernatural forces, leaving nothing but jagged spires and pinnacles. When you stand there and bring to your mind that only in the rare occasion of heavy rain a simultaneously strong blowing

CHAPTER THREE

wind could form these salt pinnacles, you get a sense for the Devil's concept of time. It's just hard to believe you are still on Earth and not visiting one of the planets patrolled by Captain Kirk and his crew.

That brings me to Scotty and his castle, another attraction we visited the following day. If you always wondered how a Spanish-Moorish-style two-story castle would look like, this is the place, in the middle of an American desert.

In 1927, the Chicago Millionaire and insurance executive Albert M. Johnson wanted his Mediterranean dream to be set in stone. Why there and not in Europe remains an intriguing mystery, still, he was a millionaire. For years, his minion Walter E. Scott, a former member of Buffalo Bill's Wild West show, had been pulling money out of his pocket by promising great paybacks from his gold mines in the desert. The fact is, he never even filed a mining claim. But he did locate pay dirt in his benefactor's pockets. Even though his fraud unveiled, Johnson continued to support the impostor and appointed him supervisor for building a private 32,000 square-foot sanitarium where desert could not be more deserted.

Here Johnson loved to listen to Scotty's trumped-up tales about desert rats the likes of 'Pike' Wilson, 'Shorty' Harris, 'Seldom Seen Slim', 'Bad Water Bill', or 'Mono' Jim. And then, after dinner, they retired to the music room, where Scotty had installed him(self) a huge music box, a complete windup orchestra, which played all by itself.

Until the day he died, Scott pretended to own the castle. History remunerated his behavior, a lifetime of shameless self-promotion, hustling and swindling, and named Johnson's mansion after him. Today you can visit the castle and find some remarkable antiques, paintings, and ceramics, though the larger attraction definitely is the unique architecture, the Spanish-Oriental mix of styles thrown into an architecturally no less amazing nature.

Strolling through a field of blooming cotton-top cacti, our conversation came to the inevitable venomous fauna. I told Cécile about my rattler and spider encounters and that I had not seen a single scorpion so far. Teaching her that you just have to turn flat rocks and eventually you would find one, I stooped down to turn one exemplarily. We were so surprised that we jumped back, routed by a baby scorpion.

On a short hike, we walked into Titus Canyon, a spectacular gorge with petroglyphs, marble-like rocks, and deep narrows. As I looked on my map, I wondered what kind of drama might have happened here; did a guy called Titus lose his wife Tita here? The neighboring canyon was Tita_not_here Canyon and after a day in Frenglish, it took a conversation with the local ranger to understand that my fantasy had become as colorful as the desert flora. The name actually related to an Oligocene mammal found here, titanothere, distantly related to the rhinoceros.

In the evening, I was invited for dinner. We shared some beers and told us our lives until last orders were called in the Badwater Saloon. Indeed, the nights I spent on the floor, and when I closed my eyes, I still saw that haggard looking man huddled under a creosote. When she left after two days, with all the pictures I had of unexpected sights and seeings, I was sure it was all real, as real as a human angel bringing water, sent by God into His antagonist's den.

04/22   OLD STOVEPIPE WELLS, 7 MILES

When she dropped me at Old Stovepipe Wells, I was back alone on the road. A rusty well pump protruded from the sand, marked by a stovepipe, which could easily be spotted by travelers. It wasn't hard to understand how lucky they must have felt at the sight of the well. From here I crossed the sand dunes, which were covered with half-buried Mesquite trees, a perfect playground for lizards. After an hour watching them, I moved on until I reached the modern Stovepipe Wells, where a motel, a general store, and the ranger station added to the stovepipe.

Between there and Emigrant, I would exit Death Valley through a chain of narrow canyons and over the Panamint Range, where the highlight of my desert trip would close in on me, but not before I had spent another night in the valley. Too much had happened in these five days since I left Saratoga Springs. I guess my mind was somehow overstrained by so many surprises. I did not really have the time yet to realize what I did, that I made it, because with finishing, I was struck instantly and lavishly by luck. I made it! I crossed that part of the desert that had been racking my brain for more than a month in a marathon-like tour de force. And now, as grateful as I was to get to know Cécile and as much as I appreciated her invitation, now I was missing that moment of contemplation every athlete needs after an excellent performance. Another night at the motel would allow me to say "Goodbye Death Valley", too.

Before I boarded the general store, I walked to the ranger station. I introduced myself as the guy who called for the water depots weeks earlier. I saw they had not quite believed I would make it that far. "Kudos to you!" yet he reassured they could not help me with depots and take over responsibility if I made my way or not. "The good news is", he said, "the natural springs signed in your map should carry water. Your only problem will be to find them." Throwing a skeptic look at my '58-maps, he continued, "Let me see that map again," and eventually convinced me to get a newer one from him.

Colin's route led across the Panamint Mountains through the untrodden wilderness of Lemoigne and Cottonwood Canyons. From there I would ascend the Hunter Mountain area, walk into Saline Valley, and leave it via North Pass until I got to Deep Springs, the end of the desert. Climbing White

Mountain would then be the grand finale of the first half before crossing over to the High Sierra. I waited for any comments like "You cannot do that. – That's impossible to walk. – No one ever did that!" I felt that somehow I had expected to be warned as the rangers strongly advised Colin not to try it, "You can't go up there! That's rugged!" It enhanced the adventure feeling when you set off to do something that others wouldn't. Still I knew at least one did it and he reached the other side sound enough to write a book about it. However, asking me three times if I had enough water was all I got for my hiker's ego.

When I came to the motel, it was time to relax and take an hour to look back to my successful crossing of the *real* desert. I took a seat on the porch, next to the flagpole, the Stars and Stripes were waving above me and for a moment, I thought, in the lower center of the blue color one star was twinkling to me. Before I could have a second look, the security guard came by to bring the flag down for the night. I suddenly felt the itch to assist him in the ceremony. When I touched the colors, I couldn't help but feel something taking possession of me, the flag's aura seemed to capture me, causing me to feel a good deal of pride.

After all the adventures so far, the land I saw and the people I met to this day, I felt proud of this country with its overwhelming untold riches, and proud of those people who value and cherish them. Exhilarated by a tremendous performance that had brought me close to the limit of endurance, having overcome all inner gremlins, and being rewarded by serendipity again, I interpreted the thirteen folds in my own soulful way. Those who know the ceremony will understand and may, I hope, accept my interpretation.

The first fold was for life, for my journey and the people I met.

The second symbolized the eternity of the nature I walked through.

The third was in honor of the history I learned and in remembrance
of all people from the first nations to our early pioneers,
who blazed the trails we walk today.

The fourth was made for the trust I had and the guidance I received
when I was at a loss.

The fifth fold represented the country I walked through,
as ambivalent and critical one might see it,
it was a land of unbelievable treasures, nature-wise and people-wise.

The sixth fold was a tribute to our hearts,
for with our heart we pledge to do good to the land.

The seventh was for those who stood up to protect its treasures,
not only for themselves but also for posterity.

The eighth was made for my mother, who could not witness my voyage anymore, the ninth a tribute to the woman I love,
and the tenth for my father, who counted his sleepless nights.

The eleventh fold resembled respect and tolerance for different-minded, different-looking, and all Godly I saw.

The last was my wish that, despite our limitedness,
with all our greatness, may we some day gain a common understanding for the Earth's values and worth.

When the flag was completely folded, the stars were uppermost. I thought of the many nights I spent out there, when I watched the real stars, recounting the past days' adventures and realizing that sometimes a good trust in God had made me venture my next step. Then the flag was tucked in, with the thirteenth fold taking on the appearance of a cocked hat. At that moment, a small breeze blew my brown leather from the porch into the scene. However, I granted George Washington the last honor, for whom it was meant, along with his soldiers, preserving the rights, privileges, and freedoms many people enjoy today.

Just as if the little oasis would be unprotected without the flag and helpless at the mercy of the elements, the breeze turned into a strong storm, blowing in swaths of sand. Half an hour later, I couldn't even see the little general store across the street. Tiny sand dunes had piled up in front of the motel doors, the pool water looked like a huge tray full of caramel ice cream. The afternoon winds had increased their power at the surrounding mountain walls. Now they came rolling and tumbling, collected sand from the dunes and eventually darkened the western valley. All that remained was a soughing wind, eerie darkness and grinding teeth; time to sleep.

Based on the legacy of 19th-century hotelier and hospitality pioneer Fred Harvey, the Stovepipe Wells motel was a little oasis resort in that land of privation. While Harvey had established service orientation to the last conceivable detail, the successor Xanterra, a park concessions company, concentrated on the essentials you needed after a desert ride, no matter if automobile tourist or walker. So I could not expect to be well announced here or be received with opulent food plates, as Harvey used to notify his restaurants before another trainload of visitors would arrive. There were no 'Harvey-Girls' animating me for another drink or more, and the dressed-up Natives, to whom he had established the best relationships, offering handcraft and jewelry, were also missing. But service was excellent, the poolside an unexpected pleasure, and the bar stuffed with friendly people, a welcoming hangout in preparation for the coming adventure. After all, I felt, I had yet got to know the true promise of Harvey's legacy in that valley called death.

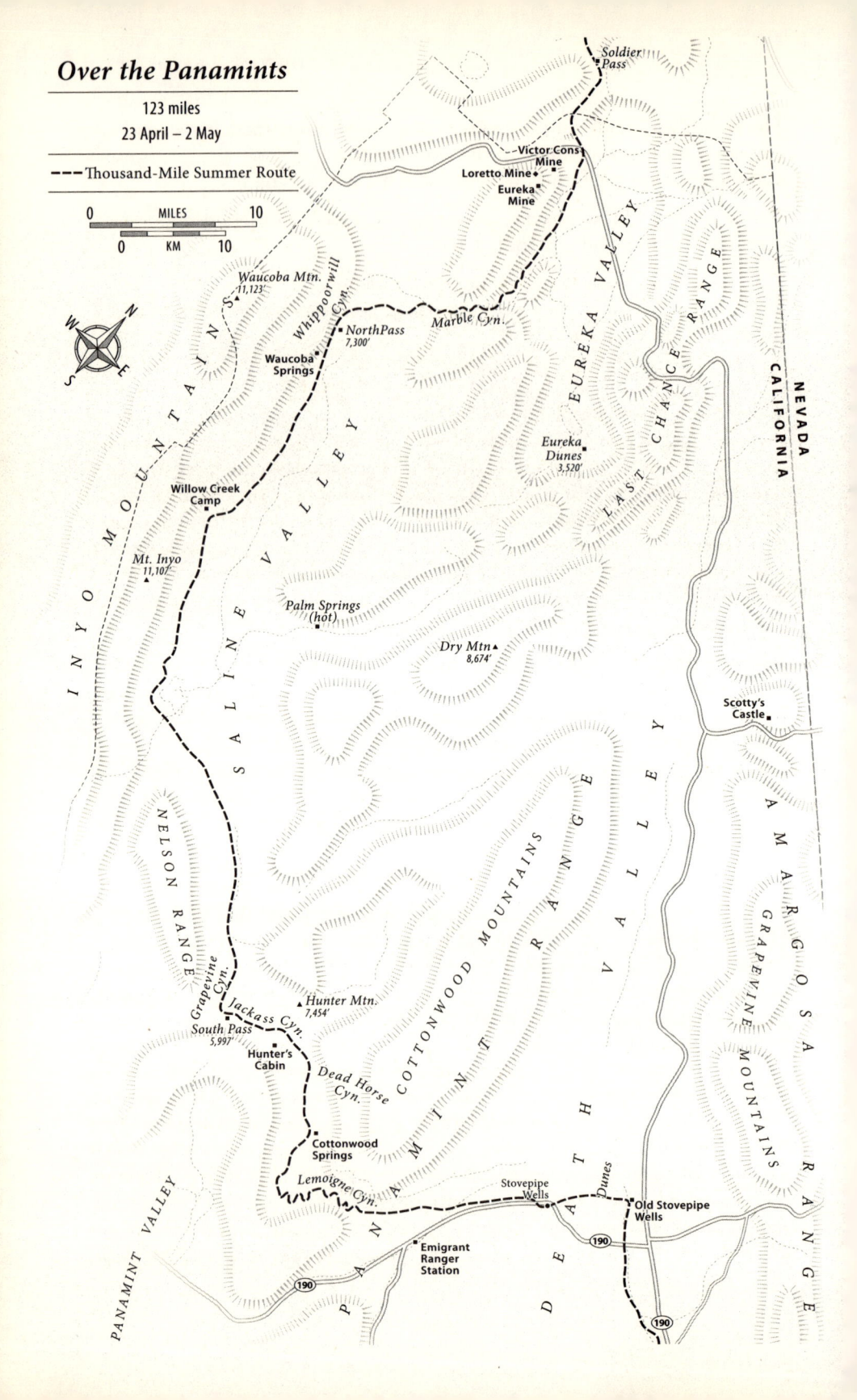

Over the Panamints

123 miles
23 April – 2 May

- - - - Thousand-Mile Summer Route

4. OVER THE PANAMINTS

To see the world in a grain of sand, and heaven in a wild flower:
Hold infinity in the palm of your hand, and eternity in an hour.

WILLIAM BLAKE, ENGLISH POET, PAINTER, 1757–1827

04/23   STOVEPIPE WELLS, 11 MILES

After a heavy storm in the wee hours of the morning, the sun came back to lay claim to what is hers in the desert. Having coffee and breakfast at the poolside, I became an eyewitness of another dramatic scene. I counted 24 sparrows gathering in the pool area. In six rows of four, they hopped to the edge of the pool. But this was a shoreless puddle, their necks were too short and none of them could reach down to paradise. It was their torments of Tantalus, and they surely had to suffer them every morning anew.

Eventually, they gave up the promised pond; so did I. After taking my leave of Harvey's heirs, I sat down at the flagpole again. Before I hit the road to Emigrant, I wanted to feel that inner gratification again, the pride and peace of mind after having accomplished a tremendous job and, in doing so, having once again stumbled upon fortune.

Watching cars passing by on Death Valley's sightseeing highway, I thought that, while for a walker time and distance in the desert expand, for them they would contract. From all regions on our planet, it was the desert which you can least meet by driving; it will always spare you its real character, its idiosyncrasies, and, somehow, release you disappointed, unfulfilled.

On the other side, I was aware that I would never have had the chance to see all these sightseeing points without Cécile and without her car. I felt shivers

CHAPTER FOUR

down the spine and grateful that I saw both, that I was struck by serendipity again. Now, I was ready for the next adventure. I got up, passed the motel office, and without an 'hallo', I called in the room behind the counter: "I don't know how you did it, but you really did outmatch Fred Harvey, to the letter. Bye now!" I had already closed the glass door, when two wondering faces looked out of the office room, then symbolizing two walking fingers that meant 'Happy Trails'.

The old Emigrant ranger station was about ten miles up the highway, a 2,000-foot ascent from sea level. About two miles earlier, I turned right into the open creosote desert, where a sandy trail led to the entrance of Lemoigne Canyon. Unlike the canyons along the big river, this one was bursting with flowers and blooming cacti. Apparently snowmelt on the much higher mountains provided for sufficient water allowing a more multifarious fauna. Spring was in full swing producing showy blossoms to attract flying pollinators as much as a hiker. While a rare ocotillo along the Colorado and cacti and yuccas in the Mojave were the stunning floral highlights, here the desert paint-box was fully opened, containing the oranges of California poppy and desert globemallow, the blues of larkspur and lupines, the violets of Mojave aster and indigo bush, and the reds of paintbrushes, which were coming in light, bright, and luscious tones. Whites and yellows grew in such a variety that I could not keep them apart anymore. Cacti and – the higher I got – more yucca went without saying.

To me, walking through these mountain canyons was the kind of adventure I dreamed about since we played Cowboys and Indians beyond the rusty gate. Pioneering through a canyon was something like the prototype of exploring for me. It was the secrecy of walking that mysteriously fascinated me, the hide and seek with the outer world as well as anticipating surprises behind every bend or in every side canyon. It was the secrets of geology unveiled by a cut into earth's crust and it was detecting so many different plants and animals all hiding in the canyons' shadow. There was an indefinite promise I felt when looking down the strips of sand as they snake away between steep walls, leading to a place that was hidden for a long time until I came to discover it.

On the sandy canyon floor, large bushes and stands of flowering bouquets found their niche in time between irregular storms and flash floods. Since the mountain lion encounter, I was overcautious and had adapted to lift my head every few steps to look up the canyon walls. There, too, I found a real cornucopia of plants, growing in all directions and angles and finding their niches on the thin layers of soil of hundreds and thousands or a million years of age, along the cross-section of earth's history. Eventually, the frequent stops and taking the pack off and on to carefully examine the canyon's flora became more exhausting than the walking itself.

Lemoigne wound westwards up the mountains, and I had to make sure that I stayed in the main gorge. Other canyons met here and there, often leading into the same direction first, only miles later turning off to another range or mountain. A couple of times I took the wrong branch until compass and map made me suspicious. But every time, I saw so many new things, I never regretted being misled. In a rather narrow side canyon I was caught off guard by a stunning fat, four-foot-long snake. It rattled the hell out of me when my right foot threatened to get too close to its hiding place. It was no more than a fair and no less than an authoritative warning with an impressive effect. In a second, I found myself at least ten feet away from the coiled-up snake. However I got there, was it running or in one big jump, my heart was still in my boots when my mind regained control over instincts, and I thanked for the warning and watched the snake wind away from a respectable distance.

Another wrong turn led me to a well-laid dinner table. Although I had realized my mistake, I paused before I would return to the main canyon. Not the most colorful Sunday tablecloth in a southern antebellum plantation house could have presented a more exclusive table pad. Violets to my right, yellows to my left, and a little garden of blooming paintbrush right behind my cooking site. Here, the desert laughed in flowers. The setting was so elegant, I decided to take some time and prepare a meal instead of just heating a pack of dehydrated food. So I boiled two handful of Spanish rice and created a fine sauce of tomato paste and canned anchovies. I know, it does not sound much different from one of the prepackaged rice dishes and their imaginative names, but in the light of these bouquets around my table, the simple fact that I prepared a meal by myself bore comparison to fine cuisine. The fireplace enlightened the chamber of canyon walls around me sort of haimish; I just couldn't keep from putting yet another log on the fire, and another, until four hours later it got dark and I stayed for the night.

04/24   LEMOIGNE CANYON, 13 MILES

Here, the canyons cut much deeper than along the Colorado, therefore I had to climb a rim more often for orientation. At the end of Lemoigne Canyon, I had to find the passage to a high valley that would lead me onto a higher plateau. To my left, a massive range stood up; according to my map, it must be somewhere here opposing its highest peak. But there were three or more cuts that could be referred to as a valley in the broadest sense. I left my pack to check the area and I soon saw that only the middle one would somehow take me to a mountain plateau.

Walking on the sandy valley floor, I passed a number of detached yucca and juniper raising a silent voice against me. Someone oversensitive would have interpreted their dirge as a warning or at least as a message, just like one cannot pass the Moais of Easter Island without a dim feeling that they had

CHAPTER FOUR

something to say. Behind the trees, after a long gradient, I finally reached the plateau and all at once at a single glance I understood their secret. There, for the first time, I saw to the other side of the world, my future world, the snow covered Sierra underlining the western horizon. The highest peaks protruded from a black layer of clouds like diamonds on black velvet. From the tension caused by these guardian yucca trees, I had felt that something was coming; they had somehow prepared me for an unbelievable view that could hit you thunderstruck if overtaken by its sight.

From the plateau where I stood to those snow-capped mountains, it was about fifty miles. In between lay Panamint and Owens Valleys, separated from each other by another lower range. It was my first sight of snow – exempt the little snow cap on Telescope Peak – of mountains higher than 10,000 feet, a tremendous foreboding of what lay before me after I would leave the desert.

In moments like these, I had to take a break, here less culinary than contemplative. I had to take some time to see it, feel it, and, however, stomach it. Usually, I would just stand still for a while until, only some timeless minutes later, I would realize that I had stopped walking. Then I would sit down and, without taking my eyes off it, start talking; things like "Are you serious? Get out of here! I can't believe it." And then after a short pause, "How did you do this?" Whether I talked to the mountain, to the planet or to a creator or God, in any case it was the helpless attempt to pay tribute to what I saw. I always had this feeling that I had to say something, that I must not just pass by without a comment, though being speechless.

After ten or fifteen minutes, I would take off my pack to get the camera and try to capture that moment. Today, these pictures are the saddest of all, beautiful though, but they cannot give the slightest feel of what one really saw. The only aspect one may capture with a photo is the contrast between the pictured view and the personal experience.

After the ceremonial break, I turned north on the plateau that should unfold into another broad valley and eventually become Cottonwood Canyon. Colin's map indicated an old trail, probably trodden by prospectors a century ago. I checked the plateau by zigzagging from one side to the other, until I was sure that there wasn't anything someone before me could have followed as such, as long as a trail is commonly understood as a more or less passable and trodden way. I didn't find one, nor did I see a single sign that anybody had ever been here. Still I thought that my route was the only way to find the natural springs at the meeting with the canyon. At first, everything went well, all geophysical indications matched the lines and dots on the map, the plateau, the valley, the side ranges. I was walking on a chain of sandy washes that found their way around and through the mountain shrub. Any one of these could have been used as a trail, but with one rain, all traces would have been swept away.

At the end of the valley, I entered a steep canyon, so steep that I climbed through it more than I walked. I was sure I must have left the hidden trail, if I ever was on it at all; but where the valley had ended, I found only rubble slopes going up and this dry fall going down. The maps were not detailed enough to show the unexpected barrier. I must have been close to the letters of *Cottonwood Springs* already, whether I ever got there would depend on my vertical fortitude.

Having climbed down the first fall, I was halfway in the canyon when I realized that there would hardly be a way back up if something went wrong. It would take me twice as long and my water was already running short. Either I was totally wrong and somewhere else but in the Panamints or those prospectors were good climbers, including their burros.

For the next ten minutes, I was consistently throwing an anxious look to an empty space one hundred yards ahead. Balancing my pack weight on all four, I climbed down large boulders and around gnarly-shaped cedar trees leaning into the abyss. As long as there were rocks, trees, and brush to hold on, I was fine. They were welcoming obstacles, like emergency brakes in case gravity should gain in on me. But the sudden emptiness, lacking any signs that there was something at all, bode ill and I feared the worst. When I reached the last big rock, a massive overhang, I held to the crooked branches of a battered cedar and leaned over to descry what would come next. Emptiness could not come across more threatening and profound, a vertical fall of some fifty feet right down into Cottonwood Canyon. How on earth should I get down there with the pack?

I knew, whatever was behind the next bend, either the springs or my vertical limit, I would not be able to come back this way. More rocks further down seemed to overhang, hence climbing up with some seventy pounds would have been impossible. Here I might find my way down, with the help of my thirty-foot rope. But the ancient fall presented a challenge I did not expect; a one-way trail if it worked out fine, or a dead end if I was wrong. I would have to take my pack off and lower things down first – but what if I myself wouldn't make it, how would I get back my pack? Climbing first and pulling it after me would have been too dangerous. If the pack would slide off and fall, it would certainly pull me instead.

I sat down, spread my maps again and gazed at them. I tried to remember everything I had passed on this day, compared and reviewed what-if scenarios. Then I was sure, this must be the way, and only around the corner there must be the springs. No other possibility. I looked down the fall again. Now that I knew that this was the only passage to the springs, that there would be no other choice, it looked even deeper and like a breakneck certainty. I kept the sleeping bag and one gallon of water with me, roped the backpack down until I had to let it fall a remaining fifteen feet. I decided to climb down the

CHAPTER FOUR

boulders to the left, crawled, slid, and clawed my way, trying to avoid starting a landslide of debris, shrub, and a hiker's limbs. Just when I paused, holding on to a thick mesquite root branch, I caught a glimpse of dark green treetops behind the next curve, the trees of Cottonwood Springs, luring me to slide into an orgy at the oasis and get drunk from fresh mineral water.

It took me one more hour to get to where I had seen the trees. Thick and thorny shrub secluded the valuable spring water; whoever wanted to rejuvenate here had to earn it. As I closed in on the oasis from high on an escarpment, I found an animal trail through the jungle of bushes and fallen trees. Hidden in a small clearing lay a natural palace of sandy beaches under a pavilion of luxuriantly growing cottonwood. I immediately recognized the sound of that little stream flowing over tiny pebbles into small pools, just deep enough to immerse a hiker's face into it. It sounded different from any other creek, because it was so special here, as much out of place as valuable. The plashing and trickling noise from that little runlet, not wider than the palm of my hand, was so clear, as if you would hear the flowing atoms of water. From this day forth, wherever I stumbled over a little creek or natural springs, in my mind I always saw these Cottonwood Springs.

In order to immerse myself in this fluvial symphony, I reclined in the sand alongside the little creek, where small cobblers were caught in a fallen cottonwood twig thus creating tiny miniature rapids. Slightly jolted from the fall, my backpack was leaning to a tree, pausing in an unusual pose, as if it was taking a deep breath. Two hummingbirds were inspecting the wondrous and colorful being. Standing in the air like tiny helicopters, their beaks were tipping at the luring colors of the pack and some clothes hanging out of the open bag. When they came to the conclusion that it was just a backpack, they lost interest in it and flew over to me. Studying me from one foot away for a couple of seconds, they couldn't find anything of interest either. With dark-brown shoes, kaki pants, a light-brown shirt, a buckskin hat, and a tan somewhere between these colors, I wasn't more exciting than plain desert soil.

However, they had directed my attention to that wondrous being I had grown accustomed to so much that it was almost a part of me. It was everything I needed, something I would defend, and, I was sure, someone I would soon start talking to, just like a good friend. It surely is a useful experience to learn that you cannot only survive with no more than you can carry, but be happy and at one with the world. In a sense, here, I had everything I needed and, according to America's most prominent non-consumer, Thoreau, I was even very rich: "A man is rich in proportion to the number of things he can afford to let alone."

I leaned back against the pack and let myself doze off until the call of a desert night bird woke me up at dusk, reminding me that I wanted to collect firewood.

With the last light of the day, I got up and picked up sage roots and some thicker sere boughs from trees that had dared to jut out of their refuge a little too far. As far as I remember, this night became the longest I stared into the campfire.

*

I have been asked very often, what I would think about when spending hours at the campfire. One thought I had to become a philosopher, if I had not agonized sooner over my own being. However, I am afraid, my answer was far from what one expected.

In general, when I sat down after a long walking day, with everything in mind that I saw and heard and felt en route, I often had no need of thinking about anything at all. When the evening came and the camp was set and the fire burned, just the delight of sitting and watching the flames amply sufficed. Some scenes and encounters were lingering on me until with a smiling remembrance I fell asleep. After an eventful day, though, the scenes might flash upon my inner eye replaying them in a slow-motion mind movie until late at night. Then I went through them again, reviewed my behavior or the steps I took, or thought about what could have happened if I had acted different, be it the rattle overheard, the natural springs missed. Very often I just felt happy that I was at the right place at the right time for another serendipitous event.

Furthermore, usually right after dinner, I spent about an hour with studying maps and drawing conclusions from the past hiking day, pondering routes and calculating risks for one way or the other.

To me, the campfire is a thing of its own. It stands alone with its immense, almost mystic appeal, secretly connecting its viewer with ancient times, with our forefathers, to whom it was everything, something like the philosopher's stone, an all-giving Pandora. Indeed, when I think of a campfire, I can only think of the most precious moments, whether with a group of people sharing stories or by yourself reflecting on your experiences as you stare into the flames. Not only on a wilderness hike, sometimes after a hard working day, I would start a campfire in the garden or nearby woods to rest the mind and make room for feelings, less for thoughts. That fire just cleans my head from every thought, from sorrow and worry, from morrow and hurry. Then indeed, sometimes an angel whispered something to me, an unexpected idea popped up and one or the other was worth reviewing. But I hardly ever elaborated these at the fire, but later when I went to bed or the next morning.

I know, for some it was hard to believe. Once I offered a more common and comprehensible example: how many of us became acknowledged philosophers by spending hours at the barbecue grill, turning bratwurst and steaks? No doubt, for some it is a philosophy, if not a religion, itself, as is the building of a campfire. But mainly it is just a rite for getting away from it all.

CHAPTER FOUR

While barbecuing also is a rite of manhood (probably because most women calculate more the risks of combining fire and lighters with beer), I recall that women were fascinated by a campfire in the same way, gazing into it and entering a wordless conversation with the flames. And, compared to barbecuing, where fifty percent of the brain capacity is occupied with remembering, which piece did I turn first, and the other half is tied up with keeping potential wisenheimer and know-it-alls off a certain zone of influence, the campfire allows something like the total freedom of mind.

In any way, it is these rite-like activities where thinking just has to be closed down, for the cause of the ceremony, or the taste. When you go hiking and cook your meals on the self-made grill, you have it all, freedom, a pinch of philosophy, and taste.

Other people saw the philosopher's apprenticeship more in the process of walking, contemplative walking, that is. "What do you think all day when you're hiking? You have so much time and nothing else to do but walk." Indeed, there were long stretches for ideas and thought, and I am sure, I somehow lived through my whole live during the thousand-mile walk, remembering situations in my past and following possible paths into my future. However, here again, I couldn't really give the Solomonic answer some questioners expected. Very much of this *thinking* did not happen consciously, but more subliminally. Angels whisper, they don't cry. Every time I felt reminded of a former situation in my life, a thought would come to the fore and pop up to the surface, to the consciousness. However, you had to have established a certain walking routine to allow yourself to look into it. Then you might think on two superposed levels, whereas the one above the surface is predominantly reserved for banal, less philosophical things like your way, water, and warmth.

Therefore, when being asked about my world of thought, quite often, my spontaneous answer was, "Not much." But at the same time, I knew it was false, that only I referred to what I thought the questioner wanted to hear. Of course, it was an extraordinary lot. There simply is not much room left for letting the mind wander on philosophical paths, when one walks into the wild. (There must have been a reason for Thoreau to just sit it out during his Walden years.)

Here, it is advisable to watch every step, every single step. The one missed could go down in one's personal history or, less pivotal, one just missed some flowers or critters. To bring up some wisdom, "You could not step twice into the same river; for other waters are ever flowing on to you," as the early Greek philosopher, Heraclitus, said. Figuratively, that applied for every act and each step; it were just a pity to miss one of the many photogenic scenes, but it became crucial in creeks, on loose gravel, steep slopes or an unfirm rock, when climbing a rock face, where each step had to be calculated with the sudden impact of 250 pounds of man and pack. Just stepping an inch too close to its hideout, the first rattling drowned in a step on crunching gravel, the fair warning overheard, could in remote places be the end.

Then I was preoccupied with calculations all day, where am I, how much water is left, how reliable is the ranger's assertion that there will be water at the springs. I navigated with map and compass, in places constantly comparing them, and predominantly above all, I just had to stop ten times a mile to have a closer look at animals, plants, rocks, and tracks. I took pictures, close to a hundred per day. Pictures of the scenery, of me and the elements, of animals and flowers, and sometimes of me and an animal and a flower. In some areas like here in the Panamints, there were so many new flowers and cacti that I had to stop every few minutes. This meant, taking off the backpack, getting the camera out, changing lenses or adjusting, making sure the pack won't roll down the hill while I was lying on the ground to sneak up to the desired object like a predator to its prey; after the capture, putting everything back together and up, pulling all laces, straps, and belts – all that, only to go under the same procedure just around the corner.

Sometimes I waited for a chance where at least two or three objects would stand close together, making my break a worthwhile photo excursion. Naturally, forecasts were difficult, though. One time I walked back a mile because the desired rendezvous of flowers didn't come. The desert five-spot was worth the trouble. After the one-mile stretch without any more of it, I thought I had probably left its habitat. I parked my pack and walked back until I found the fine elegant, blossom again, with a red spot on each of its five purple petals. You already guessed it, one mile and a few steps later, just around the next bend, there stood even taller ones, a whole group of them, proudly protruding from a collection of other flowers.

What's going on in one's mastermind then is less philosophical than pragmatic. First I had to weigh the striking object against the arduous stops and time, is it worth the trouble, interrupting the routine, taking the pack off the sweating body, unpack the camera etc. and cut down my day's output by another mile? Then, supposed the object prevailed, usually when looking for the perfect shooting position, I detected other objects, flowers or critters, and I had to weigh them against each other, who'd be first. And when I was finally kneeling over one, another member of the same species would catch my eye, being even larger, taller, brighter, or just sitting in a more photogenic setting.

One day on the walk through Lanfair Valley, a shimmering purple between two Yuccas on a hill had demanded my attention. It seemed just a stone's throw away, however, the view to that hill had concealed two deeper ditches to me, which were overgrown with mesquite. For that stone's throw I needed half an hour. Getting there I completed the hour as I descended on a beavertail

CHAPTER FOUR

cactus in full bloom with camera and tripod from all angles. On the way back to my trail, I startled a horned toad, which seemed to compensate a certain lack of agility by a dragon-like collar. It immediately lapsed into torpor, hoping to elude closer inspection through my third eye. In fact, its skin was so perfectly camouflaged that I had some difficulties focusing the subject. In the next canyon a tortoise was dragging, so slowly that I began to understand why evolution had no opportunity to make advances to this species. It was simply overlooked.

Other critters were more difficult to capture. Some bustling species were far too hectic, you could be 99% sure that, by the time you got the camera ready, they would have been crawled into a hole, at best turning around again to poke their tongue out at you; whenever you wanted to shoot, they would duck their head. Groundhogs and squirrels are most famous for that behavior; rabbits are perfectionists. I bet the only existing photos of rabbit faces are faked. How can we know that a living rabbit's face does not look like a gremlin, or a mini-elephant? You would have to shoot one and arrange it as if it was alive. Instead I could write a book about what their cottontails look like.

Colin had described a situation, when after a long desert walk he arrived at the place where he had cached water six weeks earlier. In the meantime, a couple of flowers had settled in on the hiding place. He did not – as any "sane man" would have done – check his cache first, if the water was really there, let alone drink, but he contented himself with capturing the breathtaking blooming spectacle before he would do anything else. I was as insane for sure. While it is understandable, even to sane people, that lizards, beetles, or snakes wouldn't necessarily wait until you dealt with other things, flowers, cacti, and trees and even more geology would have waited quite a while. But there was this certain magic, a matter of respect in engaging oneself with the object first, or with the landscape, in capturing the first moment, before it was maculate by my sheer presence.

One day in the Colorado River ranges, I had been so obsessed by taking against-the-light shots of an ocotillo raising its branches to the sun that I forgot to pick up my hat when I walked away with my photographic treasures. Only after a while, when I felt my brain cooking, I called Roland to stop and asked the rather stupid question, "Do you know where my hat is?" I knew instantly that this was not just having lost something. With temperatures hitting 90 and 100 F, if not 'up to', the hat was as important as water, or I mustn't walk during day anymore until I reached the next town or a hermit hat maker. I just couldn't remember when I last saw it. I sat down and thought, it could not have been long, since my brain in general was still working. The only stops we had in the last hour were for taking pictures. I checked the camera and saw the series of shots of a tall ocotillo. The last thing I remembered, I was crawling around on rocks to get the best angle. There I must have taken off my hat and put it aside, I was afraid, on a rock

154

of the same color. The file information of the last ocotillo photo taken said 12:30, Roland added, "It's 1:20 now". Considering the time between recognizing the loss and now, it must have been some thirty walking minutes away, running back without the pack, probably twenty.

Roland sat down in a wash under a palo verde tree to prepare lunch while I had to find the passage back to the place we were before. But which way did we come? Not walking on the assumption we might have to go back, I had difficulties remembering the way that led us here; the plateaus and washes all looked the same and on rocks you hardly leave tracks. Eventually, I climbed a higher bank and checked the area around. Each rock and each hollow had something I could remember, as if I had passed all of them. But none stood out as 'this is the one.' Fortunately, the ocotillo is a rather protruding plant, growing scattered sporadically and not in clusters. It hit my eye, on the slope of another plateau, tall dark-green lances with red-tipped spearheads and I remembered the background stonewall. I climbed down and up again and only when I stood in front of the plant did I see my brown leather hat, huddling in perfect camouflage between grey, brown, and red rocks. I picked it up and celebrated it back on my head like that favorite piece of clothes you found again after having missed it for a long time. Before I left, I took it off to the ocotillo again, had the photo session not been for him but a small ground-hugging daisy, I might never have found it.

Back to the wandering mind. Still there is some time left in between all these activities, taking pictures, watching your steps, and calculating the position. Sometimes in the evening, I would pick a certain subject and resolve to think it through while walking on the following day. On the evening of that new day I might have still considered where to begin with it. It was like trying to read a book but being disturbed every other sentence, rereading the same paragraph again and again. And then in the evening, of course, there was the fire waiting.

Even a couple of months was not really enough to get into a walking routine that allowed you to – no matter what terrain you were in – spend a lot of time with great ideas or contemplation. This of course would be different when you, so to speak, go for a walk, when you were on familiar terrain or when you hike for hiking's sake. But as soon as you have a schedule to walk from A to B, even more if you want to reach B, and most if you have to find your way, water, and a good place for a warming fire every evening, not too many thoughts are given a chance to diffuse from below to above the conscious surface.

It is like a job that has to be done, the best job in the world, though, because in between you see, hear, smell, and feel nature, and also, quite as interesting, your body and your inner self. In order to really think those topics through most people asked about, I would have to take a day off. One of the best experiences was that I was totally preoccupied with myself and my environment, and somehow this togetherness turned out to be pragmatic philosophy.

Somehow, the *thinking* is a higher sense, a sense with which we try to touch or feel ideas, plans, possibilities, or solutions. It can be separated from our other senses and there were situations, where, to a certain degree, it had to be trimmed back, when one was forced to use those more primal ones. By and by, all of them became more heightened and more alert along the trail; they were observing every movement, every noise, processing everything they picked up, and if necessary, reacting. They calculated, orientated, and navigated automatically, constantly checking plains, canyons, and mountain passes or looking for trodden trails. They saw a possible route, heard a rattling warning, or felt an unstable, rocky slope. They were always on guard.

Even more than the walking itself, I enjoyed feeling myself in a way that gets lost in normal life. Here, the senses became my company and after a couple of weeks, they communicated quite clearly and precisely with me when they opened up to being perceptive as instincts. At times, I could smell a subtle odor and, just by following it, find the hidden flower. I heard a beetle approaching and I saw movements behind me. I got attentive and observant to a degree, where one can feel things coming.

However, it is not only alertness what they are for, nor merely for taking up information. We often forget that it is through them that we enjoy. We may enjoy the thinking itself but we cannot enjoy other things through thinking. The more we numb our minds, the more our senses dull, the less we will be able to enjoy our environment, and in the end, the less a life is worth living. By reactivating one's ability to use the senses for more than just the obtrusive, at times importunate information overload in our civilized lives, one soon notices how much more we can feel with them and also that they are all interconnected through our sixth sense, dangling on a string that directly connects to our soul.

Only through the soul we are able to feel the gravity of silence, see the brilliance of colors, hear the sweetness of sounds, but also, somehow, to feel things coming. I am sure, reactivating these capabilities by nourishing the senses every once in a while, makes us not only stronger and more receptive but also helps to become better members of the society, who are more mindful and balanced.

Naturally, our senses are programed to receive, but in order to let them do so and tap their full potential, we have to make them receptive. At the same time, we deepen the soul. It is this sensual perceptiveness we often lose with increasing comfort in normal life that slowly moves us into a stupefying struggle for existence and repute while we unlearn some qualities that would make our everyday lives more experienceable, hence valuable. We are all just prisoners here of our own device and our limited abilities, yet in nature, we may awaken capabilities that have been slumbering within us, showing us what we really have, how we can use it, and who we really are. One may be surprised to learn that what some tend to believe to be supernatural abilities instead are simply naturally trained senses.

To me, there is no better cure for dullness than facing the unknown in becoming a temporary pioneer, pioneering one's environment as much as oneself. Last but not least, in offering ourselves to the wild, to the unknown, we will regain our sense of wonder, if only by accepting our smallness within the interactive structure between us and the concept of nature.

An outdoors trip may sound simple and banal compared to an elaborate marketing strategy, a sophisticated technical solution, or an artful piece of craftsmanship. However, I felt, it was exactly these experiences, when thrown back to one's own terms, being dependent on oneself and one's senses, which sharpen the awareness for whatever one does in 'normal life', thus enhancing creativity, courage, and self-confidence, and ultimately the highest sense, the ability to think.

In general, the *thinking* question came along with worries regarding individual perceptions of solitude. Being a solitary walker most of the journey caused some people to worry much more about my mental condition than the physical risks or dangers. "Didn't you feel lonely there, all by yourself?" or, "Weren't you afraid, so lonely?" whereas *lonely* was replaced by *alone* or *lonesome* depending on which of the three would be the least desirable state in the eyes of the questioner. My first thought was, I never really felt being in any lone state. Then I saw that the words could be seen negative or positive, and, on a peaceful morning while listening to the cheerful splashing of a tiny desert creek, I began to think about it.

Alone – I thought 'thank God'; every so often I really need it. To me, it is the prerequisite condition not only for self-contemplation but also for doing things the way you want it. Furthermore, especially in nature, your senses are more concentrated hence open when you are alone, you just get to see and hear more of her.

Lonely – when hiking and experiencing nature, I was at most as lonely as I would be when adjourning from family to the living room to indulge myself with a fascinating book. There I might immerse in a lonely togetherness with the story or the characters. Here, in fact, very often I felt being together with the nature, with a howling coyote, a trumpeting donkey, or simply the rustling garment of cottonwood trees. In this sense, togetherness won't allow loneliness. Lonely also meant to me that you had to be completely self-dependent and rely on what you already had or knew and trust on what you were able to acquire or learn, again, with the means you had or knew. It is a good self-check. I was my only companion, and it was interesting to deal with him.

CHAPTER FOUR

And *lonesome* – I didn't know what to do with it. It suggested too much sadness and boredom.

Apart from that, even in the wilderness of eastern California, every other week, I ran into a colony of snowbirds, an abandoned railroad station with minimum service, or a small town. In between I never thought I was lonesome, though alone. As I depicted, I was occupied sixteen hours a day, if not so much with survival strategies but either with comprising nature's plethora or receiving the hospitality of the people. After all, the way my solitude while walking through the vast wilderness overlapped with brief sojourns in small towns seemed to be so well-balanced that I was over the moon when I came close to civilization and after two or three days being there, I couldn't wait to be back alone in the wilderness.

04/25   COTTONWOOD SPRINGS, 5 MILES

Although today I would have a very arduous leg to go, I decided to sleep in and enjoy an expansive breakfast at the oasis. In fact, this was the kind of place where you should stay for some days. Unfortunately, when it is uncertain what lies ahead, you just don't have the piece of mind to live for the moment.

My start was held up several times by a number of vain flowers calling to be photographed. Leaving the little oasis, I climbed the slope behind to capture a salaciously blooming mound cactus. From there, I looked around and realized that the springs seemed to be walled by steep talus slopes covered with sharp, rocky debris. However, once I was here, I thought, I just keep on climbing heading north. In less than five minutes crawling uphill, the pleasures at Cottonwood Springs were forgotten, and I found myself back in the discomforts of the desert.

With refilled water sacks, my pack weight back at seventy pounds, I challenged the precipitous 50% grade of loose gravel. The only way up was to grab hold of roots, bushes, or larger rocks, secure every single step, almost kissing ground, to keep the backpack from dragging me down. The higher I crawled the more cliffy outcrops forced me to stop and reorientate in order to find a way not only around the outcrop, but one that wouldn't end at the next bigger one. Every look uphill was like studying a labyrinth, trying to follow all possible routes and remember the single one that would take you out, or here, up.

After the first half of the mountain, I had to have a short break every five steps, gasping for air. No more photos! Even if I saw the Panamintus Rex, I would not take off the pack here. After two thirds or an hour and a half, I was high enough to overlook the springs and the canyon. Down below I saw the picturesque green copse of cottonwood and, to my surprise, a thin line of trees leading around my mountain. I had two choices, continuing the ascension to a point I did not plan to reach yet or accept that I worked my way up too far, that I should have looked back earlier and walked on a horizontal line around it until where a northward side canyon joined the Cottonwood creek.

In order to get there, I climbed almost the same stretch back down since the cliffs up here and further around the mountain became impassable. I hate to admit that in two hours I had merely reached the western end of the springs. At least I had surpassed some smaller mounds and thick brush right above the springs, where a sandy trail would have taken me to exactly where I was in less than twenty minutes. It was a small comfort that with all the photo breaks I would have taken down there, I probably had not done it any faster.

Back at the springs, I refilled the water sacks with cold water before I followed tracks through the newfound canyon, the first burro tracks since I had left the big river. Soon the canyon opened out into a broad and treeless mountain valley. When I climbed a higher bank for orientation, I got a last view of Death Valley. From here it seemed harmless and inconspicuous, not much different from any other valley around. What exactly this one demands from you and likewise has to offer, you are only aware after having crossed its length, walking; having roamed its superlatives, driving; and having crawled out of the cauldron over its rugged edge. For a last time – Goodbye, Death Valley.

The mountain valley up here was full of caterpillar nests, extravagant homes of the California tent caterpillar. It seemed that this year was one of the periodic outbreaks resulting in masses of the unsightly-cobwebbed nests. On the first day, the nests seemed to be all white. But looking closer at them, I found almost transparent cocoons with a wiggly mélange of transparent larvae inside. The next day, some larvae had turned into worms and their skin began to darken. Some miles later I found nests with one or two mature black caterpillars, then ten, then fifty, and on the evening of the second day, the nests around were all black with the first inhabitants assiduously gnawing their way through the cocoon. A moment later they were overpopulating bushes and trees.

In a library I later read that their preferred host in this area would be cottonwood, furthermore that during heavy infestations, armies of them would migrate and feed on many other plants. I guessed this year was their last before Judgment Day, they sat on all plants and just as if there were not enough for all, they besieged the only signpost I saw between Death Valley and Hunter Mountain.

The sign said 38 miles to Keeler, 9 miles to Jackass Springs. It did not tell anything about what that meant, repressing the numerous washes and canyons that had to be crossed. During my race around and below sea level, I had made three miles an hour; up here I needed three hours per mile. Right before

I reached Dead Horse Canyon and another natural springs, I walked through a narrow strait of bushes, which curved and declined drastically. Again, deep down in the canyon, the inviting dark green of luscious leaves was luring, and from high above I had already decided to stay there for the coming night. These springs had no name on my map but as many cottonwood trees as the last ones. Late in the afternoon, I arrived at the oasis, named it Cottonwood Springs II, and delved into another long night with campfire musings.

Although the product range of my larder was rather meager, the evening dinner often became a real highlight of the day. Just from the names on these food packs, one wouldn't expect anything else: Southwest Salmon BBQ Inferno! This was not only a meal, it was a statement and possibly a warning. However, since I like hot food, to me the inferno seemed to be contained.

Usually, I had two meals per day. My breakfast, to start with, had less in common with the customary or continental fare. It was more a lean dinner or, as long as supplies lasted after a visit to town, a choice of cookies, granola, and fruits. In the afternoon, I only had a snack or leftovers from breakfast, but then in the evening when the campfire was burning, I always had a feast.

When preparing my journey, I had considered taking less meals and whether I needed to overcome common food prejudices. Feeding from whatever I could find along my way could have saved some more pounds. There were berries and nuts, mushrooms and tubers, roots and tree bark, many of which were edible. However, in discovering them and knowing which ones are not only edible but also palatable and providing for the nutrition a hard working body and an alert mind would need, you had to be a little botanist. One mistake could mean serious indisposition or even intoxication. Especially in the desert, nature's edibles were hard to find. I would have to complement my diet with roasted lizard tails, cooked birds and their eggs, grilled squirrels, or insects like that California caterpillar. Indeed, they could be boiled, making a fine addition to soups or even be eaten raw. In some areas large grasshoppers became frequent guests at the campfire, but as for me, despite their self-sacrificing or suicidal tendency to jump right into the flames, removing more than four legs from food source may be saved for real emergency situations (except maybe crabs and shrimps, which, unfortunately, did not occur along my route, save their petrified kin).

While preparing the hike, I had preferred to invest free time in reading about the land and the history instead of graduating in phytology or studying survival cookbooks. And on the trip, I enjoyed watching the food chain much more than disconnecting it, like on this afternoon when that fox hunted the roadrunner that hunted the iguana that hunted the grasshopper.

I realized that the pounds saved would have meant foregone pleasures too much and inconveniences by the urgency to find something, and I ruled it was OK to stick to my prejudices. After all, I saw more challenge in getting from A to B than in proving to myself that I could live off the land. Only in the mountains farther north, fish became a complementary food source and sporadic strawberries or blueberries a welcoming but rare dessert. In addition, the calls at civilization gave my diet enough variety to never really notice the persistent rice-noodles-chicken choice on the trail.

When I started looking for a place for my tent, I made sure there was no caterpillar-infested shrub around. Those tent-builders used their nests as nighttime refuges. By the time I would go to sleep, they should be in their beds too, but when the day begins, they venture out from their safety net to feed, and I did not know, whether this fellow was an early or a late riser. In good years, when large numbers of these caterpillars hatch, on and off small town papers report slippery roads caused by the colored worms commuting to and from work; a scene that reminded of that early seventies nature-revenge movie *Frogs*, starring Sam Elliott and Ray Milland.

04/26   DEAD HORSE CANYON, SPRINGS, 5 MILES

What roused me from early morning sluggishness, though, was not the hairy creature. When I first opened my eyes to reach for a bottle of water, an alarm literally rattled me out of my tent. A nicely coiled up fat Northern Mojave lay only five feet from the entrance, right in that mold in the sand from my nightly campfire session. Time to wake up! – Didn't take long this time, no morning stretching, eye-rubbing, snooze-alarm necessary. You snooze – you lose. I was up and out of the tent in no time, which made the snake kind of uneasy. Since it lay so close to the exit, I had to move the whole tent in order to get out. That was probably too big for its sensors, a warm moving rock? For a minute it remained silent, almost torpid but for its flickering tongue. Time for me to take a breath and plan further steps. I realized it would have been safer to stay in the tent until the intruder had left my seat at the pit, instead of climbing out of it only a strike away. Yet somehow I felt quite uncomfortable being trapped and captured like that, and the way I got the tent moved around and jumped out of it – believe me – not even a snake could have struck that fast.

When I stood on my feet, I felt the adrenalin rushing through my veins. For a moment, my thoughts were spinning around the *what if* question, but as the adrenalin rush started to fade, I took a deep breath and woke up to the opportunity to have a closer look at this unusual desert beauty. It was a wonderful though evil looking creature, obviously totally bewildered by the action going on here. When I pulled the tent closer to me to get my camera, the snake followed it for a foot or two, then coiled up again and rattled. Flicking the black, forked tongue in and out, it tasted odors it most likely never had before. The tail was held up high and kept vibrating in warning. In the canyon walls around this little oasis, the sharp buzzing of its rattles

CHAPTER FOUR

sounded even louder and more threatening. I picked up a stick and learned how far it could strike, and I realized it was less aiming for the stick but the warm flesh holding it. All of a sudden, with one strike, I saw the snake's mouth open wide with one fang in position, the second one just being folded forward. I stopped playing; that was all I needed to see. The mere imagination this weapon could hit me, rip my skin and pump venom into my arm was as terrifying as Ranger Marian's detailed lessons, especially out here, in view of 'rule number one', don't move and try to get help.

Somehow you expect a snake to strike with a dragon-like sizzle, but this one's came quiet and almost restrained. The second fang came forward in slow motion while the sheath around it hardly moved aside. None of the strikes was farther than half of its four-foot length. Most theories are between one and two thirds, although here, too, I heard some 'up to's' – strangely enough – generally six feet. However, in relation to the 'up-to'-lengths, at least the ratio would not have been exaggerated.

When I left the snake alone, it crawled away to a creosote bush, which it would most likely have done long before, had I not jumped out of the tent like a maniac. Then I rekindled the fire and enjoyed my coffee sitting in the snake mold.

Colin had killed the first five rattlesnakes he saw, because he was infected with horror and fear as most people primarily are. Only the ranger he met at the Emigrant station, Matt Ryan, had changed his view. He simply inquired about the sense of his doing and opened his eyes for its raison d'être and the fascinating beauty in the beast. He explained that treating them with respect and yielding the right of way would most likely eliminate all dangers. As long as we observed certain rules like staying alert and looking before you put your hands or feet anywhere, chances for an attack would be close to zero. I trusted in the ranger from the beginning, of course, I had read the book before. Ryan continued: "They're gentlemen: they'll give you warning if you give them half a chance." Indeed, all of them did, and I got to know them as an honorable species, behaving with integrity and discretion.

*

Some nature-loving people argue, 'it is their territory', meaning we would have to adapt. However, I think this is the wrong way of going about it: The wiser one gives in, would be more appropriate, at least for most people. Or, according to the golden rule: 'do unto others as you would be done by'; it works here, too. It should go without saying that just as almost any animal does – except maybe flies – we should give them respect.

I really don't think that the city is ours and the wilderness is theirs. Not long ago, most of us still lived in a wild environment. And looking at us now, with all our problems, our moods, our mental and physical excrescences, rather suggests that living in a crammed city is not really what we were made for, that maybe we need a balancing walk into the woods much more and more often than we think. I am sure, it is theirs as it is ours, as soon as we decide to venture out in it. In order to give respect, we might have to overcome a few disadvantages. While most animals act instinctively, we have lost the ability to use some senses – most of our instincts are either degenerated or concealed. Much worse might be the fact that our brain – originally and by evolution designated to compensate that loss – is increasingly being misguided and misinformed about many species, thus losing any objective means to measure such encounters or threats.

Although children stories and tales have always been altering the idea we have of many animals, it is usually to the better or, as the case may be, by adding human characteristics. What is really alarming, much more with regards to our species than to any other, is how easy our picture of other species can be changed dramatically to negative characterization through mere media sensationalism, branding snakes, sharks, and crocodiles, to name only the 'worst' guys, as monsters and killers. Granted, with regards to the last two, we would be better off being in a cage, but in fact, we don't even have to go swimming out that far. Who didn't hear a story lately about a coyote attacking a child or a pet, a raccoon devastating a house, or a recluse attack in California? How important is it to know that an eagle would be able to carry away a human baby? Why do we learn about 'river monsters', where are the fish? Why do we see people swallowing tarantulas, cuddling with scorpions, or kissing cobras on an animal channel? This has nothing to do with animals, but with our species going crazy.

Unfortunately, the educational and informative documentary that brought nature's wildlife to our living rooms since the invention of television has given way to the pseudo-nature film where brainless, self-proclaimed macho Dundees scare up wildernesses' beasts. From the safety of a well-equipped and air-conditioned SUV, they raid habitats for potential media victims, tease and provoke them until those have to go berserk, then selling the animals' self-defense as common nature reality. Who doesn't know today that places like Australia, Africa, or the Californian desert host some of the world's most venomous species – what else do they know about these places? Many people think that exploring our fauna presupposes Indiana Jones-courage. "Snakes, why did it have to be snakes?" It seems clear, Indie, when real life doesn't yield enough, reality has to be warped. That's what action movies are for, but in a so-called documentary, I think, it is rather questionable. If that doesn't allow drawing conclusions about the life we are living, unbalanced and dull?

I learned that all rattlers I came close to gave me a warning. Since I often sat in the sand, I had a good number of spiders or a couple of scorpions quickly crawling over a finger or a hand. None of them savaged me. I could have killed every single creature, but, although each startled me at first, I felt more privileged to watch and study them. Up to the present day, stupid man has been the only species that savaged others, some till extinction. If we are interested in saving those who are left, we have to understand them and their environment, and the best way to do so still is through live experience. The more facts we learn about something the more interesting it will get. I am afraid, not many of today's documentaries are good for that.

*

Today I would reach 6,000 and 7,000 feet with a much denser flora. I saw the first pine trees, scattered here and there and preferably leaning leeward to a jumbo rock. The washes and canyons were overgrown with creosote, cacti, and everything else that is barbed. According to my map, this day I had to find a plateau-like ridge that would lead me to Hunter Mountain Road, but all ridges here looked the same and rugged and furrowed as they were, I saw nothing that could pass for a plateau. Trying another ridge would have meant climbing down from where I was and up again, most likely just to see not much difference there. So I stayed where I was, focused the highest mountain around, supposedly Hunter Mountain, and walked stubbornly in that direction, at least three miles, constantly circumnavigating the deep furrows and realigning to the mountain.

Since I had left Death Valley, I had not seen a single footprint, no other fireplaces or – except the sign to Keeler and Jackass Springs – anything else that would indicate I was not the first human being here since the gold miners had left. The sign itself might have been that old, but another little plate attached to it surely was a sign of modern times, warning those who might remove or destroy markers and signposts that they would be subject to punishment. Before I started into the Panamints, I had checked three maps, and only one of them showed an old pack trail winding northwest through this area. I thought this might relate to the path that Hunter walked a century ago, but unlike so often in the Mojave, here I didn't even see relics of old times, no abandoned wagon parts or boilers, no cans or kitchen utensils, let alone a trail.

I paused in a crevice beneath large jumbo rocks when suddenly among my footsteps I recognized one that looked different, a single differently-shaped print in the sand around these boulders. Looking between the sage, I found more tracks, but they were from burros. Then some ten feet away another boot print. It somehow alarmed me, since they came out of nowhere. I walked around the rocks, and there, on the other side in a mold of sand, were hundreds of prints and impressions, totally disarranged, without a pattern, like on a campsite where tents had been built and people walked back and forth.

They couldn't be that fresh, probably a group had camped lee side of the rocks and everywhere else the tracks had been blown over by the wind or trampled down by burros. Trying to follow them I lost them again, found more somewhere else, and again the trail grew cold. I wanted to find out where they came from, if they came my way, only up through a different canyon, and if they could possibly lead me to Hunter Mountain Road. I left my pack at the memorable rocks and tried to scout.

On and off they disappeared, sometimes interrupted for no visible reason, until I found a small pile of stones, carefully put on top of each other like no happenstance of nature could have build it. Between the two upper stones was a plastic bag and in the bag a yellowed piece of paper. A group of the Desert Penguins left this note for another group. It was dated March 27 without a year, and I wondered if they ever found each other. Beyond this ridge, the tracks disappeared in the history of a long gone March.

I was still heading for the highest elevation around, although I often lost sight of my reference mountain when the hitherto sporadic pine trees began to grow thicker the higher I got. Navigating a way with map and compass is fun as long as one is not, more than anything else, occupied with correcting deviations caused by all kinds of obstacles one has to bypass. About every half hour, I climbed one of those jumbo rocks to make sure I was still right, to some degree. Eventually, Hunter Mountain disappeared and another range moved in between, blocking my view to the west and northwest. Then suddenly, north-northeast, I saw a promising long, brown snake winding down from another distant range. This must be the road that would later pass into Hunter Mountain Road. Although what I saw was days away, it was calming and the first confirmation that I was not totally wrong.

As a matter of fact, the road was so far away, I could not relate to it, or to the real distance. Yet I was overhappy to see it. I recalled one Sunday morning; I had stayed at home, although my sisters were preparing their leave to hunt some fancied bad guys who were roaming the forest behind the rusty gate. My uncle Willy was there for a visit, giving me one of his nature science lessons that caused me to devour his words and even miss my sisters' battle call. In his calm voice, he explained that it was not reality when I saw a star in the sky, but that it took its light a very, very long time to get from there to my eye, because it was unbelievably far away. I assumed that it would take me even longer to get there, but also that I was still young and at least the star was a reference point or a guidepost. Just like the star, the road meant orientation, and with gained certainty, time to get there became marginal.

From every other outlook I saw another part of the earth road and exactly at noon, I took off my pack, clambered a barbed wire, stood on the fence post and jumped onto the skid marks of a sandy 4WD road. As so often before, it felt like falling out of the wilderness back into civilization, from suspense back to security, or uncertainty to guarantee. It seemed that what I was looking for on this journey scared me increasingly the longer I was

CHAPTER FOUR

exposed to it, and still I kept looking for it. At that moment I realized that's what it's all about, commuting between the worlds, oscillating between the two, or juggling both.

After a one hour break, I walked the sand road uphill to meet the omnipresent Hunter. At his cabin below his mountain I found water, Hunter Creek, a little flow running through a grass-green alp. Behind the cabin, I surprised a group of guys with 4WDs. Apparently they were not supposed to be here, or not their cars, I remembered the locked gate about 200 yards before I reached the cabin. For a bunch of big guys, they were quite rattled seeing me and somehow, I thought, they reacted a little too reserved, as if they were caught red-handed. In their leaden silence they might have brooded over who I was, over risks and chances. But I was hungry and I had to deliver something to the woods, so after a short conversation, mainly conducted by myself, I felt I had explained enough about my kind of adventure. I wished them good day and walked back to the green where I had left my pack.

I started preparing lunch, but when I heard them leaving I paused to go behind a tree. I am not sure if anybody ever wrote about it – I mean the joy of defecating in the woods, or into the desert – but I doubt it. Most hiking and travel guides avoid this daily issue, because the majority of their overnight recommendations provides for corresponding facilities, more or less suitable. As if we got the urge only around campgrounds. Outdoor guides and even survival books ignore an issue that is inseparably linked to the essential eating and drinking, and – after taking photos and meals – the third most common event when backpacking. Instead, they discuss in whole chapters those rare situations not even one-tenth of a percent of their readers will live to see.

I will not go into details, however, as a matter of fact, it is an intensely relieving and refreshing experience to do it like Adam or Eve. Just try it, when you are sure to be alone, I mean really alone, miles and miles nobody but you and the tree; a stone serves almost as well. Either of them should be within reach and you should face it to be able to hold onto it with stretched arms, in case the session lasts longer and the knees get weak. Undress, all clothes, and grab the support tree. Before that, make sure you got the toilet paper no few steps from where you settle down. Then, let it go, while the sun kisses your back, and the wind caresses your bottom. I assure it is not only the relief in a form of less weight or less pressure, which delivers a liberating feeling of freedom. One may also see it as a symbolic act. At least you are doing something you would never do at home, although there is nothing wrong *in* it. It is natural, and with the kind of food you are having on a trip like that, even organic.

Just two quick tips: First, after everything rappelled down, possibly – after a good hiking day – making a respectable mound, you may want to consider doing one sidestep to either side. This is just to make sure you won't be landscaping that mound with the back of your hand when using the paper. Second, if you are hiking in the woods, not by yourself but with a group, you would most likely face the group when going down. You may be afraid of having to bear a joke from your comrades; therefore you keep watching *them*. Big mistake! No joke from your friends could turn out as bad as the bear itself; even more, if it was attracted by your odor, but eventually got disappointed after an in-depth analysis. With near certainty, the bear would come from the other direction, unless it had already graced your friends with its presence and they betrayed you to him. It is better to trust your partners and face the opposite side, the woods; brother bear might be waiting behind the next tree.

Speaking of toilet paper, in fact someone asked me, if I had toilet paper. Of course, how else would you do what you have to do. Without carrying even more water, especially through the desert, one cannot go without this highlight of human inventiveness. However, I did not have to carry the jumbo twelve-pack, given that I came to town every other week. Furthermore, on a physically demanding hike, your inner motor burns most of the food fuel it gets, thus disposing of leftovers less often and in form of a rather concentrated residue. Therefor one roll per week was enough, generously placed at my disposal by the last motel visited.

When I came back from the tree, I saw that the guys had given my campsite a surprise visit. Neatly placed on top of my backpack, I found their reward for my discretion, two ice-cold cans of beer.

After lunch I lay down on the green. Only then, looking up, I realized I had arrived in a different world. I had not left the desert yet, but I was high above it. Almost 7,500 feet meant no more creosote but the first forest I was walking through since I left Germany months ago. My view to the sky was obstructed by tree tops, and where I had seen an almost 360 degrees horizon for weeks, I now saw trees, more trees, and behind them eventually darkness. I felt protected somehow because of the shadow and the windbreak, although the desert was safer. There, you knew who you're going to meet the following day. Anyone who wanted to sneak up would have to wear a chameleon costume or dig himself into the sand until I would pass. With the frequent stops I made for shooting flowers, cacti, and critters, though, he would have suffered from dehydration or heat stroke before I had come within reach. Here in the woods, I could be surprised any minute. Did the guys really leave? A certain unease rose, and I did what would become a routine during the second half of my trip through the Sierra, checking the vicinity for signs and marks from other visitors, be it hunters, hikers, or bears.

I thought about what Colin said when comparing the mysteries of the desert and the forest. There, he saw only distance, with the sun displaying all secrets, she "strips everything to naked bone". Here, he saw constant dubiety, "even broad daylight never dispels all doubt". Beyond a campfire in the desert, he saw infinite blackness, here, he observed dancing tree trunks, ecstatically moving to the flickering light. As he enjoyed this show with his childhood memories of Peter Pan flooding back, I always felt like sitting in a puppet show theater, played by small kids, who would make the puppets' movements sometimes unpredictable and creative.

I had made up my mind to stay overnight. I still had one more desert valley to cross, but lying under trees for the first time in six weeks lulled all thoughts of tomorrow away. Here, I felt new life and energy infusing my mind from the trees. Lying spread-eagled on a soft carpet of needles, breathing the pine-scented air, I remembered an emigrant's report about this situation when reaching the woods after a long desert journey: "Beneath the shelter of a huge pine we made our bed, and were soon lulled to sleep by the gentle sighings of the wind, as it passed through its branches, with the sweet satisfaction that we had no more deserts to pass."[*]

Indeed, sitting in a sylvan theater, mostly leaning on a tree trunk, was more comfortable than the arid open air stadium of a desert night camp, where you rest on one elbow, constantly moving, either to examine or to avoid a cohort of bugs and spiders that were attracted by the light. As long as I did not lie down on an anthill, I was hardly approached by any insects in woods or above 6,000 feet. That's why this night should become, except the alleged recluse encounter, my first under the open sky. Generally, I preferred to sleep without a tent. So as soon as I would leave the desert and its battalion of crawling, creeping, hopping, and jumping divisions, the tent would be buried at the very bottom of my pack. Then my eyes would watch a starry movie nightly, projected to the night sky and framed by the silhouettes of trees, until they became heavy and tired, accepting the constant doubts around me as just the darkness behind trees. All through the night, the buzzing, gently whizzing sound of breezes playing with pine needles would vest in me, shaking off the silent garment of the desert. Without a tarp around my senses, I was right in the midst of these nocturnal elements and sounds, and after some weeks I would develop a keen sense of things going on around the campsite. Without seeing it, I would know it's a coyote, I could tell a rabbit from a squirrel, and every once in a while, I would open my eyes again to see, at the same moment, a star falling.

---

[*] Andrew Jackson Grayson, 1846, when following the arduous overland trail to California. Grayson, 1818–1869, was part of the trek that included the ill-fated Donner party. While this one separated from the main group at Fort Bridger, Grayson's group experienced no difficulties, and when they reached Yerba Buena (later renamed San Francisco), he joined Frémont's battalion to offer his services as a Colonel. Later on, he directed his attention to more peaceful activities like ornithology and became a talented bird painter.

I was often asked, "And what about the bears?" Exactly, this is the other reason for omitting the tent whenever possible. Here, it is not really protecting you from anything but rain, wind, and cold. You can hardly avoid smelling of something. It doesn't even have to be the forgotten Snickers bar in your pocket, or a late-night dessert, after which you were too tired to get out of your bed, unzip the tent, look for your slippers, make sure nothing had nested in them, get the flashlight, find the tree where you hoisted the food sack and put it in there. That same dessert's smell out of your mouth, the sausage smell on the knife, or the empty soda can is enough to woo an importunate guest. Brush your teeth? Forget it. Shower with soap? Same thing. Some accidents were reportedly caused because the bear liked the toothpaste. Others might enjoy an olfactory shower of your deodorant.

Think about the situation, you are captive in a tent, you hear the campsite intruder but you are unable to locate him exactly. You hear cans flying, a strange cracking sound which probably was the folding camp chair being folded improperly, and then – quiet. Unbelievable silence. The hammer in your head competes in a pulsating race with your heartbeat. The situation with the dancing trunk shadows has already been explained. You cannot be sure that the bear has left in a huff. It might sit somewhere and think, map out a strategy, wonder what's that strange colored cave without a mountain there. If then, up to 1,000 bouncing pounds decided to further analyze what is in that fabric cave but understandably wouldn't care for finding a zipper, chances are you will never touch a tent again, or worst case, will forever form a compound with it.

I heard about accidents like that twice, a dad and his two sons were killed in Canada, another couple in the U.S. To me, that's as plain as day, what else could a bear do but siege or apply force. So sleeping outdoors without a tent is not only the more exciting but also the safer thing to do. A bear would see what it got and, after taking a good smell at you, most likely leave you alone. If you are lucky, you don't even have to wake up.

This of course applies for bear area, that is, temperate and arctic zones as long as you don't have to protect from storm, rain, or cold. As mentioned earlier, I used the tent in the desert and sure enough I would do so in the tropics.

04/27   HUNTER'S CABIN, 16 MILES

I stayed at Hunter's Cabin for the night. No bear had shown up, only some deer seemed to have met at the creek to my left. The little grassy beach from where I conducted my campfire was a muddy mess. I lay long there after waking up, looking to the roof of tree tops above and listening to the constant breeze that shook the natural log house around me. In my mind, the desert whistle with its sporadic gusts was already far behind and replaced by crooning pine trees.

CHAPTER FOUR

The following days were a swing from Hunter Mountain via South Pass to North Pass, seesawing almost sixty miles through Death Valley's little sister, Saline Valley, an endorheic basin that suggested a sense of isolation, much more than its more famous sister valley. With half its size, it was bounded by mountains from all sides, the 11,000-foot-high Inyos to the west, the Saline and Last Chance Ranges to the east, and two passes letting me in and out. Both my starting point and the North Pass were on 7,300', with the valley in between being a synopsis of all desert I had so far.

The descent began with a six-mile stage passing Quail Springs and Jackass Spring, where some of the rocks down the creek bed had hidden Native American petroglyphs. Both of them nice creeks, however, due to the rich cattle activity not recommendable for drinking, unless you had missed Hunter Cabin and were totally parched. The cows seemed to be very much interested in me; probably they didn't get to see many hikers around here. A small group of youngsters kept following me through most of Grapevine Canyon and after two hours, I was afraid they would join me as far as down to the desert, where they might be screwed and suffer from dehydration.

Arriving at South Pass, I had the best view over Panamint Valley, the other neighboring salt pan west of Death Valley, separated from Saline Valley by Hunter's Mountains. I saw the dunes, the dry lake and far away the Panamint Springs Resort. Behind all that, the valley was endless, phasing out somewhere in the Mojave Desert west of Amargosa Valley. Wondering what day it was, I remembered one of my earlier visits to the resort. I had walked out on the salt lake at Panamint Springs with a cup of coffee. Right when I wanted to take a sip, I recognized a big shadow around me from above, looked up to the sky but didn't see anything, because seconds after I felt that shadow, the jet was already 1 mile ahead. But exactly when I looked up, the sonic boom hit me like a trailing ghost. On weekdays, fighter jets from the nearby Naval Weapons Center and Air Force Bases were practicing low altitude flight maneuvers, here, almost mowing the sage. Since I had not heard one that morning, I assumed it was Sunday. I forgot I wanted to time my walk accordingly to arrive at South Pass on a weekday; unfortunately, now the one out of seven chance came true.

Although I am not much into military weapons or an airplane enthusiast, I had to admit, that moment has been burned into my memory and I will never forget the goose bumps I got when the pilot returned after some minutes. He had obviously spotted me amidst the white expanse. On his next round he came streaking down the valley, a second before he was above me he did a snap roll, turned upside down into an inverted flight, waved at me and left rolling back out of the valley. I turned into stone, fascinated both by that perfected combination of power, speed, maneuverability on one side, and the sublimity and humor of that pilot on the other.

He was so low, I intuitively raised my hand as if I wanted to touch his, giving him five. Mowing the rest of the valley, in the last second he climbed before South Pass, where now my memories were still following him on his exit into the Inyo Mountains. I thought one could really be happy, associating a lethal weapon such as a fighter jet with enthusiasm and goose bumps. It would scare the living daylights out of me if I had to outrun one, especially with a seventy-pound pack on my back.

The cows didn't like that vista, supposedly having been scared away before on weekdays. They were waiting around the next bend.

The descent down to the valley floor was so steep and fast that the flora changed hourly, from juniper pines and lupines to Joshua trees and thistles and eventually to the familiar creosote and sage. To my right and well below, the small creeks had formed an amazing canyon that cut so deep into the earth's crust as if it tried to entrench itself to hide from the mountains.

Late in the evening, my knees brought my downhill schuss to a halt. Deep in my pack I rummaged for the tent that I had optimistically buried under other equipment while in the woods at Hunter Mountain. I was back down in the desert and with me the two cows. Before I crawled into the sleeping bag, I looked out of the tent for the last check routine, fire was low, no food left, no beast around, just the two of them, looking at me as if they were waiting for an invitation to come in. I am not sure if they understood that to keep the weight down I only brought a one-man tent. Their look said something else, but they accepted and finally ambled away into the night.

04/28   GRAPEVINE CANYON, 19 MILES

From about halfway down Grapevine Canyon, I could overlook the whole Saline Valley. The ranger at Stovepipe Wells had called it the most isolated spot in California. It really was a smaller, less known version of Death Valley, a wide basin surrounded by mountain ranges, a salt lake in the middle with the obligatory sand dunes north of it. Most of the larger valleys between the Mojave and here had their own dunes. They had been formed by Pleistocene winds blowing newly exposed sand, after the lakes that originally covered these valley floors were gradually drying up. There were the Kelso Dunes in the East Mojave, the extensively vegetated Death Valley Dunes, the Saline and the Eureka Dunes ahead, all of them belonging to the highest in North America with the latter placed first.

Having arrived at the valley floor, I passed the remains of its short termed busy phase, when mining companies hauled borax and salt out of the marsh lake from the 1870's into the 1930's. In order to avoid the endless winding exit roads over the passes, the steepest electric aerial tram ever constructed was supposed to haul the minerals over the Inyo Mountains into Owens Valley. One clever engineer had designed the tramway for transporting dry salt from 1,100 to 8,500 feet and back down to 3,600' on the other side. The harvested salt, however, was wet, and it had to be brought to Owens Lake where it was spread to dry. Due to the much higher weight of wet salt, his calculation was dead on arrival. Operation soon became too expensive and it ran only sporadically, probably during mule strikes.

The perennial streams from Hunter and Inyo Mountains occasionally fed the salt lake, thus creating a biological rich marshland at the valley's lowest point. Unfortunately, the gnats outnumbered the waterfowl by far, making it not really a pleasant spot to take five. But I got surprised by a sudden and early sunset. With the high-rising Inyo Mountains to my left, dusk literally ambushed me. I was forced to look for a campsite. The cut off to a legendary nudist hot springs was not far, but it would have meant another seven-mile walk tonight and the same distance back the following day. Anyway, I was not in the mood for this kind of naturism and walked the other way toward the mountain wall. I was eager to finish the final desert spurt after having smelled the odors of forest at Hunter's Cabin. Leaning against the 7,000-foot rising wall, I had a straight-back chair of a special kind. My chair-back reflected the firelight and sitting just a little bit higher than the valley floor, I could see from its southern to its northern end, with a tiny oasis in its middle.

One of the Death Valley rangers had told me about a property at the end of the flats, just a couple of miles from the hot springs road. He recommended, I might want to take into consideration filling my water sacks there, saving me the fourteen-mile detour. "It is off my routine", he said, "I have absolutely no idea what's going on there. They have cameras and dogs, but I remember seeing sprinklers. You better be careful, but you should be able to sneak up to the sprinklers and get water."

Worst case there still were natural springs after a six to eight-mile hike into McEvoy Canyon opposing the dunes. I heard the ranger's warning again: "You better be careful!" and tinkering with the idea of yet going to the hot springs, I started to cotton up to the nudist camp sidestep. Then again I turned it down, as tantalizing as a bath in this once famous hangout would have been, no bath was worth a five-hour detour on a hot saline day, as long as there were other water sources. I'd sneak up to the sprinklers.

04/29 CUT OFF PALM HOT SPRINGS, 16 MILES

As soon as I left the tent, a cloud of gnats, hitherto hiding in a creosote, paid a visit to me. I took two chocolate and nuts bars, loaded my pack and ran back to the road. Instead of becoming breakfast for the flies, I preferred to have a longer brunch break later, continued north and thought about that strange, gated place with video surveillance the ranger mentioned off the record. As soon as the ascent began, the flies were gone but replaced by another phenomenon, less annoying, though. The road was packed with grasshoppers, a fanciful kind that could have jumped right out of a *Star Wars* movie. They immediately reminded me of the sandcrawlers on Star Wars' Planet *Tatooine*, described as large, slow, and bulky, yet very sturdy vehicles that were able to travel even in the harshest of desert conditions. I bet you, they used these sandhoppers as a template.

From after the salt lake, the ground was blanketed with an armada of these battleship grasshoppers, coming in three different colors, grey, brown, and orange. I watched them jumping away from my steps and immediately turning into stone. The funny thing was, they all jumped to the right side, not one to the left. I was so fascinated by their rigor, teasing a group of 10 to unfreeze, that I had not noticed I was right at the fence of a gated property. Then I heard a for this area totally abnormal sound, the whispering of sprinkling drops splashing on the ground. I turned around, looking straight on a big rough-and-ready 'No Trespassing' sign fixed to a gate with a rusty wire. Behind two or three cabin-like houses soared a precipitous mountain wall with apparent mining activity. I was already so close to the forbidden land, I had to realize that the small camera on top of the gatepost had captured me anyway. It was too late for hiding and sneaking up to the sprinkler from the side.

I left my pack with the army of grasshoppers and walked toward the gate. A pack of hounds came running and barking at me, albeit the size of the dogs, if anything, bolstered my bold approach. They were too small and coltish to be real watchdogs, not the Hounds-of-the-Saline-Gold-Mine kind. I petted one of them and when two guys came out of the building, the dogs had already agreed to proudly escort me. Now they were barking at their owners, probably pretending they had caught me. I recognized one of them as Jay, whom I had seen a day ago on Saline Valley Road heading to the springs while obviously trying to establish a cross-country record, how-fast-can-you-wreck-a-car, from the desert town Darwin to the nudist resort. The other guy introduced himself as David, the caretaker of this mine, which the owners did not work this year.

I was invited to settle down, prepare my lunch here and make myself feel at home. The only Saline Valley resident had carved out another little oasis here named Willow Creek Camp, an almost unbelievable contrast to the desert. The creek was running along the property carrying enough water to provide for green grass and big cottonwood trees. A smaller offset from the seismic hot spot filled a cemented pool in the garden. David's masterpiece in desert living, homes and gardens, was definitely his hot tub. Under the largest

CHAPTER FOUR

cottonwood tree he had pushed a massive iron tank, which was one half of an old steam boiler. Out in the desert, along that steep mountain wall, lay a one-mile-long hose filled with water, ending in that tank. Opening the hose after a long hot day filled the whole tub, and it was too hot to just jump in, even now by the end of April. One had to wait an hour to let it cool down.

Despite the ranger's warnings, I was really enjoying their company and an unexpected refreshing afternoon. David and Jay came very close to the common understanding of a desert rat, weird and sympathetic characters. I would rate them as my first. With too much fantasy and in that environment, you'd take to your heels seeing them and make sure you get out of gunshot range. Because of a little sandhopper-related, unintended courage, I was entertained at best and again rewarded with hospitality. Both of them were hobby-mineralogists, thus enjoying desert life and talking stones. Half of our conversation centered around minerals, terrestrial and extra-terrestrial, where to find them and who of the two found the bigger piece of a certain kind. One of them asked me, "Oh you came up from Mexico? All by yourself? Did you see a meteor going down in Arizona?" Indeed I did, and now I knew – I even heard it.

We were laughing a lot about what I did and life in the desert in general, and we burst into laugh when I told them about the ranger's suspicious facts and his speculations. The surveillance camera was a dummy to keep nosy visitors off. It was one of the first camcorders ever built, an antique from the last century long broken with a cable running down the gatepost straight into the desert sand. David reported that in fact there were self-styled prospectors from time to time, who scrambled up the wall and into the mines, sometimes tourists looking more for nostalgia than nuggets, sometimes amateur-miners looking for a quick chance, regardless any prohibition signs or fences. He said, "If you want to open a souvenir shop up there, best thing you can do is, make three mega-sized roadside billboards, get them up here and write 'No Trespassing' on one, 'Privately Owned' on the next, and 'No Gold in here' on the last. You'll have more visitors than you can handle."

After a tour to the mine gallery we had lunch together and – what you could call – a real desert-rat-coffee, the spoon stood upright in my cup. With the fading sun, I packed my things, said goodbye, and joined the pilgrimage of the grasshoppers. I wanted to cover at least half of the distance to North Pass this evening.

The ascent to North Pass was the inversion of my walk down from South Pass. Soon I left the desert shrub behind, passing beautiful side canyons with juniper and ponderosa pines. When a strong evening wind came blowing up from the desert, I took shelter in a dry creek bed with an old pine tree serving as windbreak and its dead branches as firewood.

04/30   WAUCOBA SPRINGS, 9 MILES

Reaching the pass the following day, I had once again left the desert. More and more I couldn't wait to get into the land of forests. In my imagination, the land of mountain creeks and forests morphed into the land of milk and honey. Although there would be more arid sections until I got to Oregon, Eureka Valley and the Sierra Valley to name the largest, the contiguous expanse of deserts, surpassing each other with geologic, climatic and historic superlatives, was broken now by North Pass and the luring White Mountains.

I spend half the day and one night around the pass and nearby Marble Canyon, which was boasting of history in the form of mining relics. While Colin met a man called Walter Greer here, I thought I was alone since none of the cabins and shacks seemed to be lived-in. Greer made a scarce living out of gold, taking tourists' dollars for teaching them how to pan the same amount in gold. 'Learn to pan gold. You get from two to six nuggets in each pan. $1.00 in Gold for each $1.00 you spend.' Actually, a clever way of avoiding work and finding others to do it for you. Only – right here, as Greer himself had stated, 'the most isolated spot in California'? He couldn't really have struck it rich here, where the event of a walk-in customer might take place every fifty years.

Marble Canyon is a shallow trench along the northern entrance to Saline Valley. A little further down, I found a small ghost town with a lot of heavy mining equipment and machinery lying around, buildings and shafts scattered throughout a four-mile stretch on both sides of a dirt track. In these two days between here and Eureka Valley, I saw more mining relics than in the past six weeks since I left the Mexican border. The installations, equipment, and devices left were in much better shape than usually. In those places where mining activity dated back one hundred years or more, most of the iron gave way to oxidation. For a layman the rusty utensils often were hard to identify, especially everything made of sheet metal. The gold rush in Marble Canyon, however, started only some seventy years ago during the depression era, triggered by J.C. Lewis, who discovered coarse gold in various gulches along the canyon in 1934. Four years later, some twenty men were working a 200-foot-wide stream channel about nine miles long by dry washing. The biggest nugget they found was 300$ worth, in 1930's dollars reason enough to further explore this area. Fortunately for me, today the ghost town and the majority of the scattered remnants were concentrated on a one-mile gallery.

The longer I was studying the past, the more I lost track of time. Coming out of a rotten shell of a cabin, I found darkness taking over the town, creating a bleak ambiance. I was looking for my pack, had forgotten where I put it down. Strong gusts were blowing in from Eureka Valley, where I wanted to

CHAPTER FOUR

descend the following day – provided I found my stuff by then. Checking these spooky shacks, I suddenly heard a knocking. I hid behind an old tank trying to locate the noise. It came from another building across the road, but it was too irregular to be caused by a human, it didn't make any sense. Then, the knocking was interrupted by the sound of a creaking door, only, there was no door anymore. Everything but the exterior walls and the collapsed roofing had long fallen victim to time. All windows were broken and the entrance door probably blown off its rusty hinges by a storm. By now, the wind was blowing so strong, I could hardly see through the dust. Squeak – knock, knock – pause – squeak – knock, knock. The pauses were between half and several minutes. In my fantasy, I was attending a miner's meeting, one of those gatherings where a local committee got together to dispense justice, sometimes wise, sometimes timeserving and selfish. The noise I heard were the ghosts coming together in that building; each time a new member of the committee arrived, I heard the door squeaking and slamming, squeak – knock, knock. Maybe tonight they hanged a man who was innocent, just because he was in some bigwig's way. Now, once a year, they all had to get back together to speak the truth, commemorating the anniversary – or only when a lonely hiker happens to come by. Did they, by any chance, take my pack inside?

I threw a stone at the building. First it hit the roof, then obviously falling down into the scene, knock – knock, knock – knock, bang. Then silence. After a while, I got up, plucked up courage and left my hideout to walk slowly to the other side. With each step my disquiet hardened, but at the same time I knew, there must be a natural reason for it. Fighting against the wind, I reached the old building and just when I tripped over the doorstep, the noise came back. If the new member had not walked right through me, slamming the door in my face, then – it was a loose roof batten, barely dangling on two nails and banging at the wall. I laughed at myself admitting that I wasn't really sure what was going on here. I found my pack leaned to the building – it seemed untouched.

The ghosts of Marble Canyon could long be heard into the night; they did not let themselves be disturbed by my campfire. Before I fell asleep, they seemed to have moved to another building, probably the old saloon. Maybe one citizen had called a meeting to seek redress, eventually finding himself fined by the committee for daring to call them off their work. In those days the committee would have taken the fine, walked straight to the saloon to spend the sum justifiably on drinks. When I woke up again late in the night, the ghosts were gone with the wind.

05/01   MARBLE CANYON, 17 MILES

Going down the canyon into Eureka Valley did not mean that I left the mining history behind. The buildings only were longer ways away from each other. In spite of a strenuous day program, time and distance passed quickly because I found more interesting relics. I wouldn't have minded another ghostly matinee somewhere there. The canyon itself was lush and green and all I had to do was following it downhill until I saw the flats and dunes in the valley. Although I heard that the Eureka Dunes on the eastern edge of the valley would sing, I stayed on the far western side to avoid crossing the hot sand. Here, I could hunker down in one of many smaller side canyons to rest and get away from the sun. I thought singing dunes would be just another old ghost town legend until later I learned that in fact some dunes create sounds between roaring and whistling or, as others described it, between the sound of a small aircraft and an Australian indigenous wind instrument called didgeridoo.

All in all there are some thirty dunes worldwide where all physical preconditions are met to cause that phenomenon, one third of them in North America. The relevant parameters to let a dune sing are its steepness and the diameter of the sand grains hence how far they have traveled. It has to contain silica and needs to be at a certain humidity. What causes the sound seems to be a mixture of mechanical coupling between the grains and the friction between different layers of moving sand. Strong permanent wind passing over the dune can cause avalanches that build up the sound. Can you imagine early settlers or trappers being surprised by such a noise? I am sure it was those who immediately turned back and homesteaded on the other side of the big mountains.

As so often, the Chinese knew of the phenomenon much earlier than we did. It is passed down what Marco Polo heard, when he experienced singing dunes in Mongolia, "the sounds of all kinds of musical instruments, and also of drums and the clash of arms", but we do not know if he had the faintest idea of what was going on. According to a report I read when examining the cause, the sound is generated by shear stress, which means in easy words, a stress that is applied parallel or tangential to the face of a material, as opposed to a normal stress, which is applied perpendicularly. Understood? I assumed it was a misunderstanding and it should say, this sound causes sheer stress. However, later on I regretted I had not given it a closer look, since I was so close, just another day away.

In the evening, I reached another major mining district, the Loretto and Victor Cons Mines. When Colin had walked toward Eureka Valley, he was worried about his water supply and if he could rely upon Ranger Halderman, who had promised to put out a cache where he would see three shacks at the end of Eureka Valley. I thought it was these mines where he happily found it. As for me, I could travel peacefully through desert's end with refilled sacks from Willow Creek Camp.

05/02   LORETTO, VICTOR CONS, AND EUREKA MINES, 12 MILES

Today was the last day before I would set out to climb White Mountain from Deep Springs Valley and reach both the first half of my trip, and an allegorical landmark, separating not only the desert from the Sierra.

Tomorrow I would relax at Deep Springs and prepare myself and my equipment for the summit climb. I was literally jumping up Soldier Pass, exhilarated by a floral war of the reds; Indian paintbrush and mound cacti engaged in a tournament, which one would bring out a more flashy red. Often they stood close together, sometimes growing interleaved.

While taking some pictures, I stumbled over a small doll, half-buried under a mound cactus with only her head looking out of the sand. What story would she tell us, being lost and found in this remote spot of California, having a bald head and wearing a négligé?

When I reached the pass, I looked down into Deep Springs Valley and up onto a mountain range that was higher than everything so far. I settled on a rocky edge above a ranch with irrigated fields, the Deep Springs ranch college. I thought about my plan to stop by and about what a Forest Service guy I met at Stovepipe Wells had said about it. "Who would go to a remote place like that to study?" Again and again, one of them called it a strange place and left no doubt that he was very skeptical about it. Indeed, looking down at the isolated community, I started wondering, who would operate a ranch business, let alone a college, in a forlorn desert valley, surrounded by mountain ranges and passes high enough to shut off access with the first heavy snowfall. He, too, said that he didn't know what was going on there and that he didn't want to, which reminded me of the dubious camp at Willow Creek Springs. "You know, they might even force the young people to stay there and do God knows what with them." When I told him that I had plans to visit the place since an article about its founder had caught my attention, he shook his head saying: "I don't know," paused as if he was struggling for a possibility to keep me from doing it, but his best argument was an incredulous "it's a strange place."

Now I sat here, high above that mysterious place, all by myself, and somehow, I thought, I began to like places others call strange. There could be only two reasons for an institution to back out of civilization in such a drastic manner, either the forest ranger was right and the educative aspect had some dubious contents, or escapism, to retreat from distraction, to shun *wasteland* in order to find something of higher significance in the immediate vicinity of nature. I would find it out tomorrow.

I appointed the new companion my watchwoman and placed her on the highest rock on the pass before I started cooking. If only she could speak, I thought, and tell her story.

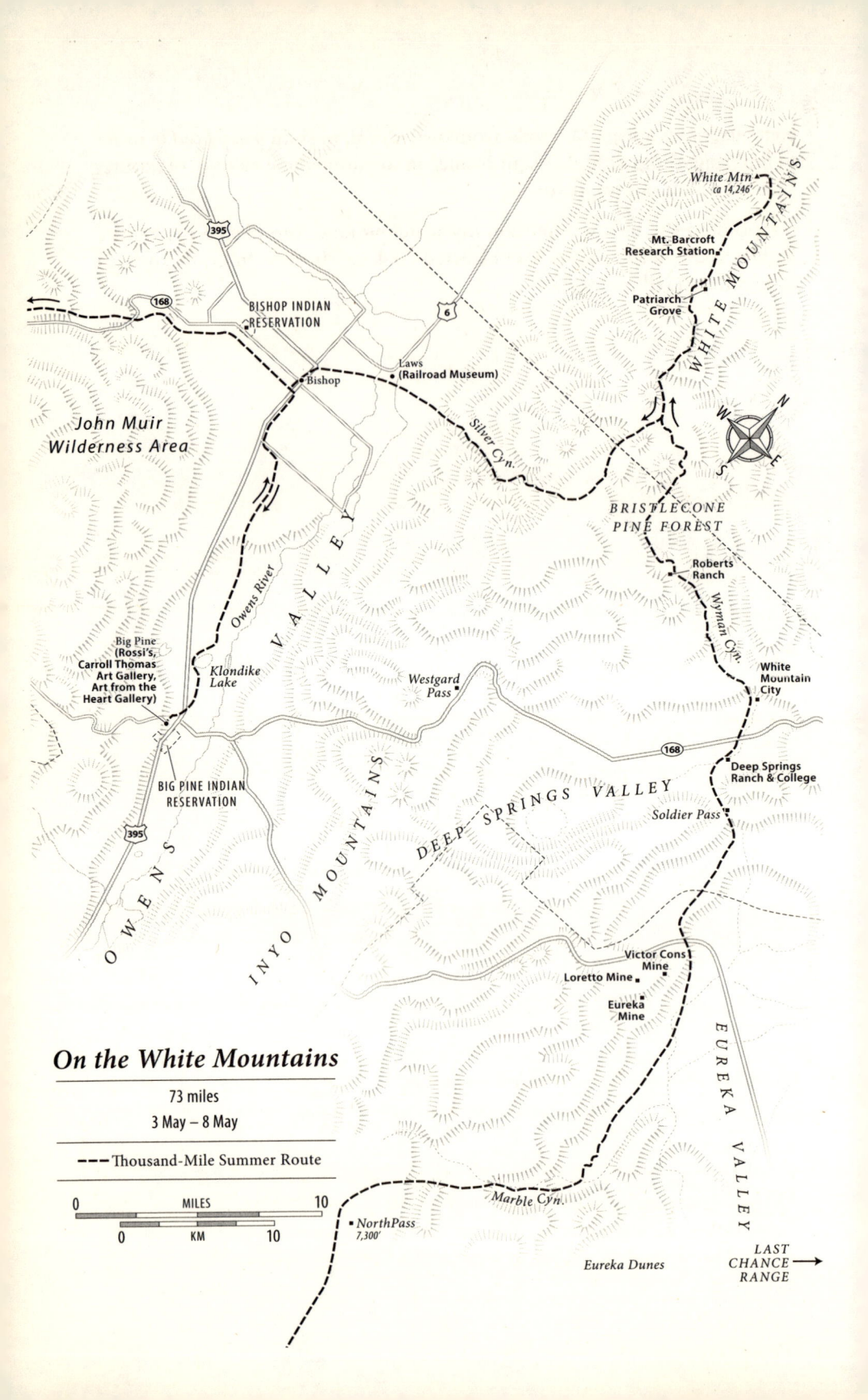

On the White Mountains

73 miles
3 May – 8 May

- - - Thousand-Mile Summer Route

5. ON THE WHITE MOUNTAINS

A leader is one who knows the way, goes the way and shows the way.

JOHN C. MAXWELL, AMERICAN AUTHOR AND SPEAKER, *1947

05/03   SOLDIER PASS, 4 MILES

In a rather chilly night on 5,500-foot-high Soldier Pass, the rumors about the valley's ranch commune had taken a back seat. I became more worried about my clothes. I had already underestimated the cold of the desert nights, where I sometimes took long sleeves and a fleece inside the sleeping bag. Due to my guideline to be through the deserts by the end of April, I had to sit out some chilly, if not freezing, nights. Apart from Hunter Mountain, the highest desert elevations had been in the 6,000s. From now on I would travel at an average of 6 to 9,000' with the passes at 10 to 11,000'. And White Mountain would take me to the skies, if they begin at around 14,250 feet. Hopefully, I brought the proper apparel for these elevations, as light as possible but as much as necessary.

In order to get warm, I explored the pass in the morning sun and climbed some rocky outcrops, around which I found a plethora of blooming mound cacti. Now in the morning sun, their petals were shining in the most luscious color I have ever seen, an almost unnatural shade of red. The little yellow pistil in its middle seemed to call provokingly, 'Touch me!'.

Examining the cacti, I stumbled over a trail and followed it for an hour until I found a cave with fireplaces and bones of a variety of animals. Between the fire pits was a small pile of obsidian fragments. Strangely enough, since the closest natural deposits for this black extrusive rock, which was used by Natives for tools and weapons, were at least fifty miles from here.

CHAPTER FIVE

Either I had found a prehistoric refectory, an Indian canteen, or someone had used the cave to reenact the life of the old days.

When I came back to the pass, six hours had passed. A gang of ground squirrels was tampering with my backpack. One of them was sitting on top of it while two or three of his buddies were investigating its contents. I couldn't blame them; who would think that I was still alive, after being gone for half a day. Though, they probably declared me lost as soon as I disappeared behind the first rocks.

I decided to walk only a couple of miles today and stay around the pass for another night to read Colin's next chapter. On the other side of Deep Springs Valley, I spotted the first of several canyons that would lead me up into the White Mountains. Following its course, I recognized several lines of old wooden poles. These must be the power lines I already saw on my map. They would be good reference points for my navigation through these canyons until I reached the dirt road to White Mountain. One hundred years ago, many power plants and power lines had been built in this area to electrify the isolated but booming mining towns of Nevada and connect them to the southern Californian system.

It was another multifaceted, charismatic character of the West, who fathered not only these power lines but the subjacent ranch college as well. Lucien Lucius Nunn lived a biography as colorful as that of an Earp, Harvey, or Scottie, though, far away from the ego cult or the opportunism of the first two, or the ne'er-do-well type of the latter. Nunn was more serious and concerned in what he did, more of a philanthropist. His impetus was to contribute and give something back to his country.

After having studied the cultivation of bees and helping his family in farming business, he had moved west to try his luck in restaurant business and real estate. Eventually, he got involved with construction and mining business, what lay only the foundation for his several other ventures, ranching cattle and developing homesteads, banking, running a newspaper, and founding a law firm. His pragmatic motive to make the expansion of his mining sites independent from the local availability of energy resources led to the first commercial hydroelectric power plant transmitting electricity long-distance by using AC current. It began operations in 1891 becoming an almost infinite financial source for his actual desire, to leave something worthwhile for future generations. He envisioned a work-study facility with the aim to educate young people, who should be, above all, dedicated to serve the community. Technologically and financially sophisticated as he was, Nunn continued investing in the power industry. But from then on, he partnered with other businessmen and got himself behind a new desk from where he managed the sustainable usage of his profits.

His frequent complaints about the lack of skilled workers of integrity made him launch the Telluride Institute, where students were not only academically skilled but also prepared for the hard labor on the plants throughout the West. To assist the students in their further education, he later founded the university-connected Telluride Association issuing scholarships and later on the Deep Springs College. While Nunn's contribution to the electric industry was epoch-making – he actually is to be awarded the pioneer in the electrification of the American West – his commitment to his students and eventually education in general was exemplary.

05/04 DEEP SPRINGS VALLEY, VIA WYMAN CANYON, 9 MILES

After a cup of coffee, I packed my things including the lightly dressed desert souvenir and descended to the farmlands below.

An hour later, I took place on a field of alfalfa, next to the college, in order to summon an unusual meeting. On the field were some fifty well-fed, assumably intellectual cows, and seeing a herd of cattle, I cannot resist sitting down and watching how they slowly turn their attention to the intruder. First they would dash away until they consider themselves in safe distance. Then, for a couple of minutes, they would totally ignore you, pretending they don't care a fig for you. But they do. After a while, the nosy characters just cannot withstand and will approach step by step. At this stage, it is important to remain as if turned into stone, or what they like even better, into a pillar of salt. The more you ignore them, best demonstrated by turning away and not looking at them, the faster they come, intermittently though. Every couple of steps they will pause for a while, lowering their head to graze and darting sidelong glances. They pretend to pluck grass or weeds even if there is nothing to pluck – that's bovine gamesmanship. Eventually, they are closing in on you, gazing at you from all sides and angles with the ones behind your back being the grittiest. Once they picked up your smell, they crowd you, examining every detail of the clothes with a marked preference for jeans and sweat soaked shirts. They just love this salty taste of sweat. Chances are, if you are hiking, meaning not taking showers very often, you make true friends pretty fast, who nip and chew on everything you wear, your shoes, laces, jeans, shirt, even the hair and everything you did not secure. Here, too, word about the arrival of a *salt creature* got around pretty fast; in less than ten minutes, I was surrounded by the first dozen while the next craned their necks from the second row.

It is amazing to look into their deep black, trustful eyes, and, excuse me, there is, somehow, a rather motherly look in their eyes. However, one mustn't forget, they are still animals, a pretty heavy kind at that. A cow wouldn't step on you, but it can get cramped when they start pushing in, jumping the queue and jostling each other to snatch the best position. Then you should have your fingers ready. When they get too importunate, a snap of the fingers or a sudden move will generally chase them back to where they started the advance in two seconds. Generally, that is, just make sure there's no bull among them, he'd be the one who stayed.

Talking to a young vet student about my bovine encounters, she doubted that cows would actually do what I described, and she saw some things wrong with my experiences, not to say fictitious. Reason being, cows were flight animals and if I were to enter their flight zone they would head the other way. Well, you may call me the cow whisperer, however, I believe, it is as with most flight species, animals or some humans, more a question of time and patience. If you don't take the time to earn the other party's trust, you won't receive it. Granted, sometimes I sat there for twenty or thirty minutes until, finally, curiosity prevailed over instincts. Isn't that almost human?

An hour later, I took my leave of the friendly reception committee and walked through an open gate to the college buildings. Somehow I had expected the typical babble of voices on a campus, here a group of laughing students, there a clique discussing, or some bawling football-playing students. None of that. It was as quiet as a schoolhouse during vacations and as loud as a lush meadow on its first day in spring. Reams of birds seemed to have taken the college by storm; they were in the bushes and on the green, large flocks flew from tree to tree as if they had to occupy all of them concurrently. The cattle were now busily gathering in a cottonwood grove, moving their lips in synchronicity, obviously all mumbling the same thing. It looked as if they had just left an international symposium on the role of alfalfa in health promotion for a coffee break. Sporadic mooing expressed they were content with the program's progress.

On the campus lawn a small girl was playing with a dog, here and there a door opened and a busy looking student with a couple of books under his arms went from one building to another. They wore casual jeans and shirts or working clothes and did not look much different from me. The only name I knew was the guy in charge of public relations. I had a short correspondence with him about my visit and in order to receive confirmation that I was welcome to come by. I sat down on a picnic table under a large cottonwood tree and waited for someone I could ask. Unlike the ebullient reception a little while ago, here no one paid attention to me. Everyone seemed to be so busy, I could probably have set up my tent in the middle of the campus without being questioned. Eventually, I stopped one of the book carriers and asked him about my contact person. "Oh, he is somewhere out in the fields, we have a problem with the irrigation system. But I'll let him know that you asked for him," said he, threw his books on a buggy and rode off on his rumbling vehicle. In the meantime, a group of students had settled around the table, obviously preparing an operation schedule, allocating tasks to names.

Half an hour later, my contact came from the fields, took off his work gloves, and said: "Hi, follow me please into the cafeteria. I'll get the president of the college for you. I am sorry, but I have to excuse myself, I have to work in the kitchen now and start cooking." I began to wonder what was going on here, at least it was quite different to our conventional idea of campus goings-on. It was quite evident that the cattle didn't serve for mere post-educative exhilaration, and the green fields weren't meant to be a pleasure garden for contemplative promenades. Both meant hard work that had to be concerted with organizing the small community and the academic life by the students themselves.

Finally, in the cafeteria it became more scholastic. There were three students debating on who was more important for posterity, Aristotle, Socrates or Plato. Walking to the next table, I felt the fact that I seemed to have come a long way was of no interest to them. When I sat down, I heard one of them whispering: "And there comes Heraclitus". There he was again, the philosopher with the flux-theory, 'You could not step twice into the same river; for other waters are ever flowing on to you', my constant reminder to always walk attentive and thoughtful. But what did they know about us? I smiled back sipping at my coffee, pondering.

Heraclitus proclaimed that change would be central to the universe, concomitantly stating that not only every life is its own universe, but also every movement within this will create its own. From my first visit to Goffs I had been experiencing my voyage just like that, every area, each day and every single person I met, even every step I took, created its own world, sometimes noticeable, sometimes concealed; all new worlds that I could have entered, some of which I did. And at the same time, they were already there, all possibilities and all endings. Behind a rock lay my slip, my fall or another step in a million, every mountain was a barrier and likewise a lookout, each day brought infinite possibilities of fun and joy, of encounters and adventures, or a dramatic peripeteia. It all depended on me, on how I walked into the world, whether it would have a positive ending or something else, whether I became part of new universes or stayed in my own, whether I set out to see the world or stay at home.

Walking in the wilderness, I became aware of that like never before. And the longer I walked and the more worlds I entered, I accepted another interpretation of the philosopher's expression: 'You could not step twice into the same river; for it's not the same river anymore and you're not the same man.'

However, I am afraid their ready wit was less aimed at philosophical deliberations but at my outfit and the little house on my back. Abhorring the superficial perception of reality and the way most people lived their lives, Heraclitus was also known as the first hermit. He led a secluded life somewhere out in a mountain cave, accordingly his appearance was kind of *outdoorish*.

CHAPTER FIVE

Until that moment, I still was not sure what awaited me here. The students were pretty much self-absorbed and not very communicative to a stranger. For sure they did not give the impression to be oppressed, though, contrary to the ranger's demurs. I looked around the campus, to the schoolhouse, to the peaceful cattle and the professionally organized farming. Everyone I saw so far had something busy to do, either academically, administrative, or hands on.

The door flew open; David Neidorf the college president came in and walked straight to me. We shook hands and sat down talking about my journey and the college he was managing. Now I was definitely immersing into the academic world of Deep Springs. With my conversational partner being a former director of both an Integrated Studies Program at Middlebury College and of the Educational Programs Bioethics-In-Action, a developer of curricular and pedagogical modules for non-partisan educational programs in the ethics of human biotechnology, I almost lost the courage to ask any intelligent questions. David has been appointed president and dean of Deep Springs only a couple of months before I started my trip. When he acknowledged that every now and then he, too, considered making a trip like the one I was doing and that he envied me for the intrepidity and the freedom to just do it, he gave me back my courage.

After dinner he took me on a tour around the premises, the classrooms, the library, and the fieldwork, and he told me how it all started.

As so often, the cause for distrust among Nunn's partners was a setting that aimed at going farther than common approaches. Nunn broke ranks with his one-track-minded business partners and swam against the current. During his Telluride projects, he had already expanded his education program to a superior academic training, self-governed by the student body. Inevitably, he got annihilated between increasing interests of shareholders on one side and his educational commitment on the other. The business operations were separated from the Institute, and the disagreements with partners and stockholders, who were less altruistic and more short-termed and profit-oriented, unhinged the foundation concept. Several attempts to found more educational programs failed. In the end he sold most of his businesses and shares to care for superior concerns, eventually founding the Deep Springs College in 1917 according to his principles that hard work along with academic study will help forming brighter minds and better personalities. I was wondering if the experiences with his partners had reconfirmed his decision, since he hoped to educate responsible, idealistic, and altruistic citizens, not the "hirelings of the avaricious" that "our educational institutions too often prepare".

"Gentlemen, for what came ye into the wilderness?
Not for conventional scholastic training, not for ranch life, not to
become proficient in commercial or professional pursuits for personal gain.

*You came to prepare for a life of service, with the understanding that superior ability and generous purpose would be expected of you,
and this expectation must be justified.
The desert speaks."*

What I saw in my first minutes on the college lawn were Nunn's three pillars the college was based on. The book carrier for the academic, the cook, who repaired the irrigation system, for the labor, the members of the cottonwood meeting preparing an operation schedule for self-governance. All of them were students.

For two years on campus, they become responsible for keeping the little ranch community working as well as addressing themselves to their course of studies. Working on the ranch means an unequaled variety of tasks, requiring above-average skills. Living together supports social skills from team playing to asserting oneself, and studying the offered courses implies great interest in science, history, and arts. On a typical day, students attend classes in the morning and work the afternoon in assigned tasks such as butchering and cooking, farming, or milking. First milking is at 4:30 in the morning, committee meetings and studies take place until late in the evening.

While the college has three constant faculties, natural sciences and mathematics, social sciences, and humanities, additional courses range from *Greek Tragedy* or *Mayan Tradition* to *The Problem of Historical Knowledge* or *Exploration and Environment during the American Frontier* to *Quantum Physics* or *The Global Issues of Ecology and Environmental Science*. If ranch life should be part of the student's future, there is a saddle making class with the ranch manager; if he is more into music, an instructor would be invited from a nearby town. It was amazing to me that in a setting where most offers were optional, up to fifty courses and studies were asked for from a body not larger than 26 students. The only musts were composition and public speaking.

Based on Nunn's idea that his students will become responsible people, when they are held accountable for all operations, the labor positions included everything that accrued in a small community, from gardener or butcher to librarian or mechanic to cowboys and farmers. All issues facing the administration of the college and the ranch were discussed within the student body and the staff, encouraging them to engage in cooperative decision-making and collective action, with the aim to keep the college's tradition and shape its future.

As I took my leave, we were smiling at the rumors and suspicion I had heard elsewhere. David said, the college had always been subject to rumors and

---

* Excerpt from a college leaflet. Lucien Lucious Nunn, American entrepreneur, educator, 1853–1925.

imputations. Having been founded in 1917, it had been accused of being a communist facility. Later on, it became an alleged commune. Beyond that, I couldn't detect any suspicious behavior today. If I were twenty again, I would definitely apply for the two years in Deep Springs Valley.

It struck me that the students I met were quite different characters and appearances, though, they seemed to form a well-tempered team of individualists. Although there was a somehow tightened atmosphere, it came across as productive, efficient, and common sense. The tension I felt might have been caused by a mix of juvenile exuberance, hard labor requirements, and the variety of characters and social backgrounds. After all, it seemed that through the college's concept the student body found a way to appreciate individual differences, different backgrounds and mentalities. They learned that although in the beginning differences ostensibly oppose each other, as you begin to understand them, they correlate, and in the end they may form a strong entity, a unity. I think it is not far-fetched to find the reasons in the combination of hard work and academic life and the closeness to nature.

Deep Springs was probably the smallest self-reliant town I came through, a little comm*unity* where every single person obtained an important role without which it wouldn't exist or depend on external services. The differences I was dealing with on my journey originated in the greatest unity, Mother Nature. They were far simpler, at least academically, though not less crucial. Mountains and valleys, days and nights, heat and cold, being alert and asleep, risk and adventure, past and future. One without the other was not possible. Each time the sun got me out of the sleeping bag formed an entity with the forthcoming campfire, at most exactly twelve hours later. Seldom was my life in such an orderly fashion, with the most consistent being the unexpected.

The first half through Californian deserts was as much a part of my journey as the remaining in the woods and over snowy mountains. In my daily routine I was now about to climb a summit that would lay the traveled world at my feet, its past and its future. The White Mountain is often referred to as a desert mountain, an allegorical partition of this thousand-mile journey. Reaching its summit, I will stand on the exact midpoint, I will have left the desert behind and enter the Sierra California.

*

Opposing the ranch, at the entrance to Wyman Canyon, lay the remains of White Mountain City, founded by Dan Wyman in the late 1850s when prospecting placer gold values. Only a handful of miners had been living there, predominantly occupied with worming out the creek's golden secret and surviving attacks by local Indians. If any, its reputation was based on its remoteness and isolation. In those days, only with a discovery of a big nugget had a small settlement like that found its way into history, or through a scandal, triggered by another creative mind in the Old West. After not getting much out of his claim, in 1861 a certain Colonel McConnel was determined to resort to a new auspicious venture by entering the political stage, and he thought he had found a shortcutting opportunity. Registering as a candidate for the Governor's office, he attached a list of 521 names supporting him, sent it to the county seat in Aurora, and won by a close vote. However, he did not reckon with his opponent's geographical knowledge. A city with more than 500 eligible voters would have been known all over the state – but hardly anyone had ever heard of White Mountain City. Its actual figure counted about today's Deep Springs Valley population or, which is the same, the College head count.

The losing candidate in Aurora was visibly annoyed and set off to find this thievishly booming city in the outlying valley. Investigating undercover, it took him only a couple of days to unveil that the Colonel wasn't a Colonel, and that he had paid henchmen to travel to the county seat, where they sought to be asked about White Mountain City, only to confirm that they delivered supplies for at least 500 men. Everything else the duped senator found here did not look much different from what we see today. Eventually, it was found that the Colonel had copied all names from a list of passengers arriving on a steamship at the port of San Francisco.

Except for this story, White Mountain City could not keep up with the ghost towns in Marble Canyon or Eureka Valley. A ghost, too, needs buildings to spook. Haunting basements doesn't seem to be much fun.

Obviously, later passersby put the remnants to good use elsewhere. Nothing was left here other than fundamental stonewalls. From their geometrical shape you might detect what it was, big quadrangle – a house, small quadrangle – a small house, circle – a furnace stack or smelter oven, a triangle, I guessed, not enough stones to build a quadrangle. Still today historians are puzzling over what the triangles might have been, also over some strange zigzag patterns, possibly walls serving as a barrage to ward off attacks by the Indians.

I was following Wyman Creek, the first water-bearing riverbed since I left the Colorado, not counting the rivulets of natural springs or at Hunter's cabin. Of course, this mountain torrent was nothing compared to the big river, but enough to make me get out of my shoes and pants for a crossing every few miles. In the Royal Gorge, the earth had folded the canyon to a deep narrow ravine with vertical slippery walls, majestically excluding the rest of the world. Here, the creek had turned into roaring rapids. With my shoes and jeans on, I kept pushing my feet against the pressing water. With every step I had to look for something to hold on, a crevice or a ledge in the wall, a fallen tree or a big rock. At its narrowest part, the gorge took a sharp right turn, the sound of gushing water bode ill. Wading around the corner, I found it filled with large boulders and debris caused by rockslides from both sides. The water came shooting from between the rocks like from fire hoses.

CHAPTER FIVE

Now I definitely had to climb out of the canyon, and I hastened to find a way before the next avalanche would force me to stay longer than I wished. Somehow the whole scene appeared as if it had just happened and, who knows, it might not have ground to a halt yet. In fact, small pebbles and granular material was trickling down the right talus slope. I climbed the left side carefully, anxious for balance and not causing another slide of debris and fallen trees.

One of the battered stems lying around was one half of an old power line mast; around the bend I saw some more swept along, some barely standing. When I finally crawled out of the canyon, I found that a flash flood must have washed away huge masses of earth, rocks, and trees. Partly dammed by the debris, the river had left its bed, flooding and swamping a large area before it flowed back into the gorge. On one eventful day, the course of the creek had been turned into chaos.

Having escaped from it, I climbed on a hill in order to get a better view of the area. Surprisedly, I could look back as far as Soldier Pass and into Eureka Valley, becoming aware of the different world I was about to enter. Leaving behind the wideness of the desert valleys and creosote flats, now entering a narrower world of mountain gorges and forests, I saluted to all the people I met so far, living or historical, fortune-seeker or pioneer, Joe Sixpack or the Plumber. Farewell, desert rats! I am a mountain man now.

From up here, the chaotic scene below looked less threatening, somehow even inviting, rough and likewise pristine. I decided to stay for dinner and start a fire to dry my socks and shoes.

Further on, Wyman took over a more moderate course. Although I passed several placid meadows with lush green grass, I forced me to move on to reach a site called Robert's Ranch before nightfall. David from the College told me that one of the cabins there was in pretty good shape for a sheltered sleep. Not only the creek was a new aspect in my traveling now, or the forest of piñon pine trees arising from the shrub. For the first time, the sky was full of clouds, not that desert kind, where a sudden wall of fast moving cumuli is but an ironic gesture, blocking the sun for a short cooling, drifting away eastwards, unfulfilled. Here and now, it was pitch dark, they were jammed and insistent, and the air felt already wet.

When I reached the old ranch site, I was over 8,000 feet high. The lonely cabin in the vastness of forests and mountains appeared as a friendly paradox, like an offered home where you least expected it. However, to me, the main purpose of an old cabin was not so much the shelter but rummaging in the past. I never slept in one, though I took my time to investigate them and spent even more just sitting and looking at the usual historical furnishing. This, in most cases, consisted of a rusty bed frame, an old wooden table with at least one prosthetic leg, a stool being hardly better off, and an iron stove. Dust shadows of pots and pans around wooden pitons and nails in the cabin wall were reminiscent of the old days, telling that once it was actually inhabited. Although one could be absolutely certain that all drawers, closets, boxes, and containers were dead empty, I had to open all of them. And I am sure every hiking inspector did that before me. Still, gazing into the emptiness there was something. It was neither the forgotten pouch with glittering dust nor the prospector's diary. It was an invisible connection to his life. By just pulling a drawer, opening a cabinet door or by untwisting a jar, you did something so ordinary that for a blink of history's eye you became a part of it. And who knows, one day you might yet find more, deep behind the dust, overlooked by all nosy fingers of the past.

I started a fire in the stove, made some tea, and took the chance to sit at a table and do some paperwork, reading in Colin's book, completing my last log entries, and studying my maps. For half a day I became Robert.

I never found out who Robert was, though. In these cases I made up my own picture of the unknown cabin hosts. In my imagination, there was the old, long-bearded Hunter at Hunter's cabin, a fur cap on his head, his brown eyes deep pools of alertness in a sunburned and deeply seamed face. Here the young Robert, whose face was marked by experiences that lay before he came into the wild; he wasn't around long enough to be remembered by his last name. Somehow, I figured, they, too, noticed that I was there. Probably, in an afterlife it falls within one's sphere of responsibility to supervise those places in particular that were named after oneself. Poor George Washington.

05/05   ROBERT'S RANCH, 13 MILES

Above the cabin, I passed several luring meadows where Wyman still was a peacefully meandering mountain creek. Since the announced rainstorm had contented itself with a few thunders around midnight, the grass was nice and dry enough for a second breakfast and an hour continuing Colin's chapter about his days in the White Mountains.

He felt he was sharing them with geographer Doug Powell and University of California scientist Bill Roche and his assistants, who were working on the research station. I did not know if anybody else was around, but I doubted that, besides Robert and me, anyone would find his way up here at this time of the year.

Due to a three-week break Colin had taken between Deep Springs and the mountains, I started my ascent about a month earlier in the year. Whatever he did in these weeks, be it academic studies in a course offered at Deep Springs or ulterior studies of more amusing character beyond the nearby Nevada border, in any case he did not consider it noteworthy. He later simply mentioned that he had to wait for the heaviest snow to melt, though, some of his photos suggest that he met the woman he considered marrying after both his outdoor and his inward journey.

When I was back on the trail, I recognized that the creek took another course. Apparently, it originated in the meadows. Had I not seen snow simultaneously, I would have returned half a mile to where I last saw clear water to refill my water sack.

A trail signpost revealed I was now in Ancient Bristlecone Pine Forest, home of the oldest trees on our planet, which did not mean that from there on you would see them. Mountain mahogany, piñon, and limber pines were the sunshades, and they would give way to higher elevation shrub long before I saw the first Methuselah tree. Exiting Wyman Canyon, sagebrush became the predominant plant – buzzards were flying in circles above to descry unwary rodents – and at one fell swoop, all trees had disappeared and I walked into barren mountains. Although it was high above the desert, I found myself on a deserted mountain. Only occasionally, trees were reaching out of a side canyon or down from a mountain that was high enough to catch water from the fast passing clouds. Stray stands of Bristlecone Pines were scattered on the farthest and highest rims. In their nugget-colored garments they stood there like eternal Indians, watching the suspect goings-on in their lands below.

It was not as hot anymore, but the constant ascent with still some sixty pounds on my shoulders made me drink more water than I had calculated. At the first larger snowfield I had to stop to melt snow, cup by cup, one cup to drink, one cup to go. It was time-killing and chilling due to an ice-cold wind from the north, but it was a sense of security to know there is water everywhere, be it in the form of creeks or in the form of snow.

The line of poles had already been discontinued since I had left the cabin at Robert's Ranch, so I did not recognize their absence until I crossed another, different line. Anyway, I had given up my plan to follow these totem poles of modern society as they were built in a dead-straight line, regardless of any obstacle, canyon or mountain, just as if people were afraid electricity would jump out of the wire in a curve. It was much easier to follow the course of a canyon, and here I couldn't do much wrong; if I kept heading roughly northwest, I had to meet the White Mountain road or fall down into Owens Valley. A couple of miles later, coming out of the sage, I stepped on a massive snow drift, stretching several hundred yards to my left and to my right; beneath lay the road, a rough service track to an alpine research station. From here it ran swinging up and down between 9,000 and 11,000 feet, either through open sagebrush or covered in deep snow.

Traveling through North America would not be that fascinating if it wasn't for discovering nature's idiosyncrasies. You soon believe it is the land of extremes, irrespective of its social or economical specifics. Each geological or meteorological form and some biological species seem to cultivate a special or unique kind somewhere here. Singing dunes, canyons as deep, rugged, and mystic as the Colorado's Grand Canyon, mountains that tower out of the plains like the Bitterroot or the Inyos, and desert valleys doing their best reversely. I already discussed 'up-to'-temperature extremes, the oldest and tallest trees, the green Mojave rattler, and there is much more like the columnar basalts of Devil's Postpile, the salt sculptures of the same fellow, and so on. Consequentially, the snowfields up here were not just plain snow but entirely shaped in a regular pattern of crevices, up to two feet deep. Crossing them turned out to be not only difficult but also hazardous. When I stepped in such a deep hole, I had to crawl out on all fours, whereas stepping on the spines turned into a balancing act, and as soon as the sun pole-jumped over the range, she hit them full-force making them slippery and brittle.

This phenomenon occurring on retreating and melting snow in early summer had a sonorous name, *nieve penitentes*, or penitent snow. Considering that a variety of factors had to coincide to create such an ordeal, I was quite lucky, although I couldn't think of a worse scourge for a mountain hiker. First there had to be large snow masses that had already formed irregularities due to its sheer mass and strong winds. Small ripples lead the way. There must be a constant wind to cause greater air movement on the ripples than in the depressions. The air must be dry enough to support evaporation, pushing the dew point below the snow surface temperature. Then solar radiation and more heat reach the ripples and, due to the dry air, most of the energy is absorbed by evaporation instead of melting. Since evaporation of snow demands a multiple of the energy than needed for melting, the ripples stand strong and form to columns while the depressions melt unhurriedly though faster than the tops. The depressions get deeper and deeper through meltwater while the tops can't cope being busy with evaporation. Once hollows are formed, they collect dirt and dust thus absorbing even more sunlight, which again accelerates the melting process. Eventually, the ripples and depressions turn into icy pillars and crevices, in largely exposed slopes several feet deep.

Visually, it was the alpine analogy to the Devil's Golf Course and as hazardous to cross. I often thought about the early pioneers, who could not explain many of these phenomena, and about what was going on in their minds. In more religious times you had to draw on Heaven and Hell, or impute bad faith to nature.

As I overlooked the area, I realized that from now on at least half of the route was snow-covered. In the Sierra I would time my hikes accordingly and do larger snowfields in meadows and on southward slopes early in the morning, before the sun would melt the surface. However, here I was on the sun-baked side until I reached the summit.

CHAPTER FIVE

Due to the absence of any serious plants, not considered the dwarf sage that anyway merged into an optically homogeneous compound with the landscape, it was like walking on the moon. Unfortunately, I could not take into account my pack being reduced to one sixth of earth weight.

When dusk fell, I had to stop for the night. I had been walking with half moon for a while but I was getting afraid I would lose orientation now. Covered by *nieve penitentes*, the dirt road had not been visible for almost an hour and a strong wind kept picking up speed and threatened to blow me off my tired knees.

The last sign I remembered seeing said Patriarch Grove, which meant at that point I had reached the upper Bristlecone Pine territory and their preferred elevation at some 11,000'. Here, I was some 300 feet higher and kind of trapped among cold exposed rock where the wind could do with me what it wanted. Ugly cold squalls were blowing, making any further steps breakneck. I was trying to find a passage back down to the Patriarch campground to be sheltered from the storm and in order to salute the Patriarch Tree, the largest bristlecone pine with a circumference of 37 feet. After a few steps, I realized I would have needed skiers to get there and in the darkness would most likely have ended all the way down in the Cottonwood Basin, if not in Nevada.

By this time, the moon had set high showing me a single pine tree, which I chose as a windbreak. Before long, I knew how lucky I was to have found that lone pine. While I pitched camp under the lee of the tree, the White Mountains were raising a storm I had never experienced before. The wind was howling in gusts, dark clouds hovered above, within my grasp if they had not moved away so fast. While I was putting on warmer clothes, I had to run after my backpack twice. Eventually, I abandoned the attempt to have dinner and coated everything I found, crawling in my sleeping bag with merino thermal underwear and jeans, a shirt, a fleece, and on top of all that, a down-anorak. Guess what, I was still freezing. And this was not just the uncomfortable freezing of a cold desert night. This night, I was on the verge of despair.

I tried to tremble me warm and into sleep until another gust lifted my sleeping bag as if it was a balloon. I crept virtually in the tree, lying between a layer of understory shoots and pine branches, with my head at the stem. There I slept by the minute, every other gust woke me up, every movement let me unpleasantly feel the hard roots, pine cones, and dolomite rocks under my back. After a couple of hours, I considered getting up and keep walking. Just when I decided to give it a try, a whole gale was blowing, patches of snow became airborne, and the pine leaned over me in a 45-degree angle. It didn't take more to convince me to stay where I was. Up here I was far too exposed, walking in the dark with such a storm would have been life-threatening. So I trusted in a tree that had been resisting such curses for thousands of years. If it would fall, I must too. On all the snowfields I had passed, I had not seen a single track. It was my mountain now as much as I was at its mercy. In this night, I was afraid, I went out on a limb, gone too far. I felt helpless and, all of a sudden, lonesome.

05/06   BRISTLECONE PINE TREE, 10 MILES

I must have slept at least a couple of hours. It was still dark when I woke up and it was dead silent. The storm had blown out itself, withdrew heading east and with it detaching its cloudy mercenaries. From their movement, I got an idea of how strong it was; in no more than five minutes, the whole armada had left California, now descending on Nevada. The curtains were open. I lay in a giant amphitheater with the barren slopes around me being the tiers. The white peaks of the distant Sierra were a dramatic background that only one stage designer could have created. The light of the moon had just been switched off, while the sun took her time to reconquer the scene. The interlude of stars I got to see in that short break took one's breath away – the Milky Way had become a clear noctilucent road.

I crawled out of the ancient tree shelter, groaning and moaning, feeling sore muscles everywhere. Rubbing and trembling all-night long must have tired me until eventually I fell asleep. Moving like a Methuselah myself, I made coffee and ate some chocolate, packed my things and explored the area to warm up again. Now I saw Patriarch Grove in a depression about a mile from here. The wind had blown so much snow in there that some larger bristlecones were covered up to the tree tops.

After a night like that and in view of the snow masses on the higher slopes, I was torn between abandonment and – once I came so far – hanging in there. The White Mountain summit was luring. Only 3,000 feet in elevation separated me from one of the highest mountains in the state of California. With the first sunlight I decided to walk as far as I could and eventually leave my pack at the first research station before I would climb the summit.

After all, this summit, albeit not the highest, was still high enough to have caused yearlong debates about which one is the number one in California, occupying a good deal of scientists. To start with, it still is Mount Whitney on the Sierra side. Photo albums won't have to be rewritten. Or maybe yes, at least the elevation. What piqued my curiosity a year ago in a bar along U.S. 395 was the comment of one of the guests, stating that only recently someone found out that White Mountain was higher than Mount Whitney. He claimed that so resolutely as if it was the most obvious fact in the world, finally proven by a fair scientist. I had spent some days between Lone Pine and Big Pine, so I had a chance to ask more people in the streets and in stores about it, not to forget the park rangers. It seemed that some living farther south or on the eastern side of the street, hence more likely to view the Sierra, favored Mount Whitney, whereas others closer to the Intermountains or

CHAPTER FIVE

rather viewing them from their veranda, favored White Mountain. Checking various written sources for its elevation, I learned that California's highest peak is between 14,491 and 14,505 feet tall. Anyone saying it doesn't make much difference? It does, physically and mentally, because it is often these last feet of a mountain that wear you out most and sear into your memory.

I checked official and less official sources while the less official more likely just quoted the more official ones. A modern way of evaluating the mess should be Google, I thought. Googling all elevations between the two variables led to two peaks with a good variance, including a negligible number of hits with homonymous street numbers, for example '14,500 Mt. Whitney Road'. A 22% minority uses 14,494', all other numbers received even less. With 15% the second place goes to the neighboring one-foot lower variant, followed by 12% for the highest appearing entry, 14,505', gladly used by adventure travel companies, and 11% for a plain 14,500, which includes the undetermined and generalists. The National Park Service, accordingly the U.S. Government represented by the Department of the Interior, is more conservative, exercising modesty by quoting 14,491', the minimum of all possible entries and with 4% not very much backed by Google.

Excuse this little statistics again, but I had been wondering from the beginning, why Colin chose the White Mountain instead of California's highest peak, and so I wanted to get to the bottom of it, of California's highest peaks.

Now, since I knew the exact vague altitude of the highest summit, I focused on the White Mountain myth. The rumor was triggered by a group of geographers and surveyors, purporting their new technology would lead to overthrowing news. Sometimes for promotion purposes false statements are being circulated, just to create vogue and awareness. They didn't do the White Mountain any good. Had it always been the third highest in the state, these rumors brought other professionals out of the woodwork. In the 1990's, a four summits expedition, organized by Nevadan surveyor Nielsen, set out to knock that myth on the head, or rather on the summit. Using the latest GPS technology and comparing standard with low-lying satellite measurements in 1998, he won the 'National Society of Professional Surveyors' Student Project of the Year Award' for reversing the order of the third and fourth highest peaks, White Mountain and North Palisades.

For Colin it was still the third highest, and planning his route it became number one, for two reasons. First, with the plan to leave the desert behind by the end of April, he was facing the Sierra too early in the year to walk its icy summits and snowed-in passes without high alpine equipment. Due to its isolated prominence, the White Mountain is usually snow-free earlier than the Sierra. Second, the Sierra Nevada is a gathering of 14,000ers. From the fifteen peaks above that in the state of California, thirteen are in the Sierra, only the volcano Mount Shasta and our White Mountain are somehow single mountains. This would make the ascent to the White Mountain summit more likely stuffed with great views, because there aren't subsidiary peaks obstructing the view.

With the White Mountain being a symbolic partition of desert and mountains, he could not have chosen better; the vistas of the deserts south represented our experienced past, those to the Sierra northwest the unknown future, both offering spectacular scenes.

Today I might add a third reason. Since Colin's days, the trails around Mount Whitney had become a major Alpine highway. Depending on the time of the year, there are conditions like at Central Station. The opposing ranges of the Inyo and White Mountains are far less visited and if you meet somebody, chances are they are locals, familiar with the area and have some interesting stories to tell. When a natural or geological superlative is being frequented like Mount Whitney, one may draw conclusions from the crowd you meet there; a vanity fair for individual records and fashion trekking rather than for the nature experience. However, to me of the greatest importance, with so many fellow hikers and park regulations being enacted and enforced, you cannot roam freely anymore.

Somehow, it is like choosing your place to live. If there are two opposing apartment buildings on a street with identical interiors, only one has a dull, grey exterior plaster, the other one a beautiful design and a newly-painted façade, where would you move in, the one with the better view or the one viewing desolation? However you may decide, the Sierra definitely is the better view, whereas the White Mountains have the better view and they are a hiking experience sui generis.

Although the White Mountains are actually a part and the northern end of the Inyo Mountains, the imaginary separation by the Westgard Pass and Deep Springs Valley leaves them isolated and lacking a comparable sustained high mountain mass like the Sierra Nevada. This in turn redounds to the described advantage.

Another method of rating the tallness of a mountain, commonly labeled as 'majesty', is the aforementioned elevation prominence, which means the height of the peak's summit above the lowest contour line encircling it. Especially for hikers, the prominence should be a decisive criterion, since it is correlated with the subjective significance of a summit. Mountains with a high prominence have less or lower subsidiary peaks thus offering better views during the ascent. A third criterion, called 'elevation isolation', marks the distance to the next higher peak.

Back to statistics, briefly. Mount Whitney is generally accepted – with an exact elevation between 14,491' and 14,505' and a prominence of 10,080 feet – as the highest in California. Mount Williamson from the same Sierra Family comes next with 14,389', but only a prominence of 1,677, isolated by just five miles. Of the same range lineage is the peak of the North Palisades,

CHAPTER FIVE

which, according to the latest research, might be number three. Sources list him between 14,242' and 14,248', 2,894 feet prominent and 32 miles isolated. With its 14,243' to 14,252-foot peak, whereas 50% see it at the lowest alternative and 50% at one of the others, the White Mountain protrudes some 7,200 feet above its base and distanced itself 68 miles from its next opponent. Motivation enough for hanging in there.

I set off into the barren landscape following the endlessly winding White Mountain Road. The lonesome pine was the last tree I passed. From above 11,500 feet, sagebrush seemed to be the only vegetation braving the elements. Much to my amazement, I saw a wild horse there, wandering placidly through the shrub some 500 feet from me. I had to surpass a large snowdrift anyway, so I left the road in order to follow the fantasy-like appearance into the sagebrush. This one immediately noticed my little excursion; it continued walking up the slope but constantly keeping a stable distance and an eye on me, picking up pace when I got too close, waiting for me when I fell behind. Only with my zoom lens I could shorten the distance. All of a sudden, behind the horse appeared the panorama of the Sierra, soaring with every further step toward the horse. It was a picture out of *The NeverEnding Story*. Had I been able to touch it, I was sure, it would have grown a straight, spiraled horn on its forehead.

The fact that the White Mountain Road is the highest road in California including the highest section of pavement was a mixed blessing for me. Instead of using map and compass, I relied on finding the road, although it was largely buried under masses of snow. At one point, it turned back to contour in a sort of horseshoe curve around a valley. Reaching from the slopes above the road, deep down into the depression, there was a large inclined snowdrift. Rather than doing a penitent walk on the sun-exposed flank around the valley, I just sat down and slid 500 feet on solid snow in a straight line, then climbed up the same distance on the other side.

Being back on the road, after two more miles on Spanish snow, I stumbled upon the Locked Gate, the end of the road in summer and for anybody who is not working at one of the research stations. While the gate was completely snowed in, I could see the upper half of a small hut, probably the highest outhouse in the world. A park service brochure said, there was a permanent bathroom located here – toilet paper would usually be well stocked. So far so true, but you would need a good sense for your needs, an early-warning system, and time and a shovel to remove three feet of snow to get to it.

After another mile, I reached the Barcroft White Mountain Research Station, located at about 12,500'. A large Quonset hut with the laboratory was attached to another building with living quarters and several storage barracks. It gave me the impression I was somewhere on an arctic research station. Heavy snow removal equipment like snow crawlers and a quick look to the summit seemed to confirm my apprehension.

When Colin came here, the station had been manned throughout the whole year. Now technology took over Bill Roche's job, the researcher he met here fifty years ago. There were antennas, instruments, and measuring devices everywhere, constantly measuring temperature, humidity, wind speed, and other information. The research teams only come when the roads are cleared or for special studies.

The White Mountains are home to several research facilities operated by the University of California, San Diego. With their multicampus research units they have been studying various altitude related aspects over the last sixty years, such as effects of altitude on organisms, physiology of the control of breathing, ecophysiology of hibernation, paleoclimate in ancient bristlecone pines, or the measurement of cosmic background radiation. Their facilities include a base station near Bishop, Owens Lab, a montane station at Crooked Creek, and the two I was visiting, the alpine station at Mount Barcroft with the observatory and the summit lab. During their history, the stations have hosted thousands of students conducting field classes. It is renowned both for field training of geologists and its open-doors day for visitors. I would suggest re-staffing the station in winter again in order to study these rare snow forms. The extraordinary size and shape of the snow columns I walked through is still unexplained down to the present day.

Today I had blue sky, and since I had no conversational partners here other than some marmots, I planned on doing the summit in the afternoon. Anyway, the wooly marmots were more interested in what I might pull out of that extraordinary picnic basket on my shoulders. Their looks told me how they wished that I would leave it here in their custody.

Below the road, I found a muddy area, fed from a tiny trickle fighting its way into spring, yet too weak to allay a walker's thirst. So I dug a hole in a five-foot-high snow pile to get clean compressed snow. Once a decent amount of water had formed in my pot, I could add looser snow.

While I was melting a cubic foot to fill my water sack, I had a good-sized meal for two. I counted 25 pots of the white powder to get one gallon of water. Then I unpacked my backpack and put only those things back in I would really need for a night on the summit. Everything else went into an Ortlieb dry bag, which was actually slated for the Sierra to get my things across a rapid creek or to haul food into trees to have it out of bear reach. I thought, it would do well for marmots too.

Early afternoon, I put everything I wanted to leave in the driver's cab of a snow crawler. Trying to spot the summit trail behind the station, I passed a domed observatory stuffed with more measuring equipment. The good thing was, the five miles went pretty much straight north, I just had to target at White Mountain. The bad thing, it was a constant up and down over rock'n'soil land. Knowing it was only another 2,000 feet in elevation was a mental backfire. In total you walk at least 1,000 feet down, which makes some 3,000 up. The summit hut is in view most of the time, and just before I left the straight line to turn in for the final climb, I looked down into another geological depression. A series of switchbacks makes sure you would remember the climb as more demanding.

In general, the White Mountain is often referred to as California's easiest fourteener, due to its gentle slopes and the absence of climbing walls or overhanging rock faces. This might be true in summer, when the dirt road prepared the ground for an easy hike to the summit. With large parts of the 10-mile stretch from Patriarch Grove being covered with carved snow, it becomes just as bad as the worst of its Sierra vis-à-vis.

When I had crossed the last depression, I stood at the foot of the summit. I realized that the remaining mile would take me as much time as the whole hike from Barcroft station, and most likely even more energy, if actually I didn't have to give up. The snow had been blown around the northeastern flank, piling up a solid frozen bank. Here, the surface was designed in *suncups*, a preliminary stage to the Spanish top form. However, by all means, this side was the only one accessible. The others had less snow but would have been a much steeper climb that you would not dare without climbing spurs. I thought about it several times, but my weaker self's chances were never as bad as here; having come so far, I just mustn't give up.

With every step I kicked stairs in the ice, balancing a totally jaded body. Step by step, breath by breath, second by second. It took an eternity to do the last one hundred feet. In a state between faint and victory, I fell down on the highest point of my Thousand-Mile Summer, my Janus summit, from where I could look toward both my deserted past and my mountainous future. The White Mountain bisected the two predominating geographic regions with the deserts south and the mountains north. *He* was the psychological half and literally a highlight of this journey.

Only now, it did not matter if it was 14,243 or 14,252'.

For half an hour, I was too exhausted to enjoy the panorama. Since I knew I was going to stay for the night, I saved the best for last and opened the small metal container first that was attached to the hut to make an entry into the summit log. Besides the logbook, its contents were an assortment of pens and pencils, various sheets of paper – perhaps for those who felt inspired to write a letter to Santa once they were here, a bottle of water, and the Stars and Stripes. These reminded me of the folding ceremony in Death Valley. What was only two and a half weeks ago seemed to be ages now. I stood up with my tripod and took some pictures of me wrapped in thirteen stripes and fifty stars, with the 51st already twinkling over Nevada.

With the last light, I turned through 360 degrees, letting out a smashing song of joy. In every point of the compass, I called the name of the persons most important to me. North, northwest, west, southwest and so on. I did it twice, first, for eight people living, then, for eight people deceased. The third and the fourth round started and stopped in the east, there was one I had to forgive, and one, I felt, I had to apologize to. Seldom in my life was I so balanced and happy. Happy about what I experienced so far and happy about what will come, balanced between yesterday and tomorrow. It felt like the median of my life. For a moment, I thought, this is greater than having reached the finish. To me, it was less a summit but a pass between my personal tides.

Nevada had already been thrown into sleep when my ceremony was over. When the sun went down behind the Sierra, I took sides with Nevada, climbed the ten feet higher summit hut with my sleeping bag and took place on the roof of the highest high-altitude research station in North America. Now I was definitely *The* third highest in California and I longed for a sound sleep on cloud nine. In fact, I fell asleep in a minute, I didn't even catch how I undressed or that I stuffed my clothes in the bag sack to form a pillow. I must have been afraid the wind could blow away my boots; the next morning I found them in the metal container. Maybe it was the thin air, which let me do some routines but spared the conscience to worry about them.

05/07   WHITE MOUNTAIN SUMMIT, 21 MILES

In the middle of the night, a rescue team with an armada of snow groomers came to the summit. They made a huge noise, engines roaring and people shouting and calling for me, a pandemonium between the summit and my roost. They could not see me on the hut roof and I was not sure if they were looking for me because they found my abandoned things in the snow crawler, or if I did something wrong, like climbing the research hut.

I had not the slightest idea of what was going on – until I woke up, confused first, then, unmasking the dream, amused. But with the first look out of my mummy bag, I became witness to a no less dreamlike experience. With goose bumps all over me, I beheld the sun standing on top of a faraway mountain range in the eastern Nevada basin, resurrecting the summits of the Sierra in the West. She brought color to the slopes of White and Glass Mountains and eventually into the valleys below and to that of death. Only me over here, she did not touch, as if I was not in this world, not part of the movie, only because I cheated the known out of ten feet.

I was looking to where I came from, then trying to make out where I would go from here, where I would be in a couple of days, in a week, and maybe where the end of my journey would be. I felt like my own little god, looking down on me and the short span of life from Mexico to Oregon.

After a feature length view onto California, I put on my pack and began stepping down the stairs I had set a day earlier. Having mastered this piece was so uplifting and spiritually conducive, I was ready to take anything. Nothing could stop me now, I thought, not knowing that a late winter revival had already deployed over the Sierra.

On the descent, I could better concentrate on the surroundings. The moonscape along the summit trail was barren and desolate with hardly any plants. Besides my backpack and my red shirt, the only things adding color to the scant landscape were lichens. For fear of being blown away, they nestled up to boulders and stones coloring them yellow and red. But the scenery around me was offering views and enchantment in all directions.

I picked up the pace to get back to my storage and celebrate the triumphal return with a bag of – though totally out of place – Hawaiian Chicken. Besides water, I had taken some food to the summit, clothes and two lighters, just in case. But I saved my appetite for the real meal I would have in company of the marmots.

When I got back down to the depression under the summit, I saw dark clouds flying above. I noticed how lucky I was last night with no wind at all. Even in summertime, the White Mountains could be one of the coldest areas in California, with temperatures down to 0 F and winds up to 140 mph or more. In a night like that at the bristlecone pine, one would have died up there, or rather had never made it up to the summit.

The occasional declines, my recovery breaks from the previous day, were the bale of today. The clouds flew in fast and thickened to form a large black anvil hovering menacingly above my head. I just caught sight of the observatory when it started snowing. Being close to the station I felt quite safe, even if all hell broke loose, here I would find a place to hide.

Was it the weight of the clouds or did I feel the first effects of the altitude, I couldn't tell. But I felt a little dizzy and had developed a mild headache. Coming up, I had been so occupied with finding my way through the snow, I never thought of the risks of altitude sickness. On such elevations and especially when climbing as fast as I did, suffering from at least one of the symptoms is all but certain. Fortunately, with the two nights at Roberts Ranch and near Patriarch Grove and the lunch break at the research station, I seemed to have been acclimatized enough to the lower partial pressure of oxygen up here to get away with a headache.

Lunchtime turned into a hail and snow inferno, and soon the whole range was softly covered with fresh-fallen snow like a bundt cake with powdered sugar. Then low-flying clouds moved in advising a quick decampment if I did not want to get snowed in. An hour later, I waved the marmots goodbye, and after only one hundred yards, the station had disappeared from my sight, swallowed by the clouds.

The White Mountain is one of these summits you virtually climb several times before you wave the flag. Coming back down from his top, I had forgotten how many times the grade had changed on my way up. Therefore, mentally my descent turned into another climb in places. I called these parts negative ascent or positive descent, depending on whether I walked up or down. There were the two larger ones between the stations, three between Barcroft and Patriarchs Grove, another three between there and Wyman Canyon, and a ninth on the way to Silver Canyon. Sometimes you have to go down to go up. On top of that, the mountain decided to hurl everything he is in control of against me. It seemed, I had to earn my night on the summit a second time. At least, his way of saying goodbye did not lack a certain sense of humor. In the shadow of a smaller range it became warmer, the wind could not blow in here, and I finally could take off the anorak and stash it in the backpack. I put on my pack, walked two steps, and *boom*, a sudden ice-cold gust hit me like a slap in the face, with the mountain's roaring laughter. I gave in and put it back on.

When I came to the single tree, a cold shiver ran through my anorak and down my back. I shuddered to think of it. A herd of bighorn sheep near Patriarch Grove got my mind on better things. Here I left the barren country again. Re-entering the piñon and bristlecone pine-lined slopes from about 11,000 down to 8,000 feet, a potpourri of odors was rising up through the air. With the retreating snow, the ground unbosomed its own earthen smell, virtually starting to breathe after long hibernation. Occasionally, a distant slope was waving with sage aroma, but the air was increasingly filled with the prevailing almost beguiling smell of pine tang. I took a little detour where I saw a group of these oldest living things in the world. As you would guess it in a harsh environment like here, these ancient bristlecone pines were looking rather unusual. I thought for a tree that old you expected a more flamboyant name, something sounding like 'Sequoia' or 'Saguaro'. Also the fruits, for which the tree is named for, are rather unremarkable, relatively small with short, fragile spikes on the cones. Yet somehow it fits to the tree that did not brag about its size either.

I was amazed by their color, not so much by grandeur. Thousands of years of windblown sand and ice and occasional fires have sculptured its wood and left weathering marks. The nature-scarred species is also called living driftwood from having been worked over by millennia of wind and sandstorms. Growing only about an inch in diameter every hundred years, the elements have a lot of time to design them to their taste. At an average tallness of thirty to fifty feet, they would not really stand out or catch the eye of someone passing by. It is the color of the wood that seems to inherit millennia, a lurid collection of historical shades of brown. When I paused to marvel at an exceptional group of three intertwined trees, I saw a maize yellow and a pueblan ocher, pottery-clay and basket-reed browns; there were reddish shades from an adobe mud-mortar to ceramic red to a Coronado blood tone; there was the color of weathered mission beams, ranch gates, and the color of gold; and the black-brown of old railroad-ties gnarling around a few green shoots – growing for many more stories to be told.

Its Latin name is *Pinus Longaeva*, Latin for ancient or aged pine tree, and with 4,800 years of age, answering to the name of Methuselah, the oldest living tree was somewhere here below the White Mountain. Somewhere, that is, because no one knows the exact location. California park service keeps it a secret with good cause. Not too long ago, Methuselah was only second in age. In Colin's days, one could have visited the even older cousin Prometheus, or rather paid one's last respects to it. In the other larger habitat of ancient bristlecone pines in eastern Nevada, Prometheus fell victim to rather disputable, if not stupid, environmental decisions. A graduate student of 'Climate dynamics during the last smaller ice age', which was some 600 years ago, thought a tree being at least five times that old would deliver the requested data. Good guess. After several unavailing tries to core the stem, he apparently got frustrated and took it personally. Rumors were, he broke two of his increment borers and was unable to get replenishment before the end of the season. Others said, his tools just were not long enough for a tree like that. In any case, he asked the local authorities for permission to chop the cross-grained tree.

He could have consulted forest service here in California, where the age of another tree had already been successfully determined by extracting cores with an increment borer. Although 90% of that tree named Pine Alpha was dead, those parts were still good for serving science through dissection and analysis. Hence it became the first tree to be dated older than 4,000 years.

Nevertheless, Nevada forest service approved the vandalizing plan and cut Prometheus on 7 August, 1964. Later on, responsible authorities excused the act as an important factor in creating the Great Basin National Park. The park was created only twenty years later, though, and I doubt that one thing had to do with the other. If so, one may call it 'enforced environmental martyrdom'.

Today the National Park Service refers to the great knowledge we obtained from the slaughtered tree, bringing into play a rather far-fetched allegorization by equating the felling with the *fire* that the ancient Greek eponymous hero stole from Zeus to give it to us humans. The correct interpretation for fire, however, would not be *knowledge* but *culture*, and beyond that, it was Prometheus' friend Athene who gave us *intelligence* and *reason*. Unfortunately, none of such qualities played a decisive role when it came to this unnecessary and rash act. Granted, once the parted tree went in sections to several institutes around the world, it unveiled a lot of knowledge to us, for climatology, paleontology, and archeology. The question remains if other trees, or even only parts of them, and a more thorough modus operandi could have provided for the same.

This story reminded me of dramatist T.S. Eliot's *Choruses from the Rock*, where the poet recited: "Where is the life we have lost in living? Where is the wisdom we have lost in knowledge? Where is the knowledge we have lost in information?" After having his chop done, the student obtained a lot of information and he proudly delivered the following surprising news: the tree's circumference was 252 inches with shoots between 11 and 17 feet high.

As an aside, it was not only some 4,900 years, as the student had already guessed before grinding his ax. With more than 5,100 years, it was the oldest living unitary organism ever discovered on our planet, exceeding our Methuselah tree by at least 200 years.

The secret of the trees' age is an attitude that is anything but vain. They let parts of themselves die off to remain strong enough to keep a smaller part alive and in balance with current climate or water conditions. Some trees have only a small percentage left of living tissue, still producing fertile seeds.

The bristlecone pine has withstood heat, cold, wind, and the erosion of time. Yet it may not escape the encroachment of civilization, or the stupidity of man. Regardless of students, atmospheric pollution poses the biggest threat to it today.

Methuselah's exact position is not revealed for fear of further vandalism or souvenir-hunters. Its exact age is as broadly spread over Google and literature as its home mountain's elevation, between 4,732 and 4,830 years. The park's custodian, the Forest Service, does not even mention an exact figure. I always trusted my feeling suggesting 4,800 years, which revealed an interesting coincidence: Noah's ancestor, the Hebrew patriarch Methuselah was born in 687, according to the Hebrew calendar, and he died in 1656 at the age of 969 years. The year of my journey corresponds to the Hebrew year 5,769. Now take that and deduct the tree's age. You'll see that the tree was born in the Hebrew year 969, prophesying its eponym's span of life. Or add the ages of the tree and its patron, you will always and forever receive the actual Hebrew calendar year, forever or as long as the tree may live. I do not know if that's of any use, but I thought it proved at least that my feeling was right.

05/08   SILVER CANYON, 16 MILES

After a night among patriarchs, I began the descent to Owens Valley through different pine tree habitats in Silver Canyon. The walk down was a wonderful trip through almost Mediterranean forests with beautiful views of the opposing Sierra and the valley. Deep down where the mouth of the canyon must be, I saw a green meander of mesquite and birch trees, the Silver Creek on its way into the Owens River. With the grade being a horizontal impertinence, I soon understood that it was advisable to concentrate on the way, though.

CHAPTER FIVE

In the middle of the canyon, some switchbacks and curves were like a flight of winding stairs. With the heavy load pushing me, I had a hard time not to reach gravitational speed. Whenever I slowed down because I saw something that caught my interest, a deer or a dramatically crooked tree, my backpack was trying to outspeed me. At some places, I could slide down on loose gravel or decomposed slate without doing anything. The twelve-mile-long Silver Canyon drops 6,400 feet down to U.S. 6, whereas half of the difference is lost within less than the first four miles. And that's exactly where most of the weird trees and browsing deer occurred.

The rangers down in Bishop had some stories to tell; stories of all too adventurous off-roaders and overheated brakes, glazed brake drums, warped brake rotors, or flat tires. I wondered how many cars might bedeck the treetops some hundred feet below where the Silver Creek flowed.

About five miles before I reached the highway, all of a sudden, the road lost its steepness, and in a sharp turn it smoothed alongside the bed of the creek. Just as I passed a locked gate, figuratively concluding my first mountain act, a breeze came up blowing into the trees. I almost overheard it, the familiar sound of a rattle. For a moment I didn't watch my step, since I was already looking for a good spot to pause at the creek. But I couldn't see a snake, not on the road and not in the shrub next to me. I checked around the birch tree when I heard it again, right above me. For a second I wondered, I rattler in a tree? Then I realized it was the breeze shaking the aspen leaves, a nice welcome but also a well-meant reminder that I was back in rattlesnake territory.

Down at the creek, it was hard to make up one's mind for where to stop. There were just too many sand banks and grasslands along the water, nicely decorated with old acquaintances Indian paintbrush and California poppy, a little farther an opulent bouquet of yellow flowers, and everywhere lilac indigo bushes, on which someone must have crashed a lavender flacon. They smelled like a perfumery.

However, I did not accept the florid invitation, I had to finish the mountain and that would not happen before I smelled the city. Having a late lunch at the creekside, I got myself ready for town, dressed to the nines. I washed my jeans, shirt, and socks, then my face and my hair what yielded about a handful of dirt. I think I even saw some gold dust being washed away with the dirt in the creek.

Right before I reached the highway, I passed Laws Railroad Museum. It was closed, but I got ice-cold water from a rancher who asked me why I turned back. He thought I had given up, that I looked like I had just left the city. Explaining that my Silver Creek bird bath promised too much, he showed me around the small railroad town, which hosted a collection of restored buildings, well stuffed with antique furniture and farming and ranching equipment. Behind the houses was a nice assortment of railroad cars and all that stuff you find along tracks. Of course steam engine number 9 attracted the child in me the most. After its final run in 1959, it had found its retirement home on the last tracks remaining in the gardened railway property of Laws. Hanging off its side, I played conductor, blowing long-long-short-long for Bishop – here I come.

The four miles to Bishop, the largest town in Owens Valley, passed by in an instant. The sudden walking on paved roads seemed to be somehow unreal. As relaxing as it was, after climbing and decelerating from my highest mountain, it just palled on me. It seemed that the longer I was traveling and the more often I hit town, the more civilization became second to nature. With that feeling, I reached city limits and with all these gas stations, motels, mini-marts, fast food restaurants, banks, and supermarkets, this town was out of my league, too big for me and too noisy. Still after almost two months, towns just had to serve the purpose of replenishing, refreshing, and meeting people. All extras, add-ons, the extravaganzas of civilization proved to be insignificant if not disturbing. It was too late to move on, but I made up my mind that I would leave early in the morning for the smaller town of Big Pine where I planned to have a few days rest.

After visiting one of the local bars, I strolled down Main Street, window-shopping and wondering what people need to live their city lives. In another two months, I would be one of them again, someone who needs a hardware store, a car service, or a boutique for clothes. It was hard to believe; didn't I already have everything I needed on my back? Yet I remembered how fast one would be drawn back to city routines when you come home, right after the backpack would be unpacked and bring-alongs be handed out.

Though, there are some things that magically get you back even faster. While giving Nathan the obligatory travel report, I happened to pass the window of the town's bakery. It didn't need a second thought, I knew instantly I had to postpone my departure till after morning breakfast. This was not just an ordinary bakery, what I saw through the window was as appetizing as tantalizing, freshly baked breads with names and ingredients from all around the Mediterranean Sea. A Cockaigne made of cookies and sweets that reminded me of those Sundays, when the rusty gate remained shut, because we decided to stay home. Then Grandma was announced visiting, and we knew she would come with a similar variety of treasures.

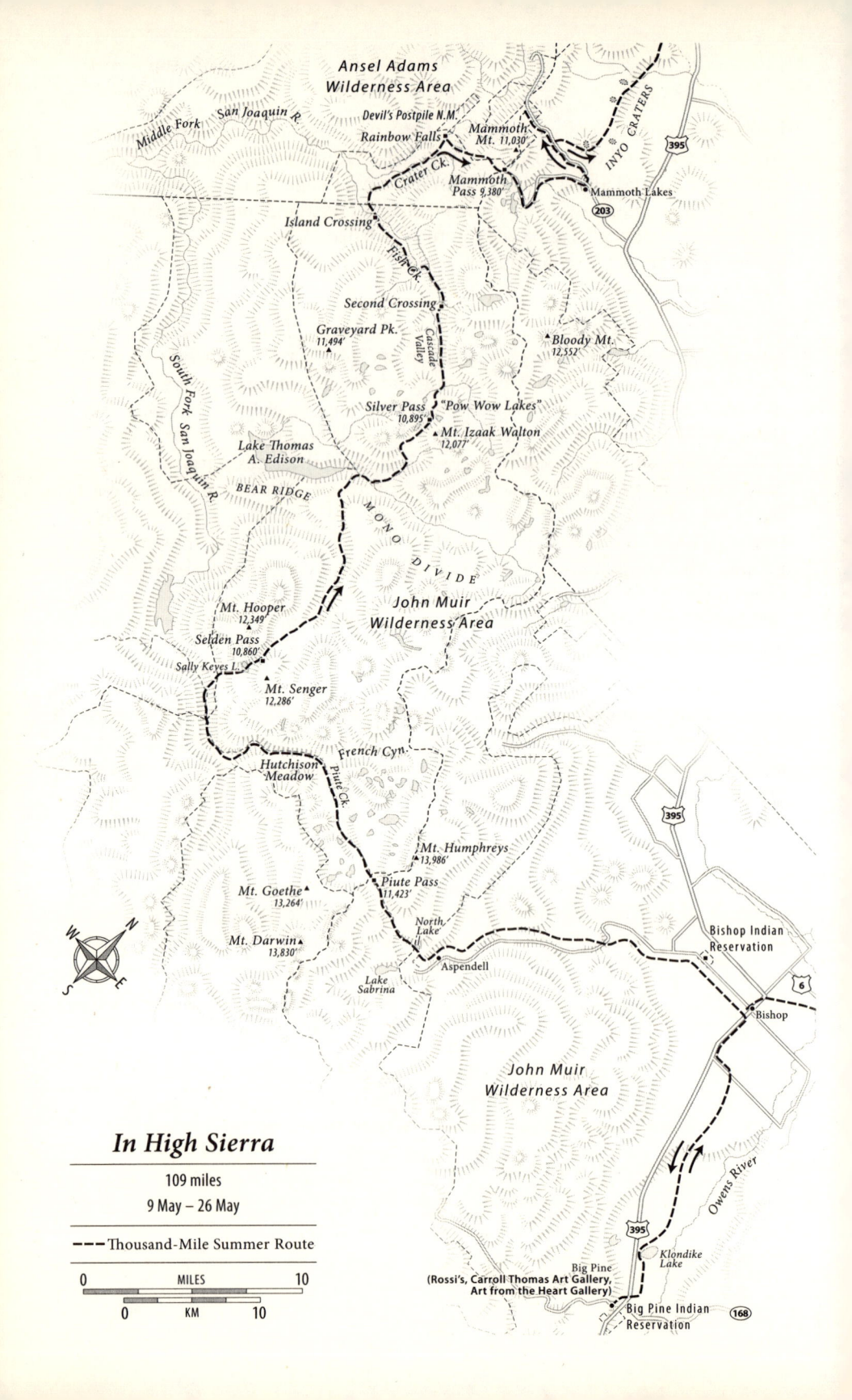

In High Sierra

109 miles

9 May – 26 May

- - - Thousand-Mile Summer Route

6. IN HIGH SIERRA

Climb the mountains and get their good tidings. Nature's peace
will flow into you as sunshine flows into trees.
The winds will blow their own freshness into you,
and the storms their energy, while cares will drop off like autumn leaves.

JOHN MUIR, SCOTTISH-AMERICAN NATURALIST AND PRESERVATIONIST, 1838–1914

05/09   BISHOP, 15 MILES

"We speak the same language," said Owens Valley's eldest citizen to me, when I told him about my journey. California artist Carroll Thomas, who had just turned 98, presided over his gallery and studio at the northern entrance of Big Pine, located some fourteen miles south of Bishop.

After a four-hour walk from Bishop, I had arrived at the small town's general store, where I delved into my usual welcome-to-civilization ceremony, reading the local papers with a cup of coffee. In an issue of the *395 Magazine,* I read an article about Thomas' life and work, that he was still active, both in painting and in hiking, and I decided that I wanted to meet this man, who spent most of his life – to be accurate nine tenth – painting wildlife and landscape images. So I walked back to his gallery and introduced my wild life to him.

Sitting together in his studio and talking for about an hour, he almost put me to shame when he said, "It's an honor to meet you, Andreas." Nothing could have borne me out more than receiving confirmation for my endeavor from an almost a-century-old, respectable, and successful man, as the history I was walking through was not much older.

Carroll Thomas is not only the oldest living American painter, he is also still working both artistically and commercially in running his gallery and shop. He is a good listener, though he really enjoys talking about his own nature experiences, many of which he portrays in his paintings. One of his best and maybe the most famous work is a painting of a bristlecone pine tree, which is, as he said, native to his backyard, the southern slope of the White Mountains. Good company, I thought, what else could have been a better symbol for his age and his artistic perseverance. Other watercolors included the Rainbow Falls near Mammoth Lakes, Mount Whitney, the Golden Trout Lake, several encounters with bear, mountain lion, and elk, and many more landscapes throughout the West. In all of them I saw his love for nature, immortalized on canvas in a clear and plain expressive style.

His ancestry is no less impressive, as I learned from a history lesson he gave me while looking at a colorful painting of a wagon. Being of Welsh-English-Scotch-Dutch-German origin, he narrated that his grandparents drove wagon trails from the East to the West, where they found home in Oklahoma until they fell victim to the course of events that later became one of the most dramatized episodes in Western history. In the heyday of homesteading, not only settlers were rushing new lands. Numerous outlaws were busily trying to run off homeseekers and secure the best spots for their own kin, among whom the notorious Dalton Gang became the Thomas family's demise.

Thomas called all of them 'Sooners' and he accentuated this word in a way so I would understand it as an introduction to the following story that should shed a different light on a common fallacy. While the word actually described those who entered Oklahoma's lands before they were officially assigned for open settlement, Thomas' personal interpretation was a more substantive one. The term originally derived from the 'sooner clause', part of the Indian Appropriation Act, which defined that no one was allowed to claim land prior to the opening by the government. However, especially state employees, who were able to enter the new prohibited land legally, were abusing their status, marking out their preferred places for themselves or acting as fences; they got company by outlawed civil war veterans, railroad workers, surveyors, and even deputy marshals; the latter were said to be the worst. Those, who entered the unassigned territory illegally by the light of the moon in order to occupy their choice before the settlers would be there, initially coined the phrase 'Moonshiners', or 'Sooners'. On the next day, when the land run officially began, almost 50% and, of course, the best parts were already taken by them. Just from the way Carroll narrated the story, from his clenched fists and an unforgiving glare in his eyes, one could tell that his own family had suffered from these events. He said they had been sent packing, unmistakably; then he lowered his voice, spoke slowly and emphasized every word. He leaned over to me and, for a short moment, I became aware of the incarnated history as he spoke: "Let me tell you this, Andreas, their behavior often was as lawless as the whole act, they'd *sooner* shoot than ask. This is why WE called them Sooners."

When we walked through the gallery, I was mainly looking for places I knew or scenes I had experienced on my walk. I found a desert landscape, reminding me of the plains in the East Mojave. There was the cougar, whose eyes reflected our encounter along the Colorado. And there were the bristlecone pines, among which I had spent my last night. But the picture that really captivated me was the falls I would hear in a week or two on my way to Mammoth. In that very moment, I could have said "Goodbye Carroll", goodbye to Big Pine, and walk straight into the Sierra to find them. I felt how I pondered my plans, what would keep me here, until I saw the next painting. Not knowing how or why, it just suggested to stay and look at it – or was it the luminosity of its colors outshining even the Falls? It was just a still life, a very vivid one, though, portraying wild roses overgrowing an old wooden coach. At its frame was a small note saying 'Rossi's'. Interesting wordplay, I thought.

After we finished the tour through his gallery, we shook hands and just as if he wanted to point out again that we really spoke the same language, he picked his walking staff and left the house with me. While I was going back to town to find a place for the night, Thomas took off into his backyard for his daily hike through nature.

Walking down Main Street, I began looking for a motel. I couldn't wait to throw all my belongings on the floor and just sit in between and browse over them, remembering all the stories that were now attached to each item from the first half of my journey. Then I wanted to check the backpack, its straps, and all equipment and make a shopping list for the next weeks, food, drink powder, chocolate, and trapper mix, but definitely no more granola bars. No honey-and-nuts bars, no banana-and-almond bars, and no chocolate-chips bars. I was so sick of these cereal treats, I would have had to stop my trip if I had to feed from them. I had brought all kinds of bars, all imaginable tastes and some beyond imagination, to spice up my snack times. My collection included the 12-pack for 3.99 as well as some trekking-energy-power-performance-bars for 2.99, each. I got sick of them all, and, by the way, the energy always came from the campfire-cooked meal and not from a bar. One lesson learned, abstain from dispensable snacks and schedule the day and the program in such a manner that I had frequent and extensive meals.

I couldn't believe it, I calculated two bars per day, one between breakfast and lunch, another one in the afternoon. For the three and a half weeks until I got to my first depot in Goffs, I had accordingly fifty bars. The average bar comes in 2.5 ounces, that adds up to some 8 pounds. To me and regarding my personal energy needs, the power bar turned out to be but an answer to a marketing-made need, at best powering the profit of outfitters and supplying companies. When a product's use as simple as that of a snack experiences a diversification like the power bar, one should have been alarmed anyway. In one store, I saw them sorted by performance bars, children bars, bars for a balanced nutrition, and – no kidding – women's health bars. I didn't get deeper into it, but I am sure there were special bars for blondes, brunettes, and dark-haired as well.

Calculating pounds and dooming the cereal bar per se, I passed a nice looking Italian restaurant. I stopped to look at the menu displayed in the window. 'Restaurant, Bar and Wine Cellar' it said, and its name was 'Rossi's, Steak & Spaghetti'. I immediately dropped my pack to walk around the house and, indeed, there was this part of a coach pictured in Thomas' painting. Only the flowers seemed to have sprung from his blooming imagination, which had transmogrified green grass into red roses. So this would be my program for the evening; studying the menu through the window, I already composed my four-course dinner menu and a premium Chianti, all that for the equivalent of just a dozen premium bars.

In most of those one-mile towns, I used to walk the length of the main street first to check out all motels before I picked the one most appealing, or where the price was right. Here, I passed three or four places, and I saw another one at the southern end of town. Right before I reached this last motel, I strolled by an arts gallery with wood-carved brown bears, furniture, and a nice display of jewelry. As so often my backpack started the conversation. "Hey, is that heavy?" asked a Viking-like appearance with long blond hair, who could well have jumped right out of an Arnold Schwarzenegger movie about a fantasy warrior in ancient times. I said, "Well I am sure you could carry it. You must be the Paul Bunyan here, is this your woodwork?" "Yes, I am responsible for the coarse stuff," he said, "my wife does the filigree." It didn't take long until after a quick tour through the gallery I was asked to sit down, have a cup of coffee, and talk about my travels.

Victorina and Robert called their place the 'Art From The Heart Gallery' and meeting them I saw their hearts brimful with arts and wide open for people. While Robert was a full-blooded Californian from Torrance, Victorina resembled the modern globo-mix with one side coming from a German-Dutch family and the other one being Indonesian-Chinese. Therefore her collection of fine art jewelry and interior design comprised both local Native American and Indonesian style. Robert was a sophisticated wood carver, his work ranged from decorative nature-related items like the bears, owls, or eagles to home-living designs, furniture, kitchen or, on special request, a bed frame or a wooden bridge for your personal garden pond.

In an hour talking, I had taken them down to the Colorado and up to White Mountain. In the meantime my pack had disappeared, and I think it was

Robert who took it to the house behind the gallery. "That shall be the hiker's night lodging", he said, "we will gear up and move to our fifth-wheel trailer," and they were adamant about it.

I was aglow with happiness and beamed to myself with a little pride. It was hard to believe, I just walked into a new town, met a century-man who honored me, and a few moments later, I was invited by a nice couple to recover from what might have sound to them like the forty days in the desert – actually it was forty, or a little more. Although I hadn't been tempted there, here I was handsomely rewarded. I thought to myself, I'd check my backpack if there was a sticker on it saying 'Please Love Me'. Besides walking with a backpack, I can think of only one other way of making friends just like that, that is walking a cute little puppy.

One of the things that interested me about Colin's trip was the fact that he did not decide to give himself over to pure wilderness hiking, avoiding any sign of civilization. I found it interesting how he constantly mixed nature and solitude with meeting the people who lived around or in it, and also with the history our ancestors had left. My earlier hikes had mostly led me into pristine wilderness where you wouldn't encounter a human being before the trip was over. This was the first time I did not walk away from other people, quite the opposite, I enjoyed the idea of walking into small towns or just campsites to see what others were doing there. Without exception, this decision was not only rewarded with great hospitality, and these moments were not only emotional highlights during the voyage; it became the logical completion of a wilderness hike on this planet, and I felt confirmed by the look in someone's eyes when I talked about my experiences. It was here that I discovered that the hospitality and the great interest of our fellow human beings made the possibilities of my trip into the unknown future so wonderful. Very often when I walked into a small town, I was a king for a day.

As we are part of nature, although some dyed-in-the-wool environmentalists do not see us that way anymore, we are also members of society, and I understood we can only get the whole picture when merging both.

When the two of them started to take the more valuable exhibits inside to close for the night, I rode the crest of the wave, crowning that day at Rossi's. I could hardly imagine a sharper contrast to my last weeks and a more luxurious reward, than indulging myself into a classy, old-established Italian cuisine. Piano player Steve took seat synchronistically with me, fondling the old saloon piano with Debussy, Beethoven, and Ravel. What a soft landing into civilization. The piano seemed to have a history too and was at least as established as the cooking. It was stuffed with sheet music, papers, and books. They lay on it, aside, underneath, and beside his feet. Piano classics, Beatles ballads, songs of the Wild West, ragtime, family songbook, Italian classics, and so on.

CHAPTER SIX

The Rossi family has been around the valley for generations. Here, they brought their rich traditions of their Italian and cowboy heritages together. When the Rossis themselves are present, the whole place becomes a living history lesson. In any case, it is a small family museum as you step back into their past by looking to the walls, which are crammed with authentic artifacts, photos, and tools. A walk to the bathroom could well turn into an interesting half-hour stroll, let alone if you're invited to visit the wine cellar.

Back at the table, food, wine, and music were so good, it wasn't before midnight when I asked for the check. Assuming my hosts would no longer be up, I went to the only saloon in town, 'E-J's Smokers' bastion since 2001', and played pool while talking about snakes in the desert and the highest mountain around. Along with the number of drinks, 'White' was gaining on 'Whitney', and when I left the bar late at night, we had found enough evidence to prove that HE is to be crowned.

05/10 – 11 BIG PINE, 0 MILES

My hosts let me sleep in. Had their dogs followed suit, I might have slept into late afternoon. When I entered the gallery to say hello, Victorina jumped up and showed me where the coffee was. Then she called for her husband and left, "We'll be back in fifteen minutes, watch the gallery, would you please?"

I was wondering if my presence gave them a chance to do, what running a retail store had made a rare pleasure. To my surprise they came back in less than fifteen, with their hands full of plates and glasses, hamburgers, potatoes, and salad.

After one day in their hands, I couldn't resist asking, if I might rest here a couple of nights. I was invited to stay until the end of my trip, if I wanted. In return I became responsible for leading half a dozen wood bears out of and into their overnight storage bin. No big deal for me, since I like animals per se. Besides replenishing my food, I spent most of the time around the gallery talking to them about the pros and cons of running an arts place on U.S. 395.

In the evening, while the bears were brought to sleep, dinner was prepared. When we met at the grill, Robert took our hands and said grace, blessing the food, a new friendship, and the second half of my journey. Then the feast started, we barbecued into the night and discussed the local history.

Nestled in alpine mountain scenery, between the High Sierra and the Inyo and White Mountains, the Owens Valley has always been my personal Arcadia. The relatively mild climate of the valley along with its friendly people and nice little towns is the perfect base for tours into the dramatically rising mountains, be it for hiking, fishing, or skiing. For lowland off-days there are numerous historic sites to explore, from the Alabama Hills to Mono Lake, or places to relax, like hot springs in the foothills, small lakes in the valley, or one good bar and a restaurant in each town. Besides the Pacific Highway 1, this most scenic part of California's highway 395 winding its way along Owens River surely is one of the country's dream roads.

Not so long ago, at the turn of the 19th century, Owens Valley was in fact a Garden of Eden, not only for visitors but also for the local ranchers and farmers. The soil was perfect and water streams in abundance. Some 5,000 settlers had made arrangements for a sound future, building an ingenious system of irrigation ditches and connecting washes and canals throughout the valley. It must have been an alpine idyll, blissful cattle grazing on the ranches and happy farmers harvesting fruits, alfalfa, corn, wheat, and making dairy products. However, the situation was too good to be true, or to remain undisturbed for long.

While the National Irrigation Association in D.C. still concluded that larger cities would develop where water was plentiful, in the same breath foretelling the valley a prosperous future, officials in the fast growing Los Angeles saw the signs of the time and did everything to desiccate Owens Valley's seed of hope by seizing its water sources. Behind the scenes, henchmen were snapping up the land for the city, county officials were taking the thirty pieces of silver, selling the valley's wealth and sacrificing its bright future to influential lobbies. Under the pretext of reclamation, the Los Angeles Department of Water and Power (LADWP) kept buying large pieces of land. Job-rotating between the agencies and authorities that dealt with water and land reclamation, former L.A. mayor Fred Eaton, his protégé William Mulholland, and water engineer Joseph B. Lippincott busily developed a plan to divert the Owens River watershed. By designing a truly remarkable engineering project, the Owens Valley aqueduct, they aimed at draining the creeks between Inyo and White Mountains on one side and the High Sierra on the other into the arid west. The geography was ideal. The whole area from its northern end to the Mojave Desert declined. There, water pressure would be high enough to lift the masses over a couple of lower barriers while tunnels took care of a few ranges. Hence no pumps were needed and even turbines could be operated to generate power at some places.

Word went around quickly and, before long, a speculation market was kicked off in areas that would benefit from the planned aqueduct. In fact, the planned acquisition had quadrupled the city's supply, and at that time the water was not intended for current needs. It was wanted for speculation and, if you will, for future growth, as LADWP head Mulholland remarked, "If we don't get the water, we won't need it." An early example of a speculation bubble; in this case it did not burst – it was overtaken by history, since the fast growing population of L.A. proved Mulholland's foresight to be true.

Some people see the reason why the valley did not become what the band of cities from Malibu to San Diego is today in exactly this story of betrayal and cronyism. Good or bad, the aqueduct project was pushed through, changing the course of Southern California's history by laying the foundations for one of the world's biggest megalopoleis at the expense of the valley's original prophesy.

All along Owens Valley, a system of diversion dams was constructed to collect water from the mountain streams. Once referred to as the 'Switzerland of California', the valley soon formed into desert with Owens Lake being the first dramatic casualty.

In the 1920s, the citizens of the valley began to protest, eventually starting sort of a guerilla war. However, dynamiting the aqueduct and redirecting water from the canals did not bring but a lot of David-Goliath sympathy. The skullduggery soon prevailed. Quite mysteriously, the local banks were closed, many farmers and workers in the valley left unpaid, and two of their more influential supporters went bankrupt. The valley economy was dust.

One wished, a Mulholland would have had a similar momentary insight as a McCulloch, "My God, what have I done?" But these circles were far from any disposition to hear the other party's case. The authorities had learned from the struggle and consequently bought the rest of the remaining private land. Soon, L.A. owned the water, the facilities, and the land.

Even though, in 1931, California lawmakers had passed the County-of-Origin statute, prioritizing local needs in areas where water was exported, two counties in the state were excluded. Hardly surprising, those were the two adjacent counties bordering Owens Valley, Inyo and Mono County. It didn't take long until one understood the lobbies' plan. After almost two decades of wet years, through the sudden drought of the 1930s, even more water was needed. Both the Colorado and Mono Lake were focused. With foresight, one Arthur Powell Davis had already withdrawn public land around Mono Lake from private settlement. His successor at the Reclamation Service, Elwood Mead, eventually realized the construction connecting the drainage systems.

The beautiful scenery is still there today, catering for a moderate but steady influx of tourism. However, ranches and farms are scarce, and Angelenos still seen with great suspicion. 'Los Angeles Sucks the Owens Valley Dry' was only one of an assortment of warfare-bumperstickers on local cars and buildings, indicating certain resentments. The historical background and its events still is a major subject when talking with locals. This kind of story can be heard at many places throughout the West. Since the first settlers had arrived along with farmers, ranchers, sheepherders, and miners, the fight for water had always been triggering crime and even local wars. By the way, the historical events of bribery and deception in this area became the inspiration for Polanski's 1974 movie *Chinatown*.

After decades of legal battle, only recently the court ruled that the city of Los Angeles had to return water into the sixty-mile stretch of Owens River. The Owens Lake, however, will remain lost forever. There is not much information available about the former salty lake, since it dried up so fast and way before anybody cared. It was probably similar to Mono Lake, hosting brine shrimp and alkali flies, nourishing a multitude of waterfowl. What we see today is a vast salt pan offering a large surface area for dust-collecting storms blowing into Owens Valley. Ongoing complaints by local people remained unheard, only when the lake dust began interfering with another powerful institution, the China Lake ordinance, the LADWP started considering dust mitigation and other measurements in fear of the courts. Today, we occasionally see the lakebed being sprinkled, a good sign a storm is gathering. Another plan is designed to plant solar panels across the lakebed as windbreaks, though there is doubt if the sensitive panels would stand the salt at all, let alone other, more aggressive minerals.

In order to avoid further environmental damage, the agency is now involved in several projects throughout the valley. If this is enough to stop the long-term trend of desertification remains to be seen. Some locals are skeptical and suggest sarcastically: "Flush twice! L.A. needs the water." Others just feel sorry for their crazy fellow citizens along the coast, since they all drank 'mad-cow water'.

05/12   BIG PINE, LAKE SABRINA, 5 MILES

Early in the morning, but not before I completed my equipment with angling gear, we wanted to go fishing at Lake Sabrina, from where I would enter the High Sierra. While Victorina and Robert were waiting at the bakery, I thought I would simply go into the store, buy a fishing rod with hooks and bait, and – two minutes later – leave. But, let me explain it this way; there are a few simple things in the world that can be discussed more thoroughly than the existence of dark matter. That includes the layout of mobile homes, barbecuing, and eventually the ordinary act of catching fish.

I was peppered with questions about where I would go and use it, if there were lakes or creeks, if I knew the elevation, and what bait I normally used. He wanted to know how long I would stay, what fish I eat, and how. I asked if he needed the color of my clothes too and received a deadpan "Why?"

I was told where to stand along the creek, what I must do and – more important – what I mustn't do. From the credo swinging in his voice, what I set out to do was a matter of life and death. I thought so too, but more for the fish. I simply thought it would be fun, making for a nice change in my outdoor cuisine. I am not quite sure if all questions were conducive to equip me properly or more for a multi-target armament, but I was ready to submit a statement, attaching my CV and medical history.

CHAPTER SIX

Some 30 minutes later, I left the store with a rod, hooks, and salmon eggs as bait and I was eager to find out whether time and money invested would simply raise the average price of calculated outdoor meals or if I would really be able to include the new resource in future planning.

We had a wonderful day at a small creek flowing into the still frozen Lake Sabrina and caught enough trout to make my first two dinners along Piute Canyon and theirs at home. To be honest, *they* caught enough fish. I had some ten near the hook, examining and eyeballing the barbed metal and bubbling up to me: "A big red salmon egg this time of the year? How stupid do you think we are?" They took the bait and left me wondering. Beginner's bad luck, I thought, probably they picked up the virgin smell of my gear and knew they were confronted with a freshman. Higher in the mountains, I hoped, I would gain more experience and my gear lose that smell.

Or maybe I found another excuse, a flimsy one, admittedly: fake fish. According to California fish and game laws, the LADWP had two obligations regarding its water-tapping projects: first, dams had to be built with fishways, that is, passage canals around them. Second, all dams had to let enough water pass to maintain a healthy fish population beyond them. No big deal for the LADWP, they got around the first condition by building large fish hatcheries, thus providing for a healthy population. Especially in summer, when the fishermen wake up from hibernation, fish trucks can be seen delivering the natural freight to popular fishing waters. Funny to think that sportsmen leave the valleys to catch fish high and remote in the silence of pristine mountain waters, fish that have been brought there by noisy, polluting trucks from the same valley the men came from.

The other condition, by the way, was circumvented much easier. That-time Fish and Game chairman Nate Milnor simply signed an agreement that let the city off the hook, claiming this exception as a part of the likewise exceptional hatchery deal.

Just when I said, it's time to leave now, it started snowing. I felt a hankering to go back with them, back to the warm and cozy home. I felt their worries about letting me walk into my destiny, but we all knew that I had to move on. In a little more than one week I wanted to be in Mammoth to meet my second companion, and between her and now lay four passes and ninety miles of High Sierra.

When I closed my pack with the trout wrapped in foil on top, Robert began rummaging in his fishing bag. Eventually, he pulled out a nice fillet knife in a handcrafted leather sheath and put it in my pack. I remembered, when they spoke about someone's birthday, a wedding, or just about doing someone a favor, they would say: "Let's see if we find something meaningful to us for him." This was their way of making presents, and I knew that this knife had a special meaning to him.

I thanked them again for their hospitality, for their art and their hearts, then I walked off into the woods toward Piute Creek. While we waved goodbye, the snow became thicker and I lost sight of them as if someone decreased the resolution of the picture I left behind. After five minutes, the snowflakes were forming an opaque curtain, separating me from the comforts and conveniences I was just getting accustomed to. For three miles, I followed an ascending forest road to North Lake where I hit the Piute Trail. It was too late to move on any further, and anyway, with the low hanging clouds, the weather was too unpredictable, so I stayed at the lake campground to wait for the next day. On my way up, occasionally, the snow clouds dispersed, allowing an intermittent view to the opposing range of White Mountain. It was a strange feeling seeing him again from up here. Although he was far away and seeming rather innocuous, the sight evoked the hardships one could face in the mountains this time of the year, and I remembered how he challenged me, in the night at the lone pine, or by the endlessly winding road covered with snowdrifts and *nieve penitentes*.

Despite the scientists' presence, Colin had felt it was 'his' mountain for the time he was there. I never established any kind of closer relationship with the White Mountain, I just developed a lot of respect and, after all, I thought that we were carved out of the same rock. But now the whole range seemed to be snowed in again and a deep apprehension about the coming days in the High Sierra resounded through the cloudy window. Without the three-week timeout Colin had taken, I was quite unsure about my departure into the Sierra.

Colin did not write much about the stretch between White Mountain and the ghost town of Bodie. Also, there weren't any maps left from this part of his journey. I only saw more recent ones, where he had marked camps and routes through the Sierra. That might relate to a trip he did later, but anyway, I thought, a trans-California walk without having crossed the High Sierra would be like driving down the coast on 101, instead of Highway 1, or, to give a European version, visiting Rome without seeing the Pantheon. So I took the liberty to complete the part he skipped. The chapter he called *In High Sierra* actually covers the lower part of the Northern Sierra. Therefore, I decided to complete his lost route between the college and the ghost town right here, where the Sierra Nevada assembled some of its highest ranges.

Unusual for the area, I considered building up my tent, in case it would snow heavier or snow would turn into rain. And I knew, it all depended on how I would wake up the next morning, how much snow I would see at this early elevation of 9,345 feet.

05/13   NORTH LAKE, PIUTE TRAIL, 12 MILES

What a wonderful blue-sky morning. I was happily surprised. The sun was touching the pine crowns while the little North Fork of Bishop Creek fought its way around freezing point. Bustling squirrels everywhere, going crazy for considering me as the first visitor who should kindly open crumbs season. Tiny hailstones lay around, where the treetops had let them through; the night frost had kept them in shape. But there wasn't more snow. I lowered my backpack down from the pine, where I had hauled the whole thing the night before. I had been too tired to unpack food and kitchenware and anyway, with the fresh fish, for a bear everything down to my socks had smelled like a nice midnight snack.

With breakfast I studied the maps I would need for the five- to seven-day trip to Mammoth. I was checking the whole area far beyond the actually planned route to look for possible exit routes to lower elevations in case something went wrong.

There were four passes around 11,000 feet and most of the distance I would walk above 9,000'. Piute Pass, Selden Pass, Silver Pass, and Mammoth Pass, sonorous names, of which any one, I was aware, could be the one impassable, the one forcing me to turn around or wait for spring. Emergency exits? Not really, if I would not put up with long detours lasting several more days. I checked my food supply; I had nine full meals and the fish. Even if on a strenuous day I had two, and as the budding fisherman I was, I should be fine.

After one mile, I walked on snow three feet deep, sometimes in and every so often almost under it. Hiking trails? Far from it. From now on, I would blaze the trail. My map suggested to stay between the two ridges, west-northwest for four miles, and pass a chain of frozen lakes to my left. The only lake I actually saw was the largest, Piute Lake at 11,000'; the smaller ones were totally covered with snow and not identifiable anymore. About half a mile from the end of the lake mounted a steep snow wall, Piute Pass, as if someone had hauled up a white drawbridge to deny access to Snow White's castle behind it. Instead of walking the frozen slope, I preferred to climb up almost vertical rocks to its right. When I reached the rim, I was already above the pass at 11,500' and had to climb the edge back down to it.

It took me five hours to do five miles; and looking down to the other side, there was snow as far as the eye could see. My mind ordered walk back – you're never going to make it to Mammoth, at least not in time. But my heart was already beguiled by mere beauty, bewitched by the winter wonderland. It was an amazing view, both backwards down the valley I came from and westwards into Piute Canyon. Bordering to the south lay Sequoia and Kings Canyon Parks, to the north John Muir and Ansel Adams Wildernesses. I stood in the epicenter of the Sierra's natural beauty, my body in a high magnitude quake of feelings. Nowhere else had I been torn so much between take it or leave it, because of the struggle with now 65 pounds in deep snow on one side, and because of the sleeping beauty, the peaceful land before me on the other. Mind and heart, let's stick together, I ordered, and try another stage, seven more miles to the Hutchinson Meadows.

Six of those I walked on snow. After the first half at around 10,400', I reached the tree line and a thickening forest providing for a hard snow surface or even, where the trees were really dense, no snow at all. Here and there I cheered "found a trail" – most often too early, and it turned out to be a dry creek bed or just a drain of a snowfield. I always tried to follow it and hoped it would change its inclination at some point, from downhill to uphill or vice versa. Then I could be sure it was the trail, as long as even in wonderland water does not flow uphill. It was a small celebration every time, a motivating achievement that meant nothing more than I found my way.

More and more creeks came running down from the mountains surrounding me. Smaller ones got lost in the snow masses, bigger ones I had to cross and some even turned into waterfalls, confronting me with a new problem. With the days getting longer and warmer, I realized this could mean a new threat and obstacle on my way, especially if I had to change sides. What would I do if one side of the river turned out to be impassable but the river itself too? I had to admit, I had no answer to that, however, the longer I have been out in the wilderness the more I trusted in my ability to find a passage somewhere, somehow.

From its unique form, I identified Pilot Knob on my map matching the peak to my right. Behind this mountain, French Canyon would open out into a delta of falls eventually flowing into Piute Creek. About ten times, I had to find appropriate spots to cross the disarrangement of the delta, usually over trunks of fallen trees. In the meadows thereafter, I finally came to rest.

So far my hike has been a chain of events that started as challenges, turned into adventures and in the end into unforeseeable natural or emotional highlights. The constant alteration of being worried and filled with awe had an effect like a natural amphetamine, a stimulant for the ego, a drug for the senses.

All these highlights had one thing in common; you could never experience the reward without rising to the challenge and without living the adventure, sometimes it was even indispensable to be in fear of what you were facing. The art of pioneering and the crucial part was to see the red light and to find the thin line between growing with challenges and overestimating one's own capabilities. As long as you are on it and balanced, you discover the hidden treasures of nature as well as a whole lot about yourself, both of which, without rising to the occasion, may elude the hesitant. In times where our lives and circumstances depend to an increasing degree on other people, here we have a rare chance to enjoy and exercise ourselves in self-sufficiency and self-reliance, finding out how far we can go by ourselves, when nothing and no one is around, that is, when you are alone.

CHAPTER SIX

Here, the thin line for me was to realize early enough when I had to give up and return. Hence the personal challenge was not so much focused on the ninety miles to Mammoth but on mastering the first half. Only when I reached the point of no return, after which giving up would mean even more hardships, apart from the psychological factor, my conscience would be relieved from the constant doubt.

05/14   HUTCHINSON MEADOW, PIUTE CREEK, 14 MILES

After a long campfire session in the snow, I had fallen asleep leaning to a fallen tree. I woke up in the middle of the night, my eyes burning like fire. They hurt so much that I couldn't open them, as if I had got a load of pepper spray. I stood up and tried to reach for water, but even though it was dark, every blink turned into horrible pains. Cursing and screaming I laid my head down and pressed a shirt on my eyes. I became scared and afraid I might have caught a rare exotic infection, I might even go blind. Maybe I was snow-blind; in fact my eyes had been exposed to sun and snow most of the day. Or it was the smothering smoke since I had been at the fire until late and, as usual, the wind had kept blowing the smoke to where I was sitting. Maybe it was everything together. What would I do if I could not see well, read the map and find my way out of here? Would I find my way back somehow, if I had to feel it back? I never thought of something like that. Rattlesnakes, black widows, mountain lion, a broken leg, or lost in the wild with no direction; everything was fine, somehow, as long as you could see what was going on. But the possibility to go blind was a horrible surprise I never took into consideration.

The pain forbade any further attempt to open my eyes. I had no other choice but trying to sleep, remain calm and hoping that tear fluid would wash out whatever it was. Between hope and despair, I dozed off until the sun warmed my sleeping bag. When I woke up, I kept my eyes closed. Although I couldn't feel much pain anymore, I was afraid I might have to realize a major damage to my vision, not to think the worst. After a while, I dared to put my hands on my face to open one eye just a little bit. But I shied away, just as if the sun were right in front of my face. I tried it again, covering my face under the sleeping bag. There, I was able to open them a slit and blink around. Minute after minute, I opened them a little more and a while longer. After half an hour, I was able to stand up and find my way to a passable spot at the creek. I kneeled down and washed them, again and again. They felt like having a muscle ache, but I could finally see again and the pain slowly diminished.

 It was a horrible night and I was worried sick. I later learned it was in fact the mixture of permanent sun and snow glare exposure and particles from the smoke that badly affected my eyes resulting in temporary loss of vision.

It was the first time on my journey that I thought I escaped by the skin of my teeth, or, my eyes.

The walk through Piute Canyon was uncomplicated. As soon as I got below 9,000 feet, I was back on a trail. I had to cover some seven miles through pine forest and isolated redwoods. Many small creeks and lime green meadows were inviting places for a break, a quick coffee or for lunch. Where Piute Creek flows into the larger south fork of San Joaquin, my path met the more established John Muir Trail, which coincides with the Pacific Crest here. Until after Silver Pass, I would walk on it, which was somehow comforting since I expected the better-known hiking trails to be more noticeable or even marked with signposts on junctions and difficult spots.

In the afternoon, I was leaving the meadows at 8,000' facing a steep climb of almost 3,000 feet over seven miles to Selden Pass. It started with a three-mile zigzag through red-barked Manzanita brush, because of its weird twisted growing another plant referred to as driftwood, in this case mountain driftwood.

Being on a southward slope for some time, I could walk snow-free trails until I had to cross a couple of meltwater creeks running down from Mount Senger. Here the idleness was over, thick snow covering the forest floor took every sign of John Muir or the Pacific Crest. In a forest where you can't see farther than fifty yards, it was almost impossible to navigate with the compass. There were too many hills and snowdrifts I had to bypass. If you start correcting all these detours, you end up making notes more than walking. It was better to follow the elevation lines in my map or climb at right angles to them. I knew, if I missed the Sallie Keyes Lakes at the foot of the pass only by some hundred yards, I would not even see them nor would I be able to find a direct passage to the pass. Looking at the map again, I realized that Selden Pass really was the only way over a long range of 12,000ers. So I had to find the first small, snow-covered lake, walk around it on its left side and find a passage over a narrow land bridge between the two lakes, without stepping aside and breaking into the ice.

Try to compare: you walk on a trail and reach your destination. You probably say something like "Phew, made it." or if you are a little more exuberant, "Okay!" with a melody. Now, you on your own, just knowing where your destination is, you set your own trail, use whatever you can, map, compass, elevation, sun, moon and stars, a tree's moss-side or leaning trees – GPS is cheating! If then, after many doubts and checks, you get exactly to where a trail would have taken you, I promise you scream or dance, and you kiss the ground. With the last daylight, around 8 o'clock I did so, reaching the shore of Sallie's first frozen lake.

From here, I could already see the pass floodlit by the moon and the best surprise was, there was hardly any snow. Having reached the lakes at 10,000 feet, I was above the tree line. A chilly wind was blowing down from the pass, but the south facing dolomite rocks warmed faster than soil and had already melted most of the snow.

I found a comfortable and windless place under a small ledge, right above the lake. When I went to look for firewood, I saw that I was not the only one to locate this spot. There were prints in the snow nearby which looked like those from a bigger cat, maybe a bobcat.

While the spaghetti was cooking, my shoes and socks drying over the fire, I studied my maps and thought of the other side; the northern slope would be quite different.

05/15 SALLY KEYES LAKE, 15 MILES

Just a quick coffee, I ruled. I wanted to reach the pass early to be back down at 9,000 feet before the sun would thaw the snow surface. One hour later, at eight sharp, I was standing on 10,860' Selden Pass, overlooking two valleys, southwards from Heart Lake and the Sallie Keyes down to the meadows along San Joaquin, northwards another chain of lakes above an equally fair and beautiful valley. Behind them lay the four recesses of the majestic Mono Divide.

I wished I had brought a pair of skiers or a snowboard. I never tried it with a pack like that on my back, but for sure I wouldn't have acted worse than sliding down on my soles. I always fell when I gained too much speed, but it turned into a half-mile fun slide down to Marie Lake, partly standing, partly sitting, or, when I really picked up speed, rolling and tumbling. A good distance from the first lake, I broke hard with my boots and walked around its western side until I reached a small outflowing creek. This would become the West Fork joining Bear Creek, my guideline for the next six miles. Somewhere underneath lay John Muir and Pacific Crest in peaceful hibernation. For orientation, the damped sound of Bear Creek was as good. Twice I saw a strange looking piece of wood on the snow, unnaturally even, like slats. I tried to pick one up, but it didn't move. I shoveled some snow with my hands and, when I realized what it was, I danced again. It was the top of a signpost marking a side trail to the Seven Gables Lakes. I was downright on the trail. The other sign was about a mile later directing to Hilgard Creek and Lake Italy. Both side trails were marked in my map saying: "not recommended for stock travel". I was wondering what that meant for human travel.

Eventually, I had to cross the creek to change sides, since the left turned into a cliffside. By now I was sure the trailmakers did not act on the assumption that someone was hiking here before late spring or until the spring runoff was over and most of the meltwater flown into the bays of the Pacific Ocean. With a late snowfall like this year and the following hot spring days, almost every little creek became a roaring torrent. When I found a somewhat adequate spot, I left my pack behind for a test run and shouldered only boots and pants.

Rolling on the rocks with ice-cold feet, wet to my shorts, I successfully delivered my clothes to the other side. It worked out once, so it would again, I thought, and walked back the same way. I did not want to lose time for warming my freezing feet, just wanted to get it over with. Facing the creek at the same spot, it looked much deeper, faster, and colder now with the pack on my back. I took a deep breath and paused for a moment, like a track and field athlete before his final heat. Then I stepped into the water, eyes riveted on flat stones and sandy spots, mind preoccupied with decisions about where to put the next foot down. I knew where the current was worst and tried to avoid getting close to large rocks. Pause and think after every successful step, while a step was completed only when the other leg has been pulled too, a stuck landing with both feet together. Now the deepest spot, two steps only before it got shallow again. You would think the flow of a creek is rather constant and unchanging, not like an ocean where the famous seventh wave is the big one. But one cold flush brought Heraclitus back in the game. For two seconds I was drowned to my hips; from infinite possibilities, I got the one *flux* with the monster wave. Don't move – concentrate, I ordered myself. If I tried to get away, I would definitely slip and swim away. Three more deliberate steps and I could reach out for some roots and pull ashore.

After all, I had spent one hour with looking for the right spot, checking every rock over and over again and doing three crossings. Another hour passed for making a fire on the other side to warm my feet and have lunch.

In the afternoon, I reached the offshoots of the Bear Ridge, where its draining creek bent to the westward rising mountains. According to my map, I had to climb up the ridge some 1,000 feet, then down a steep escarpment to where my next night camp would be, Lake Thomas A. Edison. Again the ascent was almost snow free, while, as soon as I had reached the top, the other side still lay in the deepest of winter. There, wherever the snow could fall through the trees, three-foot-high mounds piled up, whereas around the stems and under their raiment of fir branches there was hardly any. I walked up and down these mounds trying to stay on a straight line heading northeast. When suddenly the forest before me plunged down almost vertically, I knew that I had arrived at that point where my map showed a narrow zigzag line, symbolizing countless switchbacks. The actual trail might even go down as stairs here, the elevation lines were so close together I could hardly distinguish them. In half a mile I scaled down 1,600 feet and I ended up climbing down jumbo rocks until I got jammed between two. Helpless like a beetle on its back, I was hanging ten feet above the ground and waving my legs. I cannot remember – and I don't want to – how long it took me to unstrap the backpack, jump out of my bondage gear, or was it falling, and climb back up to pull the pack out of its trap. The whole slope was muddy from melting snow, and most rocks were wrapped in a slick coat of soaking moss. "Where are you?" I thought I heard my mother call. I didn't dare to look up – "Where are you, guys?" – or answer. The trail behind the rusty gate had become a one-way now. She would have called me nuts and, this time, I had agreed with her. I didn't even allow myself to look to the evening-sun spectacle going on in the west, I knew I mustn't lose any more time and that I had to get down before it got dark. So I took the rope out of my pack and tightened it at the top strap, lowered the backpack from rock to rock or just let it slide down until it stopped on a ledge. Then, with the rope wrapped around my hand, I plunged down to the next tree, hoping it would break my fall. In one situation, the backpack slid off while I was skidding down on all fours. The sudden jolt pulled me so unexpectedly that I was drawn down until I was lucky to hug a tree. Tom and Jerry had nothing on me. "Where are you, son?" – "I am comiiiing mom." I called back. Soaking wet and dirty, I arrived at the lake some time later, just in time to see the sun setting fire to the horizon behind the trees.

The big lake accumulated a lot of driftwood, accordingly my campfire was again a bigger one that night. Fire rings and picnic tables suggested that the lake was a popular fishing place in summer. At my site, someone must have made arrangements for a longer stay; I found a large boulder, which was carved into a comfortable chair, almost a recliner seat.

After dinner, four shoes were dangling over the fire from a wooden tripod, my food sack was swayed by the wind in a tall Jeffrey pine. I sat in my rocking chair, studying maps and completing my log: "From now on, I am free to only think and move forward." I had reached the halfway point on my way across the Sierra; even if I decided to give in, I'd move forward. There was no chance for 'giving-up' anymore.

05/16   LAKE THOMAS A. EDISON, 13 MILES

I wouldn't say this is a beautiful lake. Like most man-made lakes that are formed by a dam, the shores look somehow devastated. All surrounding plants were chopped up to the lake's possibly highest level, framing the huge body of water with barren land, scalped rocks, and tree stumps. This one is owned by Southern California Edison Co., which completed construction of the dam in the fifties some four miles west and down the former Mono Creek bed.

Anyway, after eight weeks in the desert, any water resource seemed to come from the land of milk and honey. I would have loved to take a swim, but after dipping my feet in the water, I was content with just brushing my teeth and splashing some water in my face. I would have enough involuntary baths on my way, I thought, and curiously enough, it never felt that cold when I had to take it, struggling through one of the creeks. As soon as it would be voluntarily, the same water felt twenty degrees colder and it cost me quite an effort.

On the other lakeside should be the Mono Trail, paralleling the roaring Mono Creek, which flowed into the eastern end of the lake. According to my map, the John Muir Trail must meet that one about 1.4 miles upstream from here, assumably over an easier passage across the mountain torrent. As far as I could see, the creek bed was filled with large boulders making the fast flowing water turbulent and footing impossible.

On this side, the trail was not visible, and trees and brush along the creek became thicker. After thirty minutes I took off my pack, placed it on a noticeable boulder, and climbed along the creekside to find a fordable passage. However, it was too wide, big rocks everywhere with a current so strong that it daunted the most lion-hearted hiker. I saw only one possibility where two boulders as big as houses, one from the other side, one on mine, came close together. Beneath they forced the creek into a high-speed whitewater. I looked at the distance and vaguely remembered my personal best mark for long jump in high school, something between 15 and 16 feet, some 25 years ago. The two rocks lowered the bar to maybe ten feet and, without a backpack, I would have jumped right here. However, it must have been about the same time when I learned from that guy with the apple. I calculated; a gravitational force of 1,000 Newton, vaguely, tearing at my pack and my own weight, sounded pretty discouraging. I was afraid the curve would go down too soon having me closely examine the other rock, face-to-face and top down. For lack of alternatives, except swimming through the lake, I did consider a jump quite a while and I walked up and down like a caged tiger. But with the raging torrent below, the risk was just too high.

I had already given up, thought about walking back to the lake and started calculating how often I would have to cross it with one hand swimming and the other one holding my things above the water; or maybe tying two or three logs together and pull them behind with my pack on top. Thinking so, I looked up the creek again and I recognized a strange looking log, apparently lying over the creek. I moved a little farther up and around the next bend, the assumed log turned into steel, and eventually steel turned into a bridge.

It might sound unadventurous, but I appreciated the fact not having to swim through that ice-cold lake. I just had to run back, get my pack and walk over a steel footbridge, ten minutes later I was on the other side, thanks to Park Service. There couldn't have been a more reliable sign for being back on the trail. For three miles and 1,000 feet altitude difference, I enjoyed relaxed hiking with a mere two wet crossings of the North Fork. Then I began the steep ascent to Silver Pass, 2,000 feet in less than four miles, where John Muir again trailed away under the snow.

According to my map, I should follow Silver Pass Creek, but this one was hard to find. Occasionally, I heard it from beneath the snow, which immediately caused me to carefully step to the side to avoid breaking in. Suddenly, the clean, smooth snowfield was torn open like a terrible scar on the winter's skin. In dashing cascades, the swelling spring waters broke through the snow, creating chaos as far as their splashes could reach. Just like in a terrible wound where the fresh blood pulsates from the vein, incrusting as soon as it leaves the stream of blood, here the ice-cold water seemed to pound from the creek while the splashes froze in no time, building up thick ice crusts on rocks, roots, and on the branches of trees alongside the flow. The cascades were not very wide, though, just four or five boulders to cross, but on everything protruding from the creek lay a sparkling, slippery ice cap that forbid any further attempt. I climbed uphill along the creek through stands of white fir, paralleling the haphazardly snaking creek in order to find an easier spot to cross it. If I broke through the snow here, I could have ended up being trapped in a jumble of rocks and branches that had broken from the trees under the loads of ice – with my feet in the water, and my body buried in snow.

After laboring uphill for a while, I finally found some trees leaning over the cascades, high enough to be out of reach for splashing water. Still they were slick, but with my feet on one and the hands on another log, I slowly moved across the barrier. Minutes later the same situation, only here the bridging trees lay nearby.

I walked westwards until after little more than a mile I should turn north into an alpine valley. Entering a wide canyon that was flanked by two ranges well above 10,000 feet, I was sure I had found it.

After a while, I recognized I was walking just a few degrees too far north-northeast, not enough to think I entered the wrong canyon, but enough to keep me skeptical. When north-northeast became too much northeast, I stopped. I climbed the left range in order to oversee the valley before me. I compared the area with my map; everything seemed to be fine, the two ranges to my left and my right with an elevation of 11,000', the small creek in-between, and small lakes right before the end. The straight line between me and the end of the valley deviated only some five degrees from the map route. The pass was the horizon, a steep mountain saddle under a prominent high-rising peak. The longer I looked at it, the surer I was that John Muir would never have put this to a hiker, not even in summertime. The mountain to its right was most likely Mount Izaak Walton, named after 17th-century author of *The Complete Angler.* Checking my maps again and again, I began to realize I had turned off one valley too early and Walton had me hooked.

In order to keep the once reached altitude, along with my attitude, I walked around the range into the neighboring valley instead of going back down to where I had turned off. Clinging to the steep rim and scurrying from tree to tree, I suddenly heard a strange sound, like a soft, spherical voice. If there had been the slightest breeze, I would have ascribed it to the wind sweeping through the firs. But it was absolutely calm and, as long as men leave footprints in the snow, there was not a soul around. Saying that, who knows. While most mysteries I faced so far were resolved, sometimes banal like the ghosts from Marble Canyon, sometimes fascinating like the singing dunes or the snow pillars on White Mountain, no one could explain this phenomenon to me. Later on, Mojave-Phil's attempted explanation was slight temperature variation between the trees and the air, causing thermal fluctuation hence a light wind that would not be felt on the ground. However, for a slight variation the sound was far too acute, sometimes ear-piercing and, to my imagination, this theory was just too simple.

After circumventing the rim, I looked into the other valley, and I almost saw a reflection of the one before; only the lakes were a little larger and the pass looked more manageable, but now the direction was absolutely on par with my map.

Due to the unintended side trip, I lost valuable daytime. I had allowed the sun at least two more hours to thaw the bearing surface. Now, the last mile to Silver Pass would become the longest mile I ever walked. Due to the south exposure, the top layer of snow melted daily and at night it formed a thin crust of ice, just enough to carry the first step. As soon as I lifted the other leg, I constantly broke in. With each step I sank into two- to three-feet-deep snow. Every effort to straighten up left me facing the same situation again and again. 1,000 squats and 1,000 push-ups later I reached the pass, totally exhausted, spent, and – absolutely happy.

The views were as beautiful as on Selden Pass. Frozen lakes clustering below the pass on both sides, fir strips vesting their outlet streams between the claws of the ranges that reached out until a faraway formation was forming another day's horizon. Here, right below the pass, lay four lakes – no more than ponds, really. Under a canopy of a glittering sheet of ice, the first drained into the second, the second into the third, the third into the last, from where the outlet stream would guide the way into the next valley.

Some basics from the desert were still valid. The sun forced you to observe certain rules here and there alike. In deserts, I avoided walking from high noon into the afternoon because of the heat. Here, by that time of the day, the sun had melted the snow surface making it impossible to get ahead remarkably. There, I was lucky to walk in the cooler shade of a mountain range, here, because the snow was still frozen. Larger southward slopes had to be done early in the morning. Wherever you could walk along northward sides, any time of the day was fine.

However, since summer came a-knocking, even the northward fields started melting now and they wouldn't carry me much longer. When I left the pass, I tried a few careful steps on the snow. First it seemed to be hard enough to carry me, I did two steps, three and four, until after at least every five steps I ended up breaking through knee-deep, sometimes up to my bottom where only the backpack stopped a further dive. In between, I lay in the snow and felt like laughing and crying at the same time. I tried to keep my spirits up and said to me, "This was your last 11,000er, you almost made it! From now on, you will go hiking." Then I braced myself, tied everything together, closed all pockets, and let it go. Sliding around Warrior Lake and down to Squaw Lake, waving to Chief Lake and with my feet high in the air flying toward the Lake of the Lone Indian, I was wondering what had been going on up here, what hat caused such a powwow of lakes.

Being back on my feet, I crossed the last lake's outlet over an ice bridge and followed the creek that would later become Fish Creek. Here the forest became unusually dense; large stands of lodgepole and mountain hemlock made sure the snow would stay until early summer. I had two miles to make up my mind whether I wanted to change the route. Here would be the only possibility to cut short to Mammoth and continue with John Muir. But it would mean, after passing some frozen lakes, staying above 10,000 feet most of the time with another 10,800' pass. My planned route was much longer through Cascade Valley and along Fish Creek, but it came with lowlandish elevations between 6,300' and a ridiculous Mammoth Pass at 9,380'. I stayed on it; I was ready for lower elevations and taking it easy in lush meadows. Crossing the 'Powwow River', I looked forward to sunbathing on a sunny afternoon.

When I was back on the trail, I understood that the name Fish Creek played down what Cascade Valley frankly admitted. The creek, or one of its many tributaries, had to be crossed at least eight times. At one major crossing the trail ended abruptly at the riverbank, its continuation luring from the other side. At this time of the year, it was the kind of passage where you would want to ask for a ferryboat. But Park Service wasn't around that time. Shaking my head with wonder and disdain, I moved on to find a better passage. I came along several rapids until I eventually reached a spot where the creek was divided, flowing around an island of trees. This was my chance, half creek meant half power. Where the torrent rested in a little side pond, I took a first step. I sank into one-foot-deep mud, the water reached up to my hips and I almost lost my balance. The whole creek side was a swamp, however, I kept wading along until I found a couple of long pine logs fallen across, a natural bridge laid out by mere chance.

Having arrived at the other side, I had enough for the day and started a fire to dry clothes and shoes and cook. After the pack was hauled in a tree, I chose a thrilling jumbo rock as my bed for the night. Quite a noisy bed-rock, since it was leaning over the creek right above a loud waterfall.

How strange it is that we can sleep with some loud noises and we can't with others. It all depends on what we associate them with. There may be something deep inside of us that relates to times when we used to sleep at a running creek, with the ocean surf, or the penetrating sound of a mating cricket. On the other side, some of us, including me, love train whistles, and find it nostalgic to sleep close to a railway. What would drive other people out of their beds was for us a childhood dream coming true. Actually, most of this book has been written in Goffs, where the BNSF is running up to one hundred one- to two-mile-long trains a day, that is every twenty minutes. Approaching the town, every train whistles four times, long – long – short – long. You would think that with the first whistle you sit bolt upright in bed. Not me! If – after falling asleep – I heard it at all, it was more like a mother's 'sleep well', gently being whispered in my ears. The railroad company was constantly checking the tracks and some difficult switches there, preferably at night when there was less traffic, meaning a train came only every thirty minutes. So whenever a service car was around, the train whistled not only four but ten times, sometimes with additional greeting fusillades to the workers. And once in a while, when a coltish engineer was really enjoying his ride, he kept pulling the whistle for the whole crossing and even longer, adding enough safety time in between the whistles that you could hear the full echoes. In a clear and calm night, following this whole scene from the train's muted approach to its ride through town until it disappears in the distance may give you an idea of the amplitude of the desert.

Sometimes you thought, the train was running through your bedroom. But the only time the railroad company really woke me from my sleep was, when they began a major track construction and stopped all traffic in the middle of the night. I guess, after 31 minutes I was up and I felt immediately that something was missing, something was wrong. Imagine someone had suddenly stopped the waterfall beside which you slept.

I can hardly imagine someone who enjoys living with traffic, metros, or any machine-like noises. Constantly barking dogs can be a real nuisance, while the casual bark or howling invests the night with a nostalgic if not mystic touch. I do know people who cannot sleep in dead silence. They would get in serious trouble being out in a desert or on a mountain in a calm night. At home they usually sleep with the TV on. A friend of mine got increasingly mad about the modern-day program; he said that *they* – meaning the advertisers – built in hidden messages, which would infiltrate your mind while sleeping. He kicked the TV out of the house – Instead he let the tap run when he went to bed. And so the wheel is come full circle: I would have a problem with a dropping faucet, but I sleep like a log with my head above roaring falls.

CHAPTER SIX

05/17   FISH CREEK, FALLS, 15 MILES

Soon after breakfast, I passed a forest of redwood trees, not the highest but still another age-superlative, and I realized that the world's oldest and largest plant species decided to come together and spend their sunset years in the state of California. There were the largest and tallest trees from the Sequoia and Redwood families, the oldest trees from the Bristlecone clan, and the longest-living genealogical tree of the Creosotes. May mankind be so caring and sweeten the evening of their lives.

The element of the day was water again, even more than the day before. Fish Creek was flowing over, flooding the valley. The first two tributaries from Purple and Duck Lakes were for warming up. Reaching another crossing of Fish Creek, the name alone perplexed me, 'Second Crossing'. Needless to say, the trail went to the bank and ended where the waves devoured it, just like that. Without a warning, without a sign, it just forsook me. The water flowed fast and furious; rocks and cobbles threw faint shadows to the surface like of jumpy, agitated fish. The deep moving blue only suggested a depth anywhere between three feet and too deep. Had I entered the water here, I would have got a quick ride to meet the Saint Joaquin. But there were good reasons for a crossing right here. Ahead on this side of the river, large jumbo rocks soared above the creek. I checked them about a mile downstream, but they only took me higher and away from my route along the water. I came back, went another mile upstream but could not find a passage either.

All in all, I spent two hours running up and down the bank without remotely seeing a promising spot. Some hundred yards from the original crossing, I spotted several islands made of stones. I thought, perhaps I could wade through in stages, from pile to pile.

I put on my running shoes to keep the boots dry, put up the backpack and trusted my luck. It just couldn't end well; it was like one of those scenes in a fantasy movie, where the hero jumps from stone to stone, while behind him the earth beneath breaks open in a hellacious inferno. Only because the script instructs so, he will be successful. In real life it just can't work. I had no script, just a thick staff in my right, like Moses; but no, mine wasn't even good for walking. I trod on a big log almost reaching to the first pile of rocks. When I was halfway out, it began moving, first just a little bit. It seemed to wait on what I would do, moved again, a little bit more – I was still standing – then, all of a sudden, it drowned completely without a warning. I leaned on my staff, it broke. Holy Moses! And with a curse and a big splash, I jumped into the creek. Still on both feet, I reached for some water birch branches and by, a hair's breadth, I could avoid being drawn from the current. I grasped for two or three thicker branches and tried to pull myself out of the water, but the brush was so thick I couldn't even push myself up on the bank. Somehow I hung in there and I regretted not having put the camera on my tripod to release it now with the remote. No, my camera was in the backpack and this one threatened to pull me back into the water. Two hopeless minutes later, either I lost strength or one branch did, I forgot, and I fell back with the pack, now completely drowned.

Then I made a quick decision, wet is wet, what was I waiting for. I turned to the creek and swam and waded, fought the rapids where I could, or let myself drift to where I was able to stand up again. In seconds it was over. I clambered the other bank and threw my pack down to open it and check the damage to technics and the sleeping bag. Everything else could dry in a day or two.

I should dedicate this chapter to the manufacturer supplying me with the backpack. Everything was dry, not a single wet spot inside, and – I swear – it really was a backpack for hiking, not for underwater exploration. Fortunately, I had formed a habit to always close all zippers well and tighten all straps. The fact that it was mainly a single bag system and that I had impregnated the zippers had helped a lot. I thanked Poseidon for waiving his claim to camera and photos and I hailed you backpack guys in Colorado; maybe you heard something.

Nevertheless, I had to start a quick fire to get my clothes and boots dry and myself warm. It was late in the afternoon, and the sun helped me only another two hours before the treetops would open the corridor for a sudden temperature fall to freezing point. I took the chance trying to get something from the creek. Thirty minutes later, I had two trout. While I cooked a pot of noodles, I could give proof whether I remembered Robert's lessons on how to prepare fish: "hold it in one hand with its bottom up, cut under the lower jaw, insert the knife in the belly bottom and slit the fish with a shallow cut from the anal fin to about one inch of the first cut; put your thumb around the first cut and hold it while pulling down all that is loose, guts and gills and blood lines. Then it's ready to be cooked and mixed with your noodles." If the taste had anything to do with the preparation, I had done my homework. Howsoever, the first self-caught fish always is the best you ever had.

The inept creek crossing, which had been my worst-case scenario for many days, only made me more venturous. In fact, I had been afraid that one creek could force me to walk back and take large detours. Now I felt confident, worst case I just had to find a passage without rapids and too much of a whirlpool and float with the current to the other side.

About a mile before Fish Creek would take a rough turn into the paralleling Fish Valley, my map suggested leaving Cascade Valley and climb over a 1,000-feet-higher range. On the other side I would follow Sharktooth Creek to its confluence with Fish Creek. Having climbed down, I struggled with a warm invitation from the Iva Bell Hot Springs, but I decided I had taken enough baths today, and I needed to get another crossing done before nightfall. So I continued following the creek's westward flow until it finally turned

CHAPTER SIX

south and away from my route. There, I would leave Fish Creek and walk north heading for Mammoth Lakes. On my map I saw a spot called Island Crossing, and it wasn't hard to guess when I had reached it. Here, the creek began meandering in two or three arms thus creating several islands. This time, I did it without running up and down the creekside in search of an easy ford. Instead, I walked straight into the brush, waded to the first island, swam to the second, and stalked to the other shore. Detecting a comfortable bridge some five minutes farther down the creek only cracked me up.

I reached the other side soaking wet, though I did not start a fire there; I just wanted to change clothes quickly and walk for another hour. When I started to take the wet clothes off, I was exposed to a sudden ambush of an airborne host of mosquitoes. I promise, you have never seen someone getting dressed that fast. In seconds I had my clothes back on, just before a thick cloud of them had deployed around me. With my hands full of gear, I ran away, the open backpack thrown over one shoulder.

There on the bridge, I thought, I could dress myself more thoroughly for, as everybody knows according to a country saying, 'there are no gnats or mosquitoes above running waters'. I guess they knew of it, too, and waited until I was fully undressed. Then a standing army of zzzzz-fighters was set in motion, and this was only the advance party. In less than two minutes, the grey haze was back surrounding me, and I would have needed hundreds of arms to drive them away.

I never really changed clothes, only jumped into a new pair of jeans and threw a long-sleeve over my t-shirt. I must have smashed some dozens between my skin and the clothes. When I undressed later at the campsite, I had bloodspots all over my body.

I ran quite a few minutes to get rid of them, but I couldn't really outrun all of them until I was back above 7,000 feet. One time, I dropped my map, which I had been using to fan them off my face. When I bent down to pick it up, they dive-bombed me in a split second. They seemed to be so ravenous that they even attacked each other causing frequent air traffic jams while fighting for their share.

The bridge theory is about as true as that all mosquitoes stay away from fire. Many years ago, at a campsite on the banks of the Yukon River – and I thought that was as bad as it could get – my travel companion Roland and I started a big campfire to keep the local state bird away from us. Instead it seemed that the fire attracted them. Before long, thousands of mosquitoes were cavorting in the hot smoke, high enough not to get burned, but circling in rhythmical ups and downs as if they were to prove their belligerence on a war dance ceremony. At irregular intervals, a stinging squad left the ecstatic ritual to savage us. But after all, ain't never seen nothing like the Fish Valley kind.

A couple of miles later, I could slow down again. Either I had left their territory by bending north and away from the creek or it was too late for these twilight creatures. I reached the tributaries of San Joaquin's Middle Fork with Crater Creek being the biggest. My map indicated I would have to ford some seven creeks flowing down the slope ahead. In that year's spring reality, though, the open slabs dotted with Western junipers had turned into a large thin fall with waters covering the whole slope. It just came from everywhere and it was too much for the existing creek beds.

Here I met the first hikers since I left the Mexican border. I came 700 miles through California without seeing a single fellow traveler. Those two, I heard long before I could see them, two men laughing out loud while building their tents on the last dry spot along the San Joaquin. It was so unreal to me that I sneaked up on their campsite. After watching them for a while, I got up and became noticeable, greeting them and asking where they were heading that early in the year.

They said, they had left Reds Meadow, some six miles closer to Mammoth, in the morning and that they were heading to the hot springs I passed earlier that day. From there, they intended to go on an alpine fishing tour. I told them about the situation and looked in four eyes wide open. I guessed they would spent more time at the hot springs than at any lake, let alone with a hook in a lake.

I continued to walk another mile or two with the full moon. Since it was hard to find a dry spot on these slabs, I began collecting every dry piece of wood until my arms were full. Eventually, I found the bald head of a protruding jumbo rock, the only place where the water masses had to give way. I hauled my pack and the wood on it and arranged this exquisite loft for the night, no more than five square yards for my bed, a place to sit, and a small campfire. Here, the mosquitoes had not heard of the fire theory – they didn't scoff at it – and it helped to keep them at a distance. To my left and to my right, the waters of Crater Creek were washing around the rock on their anarchical move into San Joaquin Valley.

05/18   CRATER CREEK, 14 MILES

In that night on the dome, I caught a strange new smell. First, I put it on the campfire, but about half a mile later, I knew better. Looking north beyond the last tall Jeffrey pines, I saw a blackened landscape. Here, the world was still in full color; there, a sad and bizarre black-and-white scene. After six years of drought, in August 1992, lightning had ignited the so-called Rainbow Fire, which burned almost 10,000 acres west of Mammoth. It became one of the worst in the Sierra's history. The combination of dense forest vegetation, a long drought, and high winds after the ignition resulted in its fast spreading.

CHAPTER SIX

On the first day, 6,000 acres burned down, 8,000 in the first two weeks. The fire took 80% of the trees in nearby Devil's Postpile Monument, which is, as so many other natural places with bizarre structures, named after the bad guy. This one is a bizarre and breathtaking geological formation of columnar basalt, giving you a hard time to understand how such structures could come into existence.

Isn't it strange that we tended to name formations we could not explain, such as the *Golf Course* or this *Postpile* after the Devil, instead of the Creator? It might have been our kind of a frivolous way of showing respect for the creativeness of nature, along with an inner conviction that there actually is no such thing as the Devil. Here, and during the conflagration, I thought, one might have been disabused; I tried to imagine this place when everything was on fire and I remembered that quote from the movie *The Usual Suspects*: "The greatest trick the Devil ever pulled was convincing the world he didn't exist."

Due to the substantial overstory burning, an unusually high amount of taller trees had been killed, depriving the seed source for a quicker forest recovery. Sixteen years later, the area still looked as if it has just happened. What I believed to smell was not so much charred trees but the absence of anything living that could smell.

Ironically, it was here where I left John Muir's to enter Ansel Adams' Wilderness, a monochrome world. Passing the half-burned sign with his name on it was almost symbolic. Even his majestic Jeffrey pines had burst into flames, leaving the tallest standing memorials of the Rainbow Fire, some twenty-foot-high black totems. The *Ansel* had fallen down. I picked the charred piece of wood that bore his forename up and put it back to the dangling *Adams*.

Without a forest cover, the sun burned like fire. I had an unpleasant feeling walking over this scorched earth. It felt like a breeze would be enough to rekindle the smoldering ground. Maybe it was the bleak atmosphere, the wounded earth, that caused me to feel all kinds of little ailments. My back said, enough, my knees were stiff, and my stomach upset. On my palate burned a permanent aftertaste from the water tablets and drops I used in order to protect from bacteria, mainly giardia. If the nasty larvae got me, it would cause diarrhea and nausea, which would most likely force me to shortcut to the next drugstore, if not a hospital. It is one of the few downers when hiking that even in the remotest wilderness areas it is recommended to purify your drinking water. After one week you establish a permanent chlorine taste upsetting your stomach. Eventually, you leave it off, when you think the spring water looks clean. Of course this is a false conclusion, but on the other side, why go to paradise if you can't eat apples.

Two hours later I arrived at an accumulation of signposts, showing various trails to the Devil's Postpile, Rainbow Falls, and to a campground with buildings, stables, and a kiosk, all of them still closed. With the post-fire coulisse and being off season, this market place of tourist attractions appeared like a long abandoned ghost town.

It was the week before Memorial Day; winter was duly in retreat, and the aftermath of heavy snow masses and a harsh winter weather became visible everywhere along the access trails, bent handrails, a broken roof above an information stand, a collapsed shelter, washed-out trails. The corrals, the stables and the cabins shook off the snowy sheathing, a mob of young deer seemed to enjoy the peaceful spring air before another stampede of vacationers would open the summer season for hiking, fishing, rafting, and horse-riding.

Park Service had not shown up yet to get the infrastructure ready for the coming masses of visitors, however, the falls are always ready and open, dropping the San Joaquin one hundred feet below and living up to their name. I saw three rainbows wafting one upon the other, painted on the spume by the sun.

I had finally arrived at this one of Carroll Thomas' favorite spots in the Sierra. Everything looked exactly like I saw it on his painting, everything but the awestruck man on a horse he added in the bottom right-hand corner to express his own amazement. Standing at the same spot, I thought, I was a worthy successor. Here, I saw that with his art Thomas created a benchmark of natural and artistic character. Through his style he simplifies the visual without taking away content, without diminishing the enchantment. Here at the falls, for his 100th birthday, he should receive a marker picturing his unique painting and commemorating his work and life for nature.

Climbing back up above the rainbows, I faced the last challenge of the Sierra, a minor one as I thought. Only Mammoth Pass lay between now and then, between purified water and another rest with culinary delights. Only one pass at just 9,400 feet. Full of vim and vigor, I took the steep grade behind the stables. The first half-mile was charred, but then a dense forest of hemlock and lodgepole brought color back to my trail, brown and green and, unfortunately, with increasing elevation way too much white. Due to the forest cover, the snow could stay here until June. Since that last mountain was more like a large mound, elevation change was not really distinctive; instead the snow piles between the trees were much more. Every twenty feet, you had to walk down and up again, from pile to pile, and when you were up on the snow you broke into it again, and again. Of course, from here I couldn't do much wrong; just by heading straight east, sooner or later I would hit one of many Mammoth's lakes and eventually see the town from up there. However, the forest cover blocked the view down to the lakes, hence making orientation difficult, how far I had come or if I was in fact aiming at the lakes. If I walked only a little too far northwards, the other side would get too steep; or too far southwards, I would have to walk around the lakes and need much more time, maybe even another day.

CHAPTER SIX

Quite unexpectedly, this last little piece of trail with an elevation that was far from the ones before became the ultimate test for me. The problem was, I was already done with hiking, thinking from the falls it would be a leisurely stroll to town. It was quite the opposite and, although the snow was still three feet from around the pass to one foot at Horseshoe Lake, where the road to Mammoth began, it became more a psychological walk than anything else. I just didn't reckon with another arctic barrier and with the amount of time it would take me to cross it.

No summit, no pass, and no canyon saw me that desperate as Mammoth Pass, only because I was too rash, because I already imagined myself being on the other side of the mountain, sipping a tasty drink in a restaurant. I had no idea how high a mountain may grow if you fail to show proper respect for it, if you do not take it serious.

After all these 11,000ers, where I had been alone in a big pot of ice and water and fifty miles away from any civilization, it was here for the first time that my mind wanted to give up, three miles from one of California's most visited recreation destinations.

I have often been asked about how was it with my energy, my physical condition. "Didn't you want to give up sometimes?" As a matter of fact, after the 'snake inquiry' and yet before 'What do you think?' and 'Didn't you feel lonely?', this is the second most common concern. My answer always is a straight no, simply because you just don't have another choice. You have to move on, or how do you want to stop – or give up – in the middle of the wilderness? Body or muscles might have suggested giving up here or there, but the mind was fueling them to proceed, two or three times to the extremes. Yet I am sure, there would still have been more physical emergency resources that I was lucky I never had to resort to. But I tend to forget about my despair at Mammoth Pass; there it was contrariwise. Here, I did not want to move anymore, fell down in the snow like a sullen child who did not get his way. Embarrassing, it was the body that urged me to stand up, saying don't be childish and get me what you promised – before I, too, cannot move on.

During all that, I had no idea if I already reached the highest point. Due to the wet snow I constantly broke in, and with frequent and longer breaks, I just schlepped from tree to tree trying to avoid the snow piles. Down on my knees, while washing my face with snow to get out of this state of trance, I suddenly noticed a wooden panel lying on the white surface. I slipped over to it, removed half a foot of snow from around it and read: 'Mammoth Pass'. Imagine the childish smile on my face, now I got my way. I could hardly believe my eyes, I was absolutely right, right on the trail, or above it. This was the stimulus board I needed, the carrot for the donkey. It was a simple brittle sign, though it emerged as trail magic, an event best described by Bill Bryson in his Appalachian Trail travel memoir *A Walk in the Woods*: "There is a phenomenon called Trail Magic, known and spoken of with reverence by everyone who hikes a trail, which holds that often when things look darkest some little piece of serendipity comes along to put you back on a heavenly plane."

Reaching the lakes fell into mental obscurity. I vaguely remember warning signs around Horseshoe Lake for its rich volcanic gas activity, I think I saw anglers at Lake Mamie and Lake Mary, and maybe there were boats on the Twin Lakes. But I do remember that I was leaning against a tree in front of a supermarket in Mammoth, holding some longed-for treasures in my hands, a cup of coffee, one coke and one beer, ice cream, and a barrel of chocolate. When I had entered the market, I just couldn't make up my mind what I needed most, so I took it all.

I must have looked like Robinson Crusoe – I had almost finished my gourmet siesta, when a young man, Chuck Norris type, stopped right in front of me. Looking me over from hat to shoes, he asked: "Wanna have lunch?"

I would have done so anyway later, but getting out of the wild and being treated to a lunch invitation five minutes later, that was pretty serendipitous. I was definitely back in the game.

Three hours later, after having lunch, coffee, and dessert, Brian and I were still sitting in the restaurant. He said, his invitation was rather selfish, that he had lunchtime and thought I would look like someone who had a story to tell. You can be sure, I didn't mind playing the bard. We talked about the Sierra, the advantages of exercising yoga on a mountain and, less abstract, the meaning of life. Before we split, Brian drove me to the supermarket to get down-to-earth groceries for some days in town. Tomorrow I would meet my second travel companion and after the weekend I should have an interview with the Mammoth Times.

When I called Nathan from the Motel, for the first time I felt uneasy about his condition. While so far, it has mainly been me talking on the phone, simply because he didn't stop to ask questions, this time it was him who gave a detailed report. I must have swamped him by talking about my ups and downs, both geographically and mentally, as he suddenly cut me off. His last two weeks must have amounted to a medicinal roller coaster ride, on which the downers where endurable only by the ensuing uppers. For the last two days, he said, he was feeling better, and hearing from me would anyway be the best medicine at all. I was in bed at 8, however, not asleep before 3 a.m. I was too hyper too sleep, a little worried but also too exited to just call it a day.

05/19–25 MAMMOTH LAKES, 0 MILES

The motel I chose in Mammoth was, like maybe half of the places where I stayed at, run by a fellow citizen from Asia. In some cases, that involved not only certain language problems, but it also drew suspicious looks from the owners, first at me and the house on my back, then outside the office as if they were afraid more of my kind would be hiding there.

While processing my credit card, the man in Mammoth, too, kept looking out of the window, totally ignoring my attempt to start the usual check-in conversation like asking for local information from the weather to a restaurant recommendation to cultural events, or just a simple 'how are you'. After the wordless check-in, I turned around to leave the office, virtually feeling how he looked daggers at me. As I closed the door behind me, I saw him leaning forward from behind the counter and all of a sudden – I just picked up my backpack to bring it to the room – he came running for the door and I heard the first words out of his mouth: "You guys wanna camp here or what?" Maybe I did him wrong, ignoring him likewise now; had an American asked me the same thing, I would have laughed, assuming it was a joke.

However, I am sorry to say, I couldn't get rid of the impression that some of our Asian friends don't seem to be the least interested in their customers or their environment, some not even in the domestic language. I am not saying they aren't, at least it appears so. Maybe it's a cultural thing, different habits in dealing with fellow citizens. Some gestures may even be intended very friendly. However, if so, not many got through to me. The following morning, when I came back to the office to get me a second helping of coffee and biscuit, um, let's say a could-be-a-cinnamon-bun, a five-footer hiding behind the counter jumped up and yelled: "Not two, one only. More guest come!" I was sure he made his tally chart there; hey Mr. Tally-man, tally me buns, and I asked him to tally me off for the second night. Surpassing one of America's worst habits, the continental breakfast, by reducing an already meager service to hardly anything, or rationing it, was one thing. However, the tone took the biscuit and here, for the first time, I chose to switch places.

Along my way, I talked to many motel owners, and I understood that times were tough and everyone was struggling to reach an average occupancy that pays the bills. An American symbol has long been on the list of endangered species, the roadside motel, squeezed to the edge of the market by big motel chains. I cannot think of a more typical American doing than cruising down a highway. Due to its large distances, highway living and thereby getting to know the country became second nature to both many Americans and foreign visitors. The roadside motel has always been associated to living this part of the American dream. Its owners were people like you and me, sometimes peculiar, quite often weirdos. Everyone who ever cruised America's backroads will remember that kind of lady, sort of ridden hard and put away wet, who would show you the way to the room in her pajamas – early afternoon; or that kind of man you would take to your heels and run away from, if you saw him anywhere else but in a motel office. However, in my memory, they all enjoyed meeting people, talking to them and giving advice, very much, and sometimes too much of it. It's in the nature of their business, why on earth would you do it otherwise? Now, if one seems to like running that kind of business, and I could definitely get enthused about it myself, I wonder why one would not take over the heritage and present one's business in this light.

For the sake of completeness, the other half of the motels were run by North and South Americans – never met a European or a Mexican, and, surprisingly, not one African American running a motel; maybe someone can explain that to me. To all of you ladies and gentlemen, I enjoyed your hospitality and your dedication, you're (still) characters.

*

For one week, I stayed in the Mammoth area, taking it easy and refueling, meeting friends and bringing my travel journal up to date. On the second day, I would welcome my friend Sonja from Germany who would walk with me for two weeks from here to Bodie. We didn't have any contact since I had left Big Pine to cross the High Sierra – for anyone following my route from afar, the most daring venture of all – and now she was somewhere over the Atlantic Ocean, uncertain whether she would find me at the appointed place and time or if, after 24 hours waiting, she would have to start a search. Such was the deal.

As the meeting point we had chosen the ranger station since I would spend half the day there anyway to check further routes, their condition, and the weather. Waiting there on the next morning, I was getting so excited to tell her all the little stories from the first sixty days that I talked a mile a minute with the rangers, telling them one after the other how I managed to be here in Mammoth now, some of which was answered with raised eyebrows. I was just re-enacting the mountain lion encounter for the third time, when one of the rangers pointed to a person behind me. There she stood in the doorway, smiling at me as if she was ready to walk. We may have stood there for some minutes to celebrate the moment; from her vibrations I felt that seeing me here, obviously in the best of health, was a load off her mind.

I, for my part, was having some difficulties to awake from my juvenile boy scout world. In any case, I was overtaken, once again, by a kind of natural beauty I haven't seen in a while.

During the next days, we made friends with the Mammoth Times staff after we did the first of three articles about the walk. We met Victorina and Robert again and visited one of the festival highlights along U.S. 395, the Mule Days of Bishop, which is known as the 'Mule Packer Capital of the World'. On Memorial Day weekend, friends Utta, Bisser, and Giovanni came from Los

CHAPTER SIX

Angeles, their car stuffed with camping and barbecue things, their minds with a vague idea that I should introduce them to outdoor living. However, it was the more comfortable variant, where the household is not what you can carry on a back but as much as the capacity of a trunk. We had two entertaining barbecue days on a nearby campground with all kinds of meat, salad and fruits, potatoes and corn, cognac, wine, and beer. It was much more than you would normally eat but it seemed that this is what trunk-supported camping weekends are for. I felt that, with my routines, I would kill the party designated to evolve into an outdoor orgy. So after some well-meant attempts showing how to build a fire, what kind of wood we should use to start with and what, to receive embers, I quit and let everybody try it. My part was supposed to be telling stories. After a while, the fire fed from everything that could burn and along with steaks, sausages, and fish, my stories were grilled above the flames until they were suitable for consumption.

While the nights had clear sky, morning fog brought rain and drizzling days. I knew what this meant to higher elevations. By the time we wanted to continue the walk, it had been snowing there for three days. Winter was back again and about to destroy a long-nurtured dream of mine. Since my first visit to Yosemite, I had planned to hike to the Tuolumne Meadows, a dreamlike place in the eastern part of the National Park. From here, the hike would lead us along some of the most characteristic Sierra ranges, the Minarets and the Ritter Range, to Lyell Creek and to the meadows and several falls along the Tuolumne River. When I had seen this area for the first time, it was to me the ultimate pars pro toto, comprising every single aspect of the High Sierra between Kings Canyon and Yosemite.

To fulfill this dream, I planned to leave Colin's footsteps here, the only noteworthy deviation from his original route. Then, coming down from Tioga Pass, I wanted to meet him north of Mono Lake again. He would excuse my idea, I was sure, since I visited the lake basin already three times before. Furthermore, he was not very enthusiastic about that tract; that had another reason, but I will get to it further down.

In Mammoth, everybody had advised us against my plan, the ranger, Mammoth Times editor Diane Eagle and her colleague Patti Cole, and outfitters. Actually, perfect preconditions for an exciting adventure. However, by now all south slopes had snow from 9,000', the northern from 8,000', three to five feet deep. I checked maps again and again; there were two possible routes to get over the highest ranges, but I realized the path to that dream was not likely to be open for us. More than half of the distance to the Tuolumnes would be snow-covered and with four to six passes around 10,000' including one or two at 11 or 12,000', there would be too many risks. Although I would have been ready for more snow, I knew we shouldn't do it, not only because I was not alone anymore. This could just go beyond the scope of adventures.

05/26   MAMMOTH LAKES, 6 MILES

The next morning we set out for Minaret Summit. I had to see it with my own eyes, the tons of snow and obstacles I just wanted to get over with a week ago. Then I could put it off for another journey, or decide, yes we can.

Late at night we reached the summit. The difficulties began with finding a dry spot to sleep. After some warmer days before the return of the cold, now the soil was wet and half-frozen. The entertaining part of that night was hauling our food supplies into a tree. For a newbie this is often the first thing remembered, when talking about a trip years later. "You mean where we put the food sack in the tree?" is, among hikers, a commonly accepted exact description of a geographical place.

It took me half the night to start a fire. When it was finally burning, we were too tired and chilled to the bone to sit there any longer. One point goes to Colin's route. Two more will make our decision the following morning, the view into San Joaquin Valley and the Ritter Range – and my new partner's veto.

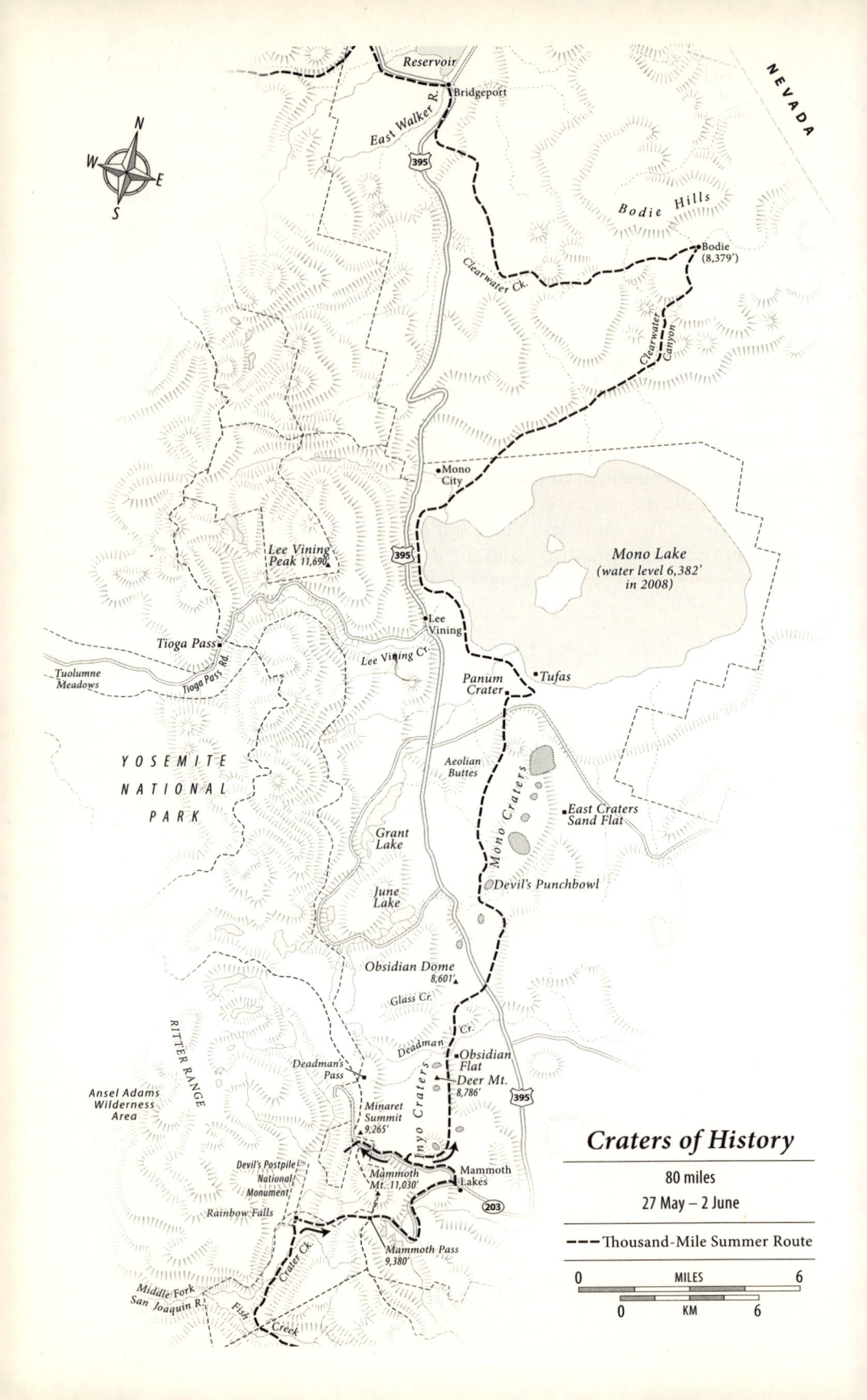

Craters of History

80 miles

27 May – 2 June

- - - - Thousand-Mile Summer Route

7. CRATERS OF HISTORY

*All the facts of natural history taken by themselves,
have no value, but are barren like a single sex.
But marry it to human history, and it is full of life.*

RALPH WALDO EMERSON, AMERICAN WRITER AND LECTURER, 1803–1882

I often heard America being blamed for having no history, its people were lacking culture or even worse, being ignorant about both, preferably brought forward by people whose countries had or still have kings and queens, thus accumulating a great deal of old stones in terms of castles, temples, and palaces.

On our way to one of the best-preserved places of recent American history, I had such a conversation with a group of visitors from Europe. They were doing a roundtrip through the Southwest, ticking off Disneyland, the Universal Studios, and Hollywood, and places like the Grand Canyon, Yosemite, Mono Lake, and the ghost town Bodie. Replying to their complaint that *they* don't seem to have any history or culture, I asked them how they managed to ignore it and if they really had not seen tracks of history on their way, or at least of American culture. The answer was a straight "In no way!"

It seemed useless to intensify the discussion. Maybe the definition of the words history and culture had to be construed more extensively for some people than I thought. How much history can a land have that has been founded a little more than 200 years ago, for the most part by European people who decided to start a new beginning? Exactly, a little more than 200 years, if we take into account only what one commonly tends to accept as civilized culture. If we added some 150 years for pre-constitutional exploration, another 600 for indigenous cultures known as Native Americans,

CHAPTER SEVEN

plus some 10,000 years for the archaic period, we are along with the earliest cultures in China, Asia Minor and way before the kings and queens, the pharaohs, philosophers, and Cesars.

As I saw it, not only California but all of North America is full of history, and just like in Europe, it can be seen everywhere, from pre-Columbian petroglyphs and pictographs to the relics of the American frontier. The people's roots are as rich and diversified as in Europe, plus remarkable influences by Native American and African people and to an increasing degree by Asians and Latin Americans.

If culture is the sum of history we preserve, what we learn from it and eventually form into habits we in turn cultivate, if it is also the sum of influences we allow or tolerate to broaden our mind's horizon and enrich our lifestyle, then the melting pot America could well be seen as one of the culturally richer and more diversified countries in the world. (If only living style would absorb more of these backgrounds and care for the influences, instead of wallowing in the common trend to generalize and standardize everything.)

In any case, I think it is not so important, how many archaeological excavations a country may file, how many Doric and Ionic columns one may find, but to know about one's roots and understand the course of historical events and the causal connections and developments. That is, *why* things happened much more than valuing it, because in passing our knowledge to the next generation, they will interpret it differently and our interpretation alike.

For example, in America's very own genre, the Western movie, one and the same historical figure has been portrayed pretty much diverse; depending on the current or popular view, from a ruthless outlaw to a romanticized desperado, or from a brutal and aggressive savage to an iconic, clear-sighted, Indian, who was defending his heritage. How can one come along at all, let alone form one's own opinion, without knowing some basics about the figure. Without backgrounds, one can only value or accept the default, but one cannot understand.

We also tend to pick certain aspects in our favor, as the case may be by either stretching the truth or embellishing a story or by omitting or misapplying certain parts. I remember my old history teacher telling us that epic story about the development of the national park idea in the 19th century. All of a sudden he got that solemn voice and he stood there like that trapper in my book about the Wild West, with both hands leaning onto his rifle, his eyes focused on something in the far distance, possibly vermin. Here in the classroom, he had his hands on his pointer stick and in the distant last row he was focusing on me because I failed to pay the appropriate attention. He placed himself right before me and began reciting this exemplary event, about a group of explorers and businessmen, who were determined to find new sources and riches in the unexplored West, furs, minerals, and land. Despite the inexhaustible resources they found, they clearly saw the real preciousness in the beauty of unfolding landscapes, the diversity of nature life, and a never before seen geology. Through reflection and foresight, they recognized a future need and became the knight in shining armor by creating the idea of protected wilderness. They could have staked claims and struck it rich, instead they went back to Washington, convinced the president to exempt this land from further exploration, and eventually their idea spread around the world. The National Park was born.

It's a wonderful story, especially the longer versions. It seemed that, every time he told it, we were informed about another romantic detail, like how they sat around a campfire or how they conferred with Indians. In other settings I heard of new characters being added, hazardous weather conditions, or rumors that they knew of treasures but never told anybody. Most of these details were not handed down but simply added by a euphoric storyteller, whereas an interesting and critical point of the matter is mostly omitted: originally, the plan of gating pristine and untamed nature aimed less at the protection of wildlife but at creating monumental sightseeing parks.

So again, without knowing much, we value, or turn prose into drama in order to create a stage adaption for people currently regarded as our heroes. A last example may be the colonization of North America; for some it is crucial to point out the Hunnish and ruthless way the frontier was driven across the continent, axing its forests, slaughtering buffaloes almost into extinction and likewise euthanizing its indigenous peoples. Others are inclined to excuse such behavior, stating that this had always happened in the history of man when peoples expanded, and that, in the long run, it was always the more *modern* concept that won through. (Q.E.D.)

Generally, in such compressed historical stages, when the conquest of a continent reached its zenith, there never was time for consideration or compromises. Wisdom often fell by the wayside, cautionary voices overheard. "Live long enough with an Indian and he or the wild things will show you a use for everything that grows in these borders." American writer Mary Austin once wrote.[*] However, too often *modernization* wouldn't allow taking 'enough' time. It always takes a few generations until we begin to review the past and work through it in a comprehensive manner.

---

[*] From *The Land Of Little Rain* (1903). In her writing, American author and playwright Mary Austin (1868–1934) described the living of the people and the flora and fauna of the Southwest. Based on a seventeen-year-long social study of Indian living, she appealed to understanding the culture and the spirituality of the Native people. Her most famous work was this account of the California desert. Austin was also involved in the Owens Valley water conflict. She co-authored a book with Ansel Adams and initiated the famous outdoor Forest Theater in Carmel-By-The-Sea.

CHAPTER SEVEN

Unsurprisingly, then, ideals our forefathers had fought become trendy, and we bemoan lost traditions and knowledge.

In hindsight, we realize that both views bear some truth. However, in order to learn from the past, it is necessary to gather historical facts and set them in the context of the respective time and its people.

Though the American history might lack some of the aspects that give value to the European self-esteem, it brings others, less known to Europeans, or long forgotten ones, perhaps the most distinctive and most impressive being the wilderness and man's interaction with it.

Traveling through California, I found a lot of understanding for the necessity to collect and preserve the history that took place on American soil, the prerequisite condition for comparing and interpreting historical events and stages. All over the country, along highways and trails, there is a great variety of well-prepared sites or just markers, designated to spark interest in the history and the land one walks upon. In fact, I have seldom traveled a place where one is invited to have a closer look so often, where both natural and human history were presented in such a multifaceted and abundant manner that everyone interested could become a little historian just by traveling and reading all the markers and plates provided. At some places, the way of presenting and how they are made accessible for everybody has been brought to perfection, not only in a rare-to-find informative way but also entertaining and interactive, easy to understand for kids and adults and as close as it gets to living history. Additionally, to satisfy a more profound or scientific thirst for knowledge, almost every little town has its own library or even a museum.

Upon signing of the Wilderness Act in 1964, president Lyndon B. Johnson said: "If future generations are to remember us with gratitude rather than contempt, we must leave them more than the miracles of technology. We must leave them a glimpse of the world as it was in the beginning, not just after we got through with it." In this sense, walking through California can be real edutainment.

The following stretch along the Mono Craters to Mono Lake and to the ghost town of Bodie, an exemplary cradle of California's genesis, bears comparison with a heritage trail, presenting geological, human, and most recent environmental history, but also how everything is connected.

05/27   MINARET SUMMIT, 13 MILES

We woke up early; it was too cold to sleep in and the sun would not rise above the trees before noon. While Sonja lowered the food down, I rolled up the tent and put it back in its bag. Behind the trees, thirty yards from our tent site, where the snowed-in summit road ended, forest's authority threatened to befall us.

A green Forest Service pickup was parked on the roadside and two ladies were watching us. Eventually, I had to give in to the commanding stare, and I walked through the trees to explain ourselves. The younger one threw an authoritative look at me stating that we were not allowed to camp out here. I did not stress out about the *why*, I just nodded and said, "OK, Thank you, we're all right and leaving in a minute." I was wondering why it shouldn't be OK to sleep here, off the road, away from the town, from private land or any facility. It wasn't even designated wilderness or a National Park. However, we had more important things to consider than arguing with the two rangers, while especially the younger one had that certain expression that reminded me of Picacho. Apparently she, too, had to prove something to herself, or to her more experienced partner. I could see it in her eyes, she wanted me. A simple 'but why not' could have started a sermon of rules and regulations and worst case, if she had found the right paragraph, a fine for committing a misdemeanor. I didn't give her a chance, said a friendly "Have a wonderful day, officers", and went back to our hideout under the trees.

It was obvious that two hikers in this area, at this time of the year, were more likely friends of nature than a marauding gang of environmental criminals. And when we later saw what expected us had we continued hiking here, I got really angry and thought they should be interested much more in where people go and give advice.

While most of them are, obviously a few are just there for belaboring a body of rules and regulations. Unfortunately, some places seem to lose their wildness as soon as they are declared wilderness. Besides the fact that some park venues are firmly in the hands of the masses, that was the other reason why I personally preferred traveling in minor-rank areas that are not elevated to the status of a park, that is, beyond declared Wilderness and National Parks, where living and everything that's intrinsically tied to it is allowed, walking where you find your way, eating where you get hungry, and sleeping where you get tired. In wildness I cannot think of being regulated in any way but my common sense. Wonderfully, this grows and one becomes wiser with every day and night spent out there. One can be pretty sure that someone who ventures this far into nature is not the kind who mistreats her.

When you hike this long, you are more likely to meet rather environmentally concerned people. With them, I often argued whether it was a shame that in order to preserve wild country we have to protect it from our species by imposing a body of laws on it. At the same time, we build feeder roads into the wild, bringing in busloads of people supporting fast-visit mentality. Is it OK to draw a net of trails and campgrounds through the wilderness?

Many people get sick about the developments in popular park visitors centers and they are right; Kenneth-Hahn Family Park in the heart of Los Angeles is wilder than Yosemite Village, Grand Canyon, or Death Valley's visitors' centers. However, keeping wilderness far away and out of reach for the masses

CHAPTER SEVEN

will not support interest in it. As soon as one walks a couple of hundred yards from the pavement or behind a rim, it will be almost as quiet as anywhere a hundred miles away in the wild.

In some of his articles and open letters, Colin was opposing plans to provide for easy access to wilderness. Today, I think, we need both. We need the purity of untouched pristine wildness, lands where you think this is just as God intended it after the earth's crust calmed down and where people can wander as He wanted it. For interest, thought and teachings, or as a quasi-appetizer, we need the accessible wilderness to spark interest for all and preserve the appreciation for awesome creation. Therefore people need to have a possibility to experience it for whatever time their limited schedules allow, from taking a photo from the car with the engine running to a four-month hiking adventure.

These accesses have to remain very much limited, though, and for the sake of the cause, we should restrain from slowly changing our natural point of interests and park visitors centers into city outposts, plastered with concrete and stuffed with all appendant facilities. Wilderness implies that there aren't many facilities for human comfort. At first sight, the lack of soda machines, picnic tables, and restrooms might create inconveniences for some. However, one soon learns that it creates more opportunities from just walking on forest soil to watching real wild life.

When planning the Thousand-Mile Summer route, visiting National Parks or any known places of interest was not an aspect. Colin's motives were beyond sightseeing or touristic needs; he just intended to walk the state. Fortunately and ineluctably, in California that still brings along a horn of plenty, ceaselessly pouring nature's wonders over you, and sometimes you just happen to be in a National Park. Then, of course, when you hike 1,000 miles cross-country, you would not walk to an entrance gate first, in order to look for a ranger station, wait for opening hours and ask for a permit before you enter the park area. You are just there and live your own 'hope they don't catch you'-rule or trust that they believe in the same mission and let you pay later. Personally, I always believed it is an unwritten law that you become part of the protected system or species when you enter and leave a wilderness by walking.

Most of the rangers I met in park systems were indeed primarily interested in my well-being, if I knew where to go or how to get there, and also in what I saw. I had the feeling that they used common sense too and ample scope to use laws or turn a blind eye to them. After talking about my trip for a while, none of them asked me for paid fees. One ranger, who caught me having a fire without the appropriate local paper, wrote me the fire permit on the spot and wished a good day, saying: "Better you have one, in case you run into a ranger …"

I understand that even if one traveler alone needs no rules because it is between him and nature, as soon as two venture out into nature, there must be regulations, first between the two, then when visitor numbers reach hundreds, thousands, and millions, between them and society. There have to be rules to protect the demands of all and everybody's right to find wilderness or a historical site just as the first visitor did. At these places the body of laws is inevitable to maintain the protected areas, as are frequent patrols by park authorities to control the masses for the sake of the protected.

Unfortunately, fees have to be raised from people who actually visit parks and do something for their physical, mental, and or intellectual health. Instead, we should consider incentivizing visits and travels to our parks and nature and fully finance the conservation by taxing, funding, and merchandising.

On most lands I came through without a park status, here in Eastern California it was actually legal, sometimes even encouraged to camp, the only rule being 'take in – take out'. The greatest responsibility, here as anywhere else, was to make sure your fire would only warm *you*, and nothing else. Especially now, when the days got hotter and the land was dry, I had to be more observant and careful about what kind of wood I was burning. Some tend to throw out many sparks or hot cinder, some even explode when oxygen or resin has been enclosed, most likely juniper, cedar, or some pines. When I felt the forest floor was very dry, I filled all water sacks and put them within reach.

Then there were private lands, fear and loathing for many a backpacker, identifiable by the ubiquitous 'No Trespassing' sign, next to 'STOP' the bestselling item for sign makers in America. Sometimes a stylized dog emphasized the warning, rarely a gun. Even in the remotest wilderness areas I ran into private lands, where a 'No Trespassing' was the only sign of habitation. Usually, that meant that someone owned the lands but hardly spent any time there. That's why one posted it there. However, I often considered them as unapologetic if not arrant nonsense, especially when posted in the middle of nowhere.

Walking cross-country, you will find that a good number of these signs more likely have a historical artifact character. The art of getting along was finding other signs or evidence whether someone was still living there or not. The problem was, if you obeyed all these signs, nowhere in California would you be able to walk a hundred miles in a more or less straight line, especially in agricultural and mining areas. On the other hand, a lot of these places were abandoned for long, activities were discontinued, or, with the help of nature conservation acts, nature has simply repossessed what once was hers.

Since it was not assigned when you would leave private lands – I cannot remember a 'Trespassing allowed in 5 miles'-sign – I certainly spent some nights on them. If someone really showed up, I would make sure to become noticeable first, then it all depended on what you looked like, how you behaved, and of course that you had stayed away from inhabited houses. I never had a problem nor did I ever look into a muzzle of a rifle or a revolver, a common bugbear among cross-country hikers. Instead, I was asked if I enjoyed the night on their land, maybe requested not to make any fire close to the house and more often treated for a coffee or a shower. Out there, it seemed, a tacit agreement held true, you reap what you sow.

The two rangers were still sitting in the car, I saw the younger one saying something to her partner, who in return waved off. Whatever the eager one proposed, they drove off and let us alone.

With our houses on the back, we left the forest cover walking to the mountain edge where the trail continued. At our feet lay once again Winter Wonderland, an amazing sight of the Minarets bordering a valley of countless lakes. It did not look much different from what I had seen two weeks before. It could not get whiter anyway. But with a snowbound trailhead on barely 9,000 feet, I surely began to entertain some doubt. There were no two ways about it anymore. My partner felt I had a hard time putting that idea out of my mind. She would have engaged in that white adventure for my sake, albeit an unpleasant feeling. But it was my responsibility, after what I had experienced in High Sierra, to resign and interpret it as Colin's call to get his son on the right track, his track. With a heavy heart, I bid farewell to the Tuolumnes again, and with the rising sun, we stepped back in his footsteps heading for Mono Lake and Bodie, where we would explore some of California's most tangible, colorful history, both human and geological.

After lunch break under the life-size bronze sculpture of the ski area's namesake, we left the Mammoth area following a thirty-mile-long fissure system, which extended northwards to the Mono Craters along Dry Creek and large sand flats. As soon as we walked out of the forest, stepping on the first of many lava fields, it felt like hot summer. While Sonja took a bath in the green water of Inyo Crater, I climbed a volcanic outcrop on Dead Mountain to get an idea of the terrain ahead of us. Before us lay large sagebrush plains, spotted with forests of Western yellow pines. The picture could have served as a poster for a new Bonanza movie about Ben Cartwrights heirs, only one aspect didn't fit in the nostalgic scene; about a mile to the right of our trail, thick clouds of smoke were rolling upwards from the forest, the first active wildfire of many more to come.

Here too, the forest floor was covered with the best fire accelerator, dried pinecones, sometimes so many that you walked on two layers of them. Some taller trees seemed to feel so good on the volcanic ground that they were growing Sequoia-like into the sky. Between the sand flats and the volcanic domes, three generations of ponderosa pines came to the fore. The younger ones had a black bark; when they came of age at around 150 years, the bark turned red; and only with more than 400 years, the seniors developed this yellowish bark, which gave them a more adequate and venerable name, the Western yellow pine. So when we passed a black one we gave him a pat on the stem saying, "hello buddy, how's it going?" Approaching a red one, we took our hat off; standing next to a yellow barked majesty commanding respect, we took a bow.

A little east of Obsidian Dome, where Glass Creek flowed into Deadman Creek, we found a campground and became neighbors to a retired gentleman, now passionate fisherman. Ken Gustavson spent most of the year traveling with his boat trailer and hopping the state's free campgrounds along U.S. 395. His motto was: "Go fishing on weekdays only, leave the weekends for the working population." Why he was there on the campground on a Tuesday instead of being out on a lake, we didn't know, until after one hour listening to him we realized that, next to fishing, he just enjoyed talking to someone even more. "Fish don't listen," he said.

Most people I met along my way enjoyed talking and telling stories about themselves and nature. And you would not believe how much one man, who spent the whole day on a boat in a lake, can tell, until you met Ken. It seemed that he wanted to make up for the coming three days alone on the lake.

05/28   GLASS CREEK, 12 MILES

When we came back to his site in the morning to share a can of coffee, Ken had already taken seat around his fireplace. He got company from the campground host and it sounded like he had never stopped talking between last night and now. At 11 a.m. Mammoth Times photographer Susan Morning came by for a photo session in the woods. This time, a prototypical hiker was needed for an article about camping and hiking. Now, Ken was convinced that he did meet a famous person. Indeed, for a few seconds he fell silent.

We left the campground at noon and crossed U.S. 395. On the other side we were entering the territory I had assigned to Ben Cartwright and his kin the day before. The smoke was still rolling above the forest, but the fire seemed to be contained. From now on, whenever I would see a wild fire, I would watch it for a while, trying to make out if it moved and where the wind might blow it. Here we felt safe, with a large sand flat between the fire and us, but still you felt one of our primal fears rising when smelling the burned wood.

Alternating with stands of lodgepine and hemlock, the crater sand flats dominate an eventful landscape. At the Devil's Punchbowl, a volcanic pit at the south end of a chain of some thirty coalesced craters, domes, and lava flows, we entered a geological study path, looking back to earth's recent history from 40,000 years ago until yesterday. With the craters to our right we passed a chain of weird looking rocky spines to the left. These Aeolian buttes are remnants from a much older volcanic activity some 700,000 years ago. What we see today are only the weathered tips of a thick layer of volcanic ash deposit.

The highest crater rises 9,172', Mono Crater, prominently standing 2,700 feet above the homonymous lake, the last remnant of an ancient lake system that covered the whole basin before the volcanic uprise. Sudden explosions created the chain of bowl-shaped cones we see today, followed by obsidian outflow rising in the cones and overflowing the original rims. Today, obsidian domes and large flows can be seen everywhere along the crater flats.

Native peoples across the continent had been using the black, glassy stone to form arrowheads and other weapons such as sacrificial tools inflicting terrible injuries. When the silicate magma cools down quickly, it cannot develop crystal structures hence obsidian blade edges reach almost molecular thinness. We were more in search of a piece of black purity. Whenever we came by a larger deposit of the volcanic glass, usually around the foothill of one of the lava domes, we couldn't resist going treasure hunting. In its purest, most eye-catching variant, obsidian is so pitch black, it does not only absorb light but traps your view alike. When we found such a mystic piece, we showed it to each other and put it in our pockets. After a while we took it out again to lay it back on the ground. Unfortunately, backpacking did not really allow taking heavy treasures.

With Crater Mountain in our back, we camped against the setting sun. Far away, down in the basin, lay Mono Lake, surrounded by open sagebrush, where a foraging coyote has started its daily mourning, remembering the golden eighties, when life around Mono Lake was just different, when its kin lived in the lap of luxury.

05/29   CRATER MOUNTAIN, MONO CRATERS, 11 MILES

Early in the morning, flocks of sea gulls were patrolling the airspace, while at eye level, we were face to face with swarms of gnats and tiny no-see-ums attacking our campsite. A sure sign that we were close to the alkaline lake body. On our way to this extraordinary biotope, we climbed Panum Crater, a didactic nature play of a two-fold structured crater consisting of both an outer tuff ring and an inner dome. With only 600 years of age, it related to one of the younger volcanic activities along the crater range, whereas the lake itself is with 750,000 years the oldest lake in the United States. The most recent eruptions created the larger Paoha Island over a longer period of time. The lava tongue now reaching into the lake came to a temporary halt only one and a half centuries ago.

Reaching the south side of Mono Lake, we explored the spectacular collection of tufa sculptures, those columnar pieces of natural art protruding from the lake. Without doubt the highlight of today's visits to the Mono Basin.

In the 1860s, one of the early visitors to California was the author Mark Twain. His first famous account, *Roughing it,* included detailed descriptions of the area. While he marveled at the picturesque forests and mountain creeks, his depiction of the lake, though, had nothing to do with his humorous style but simply showed what he saw in those days but couldn't explain yet. "This solemn, silent, sail-less sea – this lonely tenant of the loneliest spot on earth – is little graced with the picturesque." He was quite sure that "No living thing exists under the surface, except a white feathery sort of worm, half an inch long, that looks like a bit of white thread frayed out at the sides." Obviously he visited the area at the wrong time of the year. He continued that the lake "neither rises nor falls, apparently, and what it does with its surplus water is a dark and bloody mystery."*

Colin, too, complained about "the one really dull stretch of California". Neither the craters nor the lake did impress him much. "It is the one tucked away corner of California I've penetrated that hasn't seemed worth the effort," was his disquisition on the whole basin. However, Colin did not just echo Mark Twain. In fact, in 1958 there still wasn't much noteworthy around but a marshy, salty shore that made him run to escape the flies.

Likewise, the Los Angeles Department of Water and Power saw but a simple round desert lake, although in the meantime, the lake was known as a unique ecosystem, catering for millions of birds feeding from the lake. Since the 1940s, the LADWP had been tapping the lake's feeder streams. As a result, the lake level was constantly sinking and eventually the first tall tufas had become visible. However, in 1958 they were not really spectacular yet. When Colin had passed the lake, only the tips of the tallest tufa heads could be seen, like rocks floating on the surface, and so he didn't get to see but a round, salty lake in a large, dry desert pan.

Resulting from underwater mineral springs, forming limestone columns when getting in contact with other minerals in the water, the highest tufas grew to 20 and 30 feet and it needed another two decades until in the 1970s they protruded significantly from the shrinking lake.

The dramatic changes to the ecosystem threatened the birds' critical rest stop for nesting and feeding since their migrating part comes from as far as the Arctic Circle and on returning from the Equator. According to the Mono Basin Clearinghouse, without the freshwater influx, the water level dropped by 45 feet. In less than fifty years, the lake had lost more than half of its volume while its salinity had doubled.

---

* In 1861, Mark Twain (1835–1910) traveled on a stagecoach across the Great Plains and the Rocky Mountains. He spent several years in Nevada and California, first as a miner, then becoming the aspiring journalist and writer. The experiences made on his travels inspired his semi-autobiographical account *Roughing It* (1872) and several other publications.

The nice result was that hundreds of tufa towers, until then hidden below the surface, were suddenly exposed. The bad one was, due to the destabilization of the ecosystem, ten thousands of chicks died yearly and as many birds did not find sufficient food. They were too weak to complete their journey and died in the cold of winter.

For everyone interested in biological cycles, Mono Lake would be a unique and interesting lesson, especially in view of an area where you would reckon with everything but teeming wildlife.

Having no outlet streams, the lake has been collecting and concentrating minerals from the inflowing creeks over thousands of years. Based on these minerals, the lake boosts an extraordinary large population of planktonic algae. Due to the extreme temperature variation between summer and winter, the lake water turns over in early spring, stirring the water masses and bringing nutrients to the surface that feed the exploding number of photosynthesis performing algae. Along with their carnival, shrimp and fly larvae start hatching and feeding on them in such plentiful abundance that they attract not only regional nesting but the migrating birds as well. When shrimps and larvae are fed and grown by midsummer, it is time for over eighty species of birds to arrive for an all-inclusive feast. By early fall, a population of about two million become snowbirds, taking off for their winter destination, leaving behind a quiet and grazed, clear and hot Mono Lake. In the deep blue of the lake, spared algae wait for the next turnover, along with trillions of shrimp eggs and fly larvae.

For the ornithologists, only a few of these lake, shore, and riparian birds one can see in midsummer shall be mentioned: Preferring open water to feast on the shrimp, there are ducks, gulls, phalaropes, and grebes floating on the lake. Others favor the alkali flies, their larvae and pupae found at the lake's edge; among those are geese, killdeer, sandpipers, dowitchers, avocets, plovers, and willets. Along the small creeks and springs in the wetland surrounding the lake, one finds sparrows and swallows, rails and snipes, warblers, and blackbirds building their nests on the tufa towers or in the high grass.

How complex a small ecosystem like Mono Lake is, how subtle the relationships are that bind everything together and how far-reaching the results of disturbance may be, could best be evidenced by two other events caused by the drainage through the aqueduct. In the early 1980s, the water level got so low that a land bridge developed to the volcanic Negit Island. Golden years for coyotes and other predators, who had a feast savaging the birds' paradise. Consequently, their skyrocketing population inflicted humans indirectly with regards to their farming activities.

However, the newly exposed lakebed sediments and a layer of alkaline minerals were presenting an imminent and direct danger for the nearby human population. When blown away by the wind, they were a health hazard, containing toxic elements like arsenic or boron.

Mono Lake was well on its way to meet the same fate as Owens Lake. 'Save Mono Lake!' environmentalists, scientists, and many local residents demonstrated. Eventually, they founded the Mono Lake Committee and went to court. After several petitions with ongoing lawsuits and legal wrangling, in the 1990s the Supreme Court finally ordered a compromise had to be found, cutting down water exports to Los Angeles and rising the lake's level to a certain degree in order to stabilize the ecosystem on one side and secure the water needs of L.A. on the other.

However, after having interfered with nature for too long, saving wildlife was not that simple anymore. After the court's ruling, the question arose, what was to be saved, the current status or the original state before the water was redirected? What would be the consequences of each variant for the battered ecosystem? Scientists from various fields of expertise had to discuss each and every foot of a possible rise of the lake level, including considerations for seasonal fluctuations during dry and wet cycles. Each foot would cut water exports to L.A. But what would be the best water level, ecologically and economically? Soon one realized that every compromise was good for one aspect and bad for another. One target level was preferable for the brine shrimp, which eagerly demanded a lower salinity. Another one was better for the alkali flies, which depended on great quantities of shallow-water substrates. Submerging the alkali shoreline to prevent further hazards through dust storms might destroy nesting habitats for shore birds. Protecting one island to keep predators away from the nesting sites meant abandoning another, which would then be lost to wave erosion. What birds would benefit from what level?

And then there was a locally growing economical factor, the scenic value of a tufa. How much is our scenic interest worth? From all targeted alternatives, only the lowest would preserve the tufa towers as we know them today. Higher levels would erode them and eventually topple them. On the other side, every wave works at them too, only rather slowly, like every sandstorm and rain. In fact, the tufas would be better preserved below the surface than exposed to waves, wind, and weathering. But we don't really care about the poor tufas. We care to see them, because their interaction with the colors of the lake and the desert looks so amazing; submerged they have no value at all.

In the 2000s, the lake has regained a constant level, however, still only some ten feet above the historic low and ten feet below the originally achieved compromise. I wonder if human interest in nature's extravaganza, though its visibility was man-made in this case, was to be placed above environmental concerns. But aren't we part of the environment, too, with our banal voyeuristic needs.

CHAPTER SEVEN

Coming to Mono Lake, many of my generation will think of Pink Floyd's legendary album *Wish You Were Here*, according to the Rolling Stone Magazine and at least to one whole generation regarded as one of the greatest albums of all time. I still remember how I came home from the record store; I told my parents not to disturb for forty-some minutes, closed the door behind me and sat down cross-legged in front of the record player. When pulling out the inner sleeve, I saw a picture of this bizarre natural setting for the first time, a surreal scene, though, showing a *splashless* diver half submerged in Mono Lake, surrounded by far protruding tufa sculptures. I thought, "Is that art or a message?" And there was more food for thought. On the front cover, there were two businessmen closing a deceptive deal by handshake, somehow behind the scenes, because they stood behind the studios' backstage door. One of the men was on fire, or 'getting burned', an allegory for being betrayed. The back cover depicted a faceless salesman selling the band products in the desert, or selling his soul, allegorized by the absence of a face, wrists, and ankles, so to speak an 'empty suit'.

Interpreting the band's concept, the album art demonstrated the chasm between the demand of men to feed their insatiable appetites and the need for what is intrinsically natural to unfold. In particular, it condemned the market-oriented record companies' lack of understanding for musicians, and it criticized the industry's betrayal, that is, being more interested in greed and fast money than in the artists' long-term development, not to mention arts itself and its relevance for the masses. One may swap arts with nature, or water, and find oneself reminded of the conspiratorial deals that were concluded somewhere out here in the desert. The dooming absence of water, the faceless, untrustworthy partner, the absence of splashes around the diver; it is all about what is missing, life, truth, and reality, about what we wished to be here.

After so many water concerns, the question remains: Is there enough water for everybody at all? That depends less on further growth of our cities than on the way we treat our resources. If we think of it as endless and spill and spoil it with carelessness, we will inevitably run short of it, sacrificing first our wildlife, then our lands and produce, and eventually peace. If one side takes it all, the other has to suffer. If we became more considerate and renounce such faceless deals, there may be enough for all.

*

Walking around the lake's southwest quarter, we arrived at Lee Vining. The town community's hot spot was the El Mono Motel, meeting point, Wi-Fi hangout, café and library. Slightly overburdened, the proprietor Kelly was running that social market place, where a Starbucks would have needed a staff of five. Today a Los Angeles production company was casting local characters for a new Brad Pitt movie. Accordingly, there were quite some interesting people hanging around from all over the basin, killing time until it was their turn to show off. We checked in and joined the party in the motel's café, betting whether Brad would show up to go down in town's history. After pouncing on Kelly's fine selection of brownies and muffins, we browsed the small library to rummage around in local history.

05/30   LEE VINING, 8 MILES

Leroy Vining came to the Sierra basin in 1852, after the area had stayed in the news for various gold discoveries. Rather than trying to strike it rich with gold, he turned his attention to supplying the boomtowns with lumber. He established a sawmill and hoped to have found a strategic location. His guess wasn't too bad. Five years later, gold was discovered in Dogtown some twenty miles north, named after a common miners' term for camps consisting of tents and huts. Thousands of fortune-seekers were pouring into the Eastern Sierra. Shortly after, the mining town of Aurora was elected county seat for the new founded Mono district, collecting ballots as far as Bridgeport and White Mountain City. With Bodie and Lundy, two more bonanzas were springing up in the hills nearby. Leroy became a rich man, until he accidentally shot himself, being as drunk as a skunk. To the community's credit, the original Lakeview was then renamed into his name.

Although I had visited the lake several times before, even walked around it one time, the memory of these overlapping miles was faint and dwarfed by this visit, simply because I came walking, because I left walking, and because I had time to anticipate approaching it and time to be amazed leaving it.

Another quarter around to the northern lakeshore lay Mono City. Looking in on carpenter Filthy Pete, whom we met during the casting, we got the best of the sensation of Mono Lake. From his veranda overlooking the whole basin, we saw the crater domes in the south, floating like vessels in a sagebrush ocean, the snow-flanked peaks of the Sierra in the west like large sailers with white hoisted sails. Amid ships in an ocean of desert grass and sage, lay a blue and green jewel, framed by the salt-crusted shore, like a treasure on an island they were all hunting for.

It was not hard to guess why Ansel Adams' granddaughter kept a house right above Mono City. Obviously, she inherited his sense for stunning nature drama.

05/31   MONO CITY, 16 MILES

Walking up Cottonwood Canyon to Bodie Hills, sage remained the dominating cover doing a good job in lulling us until another Northern Mojave rattler reminded us to remain wary. Passing through high-desert landscape, we reached a rim at 8,400 feet, from where we looked down to California's best-preserved ghost town, the legendary Bodie. Due to the dry climate and hardly any weathering, this once booming town could have been abandoned only days ago, when we were still walking around Mono Lake. After two days in the green world of sage, the glaring, intensive colors of Bodie's historic buildings cause unbelieving amazement from the newcomer, like from a sailor who spent days on a dark ocean and, one morning, he wakes up in an emerald green bay.

Ironically, only the heartbeat of Bodie's history, the old stamp mill on a hill overlooking the town, was almost ignorable from afar, for its metallic gray-greenish coating was camouflaged by the sage.

Parking our backpacks at the old Miners' Union Hall, we delved into the colorful history of an exemplary boomtown. Everything in Bodie is so vivid, demonstrative, and touchable that you easily get lost in its past, becoming a citizen for a day.

In 1859, prospector William Bodey had discovered gold in the area, however, it did not bring him much luck. The sign painter for the start-up town could not even ask him for the correct spelling of his name. The discoverer had already died in his first cold winter. The eponyms' death should have been a warning sign to the town's growing population. Due to the isolated and weather-exposed location, Bodie citizens had to bear the cruelest winters. Severe storms and blizzards had been claiming many lives of unprepared fortune-seekers not reckoning with the harsh situation on a high-desert plateau. But the town expanded as words got around, alluring more and more miners and affiliated entrepreneurs. By 1880, the place was bursting at the seams with more than 10,000 inhabitants dwelling in and around the town. The population sprang up so fast that a majority had to live in tent cities, or dogtowns, scattered throughout the hills, facing the threats of heat, cold, and storms first hand.

Bodie became famous for attracting a lot of dubious contemporaries like the hard-bitten miner type, who was up to every trick and home in all weathers of life. Gambling, saloons, and brothels abundant, the town soon had its reputation in the West, what might have attracted even more and also non-miners. "The town too wicked to die", it was called; nevertheless there were daily casualties, suffering from a lethal combination of gold, guns, and booze. At its peak, the town had more than fifty saloons and not one church, which prompted one citizen to describe it as "a sea of sin, lashed by the tempests of lust and passion." I wonder if he took the consequences and left, or if he allowed himself to bear the misery. However, in spite – or actually because – of that, it remained a vibrant town.

Soon the supplying 'Leroy Vinings' struck it rich – provided that they did not shoot themselves out of sheer joy – since lumber for construction and firewood for ovens and steamboilers had become scarce and beyond price.

In search of other energy sources, the Standard Mining Company in Bodie had heard of Nunn's transmission line concept, transmitting electricity over several miles from a hydroelectric generating plant to the mine. My guess in Wyman Canyon wasn't too bad; in fact, in the beginning people were afraid that the power, running through a thirteen-mile line from Green Creek to the stamp mills in Bodie, would not be able to turn sharp corners and that it might jump out of the line and into the ground. In the museum I learned that, as a precaution, the power line was built as straight as possible, to prevent the electrical current from flying off. Nevertheless, with the successful electrification of Bodie, it was here that modern exploration and industrial processing of gold and other minerals resumed.

Anyway, the days of the gold-panning carriage and pair, miner and burro, were over in no time. In less than forty years, exploration and mining was developed to a degree that most of California's gold could be processed. Bodie went through many of these stages and played an important role in inventing and establishing new technologies.

During the first strikes in the fading 1840s, when individual prospectors staked secret mining claims along remote creeks, specks of gold had to be panned from creek bottom sands and gravels. In order to work larger quantities of gold-containing debris, they constructed rocker boxes, cradles or long toms. But the mystery-monger was limited in how much material he was able to shovel, wash and rock, and sort out. Some disclosed their secret to associate with others, to rationalize work and allocate activities like hauling the debris, diverting water to the find spot, and shoveling it into sluice boxes, which were extended flume-like rocker boxes with riffles at the bottom, where the heavier gold could be collected. Of course, the latter usually remained the discoverer's prerogative. In some locations, formerly panned streams were redirected, and the whole exposed riverbed was sluiced.

The stampede into California caused by the first bonanzas was so immense that in only ten years after the first discovery, hand-held pans and sluice boxes had washed most of the easy to find surface and fluvial gold. Dogtowns and wooden shanties had popped up along virtually every creek, river, or canyon, and the lone wolves and solitary miners were well advised to resort to new businesses. A growing population provided for enough customers to make fortunes in other endeavors such as manufacturing shovels and pickaxes, which were in high need for both digging for gold and graves, or in areas involving logistics, transportation and even entertainment services.

Due to the essential higher investments in mining machinery, more companies were now entering the market. While in the valleys west of the Sierra, huge dredges moved along current and ancient streambeds, lifting the dirt from the ground, washing and screening it, in the mountains, hydraulicking became the major method by pumping water through a high-pressure hose and spraying the gold-bearing slopes and hills. By the 1860s it was these small companies or groups of people, who took the biggest share of the precious resource. Having excavated down to bedrock, they were stumped again.

Eventually, mining operations went to the bottom of its source, finding more gold buried in the hills around the streams. Digging the ore out of shafts and adits, they either transported it to the creeks or pumped water to the hills to wash and separate it at the spot. The deeper they dug the more gold-bearing rock, mostly quartz, had to be excavated. With the so-called quartz-mining, various methods of crushing the rocks mechanically were established and the hunt for the source rock began, the mother lode, often assumed as a vein of pure gold, somewhere upstream from where the creeks had eroded the specks they had panned before.

With pan amalgamation and chlorination to separate the gold from the ore, chemistry had found its way into mining. All kinds of crushers, mills, or the Spanish-American arrastras, where the burro came into action again by pulling a heavy millstone crushing the rocks, were used to pulverize the debris to the desired particle size. Eventually, the mechanized mill became the more effective tool, where heavy stamps were lifted and dropped to crush the ore.

Two major inventions, both brought to perfection at the Standard Mill in Bodie, catalyzed the industrial process, thus increasing the efficiency of operations. These were shifting the mechanized process from steam engine to electrical power and using cyanide to separate the precious metal more thoroughly. The latter included reworking older material, wastes that had been stored aside with foresight, when current methods had reached their limits. Huge piles of discarded rock, called tailings, were now waiting to be reprocessed again. The environment was treated with less foresight. Large amounts of heavy metals, toxic chemicals, and other pollutants were flushed away with the rivers, increasingly destroying animal habitats or ending up on agricultural lands. Still today some areas are heavily affected from either chemicals or the hydraulic mining, which often left barren, soilless lands.

Having pulled out $16 million in gold, the largest operator withdrew in time. Due to the effective processing, the mines were depleted to a degree, where only new technology or a skyrocketing gold price would make reprocessing profitable by moving tons and megatons to receive an ounce. In 1914, a long-time Bodie citizen, James Stuart Cain, bought the Standard's facilities. He operated or leased the facilities intermittently until in the early 1930s several effects drew operations to a close. Another cruel winter had scared away most of the remaining workers to modern boomtowns along the coast. The few who stayed had to fight several fires, which destroyed major parts of the town. Eventually, with the upcoming war in Europe, the government ordered to focus all mining capacities on 'strategic metals' needed for warfare. Days later, the town was abandoned for years, until in 1961 California State Parks took over and arrested decay.

With the exodus from Bodie, the population of the neighboring towns and supplying businesses in the valleys below dwindled as well. Many people moved away after they had sold their land and water rights to an institution that was, surprisingly enough, willing to buy now useless land at high prices, the Los Angeles Department of Water and Power. Through this and the conspiratorial land sales farther south, the city of Los Angeles had become the largest landowner along U.S. 395.

From a Bodey, squatting at the creek's edge with a hand-held pan, to crude mills and arrastras to the Standard Mill's capacity of processing 500 tons of gravel daily, all these stages of gold mining in the West can now be seen in one of its greatest outdoor museums. This is not merely a visit to the gold rush past but to the beginnings of today's California and the events and principles the state has been founded on. Park rangers did a tremendous job in preserving the state of almost 200 relatively unweathered buildings and structures. Nothing was repaired, but from that time on, nothing is allowed to fall down either.

When you stand on these Bodie Hills, no more than a day hike from either arid desert, alpine mountains, or lush valleys, when you look down to this town and visualize that almost overnight, a booming city of thousands of people came into existence (at that time, after the Bay Area and Sacramento City the third largest in the state), that in another night, all of them were gone, then you begin to comprehend the special character of California history and you see some of the reasons why it developed its own mentality.

The big bang of California history took place near Fort Sutter on January 24, 1848, a distant outpost run by an entrepreneurial Swiss immigrant. With the news about the first discovery of gold there, the trickle of Americans emigrating to California had turned into a flood in no time at all. The immense influx of people from all over the world advanced the accession of the territory and eventual statehood as the 31st state in the Union on September 9, 1850. Otherwise, it would most likely have remained for much longer a far-away land, far too difficult to reach, being cut off by the harshest deserts, the highest mountains, or several-month-long sea travels. While the state's pre-gold population of Americans and immigrants was about 15,000, thirty years later there were more than a million arrivals. Montalvo's legend of the land of gold had finally come true.

Pushed by greedy newcomers, everywhere the westward movement was driving Native Americans from their lands, who in return attacked miners and settlers to defend their hunting and living areas. The endless chain of violence, including diseases, massacres, genocidal attacks, and starvation, is history, having gone down as the darkest chapter of the American frontier. When Frémont and Carson explored the land, Native Americans were estimated at 150,000 in California. When the gold rush was at its peak, one fifth had been left.

CHAPTER SEVEN

With 300,000 citizens, San Francisco had virtually erupted in the 19th century. It was the largest city in the West, growing bigger daily by frequently arriving steamships bringing in new fortune-seekers. A fast growing population needed infrastructure; roads, schools and churches were built, civic institutions came into action throughout the state and in the lower valleys, large-scale agriculture developed to cater for the growing needs. Due to its rich resources and the strategic location facing the Pacific Rim, in the East plans were made to connect the new state to the Union's railroad system.

Many things were different on the West Coast; many developments moved faster here. Chances never dreamed of before needed immediate action. The kind of people it took and how those characters who made it influenced the formation of a state's own mentality was put in a nutshell by an early, rather observant visitor, Scottish travel journalist J.D. Borthwick: "The men who settled the country imparted to it a good deal of their own nature, which knows no period of boyhood. The Americans spring at once from childhood, or almost infancy, to manhood; and California, no less rapid in its growth, became a full-grown state, while one half of the world still doubted its existence."*

Quite an interesting aspect, in these days, many supplying businesses were run by women, mainly laundry services, boarding places, and food caterers, and not least brothels to entertain the male crowd. Although most women had set off along with their men, quite a few arrived alone in the West, having lost their husbands to the hazards of the trek or to the craziness of the gold. Thus women became an important entrepreneurial factor in the American West, being far ahead of their East Coast or European sisters.

The events around the first rush of people into the *Eldorado State* seemed to have formed the land and its people sustainably. The Californian Dream was born as well as a Californian style, reconfirming and fulfilling itself again and again through further rushes and superlatives.

At the same time when people were swarming into Bodie, Los Angeles counted only about the same population, around 5,000 citizens. With the first boom hitting the small settlement along the coast, it was the same concept that made the city what it is today, in terms of surface area the largest in North America or, if you take the Greater L.A. area, with 10 million people the most populous county. Here, it was not the gold, but other resources which were, with regards to current needs, demanded much more than gold,

---

* From: *Three Years In California* (1857). At the age of 21, Scotsman John David Borthwick (1824–1892) inherited a small fortune, which he used to travel the Americas for some ten years, three of which through California. Discovering his talents for both writing and illustrating, he began portraying his observations and eventually published this autobiographical classic about his experiences during the gold rush. Enriched with detailed lithographs, the book offers an entertaining in-depth look on the work and the social life in early California, from mining techniques to leisure and crime.

such as oil for mobility, creative minds for entertainment, and eventually bits and bites for information.

From the discovery of gold in the mountains, to large-scale farming in the valleys, oil along the coast, movie business and entertainment in general in the cities to the outsprings of Silicon Valley and the *dotcom* rush, the whole state seemed to inherit serendipity falling from one lucky boom into another. The Californian Dream became a driving force itself, attracting more and more people, some of whom believed that by just being here one deserved a share of it, or at least that one could buy in on it. For a long time, just jumping on the band wagon worked fine.

Almost every spot throughout the state has been experiencing a boom, apparently a process still going on. While Colin hiked through a state with 15 million citizens, today we count 37 million. One starts wondering, if the fate of Bodie could happen to the whole state, if sudden rise implicates a harsh fall, from boomtown to ghost town, a place that solely lives from its past but does not bring new ideas, impulses and inspiration anymore.

What had caused the abundance of gold in the state, the resulting boom and consequent Californian Dream, could indeed become its doom. The same tectonic process that has been constantly pushing the seafloor under the continental mass, thus bringing up minerals-bearing magma, keeps Californians on the edge, here geologically, and exposed to permanent threat. However, despite factual geology and unperturbed by aggravating economical warnings, Californian population was never put off. From the beginning, it has been living with imminent hazards, resurrected from fires, floods, and earthquakes, and it survived several rushes' rise and fall, some of which were declared dead soon after they started. In the best tradition of the first newcomers, it has always been able to recover from crises and reinvent itself. Therefor, the prerequisite seemed to be a common optimism planted into the California bone, which related to everybody's chance to strike it rich, if willing to work hard and trusting in one's luck as well as to living in a land of freedom, of abundant riches and entertaining attractions.

Ever since, exercising itself in *weebles*-mentality – it might wobble, but it won't fall down – California has been residing on the edge in more than just a geological sense, and somehow it still is the ever-growing community of fortune-seekers to the present day.

As a sign of our times and not limited to California, on the crest of the economic wave, mere consumerism closes in on creativity, advancing to become the main purpose in our lives and a *perpetuum mobile* of economy. Worldwide, at a point where every place is pioneered, where everything seems to be accomplished, *wasteland* spreads out conquering our mentality and dominating our orientation in life, slowly weakening such qualities, for example, on which this state was based on. Unfortunately, to many people, chilling on past days' reputation while wallowing in vacuity, and letting oneself distract by non-issues instead of facing current threats is today as much related to California lifestyle as its golden heritage. The fact that all that glitters isn't gold, struck the state only recently, as the rest of the U.S and the world. However, when you are sitting on an edge, you are likely to wobble more than on a sounder foundation. Suddenly, the other side of the golden coin became visible, the consequences of living beyond one's means, of carelessness and outdated structures. Suddenly, Californians, rather unversed in giving up claims or aiming lower, have to put up with severe restraints and cutbacks regarding the lifestyle. In these days, many citizens are asked as never before to waive accustomed rights while the state is struggling with long-established but stale practices that were approbated in different times. While the economic wheel has continuously taken up speed, legal and political structures are still pretty much the same as when the state joined the Union. It didn't really matter for as long as things went well, as long as the only way was up and farther.

However, as so often, things went well until they didn't, and all of a sudden, the dream came to a standstill, uncertain which will be over soon, the crisis or the dream. In many other, though less dramatic situations, California has found a cure, based either on its natural riches or its more human ones, optimism and creativity.

The gold has gone, oil is marginal, movie, entertainment and web-based activities found great competition all over the world and the aftermath of its explosive genesis along with the budget disarray imposes perhaps the biggest threat ever to the state and its people, especially in the face of global markets and the advantages other parties might take of the situation.

Despite the depletion of older resources or an ongoing devaluation through worldwide competition, there are two boundless sources of riches that will remain in the state as long as people care. One is the human capital and people's mentality, their openness and creativeness and the ability to break new grounds – proven by so many historical masterstrokes that influenced trends well beyond the state's boundaries. The other is nature's unique performance throughout the state, presenting superlatives in abundance and dreamlike lands as seldom seen elsewhere. Actually, these are good foundations for finding solutions for current problems and setting new trends. Perhaps an old acquaintance had already recommended one; when Amadís roamed around the land of fantasy to find out more about himself, he masqueraded as The Knight of the Green Sword. Why not – in the best pioneering tradition – procure for solutions, since the world is demanding for it.

In any way or manner whatever, whether serendipity will prevail, whether the old dreamland may remain Neverland, a place whatever you wish it to be, depends once again on its creativeness, the willingness to give up outdated conveniences and move toward new chances and markets, before one is overrun by more modern times, by another far-away country.

Contrary to common belief, serendipity is not accidental; it is not mere fortune, but more a coincidence and the consequence of a movement, but also of the way one moves. What might have seemed to be luck to Bodey and other discoverers was only a logical sequence in the westward movement. The important catalyst was that the people did something, that they set off and gave room to possibilities.

*

Coming down from the look-out hill, we went back to the Miners' Union Hall, where our backpacks were waiting. Today it hosts the town museum, where Colin had read a book about the local history, written by 1881 born Ella M. Cain, James Stuart Cain's daughter in law. In *The Story of Bodie* she portrayed the work and the people of this mining district and Mono County along with first-hand stories about life in Bodie and some louche, shady characters.

By nightfall, the museum was locked, and when the last visitor was gone, we found ourselves a place for the night, where the original tent city had spread out. Bodie was closed.

We set up tent on a spot that must have been a preferred site in those days. Located on a small mound about half a mile from town, from here one was able to overlook not only the former dogtown but as far as the cemetery and the streets of Bodie. Suddenly, another one of Pink Floyd's masterpieces leaped into my mind. The melody in my head started with the *ping*, when I drove a rusty, most likely 150 year-old nail into the ground to anchor the tent for an upcoming storm. It was the same ping that opened the band's side two of the *Meddle* album, or for those readers whose discs only ever had one side, the bit after Seamus, marking the beginning of the legendary live version of *Echoes*, performed at the ruins of Pompeii in Italy. Once well described as "a soundtrack to a non-existent movie" (Melody Maker Magazine), the mind song prompted me for the first and only time to start the iPod and having taken a front-row seat on our mound, we switched earphones, rewinded several times, and watched the whole movie come into existence on another stage setting designed by history.

06/01   BODIE, 18 MILES

Leaving Bodie, sagebrush again covered the rolling hills on our way to Bridgeport. The hills were gentle enough to allow its creeks some breathers thereby creating small meadows here and there. The shrub became greener along Clearwater Creek and turned into grasslands and tree stands when we

CHAPTER SEVEN

reached the valley of East Walker River, close to where the hydroelectric transmission plant had been built to electrify the Standard Mine.

At the northern end of the valley lay the town of Bridgeport like a farmstead, framed by grazing lands as far as the eye could see. The view was so amazing that we decided to spend a night on the hills beyond city gates, overlooking the scenery. When the town hall bell told 8 o'clock, the sun had drawn the curtain and we had settled for dinner. With every light switched off in town, another star mirrored in the waters of East Walker River.

After Jedediah Smith's crossing near modern Sonora Pass in 1827, Joseph Walker was the second American to find a passage over the Sierra Nevada. He came down this Walker Valley from Nevada, was the first one to see and explore the Tuolumne waters, and he proceeded through Yosemite to San Joaquin Valley.

06/02   EAST WALKER RIVER VALLEY, BRIDGEPORT, 2 MILES

When I heard the mission bell again early in the morning, I opened the tent to look over the valley. With the rising sun behind us, the view was even more breathtaking, and I was thinking to myself, somehow it is a pity that we do not just stay where we fall in love with a place anymore. I envied the emigrants for that freedom, the be-all and end-all of their trek existence was to find that one place, a motivation so huge enabling them to walk through the unknown and face the greatest hardships on their way.

Climbing down to the nice little town, we had to experience the other side of the coin. The idyllic location redounded to some surprises. The breakfast was the most expensive I had in two and a half months, and so were groceries and the motel. We checked all of the four motels; not only did they demand the same price, but their counter staff was the same kind as well. A young girl would tell us the rate but be unable to answer any further questions, be it because they were not from here and just being trained for the season, or because they were afraid to say something wrong, afraid of the dragon behind, the old lady of the house, who was monitoring them with distrust.

Questions like a price for two or three nights, where the ranger station was, or anything about the town were answered with a quick "Dunno" or simply remained unheard. One hotel had a sign saying 39.99. First I wondered if it was an antique enamel sign, but knocking at the door I was sent to the neighboring bar for more information. The information I got there and the way it was said was so unaccommodating that I was happy to pay fifty dollars more somewhere else.

Unfortunately, we had two days in this town since Sonja would take a bus from here to Reno. Walking down the town's mile, after two hours we had visited every store. The ambiance did not change much. The girls in the café were right stroppy cows. No 'How's-it-going' in the supermarket, no 'How-do-you-do' in the souvenir stores. We started wondering, what happened to that town; was it under an evil old-days' spell? Indifference and unfriendliness blew through the streets of this romantic little Western town with unequaled alpine scenery. We decided to get to the bottom of it and visited the town museum. The museum lady seemed to be exempt from the curse, maybe because she understood history and had came to terms with the past. She was the first friendly person, pulling out all the stops, where we were from, where we would go, if we were interested in the history, let me show you this and that and give you these brochures, and so on. One brochure portrayed some important people in the town's past. I think there we found a semi-scientific approach.

Bridgeport pretty much depended on the mining boom in the mountains around. Early settlers soon recognized its potential for farming and grazing cattle, and with the first discoveries in Dogtown and Bodie, it became the major supply hub and a wagon port for transiting travelers and businessmen. The former settlement Big Meadows now was the 'port with a bridge' crossing East Walker River. All businesses and institutions that did not have to be on the spot were concentrated in the more agreeable climate of Bridgeport Valley. Sawmills were built along many mountain creeks.

At the same time, Aurora was at its peak with some 5,000 citizens and remained the county seat, whereas serious disagreement arose about whether it was situated in California or Nevada. For a short time, both states had governed it simultaneously. In 1863 a survey had been completed that assigned the mining town to Nevada jurisdiction. Bodie took over only for an instant, but due to the bloodcurdling conditions, the new county seat was quickly moved to Bridgeport.

That, of course, did not mean people down here were more likely to go to heaven. They were just businessmen and politicians, working less hands-on and more subtle. Browsing the town's history unearthed a who-is-who of scalawags, criminals, and city officials, with some of the latter being a sub-category of the first-mentioned. In the ongoing battle for mining claims, county seat and business interests, the town seemed to have been buffeted by corruption so heavy, it might have had an impact on the descendants. Best case, we thought, it was only shame. Still being upset about our reception, I presented the wry theory to the museum lady. However, she came to defend her fellow citizens and blamed it on the dulling consequences of tourism, since their town still is something like a modern port for visitors, a gateway to the Eastern Sierra. She recommended looking at the town's manifest history; besides the museum, which was the original 1880 schoolhouse, there were many other 19th-century buildings in a remarkably good shape, including the second oldest operating courthouse in the state.

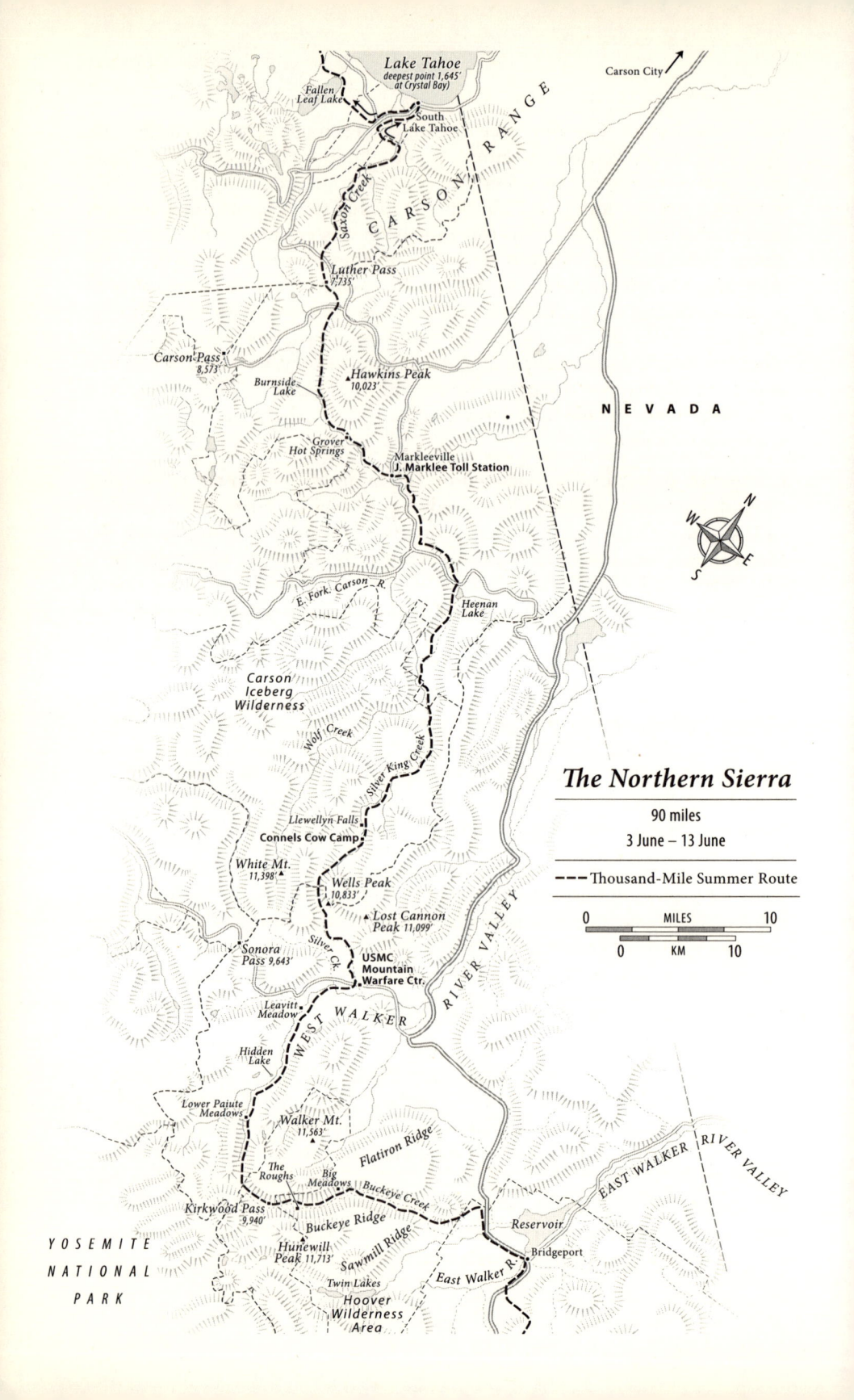

The Northern Sierra

90 miles
3 June – 13 June

--- Thousand-Mile Summer Route

8. THE NORTHERN SIERRA

Behold this and always love it!
It is very sacred and you must treat it as such.

SIOUX INDIAN

06/03 – 04 BRIDGEPORT, 14 MILES

After I brought Sonja to the bus station, I picked up my pack and walked across the fields toward the next mountain range. I almost felt sorry to leave that town, although, I am sure, that was rather due to the partner I was missing. Again the first steps alone were hard. With such friends by my side, being suddenly left alone after having company for two hilarious and eventful weeks, I felt myself hovering in this social vacuum for the second time. Knowing that she was my last companion and assuming that with the desert and the High Sierra I would have passed the highlights of my journey, this one turned into a sudden super-massive black hole. A strong melancholy took possession of me as I left the outskirts of town, and it grew deeper and deeper until I even noticed a small doubt lurking in my mind, whether I should walk into unknown terrain, alone, whether I should continue at all.

I had to make sure to quickly find appropriate distraction in order to keep the spirits up. Fortunately, the last phone calls to my fellow traveler-in-mind were uplifting. Besides the museum lady, Nathan's was the only friendly voice I had heard in that town. He said he would do OK, and when I spoke about my doubts, he even encouraged me to hang in there, he would need more adventure reports since it was this what made him hang on. Nature, too, didn't keep me waiting very long, and before soon, I was collecting new material for stories at another shared campfire.

Since I came down from White Mountain, a strong permanent wind had been blowing through the valleys east of the Sierra. Here and today, it felt

CHAPTER EIGHT

like a new season had started; in fact, it was the first nice and calm summer day. It was moderately hot with just a low breeze, enough, though, to blow the scented air of summer from the green fields across the town. The birds were agitated, capering between fence posts and welcoming the new stage with musical triplets. Cattle were grazing devotedly on lemon-green meadows along East Walker River, and with its waters all bad thoughts about the inhospitable reception seemed to flow out of town.

Walking toward a landscape that didn't fall short of the Alps, the sour began to turn to sweet. As I ascended into the forest to Buckeye Creek, bouquets of sunflowers, lupines, and Indian paintbrush were adorning my way. Every little runlet was lined by birch trees, forming small forests of their own, whereas Pine trees dominated the hills and slopes. I passed a campground where I was welcomed by a group of soliciting ground squirrels. "There you are, finally," I heard them say, "did you bring food crumbs?" I was happy to face the Sierra in spring now and abloom, only two weeks after the depths of winter. Bound for solitude though, I felt that nature had already started to take my mind off the farewell and that she appeared at her best to cheer me up.

When I left the site passing a cattle gate, I met two cowboys, who just came back down from Buckeye Canyon. They said, there still were patches of snow up to the cabin at Buckeye Forks, but the trail was always visible. How it would look like beyond the cabin and approaching the pass, they didn't know, but they called attention to the fact that this was the longest winter they had seen here in a while.

Closing the gate behind me, I found myself entering hobbitland. Through an endless bed of grassland flowed the valley's lifeline, snaking around gentle hummocks, seamed by lemon-green stands of water birches and dark green piñon pines. As far as the eyes could see, the meadows cradled small ponds. Their green carpet covered the whole valley floor and reached up to a line of aspen and Jeffrey pines that separated the valley from the grey mountains.

At Big Meadows I had to ford the Buckeye, a wading pool compared to the cascadesque creeks before. Here I set camp in a loop of the snaking river. I was encircled by ridges, the Flatiron in the north, the Buckeye in the south, and the Sawmill farther east, their peaks between 11,000' and 12,000' with snowcaps reflecting the sun long after she had left the valley floor.

Compared to the weeks in desert and snow, it was like moving into a five-bedroom luxury estate after having lived in a shack, where it always lacked of something. Here was everything. I had running water, good firewood, and a super soft king-sized grass bed with flowering bouquets on the night table. The mountains seemed less ominous and the meadows more inviting. The sun was withdrawing the last snows from peaks and passes, filling the creeks' little pools.

I crossed the creek again to check a group of firs for a good-sized, higher branch. Then I threw one end of my rope over it and tied the other around the stem. Twelve feet high, that would do it. The cowboys at the gate had explicitly warned me about bears, "There is bears around here, be careful with your food, and yourself!" They had seen tracks and scat and trees with scratched bark, where the bear had sharpened its claws. So they were definitely awaken from hibernation and most likely hungry after a long winter. I made sure my food was high enough in the air. "Be careful with your food," he said, "and yourself. Look for marked trees." Should I haul myself too, next to the food?

Bears use trees for various purposes. I am not sure if climbing them for food bags is part of their foraging strategy, but they rub their backs against them and use the bark to sharpen their claws and teeth. Both, at times, would not leave much of the tree, depending on its stamina and if it can cope with the pressure of several hundred pounds scraping against it. They also use them as signposts by marking them with their odor to either define their territory, place a lonely hearts ad for a mating partner, or to let their buddies know that – hey, there's a fresh hiker out there.

While preparing my *last* supper, the Sawmill Ridge adorned itself with a crescent. I crouched at the campfire, fueling it with nostalgic ideas until late into the night. I must have dozed off halfway, when a loud crack woke me up in the middle of the night. I listened into the dark; there again, it came from the group of birches on the other side of the creek. I got up and threw a piece of wood across it; three or four cracks, something was lumbering away.

On the banks of the creek, tiny waves were forming a pattern of frozen ripples. Only at one spot in the mud, the thin ice was broken, and about ten inches from the shore, the waves were slowly filling a small puddle the size of my palm. It was obvious, I had someone visiting me.

Quiet as a mouse, I sat there for another couple of hours pricking my ears at the slightest sound. When the last piece of wood had burned down, the cold drove me back into the sleeping bag.

06/05   BIG MEADOWS, BUCKEYE CREEK, 17 MILES

Although I had been burning the midnight coal, I got up early. Before setting off for the pass, I wanted to find out who had knocked around these trees. I checked the vicinity for any tracks, and in the mud, between the creek and the birches, I found four more prints. They were rather indistinct, but from the size I would think it was a medium-sized bear. Behind the trees was high grass, the tracks disappeared. On my side of the creek, the little footprint puddle had filled with water now forming a perfect frozen cast for further

CHAPTER EIGHT

forensic work. However, the rising sun has already begun to melt the evidence and here I couldn't find any more tracks. It seemed that the trespasser had changed his mind and turned around immediately.

Soon after I took off, a narrow canyon passage called 'The Roughs' psyched me up for the pass. It was filled with large boulders on which I had to crawl and climb on all fours. Having left the canyon, I found the small cabin at Buckeye Forks. It was the last stop before another steep ascent through snow, 1,600 feet in 2.5 miles. I looked back into the valley that could not have been painted more fantasy-like by Tolkien himself, and I hoped it would be the same on the other side of Kirkwood Pass.

Spending some time around the cabin, I did the routine check-up for nostalgia around old buildings. I did not find much of interest but scattered unidentifiable wooden and iron remains. Only a brown tuft of hair lying on the ground grabbed my attention. I doubted the collapsed cabin had been a barber shop, and looking up I saw a tree some thirty feet away, full of scratches and more hair on the ground. The scars on the bark were shining in fresh orange-brown, one loose piece still felt smooth and clammy on the inner side. It could not be long since the bear was here. The scars on the tree were about six feet from the ground; I thought I was exactly his size. Habitually, they stand upright when marking a tree. I hoped that this one had not stooped down then.

Due to the snow, the steep climb took me more than two hours. The pass cut through a range which was some 1,000 feet higher. Dragging from tree to tree, I aimed at the notch. On the last hundred feet, a snowdrift had been blown at the rim building up an icy chute. Again, I had to kick stairs in the snow. Every few seconds, I stared at my hands only to see something that's not glaring white. Even the sky was a white overcast with no patches of blue. There was nothing to hold on, neither physically with my hands nor visually, since contours got lost in white monotony. Keeping myself balanced with the house on my back became the real problem for one hundred feet and half an hour. One false step would have brought me be back down until the first tree stopped my slide. Everywhere I saw blood red dots in the snow. Although I knew that it was an algae, I couldn't help but think of blood spots and what it meant to be overtaken by a bear up here. The snow algae, also called watermelon snow, grow on summer snows at altitudes from 10,000' to 12,000'. Accidentally eating it or drinking the meltwater would cause similar impairments as giardia.

At 9,920 feet, Kirkwood Pass was my fifth, but far from the drudgery the previous passes had demanded from me. It was a single barrier on this leg, and, to my knowledge, there was nothing else that could become insurmountable thereafter. I think the possibility that I might fail only at the last of several obstacles had been the real head-scratcher in the High Sierra. Again, it was an exhilarating and, quite literally, an uplifting feeling to look back to where I came from and forward to where I was heading. Reaching a pass always was like having passed an examination, summa cum laude. From here, you saw what you did and, at the same time, what the grade-grubbing was for. Here you remembered your ups and downs, and you took the achievement and transmitted its outcome, its emotions, to what lay ahead, to move on imbued with new strength. On a mountain summit instead, you reached your final destination and would generally walk back the same way, somehow your journey, or rather your adventure, ended on the peak.

The mystery of climbing a pass was its rubber band effect; you pulled it until it almost ripped and when you reached the pass, it would catapult you ahead with all the emotions you picked up there. The more you were strained from the ascent, the more energy you received by reaching the edge of the mountain.

I walked down in the cold shadow of Hawksbeak Peak and its range bordering Yosemite in the south. Meltwater creeks kept tumbling across the trail, determinedly breaking the seal of winter. Most of them were not visible yet, flowing in icy tunnels or still snowed in. However, it seemed that with every moment they were getting faster and louder, from a soft splash below the pass to a menacing roaring further down. In the end, they all united as Kirkwood Creek, flowing northwest to form the Upper Piute Meadows at the confluence with West Walker River.

I followed the meadows looking for a spot where I would stay for two days. For the first time, I did not have to think of any threshold ahead; there was no deadline to avoid desert heat, no snowed-in passes, and no impassable creeks. I had no rush at all. The mountain valley's meadows outranged even the Buckeye Shire and, I knew, I saw it, it couldn't get any better.

At the end of the Lower Piute Meadows, I realized that I had been passing the most beautiful places all day. I was already about to walk away from the river, having seen at least ten sites where I should have stayed some days. But I enjoyed walking so much here and I was constantly curious for the following spot that I kept moving on, always with the intention to stop at the next one.

When I reached a cutoff to the small Hidden Lake, I finally ordered myself to do so. After a short visit to the lake, which is half a mile off the river, I preferred to spend the night at the running water. When I had the choice, I always preferred a creek or a river to a lake. One reason was that it brought fresher water, but even more important was its sound and its movement. Listening to it and staring at its flow, it just seemed to be more vivid than standing water and likewise more inspiring. And who knows, the next wave might bring a new idea, for here you never stare twice into the same water.

CHAPTER EIGHT

06/06   WEST WALKER RIVER, HIDDEN LAKE, 4 MILES

During an extended breakfast, I completed the diary and studied my maps. As much as I enjoyed staying, I also felt the urge to see more of the beautiful land to find out what came next. I was driven by persistent anticipation, a faint idea of the unexpected, that it might be even better, greater, and maybe waiting just around the corner. What I already saw was more than I had expected, though I was still afraid of missing something. I thought, it amounted to greed, our fatal but crucial nature, depriving us of being happy with what we have, rewarding us every so often with even more.

Around noon I gave in, put out the fire and left – the explorer's spirit prevailed. However, this became one of these days, when I did not get farther than an hour's walk. Just like with the flowers in the desert, I found 1,000 reasons to stop and look, explore and take pictures, or just sit down for a while and wallow in pleasure. When I was crossing a creek, it was the skunk cabbage and water lilies that engrossed me, on barren slopes, it was the patches of phlox in all pink variations between snow white and dark violet. In the forest, tall yellow wallflowers were greeting from the trailside, forming a guard of honor, ambitiously craning their necks as if they tried to grow as tall as the pine trees behind them. The grass along the river was just grass, lush, inviting, luring me no less to halt.

Four hours later I had done just as many miles. Then I saw the surpassing spot for an extended sojourn at the river, the place I had been afraid of missing. This was the spot where you hoped to have kept all cares for, only to be solved here.

Between a miniature forest of birch trees and a group of pines was a sandy hill in casting distance for my fishing rod. I emptied my backpack, washed some clothes and allowed myself the luxury of calling it a day in the early afternoon. This was the place to linger and take it easy for a while. With a cup of coffee and a chocolate bar, I leaned against a tree and immersed myself into Colin's book, flicking my calendar back fifty years. I was sure, if Colin had to wait for me somewhere along his route, it would have been here. Even the fish were happily taking a hearty bite. I had to stand up three times to get one off the hook; finally my rod seemed to have lost its virgin smell. Tonight's dinner was noodles a la trout, the natural sommelier served a blanc de blanc West Walker 2008.

06/07   WEST WALKER RIVER, LEAVITT MEADOWS, 0 MILES

When the first sunbeams entered the valley, I woke up but stayed in the bed of high grass for a while. I pricked up my ears picking up an unusually loud honking of geese. One was standing on my side of the river, the other one some twenty feet across on the opposite side. They seemed to have a lively discussion, heatedly arguing over who had to come to the other side. Screaming themselves into a rage, they couldn't come to an agreement, though – understandably a compromise would have been absurd. Eventually, a group of five or six feathered fellows, who had been rubbernecking the fight so far, horned in, creating such a tumult that I felt compelled to get up and see if maybe I could help. It was the funniest scene I had seen so far, like one of these TV shows where at the beginning two parties exhibit their issues until after fifteen minutes the whole audience descends on each other yelling, crying, and spasmodically sobbing. When I walked down closer to the river, the two protagonists flew away, whereas the supporting actors now really started a duck fit, honking even louder while flapping with their wings and biting each other's necks. At the edge of the forest a group of deer was grazing, lifting their heads with wonder.

I had not the slightest idea what the bone of contention was, and I deemed it was advisable to stay in due distance and mind my own business. I walked back to my campsite to rekindle the fire and make coffee. While the water was boiling, I walked down to a curve of the meandering creek, where its flow slowed down thus forming a little pond. When I bent down to wash my face, I saw these tracks again, this time more clear. Out of the water's secrecy came a trail pattern of five- to seven-inch-long tracks. I held my breath; following them, I saw they went right to the place where I had been sleeping. There, the soil was too dry to detect them, but ten feet behind my sleeping bag, I picked them up again. Then they turned off to a stand of birch trees. I thought, I was lucky to have enjoyed a sound sleep and continued my washing ceremonies. Fortified by a hearty breakfast, I further followed the tracks. Obviously, I was of no interest to him. Behind the trees, I found the pattern again, leading back to the water where the creek had washed them away. I doubt it was the same bear since between that tree at the cabin and here was the ridge I had crossed. Unless that one was following me?

While the alertness in the desert was mainly focused on rattlesnakes and venomous insects or the rare chance to meet a mountain lion, from now on, in mountains and forests, it was the bear. As most other predators, they would sense me way before I noticed them and most likely consider a human as unenjoyable and stodgy. In most cases they elude us, but you could not rely on 'most cases'. I felt that the outdoor adventure – at least for me – was pretty much connected to this uncertainty, to the chance to encounter wilderness where it surpasses even the impressive scope of mountains and canyons. Somehow, just knowing that there were creatures that outmatched a human, just being aware that there were natural challenges one might not be able to tackle, quickened the pulse as much as it heightened expectations, thus, in a figurative sense, making mountains higher and canyons deeper, forests darker and, quite prosaic, every evening's campfire equivalent to a safe homecoming.

CHAPTER EIGHT

All close bear encounters I had on earlier hikes happened for the same reason, because I was walking through brushwood, bushwhacking my way to reach a river or a clearing. Most likely I was walking against the wind, which took my smell away from the bear. In one situation along the Yukon River, I just got out of the wood, jumping down a bank to a creek. He was already there, right there, stopped drinking immediately, turned around and stood up to his full height, completely filling the field of view. They do that only to threaten – it sure as hell did – and also to pick up scent.

Apparently he did not like the smell or was as surprised. He shook his head three times, and with two darts he jumped away into the woods. Another memorable encounter was a little friskier. I was walking on an animal trail, the only possibility to get ahead in these primeval taiga forests. Suddenly I heard two cracks, the sound of bursting trees. I looked ahead and only then I realized I was walking right against a seven-foot grizzly. This one ran off the path and stopped behind a larger tree. I could see his face, peeking from behind the trunk, as if he wanted to invite me for playing hide-and-seek. In fact, I accepted and moved behind the closest tree, not so much for playing but in order to literally disappear.

While the rattlesnake was the protagonist in desert tales, the bear is definitely the main character of the northern fauna. Along with lions in Africa, tigers in Asia, jaguars in South America, and sharks in between the continents, they all are the chairmen of the food chain in their respective territory, and somehow they are the stewards of adventure. We proclaimed them kings of their territory, due to their obvious physical advantages along with some other blessings, making them the best subject matter for suspenseful travelogues. In many cultures it has been – and still is – the ultimate proof of courage to dare that king and hunt him down, mostly by unfair means instead of a fistfight. But the real trial of strength between human and animal is tracing and watching the potential opponent, and then behave in a way that the he decides to leave. The reward for such a thrilling encounter is worth much more than a trophy, it is the chance to watch a predator in its natural environment.

By the way, attacks or injuries by other less spectacular species are way more likely, also possibly lethal. In Africa or Asia, for example, attacks by hippos or elephants are more often than those by lions and tigers, everywhere in the world by unspectacular insects like mosquitoes or flies, and in populated areas by our cute best friend, the dog, not to mention our own kind.

Unintentional attacks by venomous spiders, centipedes, or scorpions are most likely caused by us freaking out, thereby provoking the achy reaction, a bite or a sting, whereas the multi-legged visitor was simply out for a flying visit.

According to statistics about the most common causes of death due to injury in the U.S., from all unintentional or accidental lethal injuries (omitting suicidal, murder, and legal intervention), traffic or transport accidents make

50%, roundabout 50,000 per year. The other half include a great variety from falling from bed or chair (however that works), explosions, drowning in a bath-tub, ingestion of food or other objects causing obstruction of the respiratory tract, exposure to heat and cold or to alcohol and drugs. Every single variant exceeded the number of animal attacks by far. The total percentage of all mammal attacks (excluding dogs) plus venomous snakes and insects comes to 0.08%, or in other words, chances in a year are one in 3.5 million.

Even if the Safety Council compiled the same statistic among hikers, I am sure there's much room for happy ending adventures.

To a large part, it is our sensationalistic media and television world creating a wrong-sided picture of many species and their alleged dangerousness. As discussed earlier, the style of many today's documentaries brings it that we lose knowledge of domestic species and become scholars of the rarest, most flamboyant deep-sea creatures or reclusive but venomous animals, while the documented aggressiveness is merely caused by intrusive, meddlesome film cameras and an ever-annoying documentarian. To put their reaction in a familiar context – some humans have been reported to display a similar aggressive behavior, beating up paparazzi or wrapping their cameras around a tree.

Compared to being in a zoo or watching these pseudo-documentaries, observing an animal in its natural environment is something totally different, just like the chance to get to know a famous actor personally after only knowing him from the movies. The bear, however, did not invite me into the auditorium until some days later.

After breakfast, I unstrapped the top bag off my backpack, packed it with camera, water, and a piece of chocolate, and crossed the creek to explore the valley along West Walker and the secrecy of its bounding forests.

One hundred years before Colin had walked along this river, one of the first illustrated magazines about California's nature, the Hutchings' California Magazine, had quoted an emigrant's travel report about these meadows: "… we descended suddenly into a large and beautiful valley, and through which wound the river, now quiet and noiseless … This little valley, or basin, was one of the few truly beautiful spots in this wild region, … and at the northern extremity a little miniature lake, the water cool and clear as crystal, and floating upon its surface was a little flock of ducks, which gave life to the picture. On the south and east, and rising abruptly from the little grassy meadow, were high barren peaks, while on the west was a low sandy ridge, over which lay our trail."* Nothing had changed here.

---

* From: *A trip to Walker's River and Carson Valley,* Hutchings' California Magazine, June 1858

CHAPTER EIGHT

06/08   WEST WALKER RIVER, LEAVITT MEADOWS, 11 MILES

Leaving the river, I hit the trail above the end of the meadows. Before I got to Sonora Pass Road, the West Walker River had dug its bed deep into the valley. From high above its course, I saw some 120 marines in olive-green shirts and shorts, training how to ford a river. One after the other walked into the stream and tried to breast the rapids. Then they walked in pairs, obviously one rescuing the other. I sat down from where I had a good view and couldn't help but smile. As often as I had to do that in the last four weeks with my buddy on my back, I was sure I could have been of some advice. When I got up and moved on, they saluted to me, exposing the two waterborne guys to an unintended, extended, ice bath.

Where the river bounced against the mountains, then turning away to the east, I climbed out of the valley onto U.S. 108 and the historic Sonora Pass route. Just a little north from here, the first California-bound wagon train had crossed the Sierra, organized by 21-year-old John Bidwell, after he had founded the Western Emigration Society in Missouri. They had to abandon their wagons in the desert heat of summer 1841, but they eventually arrived at the Sacramento River.

Reading biographies of people who played an important role in California's early days, pioneers, guides, or trek leaders, at every other you stumble across the name John Sutter and his Fort, where the first California gold was found. This Bidwell stayed and worked for Sutter until he himself struck it rich with gold.

Due to the immense difficulties in crossing the Sierra via his route, later groups traveling west used other trails. Only nine years later, the Clark-Skidmore party from Indiana and Ohio thought they had found a more passable route right here over Sonora Pass. The emigrants, who were aiming for the mining towns of Sonora and Columbia, had been infected from the gold virus, shrugging off the hardships they would face on the trail. However, their enthusiasm was soon restrained. The steep grade up along West Walker River had often stopped them in their tracks. Progress was painfully slow. The party ran out of food and, after eventually slaughtering their oxen, they were forced to leave the heavier stuff behind. Getting over the mountains required easing the wagons down steep descents with ropes, building plank bridges, or even filling ravines with rocks and boulders. When they arrived at Frémont Lake, they had to lower its level by diverting the inlet creeks in order to make a path wide enough for the wagons. Having promoted his route across the mountains as a ten-day travel to the mines, their last scout didn't need to ask for trouble; it took them more than a month. From the 62 members leaving Indiana and Ohio only 24 made it to the towns. The rest had given up, one way or the other.

Despite their experiences, merchant interests and the rich mining activities kept the new 'West Walker – Sonora Road' open until in 1853 another party almost met the same fate as the Donner party. Years later, an Atlantic & Pacific Co. railroad surveyor had sent this report after having followed a trail of dead animals and broken wagons: "This route is the worst that could be found... I advise no emigrant to take it." For many years, the trail was abandoned until, in the heyday of Bodie, gold fever again raised the threshold of pain.

Walking east on the highway, after five miles I reached the Marine Corpse Survival Training Center. With its red-roofed barracks, from afar, the small settlement adorned the mountains like a Swiss village with geranium balconies. In cooperation with Forest Service, here, the USMC is training for survival in mountains and cold, as I had the chance to witness along the river.

A friendly marine saw me passing the entrance gate, behind which the trail to Silver Creek began. He became interested in my gear and asked me many questions in a yet untrained commanding voice. He was a freshman for sure, however, he left me no choice but to answer all of his questions, what I had for food, if I ate plants or hunt animals, how I crossed the creeks and the passes this time of the year, and most of all – why would one do what I did?

Another one came by and, after repeating my report to him, he offered me his old snow shoes. I thanked him and kindly declined, it would be too late now, and, furthermore, they were too big and too heavy. Had I known that there was still so much snow, I would have brought a pair before I entered the Sierra. Now there was only one pass left and the days were getting hot enough to be optimistic.

Instead, he opened his survival backpack and passed me one of his MRE food packs – meal ready to eat – saying, "The cookies are OK, everything else only before you die." I asked him about the essential contents of his survival pack, the items needed most, when you get lost in the wild or on a special mission in foreign land. I had to admit, it came much lighter than mine. Basically, I had all of his small gadgets like a compass, two fire starters (waterproof matches in my case), a signal mirror (which was included in my compass), a knife, a mini wire saw, a whistle, a rope, fishhooks, and an aluminum tarp. But with the clothes I brought, I could have vested the two of us, and of course he had no camera or any fancy technical devices like a laptop or an iPod (which I, by the way, never used again after the *Echoes* at Bodie). Yet looking in his pack, one item had arrested my rapt attention. I picked an eight-inch-long hand broom and examined it curiously. "This is a broom," he said, recognizing that I had no idea what it was. Actually, I had no idea what it was for, so he continued, "to sweep snow out of the tent."

06/09   SILVER CREEK, 8 MILES

Entering Alpine County, the landscape was almost a continuation of the days before, a rugged range of snow-capped peaks and lush valleys with meandering creeks, on the level an Alpine area.

When you experienced something you rated as your personal highlight, it is often hard to give it away or swap it with a new experience. After the days in the meadows of West Walker, I would hold on to them, unless I saw something I had not yet imagined. Accordingly, I was very skeptical about Colin's ardor for the Silver King Valley. It would now take a lot more to impress me as much.

A steep ascent along Silver Creek brought me up to the last 10,000-foot barrier below Wells Peak, which separated me from Colin's favorite spot. Up here, it was a strange and tangible silence, caused either by the sudden absence of the many small creeks below or a sudden purplish overcast swallowing every noise. In the same year Colin stood up here, Jack Kerouac had published the *Dharma Bums*, based on his hikes across these ranges with the Zen poet Gary Snyder. Fifty years later, I understood what he wrote, "The pinkness vanished and then it was all purple dusk and the roar of the silence was like a wash of diamond waves going through the liquid porches of our ears, enough to soothe a man a thousand years."

Around the pass, there was still pretty much snow, though the last days had been warm enough to prepare at least snow-free paths almost to the top. Admitted, the view down into Silver King Valley, a snaking creek through Alpine meadows, was a wonderful scene. However, as I already *knew* before I saw it, it could not keep up with the Piute's or Leavitt's. Indeed, here too, the creek invited to set camp at each bend, which could easily turn a planned night along Silver King into a fortnight. The enchantment was still there, though, I could not feel the magic anymore. Maybe the spell had been expelled by too many visitors, people who came here for the rare Piute trout. In the 1960s, the rare species, which was endemic to only the upper part of this valley, was listed as endangered, ten years later as threatened. The causes of nearby forest fires eventually finished the creek and consequently any fishing. Or maybe it was just the fact that everyone has to find his own little paradise and that I had already found mine.

Colin had really taken the bait here. I passed three of his campsites on that day, each no more than one mile and a half from another. He had spent six days fishing in Upper Fish Valley, as his San Franciscan friend Herb Pintler had predicted he would when he was still planning his route in San Francisco. Pintler had told him about the legendary Piute trout, a subspecies of the common cutthroat that developed in the upper creek section after erosion and landslides had created a natural barrier for the fish some 8,000 years ago. Due to the shallower water upstream, they changed their camouflage, lost the heavy spotting of cutthroats, and assimilated by a lighter almost purple coloration.

Thousands of years later, the arrival of Basque sheepherders seemed to have secured the population by planting the unusual looking fish above a yet higher barrier, the Llewellyn Falls. Nature did not intend so, since at the same time she had begun to wash the land barriers away and reconnect the lower stream systems again. Now, below the falls, diversity developed, a genetic mixture of Lahontan cutthroat, imported rainbow and golden trout, and the temporarily native Piute trout. At the turn of the 19th century, it was also newly arrived settlers who had been stocking the rivers with other trout species thus catalyzing hybridization. It seemed that only the Piute population above the falls remained isolated, except for one single hybrid that mysteriously had found its way over the falls, caught by Colin Fletcher on a Sunday in June in the year 1958.

When I came through this area, there weren't many fish anyway, instead I picked up heavy discussion about them among the local population. The California Department of Fish and Game and environmental agencies were designing a natural plan to take out some of the threatened native Piutes, store them in hatcheries, and kill all remaining fish, preferentially, since most efficiently, by using pesticides. After a while, when the chemicals were washed away, the parked population would be replanted in the streams. I couldn't help but think that somehow it did not sound quite *natural* to me.

Considering the drastic impacts on other fauna like amphibians and mainly everything that lives in and around the creek, the required neutralization of drinking water and temporary full closure of the valley – could that be *natural*? Can we go that far and still be in line with environmental concerns, when saving becomes interfering, especially when the corrective means would be anything but natural? With a little evolutionary fantasy, one may see a different plot; maybe nature, too, had her moods and on one bad day, in a freak of nature, she had caused the landslides that forced a part of the cutthroats to live in horror for many generations until they finally adapted to the harsh conditions of shallow waters with less hideouts and less food. Maybe now, by washing away the barriers, nature was mercifully bringing the long separated relatives back together. And here comes man interfering with nature's plan.

However one sees it – and since I wasn't that good at identifying the various types from hybrids to Piutes, fishing a species declared threatened was out of question. That gave me more time to devote myself to the other Basque heritage, the vestige sheepherders had left along their traveled paths through mountains and valleys between here and the Warner Mountains. While pine trees would have reminded them much more of their homeland in France and Spain, they had carved their stories only into the parchment bark of aspen trees. Rarely were there sayings, sometimes drawings, but mostly the story told was just a name and a date. Nevertheless, while the occasional finding of an obviously modern entry into the aspen logbook seemed to merely tell trivia, the Basque carvings transported the yearning of people who left their home to make a living in solitude and in a harsh environment. They also told of people who found themselves in an unimaginable setting of natural beauty, and of the melancholy from being torn between the old and the new.

In their sonorous names, I read the loving thoughts of a girl at home, devoted thoughts of the family, and the poetry of letters never sent to loved ones about a nature where words just fail. Some had been carved tentatively, almost indecipherable today, their stories outtold. Others were determined and deep inside the bark, destined to last for a century. Gnarly framing around the letters, the regrowing bark elevated them to calligraphy.

Perhaps I read too much into a few letters and numbers. But when I saw how filigree and sophisticated some carvings were designed and how much time and devotion must have been exercised, I thought that, between the lines, I could hear of the lives of mountain shepherds, pioneering between then and now. I felt sorry that I wouldn't be able to meet one of them anymore; all the more I wanted to read their stories as often as possible.

Since the early 1800s, Basques had been involved in the Spanish exploration of the Americas. The gold rushes of the mid-19th century lured many more away from their homeland around the west Pyrenees. Coming from this rather rural area, they brought a certain skillfulness for livestock, first concentrating on transhumance and in the course of history becoming experts in sheepherding. During the peak of the California gold rush, they moved large herds of more than 1,000 animals from winter quarters in the desert to the summer quarters high in the Sierra Nevada, White Mountains, and Warner Mountains, thus becoming another important pillar of supporting the frontier.

With a growing population, conflicts of interest arose between farmers, cattle-ranchers, and the sheepherders. Anti-Basque sentiments were fueled; their sheepherding routes became increasingly restricted by civilization growing into nature on one side and land allocation to the agencies (National Park, National Forest, BLM) on the other. The era of nomading *Amerikanuak*, as they were called at home, came to an end.

For a short time around and after World War II, the need for sheep grazing exceeded environmental concerns, hence Basque immigration resurged. However, shortly after Colin wandered along their routes, grazing permits were again so limited that he might have seen one of the last men standing at the end of a flock of a thousand white sheep.

At the junction of Bull Canyon on the west side of the creek was Connels Cow Camp, the place where Colin met cowboys Charlie Roberts and Sid

Henderson. The cattle were long gone and with them the cowboys. The camp was now owned by Forest Service and used as a patrol station. The Wilderness Act was visible here, the grazing was stopped, trails were not maintained more than a minimum and 4WD roads were cut back. Good for the wilderness, and yet this might have caused the magnitude of another devastating wild fire.

One man I met on Sonora Road talked about the 'good old days', when he drove cattle in these mountains. He had spent many nights in a small cabin, he said. Whenever he felt that his animals were anxious, he stayed up there overnight to guard them. But quite often he would just have sat at the creek for too long, lost in reverie, until it was too late to ride back. The cabin was still there, but since the dirt road was closed, he could not get there, because he was not able to walk that far anymore.

I stayed overnight at Colin's third camp, gazing in a beautiful but empty river, overloaded with high expectations, but not a single trout.

Colin was often very contained in disclosing the exact location of some of the natural highlights he found. In his *Thousand-Mile Summer*, he actually admitted keeping one as a secret while he left no doubt that his favorite would be the Silver King, praising it as the most wonderful spot along his way. There is no place he wrote more about than this remote valley, which was home to the rare trout species. He even wrote an article for the fishermen's scriptures *Field & Stream* Magazine, giving full particulars about his alleged Arcadia, including a map. I started wondering, what his favorite, his secret, really was, maybe the meadows along West Walker?

06/10   SILVER KING CREEK, CONNELS COW CAMP, 18 MILES

I forded the creek at the cow camp, reaching Llewellyn Falls after one and a half mile. I knew that Colin had not waited long to ensconce himself for another break so I had saved my breakfast to join him at the falls.

From there it was a wonderful walking day through Lower Fish Valley and Long Valley. I enjoyed each step and every detour around the creek's numerous bends, all of them inviting places to set up camp for another night. Something kept me moving, though, somehow I felt pleasantly uneasy.

06/11   HEENAN LAKE, 11 MILES

Eventually, Silver King turned west, joining the East Fork of Carson River. The thick forest had a medieval atmosphere, telling stories from a past, when they were the natural roof for travelers reaching from city to city. It felt like time stood still, and it could have stopped today, fifty years ago, or five hundred.

CHAPTER EIGHT

Descending to the town of Markleeville, Carson River was suddenly forced into a deep ravine virtually foaming at steep rock walls. Only when reaching the large ranchlands around town, it was set free and fell back into its contemplative meandering.

The reception in Markleeville was just as one would expect it from a hamlet hidden in deep forest before the arrival of modern times, or any time at all. The streets were empty. It was a regular weekday, but everything was closed. General store and post office – closed. Hotel and Motel – closed. The restaurant – closed. There was a mini gas station with a sign in the window saying 'Always Open' – it was closed. I thought, either everybody was out of town working in the fields, or there was a spell on that remote, little village in the mountains.

I sat down on a bank enjoying but wondering about the quiet. An hour later, the first vehicle rolled down Main Street, it was a carriage pulled by a horse. Yes! I was ready to believe I had walked through a time warp, now having reached the apogee of my adventure. I have gone back in time – then, no! I did not; there came the first of several cars following patiently behind him. In three minutes, five pickups had parked around the junction of the only two streets. Simultaneously, both the restaurant door and all car doors opened, men and women in working clothes and boots jumped from their seats, beating a path to the restaurant doorstep. Stories from the day and loud laughter filled the street with life, but for a short moment you could feel how the stories stumbled and the laughter stalled, when my appearance caught their eye. They slackened their pace, we were eyeballed, my dusty backpack and me, until the door fell closed.

A little later, I went inside, too, to hear what the stories were, what everyone was laughing about and to get a drink and something to eat. Somehow the place seemed to be run by everyone, by everyone but me. Although there was one girl behind the counter serving some guests, the majority helped themselves. People streamed in and out, at the bar and behind the bar. Everyone was telling his own story at the same time and somehow it seemed that they all heard and understood everybody's words.

"Excuse me", I called twice. "What can I getya?" came the reply while she was listening to three and talking to two others at the bar. "A Sierra Nevada and the menu, please." The beer I had in half a minute, but, "oh, did you ask for the menu – today's salad only," said she, looked me in the eyes, took my astonishment as an order and back she was in her conversations.

With the beer in front of me, I must have come across more sympathetic somehow. After a while, one of the men, sort of a mountain man type, turned on his barstool and looked at me. I think, what I understood from under his humongous beard was: "Are you a hiker?" He caught me by surprise and I thought, this is not the time to answer funny things, like, "No, why do you think so, I came to rob your bank." "Yes I am," I replied, gazing at this forested face reminding me of that medieval forest I just came through. The longer I thought about it, what he said or how he said it sounded more like "Eureka!" But I doubted that he would have shared his discovery with me. However, it seemed that his curiosity was satisfied and our conversation over; he nodded, said okay, and turned back to the crowd.

In any case, I felt I was accepted now, I was just a tourist, a nature-lover, and there was no reason to fear the worst, a vagabond that would hang around town. Because of our little dialog, from now on everybody smiled and greeted with a look on my heavy pack meaning, respect, that's a load to carry.

Having finished the meager but excellent and hearty meal, I got a room across the street at a motel called J. Marklee Toll Station. The owner was not there yet, but the daughter told me to take a room and talk to her mom next morning. I chose the room on the far left with the best view on both sides of town and went to bed with Colin's paragraph about Markleeville. He had stayed almost a week here, but after that evening I did not expect to meet anyone who remembered him coming through or, if so, who would divulge it to me.

06/12   MARKLEEVILLE, 0 MILES

I woke up at cockcrow. Here in Markleeville, that was 9 a.m. Going for a little stroll through the two streets, I passed the museum, the library, and the café; everything did not open before 10 or 11. The only busy place was the general store, where I knocked my breakfast together.

Some minutes after 12, I went to the post office to send the MRE to my Bowie-knife friend in Germany. I thought he might like the funnily packaged cookies too. The sign at the door said it should open at noon, but I understood that opening hours here were only recommendations. Three people I had seen at the bar the night before came to check their mailboxes. Now knowing who I was, they were greeting me as if we knew each other for years and confirming, "she'll come, maybe coupla minutes later".

'Coupla' turned into thirty, again, and I was just about to leave and cram my mail back into my pack. Something had made me add another five minutes and another until she came, serendipity Mrs. Margaret Daniels, in her capacity as postmaster of the year 2006. My visit to the post office opened not only the world of Markleeville to me but also Colin's sojourn in the unobtrusive hamlet. Margaret was a cascade of words, like obviously everybody here. Only now, I was the subject.

She knew everything about the town, all stories, all people, and in one hour I knew probably more than all the guys in that bar together. In that informative hour, I also learned why a tiny branch like hers, catering for a population of just 200, was at times more busy than some I saw in downtown L.A. People did not just go there to drop mail. They talked and exchanged the talk of the

CHAPTER EIGHT

town, news from the last court meeting or the re-opening of Sandy's Café – and they were laughing non-stop. There was one lady who came in, looking really frowning and serious and unsmiling. It was quite obvious that she was not in the mood for small talk. Ten minutes later, she left with a smile in her face, wishing everybody a wonderful day. When I asked Margaret if that would be her mission, she told me her story. Twenty-one years ago, she came from Canada to Markleeville and ever since she was the postmaster of the town. She was an active member in the National League of Postmasters of the U.S. – I didn't even know something like that existed – and had already been nominated postmaster of the year in 1995. That time she missed out. A dozen years later, after having delivered the highest sales increase of California, Hawaii, Nevada, and Arizona, she was finally rewarded the title in 2007. She pulled a plastic zipper bag from under the counter, opened it, and took out a photo showing her with former President Bill Clinton. "That was after the awards," she said, and "Keep it for your book." I couldn't imagine a nicer present from the postmaster of the year. Whenever new customers came in, she asked me to show my copy to them, so she could tell the story again.

We left politics and discussed my concern, that I was interested in someone who might remember the Mrs. Brown, Colin had mentioned, the lady, who had run the motel I was staying at and who had been the only woman sheriff in California at that time. I was told to be back at the office the following day, same time, around noon. "Noon or same time?" I asked. She laughed and waved me goodbye.

Before I went back to my room, I had coffee and ice cream at the small café, maybe for an hour or two, in any case enough time to let the news about me spread through town. When I came to the motel, Sandy Matlock, the new owner, was there, and before I could introduce myself, she already called me by name. She knew everything about me, and she had a message from Gary Coyan, who was here asking for me to talk about Mr. Fletcher.

Now I was the talk of the town. I called Mr. Coyan and made arrangements with him to meet at the motel. "He is the last old timer in town," Margaret had said, "if there is anybody who knows anything about 1958, he will be the one to ask."

When he came to the motel, I saw him walking around the building as if he was indulging in reminiscence. Then he called: "Are you the guy tearing off the taps from tea bags?" Colin had described that he got in a state of fussiness during his walk, tearing off everything dispensable to get rid of unnecessary grams; he thought that, "If you look after the ounces the pounds look after themselves." Obviously that had impressed the young Gary Coyan most. When he was in his twenties, he recalled, a hiking man had spent a week in town, stayed in the same motel and, as a matter of fact, in the same room as I did. In the afternoons, that man used to come to his grandma's porch to talk to her. Elizabeth Coyan was blind and enjoyed listening to his descriptions of nature.

He regretted that the man forgot to mention his grandma in the book, though, since he spent almost every afternoon in a week's stay with her. But he did not forget her; one day, a parcel was delivered containing a book titled *The Thousand-Mile Summer*, and it was personally signed.

The next day, he took me to Jim Long's house, whose grandfather was the judge of the town from 1907 to 1947. With him lived Dick Edwards, the museum director. Gary and Jim left us alone, and I immersed into the history of Alpine County. The museum was closed, of course, but Dick gave me an exclusive tour through a very sophisticated and unobtrusively arranged house of history. Instead of being swamped by a vast, unmanageable collection of relics and paraphernalia, you were guided and informed about essentials. "If you have five old coffee makers, you don't need to display all of them," said Dick, who had an eye for allowing each item enough space to bring it back to live, or the story it had to tell.

Having led emigrant treks into California since 1849, a Jacob A. Marklee decided to settle down and benefit from the silver rush in this area. At the peak of the Nevada silver boom, in 1861, Jacob Marklee had built a toll bridge over today's Marklee Creek. One year later, he recorded his land claim in Douglas County, Nevada. When he came back, he had to learn that, after the latest boundary survey, his land was now in California, and before he could react accordingly, a Mr. Tuttle rushed to file the same spot in Placerville, California, a.k.a. Dry Diggin's, a.k.a. Hangtown, another hub for mining operations and, for a short time, the young state's third biggest town. Tuttle and Marklee fought it out, eventually shot it out, and Jacob Marklee got killed. Tuttle was taken to Bridgeport but set free, showing credibly that they had a fair fight. Did I say Bridgeport? Anyway, Tuttle disappeared and so, in the end, or historically, Marklee had won; the people named their new city after him. For a short period during the silver boom in Nevada, Marklee Ville became the major supply station for the mining sites and with a population of 12,000, the seat of Alpine County.

Covering the official part of the town's history, Dick asked me if I had seen the bridge over East Fork Carson. He told of a shooting, where a miner had killed the local barkeeper in an argument. "Presumably, here, not a good idea," I said. "In fact," he continued, "town people liked him and tried to lynch the shootist, who then turned himself into sheriff's custody. Worse idea!" Dick stressed the last words with raised eyebrows. "This one either had looked the other way or he even helped the mob. Minutes later the unlucky fellow found himself hanging from the toll bridge, and from that day on it was called Hangman's Bridge." I sure was right, I mumbled, last night in the bar, not to give foolish answers. But wait for the unofficial part; there were rumors that the rope had been too long, that the hangman's

CHAPTER EIGHT

feet landed on a rock in the creek bed and that he was stoned to death. Understandably, this part of local history was relegated to the land of myths.

At the end of the tour, we stumbled over an old acquaintance; when the bottom fell out of the silver market, a certain William Bodie found gold not too far from here. Within a few days, the local newspaper got their printing press and tools and supplies on a wagon, and off they went for Bodie, followed by thousands of loyal readers.

When he closed the museum, Dick completed his lessons with essential statistics; in Markleeville, everything existed only once. One museum, one restaurant, one courthouse, one hotel, one motel, one general store. There also is one town bear and one town raccoon. Every evening they would come for a visit, the smaller guy around 7, the bigger cinnamon fellow at 9.30 p.m.

The reason for the empty streets during day might have been that many of the town's population are artists who spend daytime in their studios. Until recently, not much information was available about that secluded mountain village in a rustic countryside. Only in the last years, some of the citizens added a second string to their bow serving summer tourism. Today, no friend of the eastern Sierra can just pass through but will succumb to the charm of the Alpine village, stop for a coffee, sit on a bank wondering, eat a salad, or even stay overnight at Sandy's Toll Station to await the cinnamon bear.

In the evening, I became part of the bar talk and had to tell my story to three people at the same time. Since all three sat at different places and were themselves involved in other discussions, I offered modules. One got the desert stories, one the High Sierra, and one the rattlesnake encounters. I was upgraded to receiving a beer without asking for it and, I was sure, after two more nights I would have helped myself.

At 9 p.m. the bar closed. I walked back to the motel, grabbed a chair, and sat behind the room to await the town bear. Half an hour later, he sneaked around the building, a good-sized cinnamon bear. I was quietly watching him on his evening routine checking the motel's backyard. He was so concerned with poking his nose into every corner, snooping at all these wonderful odors, that he didn't even recognize me. When he reached the second to last room I got nervous. I slowly moved one leg forward to be in a position where I could jump into my room, but before my leg was stretched, he noticed a movement, threw me a sharp glance, and took off into the dark.

06/13   MARKLEEVILLE, 7 MILES

Weekend was in the air. Sandy was busily working to reopen the breakfast café for visitors, and the Wolf Creek bar put signs on the street corner, announcing live music on Saturday. Filling its boardwalks with tourists, the town suggested to stay for an entertaining weekend, but I felt the ants in my pants and prepared my leave. When I passed Gary's house to say goodbye, he offered me to use one of the pack goats, he and his wife were raising, for the remaining stretch. He said they were good travel companions, gentle, docile, and frugal characters. They eat while walking and whatever they find, they leave only small pills, carry up to eighty pounds, and they even give milk; almost a Swiss army knife, born to multitask. I only had to eat secretly because they liked to share. At night they would nestle up against me and make it warm. The thought was tempting, however, I wanted to consider the offer for another journey.

When I knocked at the museum to say goodbye to Dick and Jim, I received a luxurious farewell present, a bottle of red wine; a weighty luxury, that is, I would have to empty it the first night, since I had turned down the pack goat.

When I went back to pick up my pack, I passed the gas station. The 'Always Open' sign was gone because the door, on which the sign was attached, was open.

Leaving town westwards, I passed the Grover Hot Springs and followed Hot Springs Creek until I turned north to climb up rocky switchbacks to the next pass. On the other side lay the small, beautiful Burnside Lake hidden amidst thick pine tree forest. I did not know if the famous Civil War General Ambrose E. Burnside had been here to name that lake – due to a couple of tragic defeats, he was better known for his weird looking facial hair-do – but when I bent down to fill my water sacks, I saw my face in the reflection of the lake and I knew, it was time for a decent shave. Then I started my Italian feast, spaghetti al canned tonno and a bottle of Chianti.

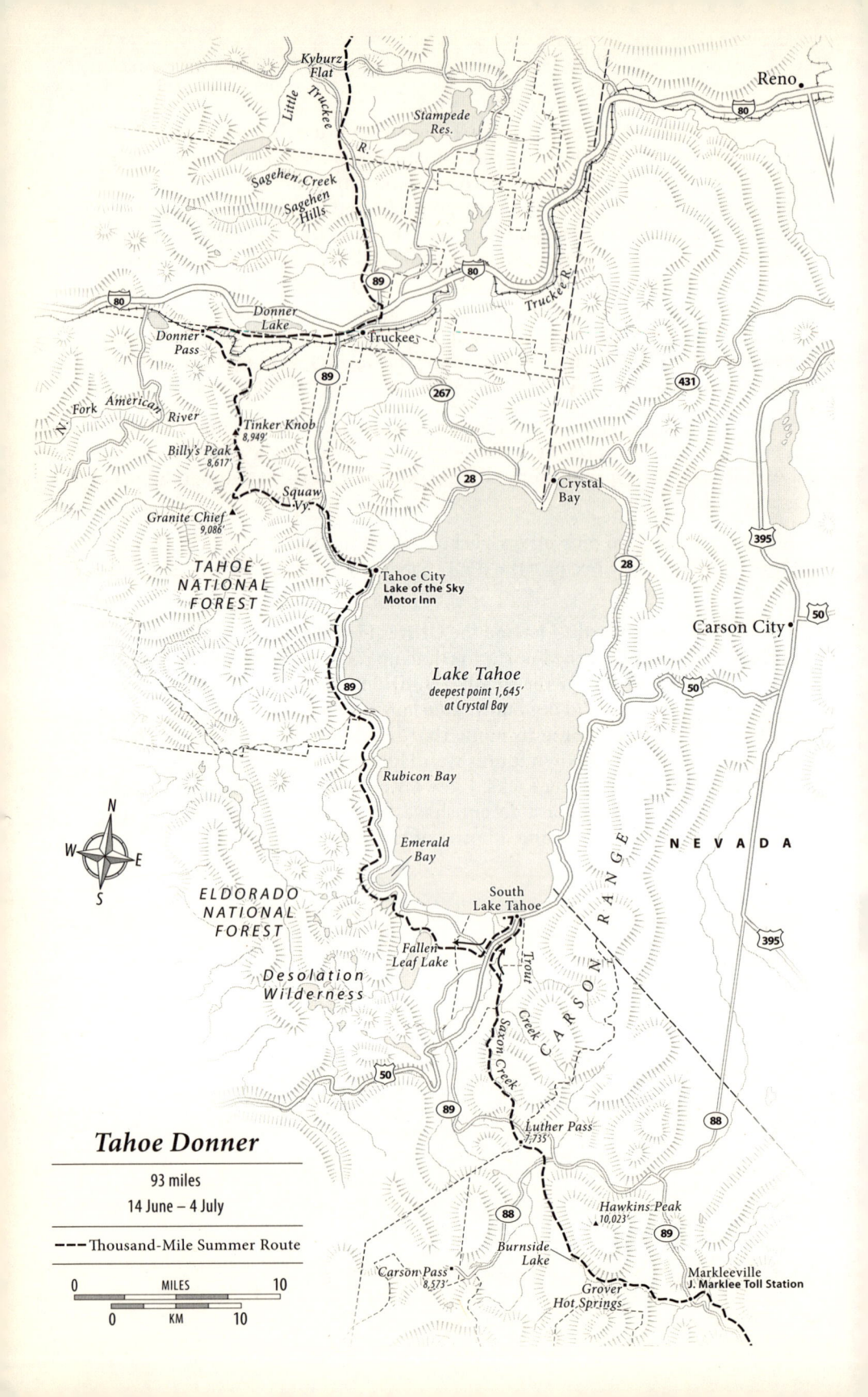

Tahoe Donner

93 miles

14 June – 4 July

- - - Thousand-Mile Summer Route

9. TAHOE DONNER

There is no such thing as death.
In nature nothing dies.
From each sad remnant of decay
some form of life arise.

CHARLES MACKAY, SCOTTISH POET AND JOURNALIST, 1814–1889

06/14   BURNSIDE LAKE, 15 MILES

The fire was still smoking too much to get away with "No Sir, I have no idea, it was already burning when I got here." Early in the morning, the forest ranger came driving down the dirt road along the lake. When he saw me, he parked his ATV and came to my site.

I never really knew if I was on park or BLM land or just in nature, if it was right how I slept or legal to have a fire; I thought, I just did what a cross-country hiker had to do, and I made sure I was always careful with fire and that I did not leave anything but tracks. Nevertheless, seeing a ranger often caused me ambivalent feelings, especially after the encounters at Picacho and Mammoth. But this one was easy-going; he was the one who issued me the fire permit since 'obviously' I had lost mine somewhere.

Eventually, our meeting evolved into an interesting conversation about the local flora. We were standing there like two trappers who had accidentally met, now exchanging their observations about trail and weather conditions along the routes. Treating him to a cup of coffee, after the fire was legalized, created a scene reminiscent of those old-day Marlboro commercials. Two men kneeling down at the fire, their hats throwing long shadows on the perpetually tan faces of someone who lives outdoors. For a short arresting

CHAPTER NINE

moment, they enjoy a cup of coffee and a butt. They kneel, that is, they mustn't sit, because they always have to be alert and reckon with something, here in the wilderness.

Before he left, he mentioned that in this area I would definitely meet hiking rangers every once in a while, then I would need the permit. Having lost it wouldn't count. I didn't think so. He was the first ranger I saw in real wilderness away from park sites or established roads. And still, he was driving. A ranger with a backpack – like in Canada – that would be something, I thought. It seemed that most U.S. rangers could only look to handle basic things like manning the stations and visitor centers to collect park entrance fees and give information. However, in times when their budgets and headcounts are constantly being cut, how could they do more, like maintaining trails and checking their wild territories including its permanent and temporary residents, its animal world and hiking visitors. Also, I haven't even seen a hiker so far but the two at Crater Creek, who wanted to go fishing south of Mammoth. Somehow it was great to be the only one out there, but at the same time, it was alarming; don't people do that anymore?

After I had left the lake, I strode on a carpet of yellow flowers for several miles. Besides dandelions and sunflowers, due to the shape of the leaves, here also called mule's ears, there were at least three more species, coming in light yellow, lemon, or dark yolk yellow. Between them stood a few disruptive violets, but totally narcissistic and out of place were the first red snow plants. Protruding from the forest soil like miniature firs in red, this strange looking plant with curly, glandular-hairy leaves became a fairly common sight in the woods around Lake Tahoe. Growing one foot tall, it angled for attention, and in this regard it relegated the highest pine tree. John Muir once described the flamboyant plant as a "bright red glowing pillar of fire". As soon as the snow cover was gone, the little flesh-red bonnets worked their way through a decaying layer of pine needles and forest litter. In only two to three weeks, I saw them grow from the size of a small mushroom to one foot and a half, glowing like an over-decorated Christmas tree.

The plant per se is redolent of a fungus, but as a matter of fact it neither belongs to the plant kingdom nor to the fungi; instead it parasites on the symbiotic relationship between the two, between conifer and fungus. For a healthy living, the conifer is dependent on an underground fungus that helps the tree to get enough water and minerals through its net of fine root hairs, the mycelium. In return, the conifer shares some of its photosynthetic products with its associated partner, like sucrose and glucose. Since snow plants, too, have no chlorophyll, hence unable to photosynthesize, they take advantage of the win-win-situation between tree and fungus, sharing their mycorrhizal liaison by branching off the nutrition they need for themselves. That's why the fleshy – no less flashy – fellows are always seen beneath conifers. Like all members of the Indian pipe-family, snow plants do not return their hosts' favor but with a wondrous sight.

Although you would never think of eating a plant that comes in such a warning color, parts of it are edible. However, only Native Americans were able to acquire a taste for it before it became protected by law. They also used to grind dried plants into powder that relieved toothache and other pain. The emergency tablets I took with me had the same color, and my doc had told me they were only for the rare event when I had to chop off an arm or a leg; then, with these red pills, I would still be able to make it a couple of days. The only problem, he said, I would act as if I still had all limbs, which might cause other tricky situations.

Reaching Hope Valley at the junction of 88 and 89 highways, I crossed the Carson River for a last time. It was here where the eponym drew hope, seeing the first lush valley after an arduous winter march across the mountains. It was pretty impressive how often he engraved his name on local history, from here I saw Carson Pass, I had forded the Carson River and crossed the Carson Range, behind which Carson Valley declined to Carson City. A little further west from here near Silver Lake was the town of Kit Carson. Why so many Carsons around here?

The omnipresent Christopher Houston Carson, better known as Kit Carson, made his living as a trapper and mountain man, Indian agent and mediator, explorer and soldier, no easy introduction to briefly describe this man and the complex role he took in the United States' Westward expansion and the consequent Americanization of the West.

While here, too, Jedediah Smith is to be seen as the earliest pioneer, exiting from San Joaquin Valley after his first Mojave crossing, Carson had really roamed this area several times. At the age of seventeen, he left his home in Missouri and came to the Southwest. The Westward drift kept him restless, and with only nineteen years, he joined one of the first fur-trapping expeditions into California. In the 1830s and '40s he was trapping the mountains as far as the Sierra Nevada, earning him a reputation among his peers as a hard-to-find reliable, honest, and courageous Westerner, a man whose "word was as sure as the sun comin' up". In the 1840s, Frémont hired him as the chief guide for his expeditions to map and explore trails to the West Coast. Frémont's detailed epic reports made him an icon of the new world, the first American superman.

Carson guided Frémont when he joined the bear-flag rebellion as well as General Kearney's troops in the Mexican-American war. He never tried his luck in California's newfound golden treasure, though he profited from his excellent knowledge of the area and earned some good pocket money from driving and selling thousands of cattle to the hungry miners.

He had lived among Indians and married Indian women, yet ultimately, he was not their friend in general. During federal campaigns he found himself conscripted to fight a bitter war against fractious and rebellious Natives throughout the Southwest. Since he was soon appointed to higher ranks in the U.S. Army, it was among his duties to assist in displacing them into reservation, be it through mediation or brute force, possibly against his will but by the order of his employer.

Yet, everyone who witnessed Carson had described him as an outstanding and honorable man of the West, "a gentleman by instinct, upright, pure, and simple-hearted, beloved alike by Indians, Mexicans, and Americans." One contemporary went as far as appealing honor to those who suffered most from his army campaigns: "The name of Kit Carson is to this day held in reverence by all the old members of the Navajo tribe. They say he knew how to be just and considerate as well as how to fight the Indians".

In recent years, several allegations have been brought up, disputing Carson's integrity and superhuman attitudes. As humungous a persona as Carson probably was, it is not unthinkable that, in the course of events, he had to fall victim to the whims of other interests, making him a pawn in the confusion of the Westward movement with all its conflicts of interests and wars.

Along with the romanticized stories of Buffalo Bill and Wyatt Earp, Carson's legacy can be seen as the incarnated ambivalence between fact and fiction. After the real person had been glorified and his stories romanticized in various ways, his character was woven in a multitude of historic events, according to respective contemporary ideals. When Carson's role found its way into dime novels, comic books, and later on into music and television, the created image came up to the people's expectations. There were times when a white superman killing bears and Indians alike, while rescuing damsels in distress, resembled carrying the nation's banner into the frontier. Titles like "Fighting with Kit Carson", "The Return of Kit Carson" or "Prince of the Gold Hunters" were devoured feverishly and regarded by many as biographical literature; thank God and with credit to a sober-minded Hollywood, we were spared "Kit Carson meets Godzilla".

Carson biographer Harvey L. Carter stated in 1968: "In respect to his actual exploits and his actual character, however, Carson was not overrated. If history has to single out one person from among the Mountain Men to receive the admiration of later generations, Carson is the best choice. He had far more of the good qualities and fewer of the bad qualities than anyone else in that varied lot of individuals."

On one of Frémont's journeys back home to Missouri, he wanted to find out if there was a navigable connection between the Great Salt Lake and the Pacific Ocean. Guided by his best man, they circuited this area around Carson

River Valley for several months, eventually arriving near today's Markleeville at the Grower Hot Springs where they set up camp. It was already in the middle of the winter 1843/1844, impossible to cross the Rockies before spring. Meanwhile, Carson, who was somehow familiar with the area, climbed several passes and mountains for navigation purposes, casually discovering Lake Tahoe and the Sacramento Valley. Early spring, they left the Sierra this way and surpassed the mountains southwards through San Joaquin Valley and back east across the Mojave Desert.

Further following the Frémont/Carson route, I, too, was heading for Lake Tahoe, the alleged jewel of all lakes in California. Right behind the crossing, I found a welcoming shortcut to the heavily used four-lane Highway. Snaking up the mountain to Luther Pass, an old section of U.S. 89, or Carson Road, was abandoned long enough that it had replaced the yellow markings with yellow flowers protruding from the broken asphalt. Reaching the pass, I cut straight through the woods heading north to climb the last range before descending on the emerald lake. Luther Pass was most likely named after Irish emigrant Ira M. Luther, who crossed the range here in a wagon in 1854 and later became a busy tradesman between the goldfields of California.[*]

Being close to one of the state's most popular summer and winter destinations, I found a network of trails in the Tahoe Forest. The Tahoe Rim Trail was the newest project, a summit trail surrounding the lake from peak to peak. Although it has been promoted quite a bit since it was opened in 2001, I still did not meet any hikers. Instead, I bypassed a group of Basque mountain bikers who had difficulties with the steep grade. So they ended up hiking, at last.

After a three-mile ascent, we all arrived at the junction to the rim trail, walking. While the Basques dashed away starting their 165-mile tour around the lake, I was looking for the springs of Saxon Creek to follow it straight down to the lake. As soon as I had left the last snowfields behind, I set up camp at the first small tributary to the Saxon.

In the desert, I had an open sky above me, where more stars were switched on the darker it got and the longer I stared. Eventually, I saw the Milky Way and an unfathomable chaos of stars and signs from horizon to horizon. Since I walked through the forests, each night I saw another part of the whole sky picture, set in a wooden frame of treetops. Chances for capturing a flaming star here were rather low, but in that night, they had all agreed on falling through this window. One was blazing so bright I instinctively leaned to the side in a knee-jerk reaction.

---

[*] Other sources mention a Lieutenant Luther, who came through here looking for the best route to Hangtown and Sacramento, or also a Sacramento citizen with the same name, who crossed this pass around the same time.

CHAPTER NINE

06/15   SAXON CREEK, 19 MILES

Reaching the outskirts of South Lake Tahoe, I walked along holiday homes, where I passed reserved, incommunicative people preparing their homes for summer. Everyone seemed to be so self-absorbed; two neighbors could stand back-to-back cutting their hedges without saying a word. Trees were cut, boats cleaned, homes constructed, gardens designed, but not a word spoken. Here again, like at Walker Lake along the Colorado, the only, albeit nonverbal communication with me was a suspicious look.

Along highway 89 into South Lake Tahoe, the streets became busy and anonymous. The first traffic jam since I had left Los Angeles three months ago reminded me that I was not a 19th-century pioneer but a modern hiker in Colin's footsteps. I walked down several miles along the resort's restaurant and motel strip. The closer I got to the shore, I smelled sweet summer sweat and sunscreen odors, just like you breathe the salty air when you approach an ocean. Passing a sign saying 'La Baguette, a Tahoe Artisan Bakery', another rare odor reached my nostrils. The warm smell of pastries was beckoning to me so intensively that I had to stop for a second breakfast. Having received my choice of muffins, a fruitcake with cream, and a chocolate croissant, I took seat and wondered, who had bought all that stuff. It was more sweets than I could eat in two days. I just couldn't resist, when I saw the variety of pastries, cakes, and cookies luring at me. I didn't stay alone for long – was it the backpack again or my shopping spree – and the owner, a French chef, joined me for conversation. I assured him that, although I would not know anything about South Lake Tahoe, I learned at least that his sophisticated, artful assortment of little sweets was the best bakery for the last 300 miles. In return I received a lot of tips for where to stay, what to do, and how to spend the evening at the lake.

But the town at the southern tip of the lake was not much more than a residential colony of log mansions and million dollar houses, not Beverly Hills but Beverly Woods. At most places, access to the lake was refused by private properties. The public beach in its center could have been somewhere in Malibu. Two miles to the east lay Nevada, easily identified by a row of high rising casinos situated right behind stateline. Those were the ones causing the traffic jam, and to me they were likewise unreal. I felt alien and bewildered, and after an hour sitting at the beach promenade, I just got up and left the town. It had nothing to offer for a hiker but expensive motels and groceries, with everything being a long way away from each other, scattered along a 4-mile business road.

Walking over Tahoe Mountain to Fallen Leaf Lake, I rested at a lake cabin operated by the Tahoe-Baikal organization, which was running a Russian-American exchange program for kids. I decided to find a place for the night at the smaller lake, and, only when I settled down, I realized I had not only left that town but this popular lake without a feeling. I had felt no amazement, no surprise, where I had originally anticipated that touching experience I had had so often when seeing an unexpected scene of natural beauty. Here, I was not even disappointed. I just walked away.

I think it was the urban environs, the traffic and the buildings, that made me dismiss that visit as not being a part of my travel world. Besides nature, I seemed to accept only small towns whose size did not exceed the degree where people know each other after a while. With a population of more than 20,000, South Lake Tahoe was the biggest Californian town along the thousand-mile stretch, and it just didn't count.

06/16   FALLEN LEAF LAKE, 9 MILES

From here, Colin stayed away from the lake. His route from Fallen Leaf Lake along the Rubicon River to Donner Pass paralleled the shoreline of Lake Tahoe in due distance. However, later at night, I began to think whether I should give it a second chance, or rather me, to find out about its reputation. Until a day ago, from all that I heard, I could hardly believe that someone seeing the jewel of lakes would not feel obliged to walk its shore. And I was about to leave it without really having seen it. Somehow, I couldn't let go of it, there must be something more than I saw at its southern tip, and tomorrow I would try.

During breakfast with two girls and two boys from Russia, we mainly compared the sizes and the "dangerosity" of American and Russian brown bears. They were lucky kids, whose parents took them on yearly family trips to Lake Baikal, and I think it was their vivid stories and depiction of that Siberian variant of Lake Tahoe that confirmed my idea.

Two hours later, I was back at the lakeshore. A steep road ascended to a cliff high above the lake, slowly disclosing what it was all about. The lake needed scenery to come to live, dramatic cliffs, an island with a stone hut, and a dark green frame of pine forest. Looking down to the Emerald Bay, I saw the jewel shining in green and blue, as if the Caribbean had an outpost in the Sierra Nevada. The surrounding band of conifers seemed to appear in humble black, enhancing the lake's play of colors even more. At the end of the bay, two forested arms were grasping around its waters, virtually protecting their treasure, but there was even more value behind these arms, where the lake opened up wearing a waved cover of dark blue velvet. If not the largest, for sure it was the bluest since, with more than 1,600 feet, California's deepest lake.

I was reconciled and glad that I had stayed close to the water. From the rim trail in the south, which had about the same distance from the lake as Colin's route here, I had already seen it, but it was too far away, and a closed curtain of trees had never really allowed to see the whole. I decided to keep paralleling Colin's route walking around to the northern shore, where I expected the Alpine

CHAPTER NINE

scenery in the south to augment the picture with a crowning background. On the other side of the little bay was Bliss State Park, commemorating two 19th-century pioneers of the West, Duane Leroy Bliss and his wife Elizabeth Tobey, who had the vision to preserve the native landscape of the Tahoe region.

06/17   EMERALD BAY, 8 MILES

For two days, I was lingering on the Rubicon Trail along the shore. A couple of lakeshore communities did not stick out much, consisting mainly of some log houses and cottages discreetly pasted in the forest. Wherever possible, I walked down to the lake to enjoy an Arcadian pause between the whispering wind through fir trees and the sound of the surf.

06/18   RUBICON BAY, 12 MILES

Since I did not expect much from the second biggest city, but a reflection over the lake of South Lake Tahoe, I was pleasantly surprised by that nice little town with nicer restaurants, cafés, and shops, and basically a friendlier atmosphere. Sunnyside and Tahoe City had more to offer than just a Malibluish beach. Whereas the city at the south shore had the charm of a supply and logistics zone, here I found a nice town setting with everything in walking distance. I admit, 'walking distance' may sound ambiguous in the context of this book; to make it clear, Tahoe City was another one-mile town.

'Fanny Bridge' was the entrance to town, named after the line-up of fannies you see when crossing the little Truckee River, the lake's only outflow. On every side of the bridge, usually some 10 people lean forward and look down, watching and feeding the famous large trout.

I walked to the other side of town and began to fancy staying for a night. When I reached the last motel, there was this sign again, 'Back in an hour'. After all, I thought an hour sounded more reliable than five minutes, or 'in a minute'. I don't know why, but I decided to wait that hour instead of checking in at one of the other four places. Somehow I trusted in my habit to walk through a new town first before knocking in, and at least three times it was worth the mile. I parked my pack at the office, raided the bakery for coffee and muffins, and sat down on the next pier. The boats were still floating unaffected by the first envoys of spring. Blue jays and squirrels were more on the go. While I called Nathan to let him know that I had arrived at the emerald lake where we always wanted to go fishing, the little gnawers took great care of my muffins and kept me company until the objects of desire had disappeared. With the Alpine background, I felt reminded of the

Lombardy lakes in northern Italy, Lago di Como, Lago di Lugano, and now Lago di Taho, and I was glad I had given me another chance.

Three hours later, I had checked in, lay on a king size overlooking both the pool area and the lake. And no, Randy, the motel manager, was not two hours late to open the office, but we had a nice chat about my trip and made friends just like that. I did not only find a wonderful place to relax and squeeze in a writing day, I also had rambling conversations with him, and his black German shepherd Emma loved me on the spot. I could hardly wait to sit down in the evening and start writing in this inspiring ambiance. However, there is one thing we allow to interfere with our plans, even with our favorite pastime, and that is getting to know someone as a new friend. Randy invited me for a glass of wine, which turned into a bottle along with dinner, and the following day I was invited to move to the guesthouse.

06/19   TAHOE CITY, 0 MILES

After a short night, Randy presented himself in the best light, preparing a continental, yet opulent, breakfast for the motel guests. From 8 o'clock, every five minutes someone was coming into the office, so we ended up having breakfast with a variety of people at the bell desk. Around 9, it was so crowded that you couldn't see someone coming in anymore, you just heard the doorbell and knew that someone new had arrived.

There were people checking in, others checking out, or just stopping by to say hello and drop something into the conversation. However, the life of the party was some visitors asking more or less intelligent questions such as: "Do you rent rooms, too?" or "Are your rooms quiet?" probably meaning, are they far enough from this convivial gathering. I think it was the mixture of people with their stories and their concerns, why I thought, everyone running a motel should write a book. Just for the fun of it, I would like to run one for myself for a season.

Among our coffee guests were annual visitors Paul and Mary from San Jose, who corroborated that my instinct was right, I had chosen the best and most vibrant place in town. So did the owners, Paul and Terry, when they showed up on their morning routine. Emma the shepherd did a great job in handling new guests at the reception desk, people from North and South America, Europe, and Australia. Standing on her hind legs, with her paws on the counter, she soon turned the office into the main attraction for visitors.

When the last muffin was gone and the office was empty, I adjourned to the poolside to do some writing. For a creative break, I enjoyed strolling down to the lake or just down Lake Boulevard to one of the small European-style cafés. In one place, on my way to the bathroom, I passed a large wide-angle panoramic photo of a snow-covered mountain range. I was in a hurry and just caught a glimpse of the picture, but relieving myself, I recognized that it reminded me of the Alps. I thought, how funny, somehow they all look the same. Of course, I was sure this was a local panorama. Coming back, I had a closer look, and I was surprised to read the little plaque at the bottom, it was the Alps. I could not tell what the difference was in comparison to a similar shot of the Sierra. It was not like comparing the characteristic Matterhorn with Mount Whitney, there simply were thirty peaks in a row as one could see them in any higher mountain range around the globe. It was something else, like a certain connection, something you would only feel after you have walked there for some time.

06/20   TAHOE CITY, 12 MILES

After breakfast in a restaurant overlooking the lake, it was time to say goodbye. Just as my life was enriched in these days at Lake Tahoe by Randy, I felt that, with my next step into the wild, the list of people who would be worried about me had increased by one, or by two including Emma.

Back at 'Fanny Bridge', the little river's name pointed north to my next stop Truckee, a small town right below the notorious Donner Pass. Along the river, summer was celebrated by a hodgepodge of families and children, floating up and down and in circles on that first hot summer day around the lake. However, I would not follow Truckee River but walk back into the mountains to hit Colin's route on Granite Chief Trail.

Halfway up to the rim trail lay the estivating ski resort of Squaw Valley. Now in late spring, it looked like a modern ghost town. After another three miles and a 2,000-foot climb, I was up on the rim and back in the wild.

With close to 9,000 feet, Tinker Knob and Anderson Peak were the highest peaks along that range. A higher experience of almost supernatural character was the white-bearded man who came toward me, right when I stepped back on Colin's trail. I had just turned around a bend when I saw him approaching, struggling over a larger patch of soft snow. We were some 200 yards away from each other, which gave me enough time to assume that this was Colin himself, taking me to task for having left his trail for a couple of days around Lake Tahoe.

With his long beard and a time-worn equipment, which in fact looked like what one would have worn half a century ago, no bright colors and no tags with buffaloes, claws, or stylized mountain ranges, he could definitely have been wandering around for the last five decades. We met at the narrowest part of the trail, stopped and asked each other how much snow there would be in each other's direction. When we finished discussing trail conditions, we exchanged our motives, and I learned that I met quite a walking personality. His name is Billy Goat, and he is something like the good soul of that trail.

Every year, he said, from April through September, he would be on the Pacific Crest Trail, which coincides with Colin's route between here and Donner Pass. There is one stretch in the Marble Wilderness that he had walked over 150 times, once three times in a row. We talked about backpackers' stuff, why we did what we did, and what we used for food. Having hiked more than 30,000 miles on the trail, Billy was adapted to living there. He knew better what you could eat and where hidden water sources were than anyone else. Everything he brought with him for food was dried beans and buckwheat groats. He was the one who knew where the bear shits in the buckwheat.
I forgot to ask him, if the mountain to my right was named after him, my map called it Billys Peak, 8,617 feet. Anyway, I would not have been surprised to find him later in a book about pioneers of the Wild West in the 1800s.

A couple of miles later, I set up camp. From a higher ledge of boulders, I could overlook the valley of the American River. Somewhere farther down was the site of Sutter's Mill, the place where the Golden State was born. While scanning the landscape near and far, to my surprise, I spied a couple of hikers building their tents nearby behind a stand of pine trees. For the first time, except the legs with Roland and Sonja, I would not be alone at night. I would have to share the night sky with neighbors, with strangers. In order to find out who the newcomers were, I paid them a short visit exchanging the latest weather and wildfire news. After a shared beer, I walked back to my lookout, right in time to watch a spectacular sunset. One half of the horizon was clear and slowly colored by the sinking sun. A wildfire some forty miles away had filled the other half with thick white smoke resisting the blaze of color. Right in the middle, the American River cut through like a natural divider between the worlds. Meanwhile, the hikers, too, took place on a larger boulder to watch that play. They were far enough to not really disturb my solitude, though I felt it was different, as if I had to share a treasure that has been all mine for a long time. Just before *my* golden ball disappeared, it was reflected in the meanders of the river like glistening patches of gold. Now the left side of the horizon glared orange and red while the other struggled in nondescript pastel colors. Then, all of a sudden, darkness had swallowed the world and, although it was quiet all during sunset, only now it felt silent. I was alone again, climbed carefully back down to my pack and crawled in my sleeping bag.

06/21   NORTH FORK AMERICAN RIVER, 9 MILES

I woke up with dawn and started a small fire to have a cup of coffee. While the water was heating, I checked the area to find the little pond marked in my map, the last water source in a dryer mountain area until I would reach Donner Lake. From here, most of the trail to Donner Pass would be through open terrain. Therefore, I wanted to be closer to Timber Knob, a bald mountain

CHAPTER NINE

some 1,500 feet higher, before the sun got hot. Millions of mule's ears populated the slopes as if someone had thrown a thick yellow duvet over the mountain. Just on the marge along the trail, a panoply of varicolored flowers had found a narrow niche.

Passing Anderson Peak and Mount Lincoln, more and more weekenders came by, the closer I got to the Donner area. I met families and groups, a woman with her daughter and a daddy with his son. One woman practiced infantile outdoor education, carrying her baby like a backpack as she was running down the trail. I couldn't help but remember that cartoon with the puking kangaroo baby.

06/22   DONNER PASS, 9 MILES

Reaching Donner Lake, I ran into a jocular group of six high-spirited guys returning from a walk into the woods. They came from all parts of the country and had met in Truckee to celebrate the birthday of one of them. As they declared, this alone wasn't reason enough for the kind of celebration they planned to have in their holiday log house. Having passed a fairly strenuous day hike would surely serve as a justification for a wild party. We were mocking hiking in general and a clique of city slickers doing so in particular. Our exchange of less useful information but funny hiking trivia and anecdotes eventually turned into an invitation for pizza and beer in the first saloon in Truckee.

According to the questions and the discussions we delved into, predominantly, my journey must have seemed to them as a yearlong abstinence from some basic things. With the second round, an advisory council was set up to create a more or less scientific approach for how I would win one of the waitresses over.

Early in the evening, we had in fact developed many how-to ideas, and one curvaceous lady was singled out. However, granted she got the Mercedes bends, I was poised to leave alone and instead of staying in a motel, I joined the guys' party at their house in the hills around Truckee. Lucius and Scott and four brothers Dan, Jim, Mike and Bill. That sure sounded like the 'Wild Bunch' and although planning a robbery was not part of the saloon committee, we partied as if we already did. While the four brothers were in charge of organizing the food, drinks, and music, Lucius and Scott bore the brunt of the work, talking politics. In between, I had to give reports on the peculiarities of living in the wild and, I think, I never talked that much about my journey; at some moments, I was answering four questions at the same time. Later in the evening, Dan recorded part of a session-like interview, when all six of them interrogated me more or less simultaneously. This recording, however, or any excerpt, is not slated for publication at this point – or any time later.

06/23   TRUCKEE, 0 MILES

After sleeping the Wild Bunch night off, I received an opulent brunch. With six farewell-handshakes and their sober respect, I walked back into Truckee to spend another night at the Cottage Hotel. Ten days earlier, I had called the owners, Bill and Joan, to ask if I could have somebody mail my last replenishment package from L.A. to them, announcing that I would walk into town in some days. When I came to the house, they were sitting on the hotel porch and on Joan's shoulder a large white parrot. They saw me and knew right away who I was, "Look, the hiker Andy, the guy with the LAST ONE package." The parrot approved it. "Sorry Andy," Bill continued, telling off the cheeky bird, "we are fully booked for days", long pause, "but we kept one room for you free." He added something like, someone who walked that far deserved a room, but the parrot kept interrupting him.

Indeed, the hotel was a cottage, one of the smaller old buildings in town that apparently had not received much renovation, or redecoration; it was just well preserved. The owners must have been the eldest of the town. They sat on their porch as if life has been good to them, constantly smiling and always having an advice down pat, or a good joke.

Having thrown my pack into the room, I walked through old town Truckee along Donner Pass Road. I noticed many historical buildings, all in pretty good shape. It reminded me of Bodie; I imagined a city clerk there had just turned on the main fuse, and in one fell swoop, all streetlights and shops were brightly lit, people walked through the streets and amused themselves after a hard working day.

Even modern businesses seemed to be cautious about displaying their products and services in order to not disturb the historical ambiance. While all shops and restaurants were on one side of Main Street, the tracks and the station made up the other side. Like in Goffs or Nipton, here, too, the railroad had been the heartbeat of the town, a town with a past, namely one of the most dramatic chapters of Californian history.

"Tro Kay!" yelled the friendly local Piute chief, in our words "Everything's all right!", when he saw the first settlers crossing the Sierra. The emigrants thought he was saying his name, which actually was not far from that. So they named the site after him, Truckee. Chief Tru-Ki-Zo gave them a warm welcome. He had even served as a guide for Frémont later, however, due to white men's behavior, the friendship did not last very long. When twenty years later, in 1846, the Donner Party came through, his son Winnemucca did see what was going to happen, but he left them stranded and abandoned them to their fate.

On their 2,500-mile journey from Chicago to California, the original trek of Donner's and Reed's families had grown to more than eighty people by joining another trek. Plans were to arrive in Western California before

CHAPTER NINE

summer would draw to a close. Alarmed by cold weather and the first snow in the mountains, the party rushed westwards as fast as possible. However, too many people had too many opinions and unexpected situations increasingly wrecked their nerves.

On their way West, the party was further ruffled. A shortcut to a shortcut had cost them almost a month. Most of their cattle had either been taken or killed by Indians, or they were just fed up with being chained to the oars and took off. As a consequence, the settlers had to leave wagons and belongings behind and cache their values. However, as with every travel preparation, people had forgotten things, needed something they cached, and eventually kept losing more crucial time going back and forth.

There were at least three killings, two resulted from ongoing arguments, another one was accidental. With increasing stress, the party's inexperience made for accidents and misfortunes. While repairing the axle of his wagon, Captain George Donner himself had cut his hand so bad that he had to stay behind with his family until he recovered.

After having traveled for many weeks through incalculable wilderness and a never-ending succession of daily ordeals, both humans and livestock were already mentally and physically strained when they left the Great Basin desert of Nevada. However, it was not before early November when they arrived in California and here, the worst was yet to come.

While the first difficult topographical barriers in the east had been timed early enough, ongoing unpredictable events had caused crucial delays. Like many other treks, they had underestimated that last most grueling leg of their journey peaking in the Californian mountains and deserts. The ascent of this last barrier was unexpectedly steep and dangerous, and the heavily forested slopes were filled with large rocks and boulders, which made driving the wagons almost impossible. Consequently, they had to be carried piece by piece in several passages and reassembled when the obstacle was overcome, never knowing if it had to be done soon again.

The majority of the trek had to stop over where Truckee is today. A smaller group tried to go for help and organize food, only to get stranded somewhere else. By now, the sky had darkened over what was to become Donner Pass, ominous clouds brought an early winter arrival, and along with the greatest snowfall in the known history of the Sierra Nevada, the disaster took its course.

By late October, one member reported five feet of snow; the scattered groups had to make arrangements for a long hard winter and build camps close to the lake. By mid December the groups were snowed in eight feet deep, the nights got awfully cold. Food supplies were about exhausted, and the first weaker members died of malnutrition.

During several attempts to reach the summit, small groups sent for help got lost somewhere below the pass. Meanwhile, the trek was split into several groups. Nine feet were reported. In snow that deep, it was almost impossible to chop a tree and dig the fallen stem out of the snow to get firewood. Trees cut at the surface of the snow left stumps between twelve and twenty feet high, some of which can still be seen today.

Further desperate attempts from single members to escape the hopeless situation ended in odysseys and starvation. Those who hung in started discussing whom to kill for food and drew lots. But no one could act it out, until that night that became known as the 'Camp of Death'. Around midnight, the storm had blown out the fire. The members of the main group moved together in a circle, covered by blankets and buried from ongoing snowfall. Two more had died on that Christmas Day, and on the day after, "averting their faces from one another and weeping"[*], the first group resorted to cannibalism.

Somewhere farther up the mountain, another group proposed to kill two Indian guides for meat. Sensing their fate, those were taking off to the woods, however, their luck was short-lived. Two weeks later and totally exhausted, they ran into the arms of the first group, who killed them for food.

It was January 17, 1848, the Mexicans had just lost the fight for California in the coastal towns, when seven famished characters of a group of 15 made their way to the other side of the Sierra. When they arrived at Fort Sutter, it was its proprietor, who funded and called upon organizing a rescue team. Due to the extreme weather, though, the rescue teams could not set off before three weeks later.

The first group was found on February 19th, but only two months later, the last refugee arrived at Sutter's fort. From the 81 members, who got snowed in at Donner Lake, 36 had died, among whom more than 20 secured the lives of the others. Three years later, on his first trek into California, Jacob Marklee had come by the Donner Camp site where they found human bones. One of the emigrants reported: "There were piles of bones around but mostly of cattle, although I did find some half dozen human ones of different parts. Just to the left of these was a few old black burned logs ... Here was nearly the whole of a skeleton. Several small stockings were found which still contained the bones of a leg & foot... I came to another of the cabins ... Here I also found many human bones. The skulls had been sawed open for the purpose, no doubt, of getting out the brain, & the bones had been sawed open & broken to obtain the last particle of nutrient."[†]

---

[*] From *Patrick Breen's diary*, who was a member of the Donner Party along with his wife and seven children. The entire family was brought to the settlements by Sutter's rescue parties. Written on eight sheets of letter paper that were folded to a small book of thirty-two pages, Breen (1806–1868) delivered a detailed report of the circumstances that led to the drama. Parts of his diary were first published in the *California Star* in May 1847.

[†] From the diary of Wakeman Bryarly (1820–1869), published in *Trail to California: The Overland Journal of Vincent Geiger & Wakeman Bryarly*. In 1849, Vincent Geiger & Dr. Wakeman Bryarly joined an organized emigrant group to the California gold fields.

CHAPTER NINE

It is hardly possible to imagine what these people had to live through. Perhaps another witness' report helps to understand a little: "And the worst of it all now is to see, every few hundred yards, the grave of some kind brother, father or mother, and even some who have not been buried, but have probably been forsaken when sick or faint, and left to die and waste away in the winds and rain of heaven. But the sight of the dead is not so fearful as the living dying. God of heaven! Could human suffering appease their wrath, the world would soon be forgiven."*

Almost exactly a year after the first rescue team got through, Sutter was to be rewarded for his stake in the party's rescue. On January 24, 1848, his partner James W. Marshall, who had also served under Frémont during the Bear Flag Revolt, discovered the first grains of gold while working on Sutter's sawmill. Sutter was not too happy about it, though, fearing an influx of miners disturbing his agricultural business. He began to claim title to as much land as possible, making no mention of the gold. However, word of mouth was faster than bureaucracy, and in the following months masses of prospectors were arriving and camping on his lands. "Ho, to the diggin's!" became a common greeting in the Nation. Within weeks, all of America turned its eyes to California, once again *El Dorado*, the legendary land of gold, and the rush was on.

Deeding his remaining land to his son, Sutter died almost poor, while junior had realized the signs of the times. He planned a new city nearby and set the foundation for Sacramento. Six years later, the California State Legislature moved from Monterey to the new city along the Sacramento River.

The events at Donner Pass had shown vividly that it is less the animal beast we have to fear but first of all ourselves and a lack of understanding nature's elements. Most accidents and fatal events, historical or modern, resulted from tragic misjudgment and overestimation of one's own capabilities. I couldn't help thinking of my days in the Sierra and what would have happened if another snowstorm had brewed.

With dinner I read Colin's last chapter, realizing that our journeys were about to come to an end. Outside, the antique façades appeared in a strange sepia tint, somehow in line with a rising mélange of nostalgia and melancholy inside of me. It was only afternoon, but the sun was gone; the streets of Truckee were filling with smoke from a nearby fire, smothering the old town in a Saturnine atmosphere.

Late in the evening, I got a call from L.A. that derailed me from my train of thoughts. My friend Nathan's state of health had changed for the worse dramatically. The bitter reality of two weeks seemed to have closed in on the hoped-for two years.

---

* Emigrant John Wood's report, dated 1850

While half a year ago, the fact that they mentioned a possible end at all had scared me more than any period of time, now I was scared by not receiving an idea at all. All good hope we had, before I left for my journey, was shot down by a call. I put my maps aside and thought about how and when I should interrupt to go and see him in Los Angeles. When I called again to find out how serious it really was, I felt that they went easy on me and that they did not tell everything, like obviously he hadn't done either. I later learned that in the three months I was walking, he had ups and downs that would have called me back to L.A. quite regularly. Whenever we talked on the phone, he let me believe that he was just recovering and doing much better. He said, we would talk again next week or whenever I got into a town, and his last question always was, "how many more weeks you got?"

I was in such good faith that two weeks ago I did not hear him saying, "I want to see you". I mean, I heard it, but I understood something else, like 'I would like to see you,' or, 'when you're done'. Now with this information, and since it was the first time I did not get it from him personally, I knew I was overdue.

After a short walk down to Truckee River, I went back to the hotel to make preparations for taking the next morning train to L.A. In my room, I put a few things together for the ride home, the backpack I wanted to leave with Bill and Joan. When I had closed the pack and pulled all straps tight, I stared at it, was it for minutes or ages, I didn't know. It was the strangest feeling to put away my house on the back for an indefinite time. I walked down to see Bill and Joan and handed my pack over to them. When I turned around, a sense of foreboding befell me, a fearful expectation of the days to come. In this moment, I felt that the fear of loosing him and my fear that from tomorrow I would not walk into the wild became one and the same. And I realized that, somehow, it was him why I was here.

Arriving at Truckee, I believed I had covered all highlights of my journey, had disclosed the secrets of the desert and pioneered untouched mountain wilderness. From here, I thought, it would be an easy-going to the end. I was high flying and happy about the friends I made and the hospitality of the people en-route. I believed in my wildest dreams, and I could have moved on forever and live from walking. I was so rich of good experiences, and I accepted my greatest talent in receiving them. Though, reading Colin's last chapter in these days had sparked a certain wistfulness in me, a nostalgic feeling and the big question, how am I going to compensate all these lucky days once I reached the final destination. Now, I suddenly had to face the biggest and unexpected struggle of all, and I was unsure, after this bad news, would I be able to finish the walk at all? What would happen now, and where I would go from here, being on top of the world, my view was anything but clear.

CHAPTER NINE

06/24   TRUCKEE, 0 MILES

It was before sunrise, when a freight train crashed past, rumbling through town and shivering the dreamful sleep of the pure morning hours. Half dozing, half waking, I thought the walls of the little cottage were shaking. A train whistle was blowing forever like a siren.

I must have fallen back asleep but the whistle kept blowing in my dreams until eventually it became a ringing. My phone! I woke up with a start, answered the phone and looked out of the window to see if that train was still there. But the station was abandoned. It was dead silent. The air was thick of smoke, swallowing every noise and my voice alike. The sun could not get through, she was wearing sables.

"One hour ago," said a sad voice, "one hour ago, our brother had passed away."

I couldn't talk; in my numbness I realized that the train had delivered me the message in the moment he died.

I was already on the home stretch, but he could not go farther. I mumbled a Bertrand Russell, "A train crashed past with purposeless speed, hurrying from one abode of sorrow to another. Even so Fate hurries on, and its rails are built of human souls", and hang up the phone.

For the first time, I really felt lonesome. Or had I left him alone? Under the canopy of smoke and sorrows, I sat down at the creek to drown my tears in the consoling waters of the Little Truckee River. When I heard the whistle again, I got up, shouldered my bag, and took the train to Los Angeles.

I had taken all kinds of interruptions into account, weather, illness, or injury, all potential obstacles but not the loss of my friend. Now I knew that the possibility had always been traveling with me. It was Nathan's decision to let me wander as long as he could weather through the drought of deserts and the snow on the passes, all of which he took to his dreams whenever I called him. His strength and his hope was that I was doing fine and that I would greet him with a bouquet of roses, as I always did when I came back from a trip.

I can't remember much of the train ride; I was engrossed in thought, any clear idea faded immediately along with the zooming landscape. But there was one experience I would never forget. One of our first stops was at the town of *Roseville*. A twenty-minute break was announced and everybody got off for a stroll or to stretch the legs. I was doing fine somehow, the monotonous rumble seemed to have a soothing effect on me and the ride gave me some time to travel from my past months' elation to my brother's salvation.

After a chat with some passengers in the concourse, I had gone outside to the forecourt and leaned to a pillar, when suddenly an old lady stood right before me. The collection of poor clothes she wore was as close as she could get to display a suit. She looked at me quietly, opened her purse and handed me a brochure. When I saw the title, I was so puzzled that I didn't notice she left. I turned around but could not see her. She seemed to have simply disappeared, faded away like most of that day had with the airstream. I looked at my hands holding the brochure, and I read: "How to cope when you lost a loved one".

*

I spent five days with the Hall family, a one-of-a-kind get together that indeed helped to cope with the loss. For service, more than 200 friends and members of the family came to pay their last respects and say goodbye. I knew for sure that the deceased was in better hands when I witnessed this family-and-friends reunion. The persuasion, with which everybody helped arranging a day just like Nathan would have done it, resolved any doubt. Occasional tears were drowned in common laughter and story-telling, remembering and toasting to countless stories of his life, which had made more than these 200 people happy. When I drove our friend Linda home – one of the last living blues legends – she took my arm saying: "I am so happy you brought me, I had the happiest day in my life." She was indeed – coming from a funeral – all smiles.

07/02–04 TAHOE CITY, 0 MILES

A week later, I sat in the train back to Truckee. When I called Randy to tell him about the interruption, he offered to pick me up with my backpack and stay with him for Independence Day. He would then drop me in Truckee again where I could continue my journey. It was exactly what I needed to get back into my routine and be able to bring to an end what I started.

Nathan had always been an anchor in California, my mental supporter and the one who understood whatever crazy idea I had found to leave with nothing but a backpack. With his simple "You are my rebel!"- phrase, everything was excused, blessed, and sanctified. It took me a while to regain my credo and enthusiasm. Whenever I had called him from one of the towns, I felt he was taking part in my journey, so much that, in fact, sometimes I thought I would do it for him.

In terms of people, it was Randy, who got me back on track. In terms of nature, the far northeast of California turned out to be a real surprise, another forgotten land, awaiting me with some unexpected events.

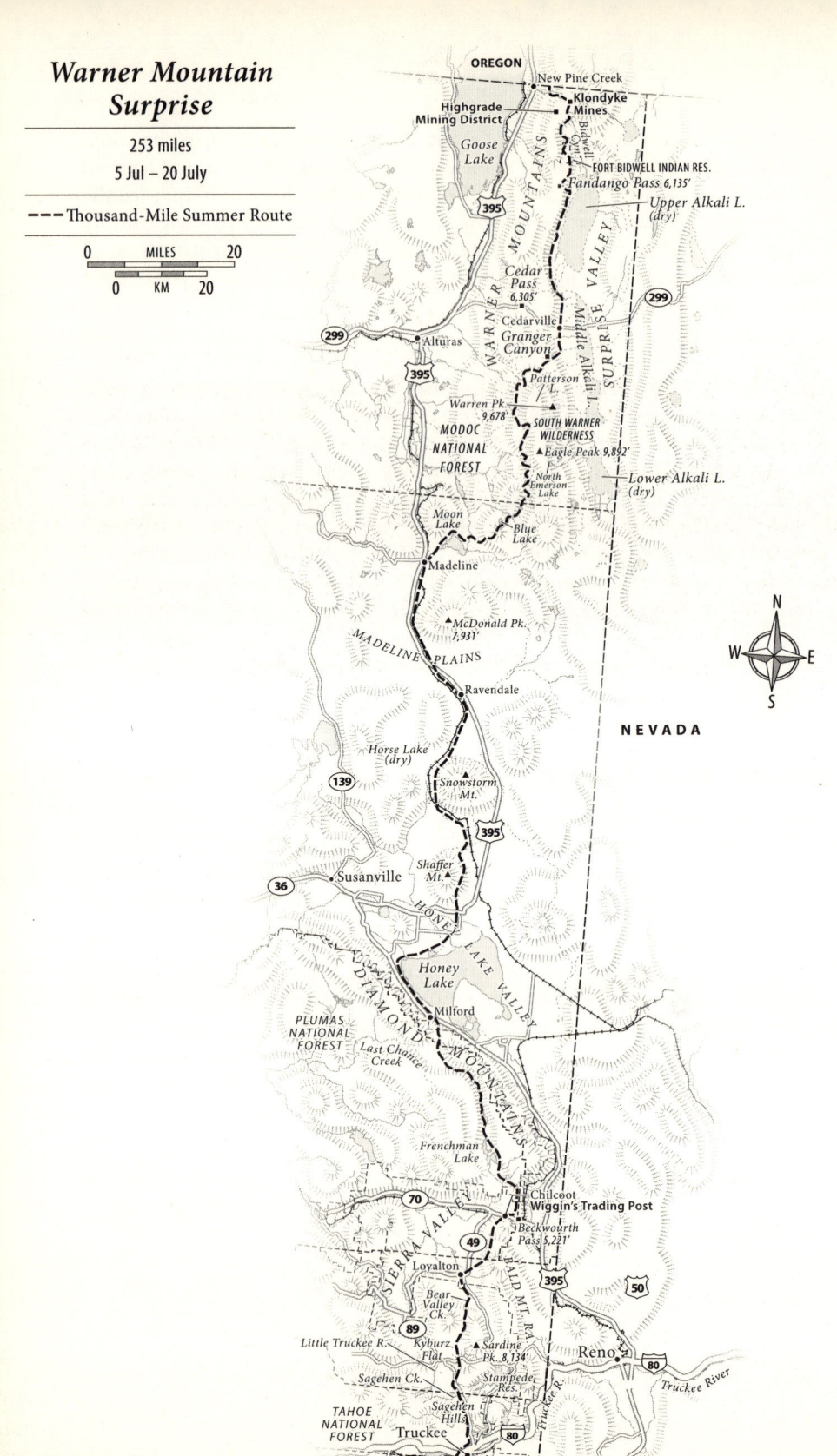

Warner Mountain Surprise

253 miles
5 Jul – 20 July

--- Thousand-Mile Summer Route

10. WARNER MOUNTAIN SURPRISE

When you have worn out your shoes,
the strength of the shoe leather
had passed into the fiber of your body.
He is the richest man who pays the largest debt to his shoemaker.

RALPH WALDO EMERSON, FOUNDER OF THE TRANSCENDENTALISM MOVEMENT, 1803–1882

07/05   TRUCKEE, 15 MILES

North of Truckee, Colin's route led across a 7,000-foot ridge, the Sagehen Hills. While he followed the homonymous creek into Stampede Valley, I had to deviate a little, as I could not walk on water. Completed in 1970, at the confluence of Sagehen and Little Truckee Rivers, the Stampede Reservoir had been formed as part of the Washoe Project, which comprises both the Carson and Truckee Rivers. Regulating water flows in an area of extremes, where arid basins face high alpine mountains providing for only seasonal meltwater, the project was designed to fulfill year-round needs around the Tahoe-Donner leisure park, thus ensuring supplies for households and power production as well as for habitat improvement for endangered species and for fishing, boating, and camping aficionados.

I left the Sagehen and turned north at the conjunction with the new lake. The area spurred me to quicken my steps since there were vast burned stretches and where there was nothing to burn, sagebrush steppe.

Although, after so many days in the city, I set off with sunrise and full of excitement and energy, I had to call it a day early afternoon. Somehow I felt drained. My head grew heavy and my sight grew dim, I felt the constant smoke in the air and its tiring effect on my eyes. Since I had arrived in Truckee for the first time, there were large wildfires burning in the western Plumas and Lassen forests.

CHAPTER TEN

07/06   KYBURZ FLAT, 17 MILES

Sage became the dominating brush again, interrupted only by a few thistles that were rising up to the sky like a standing firework. Unfortunately, more smoke was hanging in the air. I could see it being blown in from the west, increasingly covering the firmament. As soon as I would hit the next town, I had to ask somebody about the fires to make sure I wouldn't have to be worried. The sunsets were spectacular, though, dramatically staging the dark red star in a nebulous setting.

My arrival at the town of Loyalton only added to the scene. With two churches towering at the town entrance and the setting sun behind them, it became a scene of doomsday. There was no one there, no kids playing, not even a barking welcome from straying dogs. I walked through the empty streets of what seemed to be a ranching and logging community. After the compulsory one-mile inspection, I reached the end of town without having noticed any signs of life but the asthmatic breath of a cooling unit coming from a forlorn soda machine. I gave the android what it wanted, and after receiving a chilled coke, I started talking to it for lack of another person.

Further down Main Street was a saloon; maybe there I would find out what happened to the town. The machine wheezed good-bye and finally cut out with a last metallic clunk. When I stepped into the saloon door, I was virtually entering the opening scene of a bad Western movie. The door fell slowly back, its creaking an almost melodic score. A sudden gust blew sand into the room and from one of the tables three stone-faced men turned their faces around to me. For a second I paused, six eyes were looking me over, their last spoken words seemed to have frozen in their open mouths. Then they turned back to their conversation. I did not seem to be a threat to them, but their surprised look suggested they were expecting somebody. The rifle leaning in a corner behind their table did not add to easing the situation. I leaned my pack to the counter and went to the bathroom. When I came back, the men were gone and I thought I was alone. I called for somebody several times, but I received no answer. After ten minutes sitting at the bar, I put some dollars on the counter and grabbed a bottle of beer. I started cleaning my backpack, checked my maps for the coming leg and browsed through some local papers. Suddenly the door was thrown open, a small kid ran into the room, looked around and sallied out again. The door squeaked until it snapped in, the final theme for me. I sure could have taken over the place, but it was all so weird and I was too tired to watch the whole movie. I left some more dollars, took another beer and my leave to sleep in the sage.

Later I learned from a farmer that there were 'post-independent' fireworks in another town and that everybody had gone there to attend it. About the three men he asked pretty much for a precise description. However, when I asked him what he thought, he said he had never heard of such men and changed the subject.

07/07   LOYALTON, SIERRA VALLEY, 18 MILES

Without the curtain of trees I was used to, I woke up with sunrise. I took the opportunity to start early and cover a long walking day in order to get out of the sage monotony; eleven straight miles to Vinton, two more to Chilkoot, and another five uphill to the outskirts of the Diamond Mountains. I established a walking trance, a much better way to get through long unchanging landscapes than counting mileposts or street markings that only show the psychological infinity of walking on a straight line quite plainly, if not painfully.

My only noteworthy stop was at Mr. Wiggin's Trading Post in Chilkoot. With a cup of coffee, I came to talking with Mr. Wiggin. From a collection of newspaper clippings in the store windows, I saw that he has been here for half a century, and I thought maybe Colin stopped here too. Unfortunately, he took over only a few years later, becoming the fifth owner of the 1894 founded station. Running one of the few rural gas stations left in California, he had just got in the news after having made a good point about tax-exempts for rural stations. Providing services for small populations, many of them would not be able to comply with costly state mandates. A new law required reducing emissions by upgrading gas-dispensing nozzles in order to capture 98% of the gas vapor instead of the current 95%. Mr. Wiggin made clear that, if the rural stations were driven out of business by costly updates, the customers would have to drive much farther to get gas, emitting a multiple of what would vaporize at his station. Consequently, another bill now allowed those in sparsely populated counties and with a limited output to operate without installing the costly technique. I wondered if these exemptions bred the cluster of gas stations at some places. I couldn't see any logic in operating 4 gas stations at one intersection, sometimes two or more run by the same petrol corporation.

Late in the afternoon, I arrived at Frenchman Lake, another dammed creek. In the days of Colin, the valley was quiet and empty, its name *Last Chance*. Colin took it. Before long, construction began for a well-visited vacation area.

As at the Stampede Reservoir, this lake, too, was amply utilized both by waterfowl and water sports enthusiasts. When turning north into Frenchman Lake Road, I saw hundreds of cars coming from or driving to the recreational area, most of them pulling trailers, hauling RVs, 4WDs, boats, jet ski, or tons of fishing equipment to the vacation land.

Almost all of them blew their horn, shouted good luck, or tried to cheer me up in any other way. It goes without saying, the majority were male drivers, but I remember noticing one car where a young woman sat behind the steering wheel. There, for once, the greetings came from the passenger side.

CHAPTER TEN

07/08   FRENCHMAN LAKE, 15 MILES

Frenchman Lake is fed by Last Chance Creek. However, when I reached the small estuary at the end of the lake, it seemed that I had missed mine. Walking deeper into the Diamond Mountains, I had expected more water as the vast flats of sage and green grass would have suggested. But most of the creeks had already dried up. And although Last Chance was still carrying a little, as soon as I passed the first cattle, I understood that they had many uses for the water. Anyway, it was more a body of standing water than a running creek and the river's name did not give much cause for hope. I left my pack behind and walked back a mile or two to fill my water sacks.

About halfway in the mountains, I saw two cowboys droving a group of lost cattle from the woods back to the herd. I sat down between two trees at the edge of the forest to take some pictures when suddenly a bull on his zigzag attempt to escape came to stop right behind me. There were numerous other possibilities to hide from the cowboys or find a passage elsewhere, but the bull decided it had to be between these two trees. Face to face with the angry buck, I tried to stay calm; anyway I didn't have another choice. Pointing his two weapons at me, he snorted and moved forward, slowly making his position clear to me. If cattle could read, I had assumed he wanted to discuss John Muir's saying: "Between every two pines is a doorway to a new world." However, this would not be the case for this one – I proved him wrong. When the black hulk came into reach, I flipped with a stick against its neck. The bull rose like a rocketing pheasant and, after all, found itself another doorway.

The cowboys were visibly impressed. We said hello and I noticed it was a cowboy and a cowgirl. The married couple ran a ranch nearby with the sonorous name Flying Diamond J. I told them that I used to spend off-days in the Alps to take close-up photos of cattle and that this was not my first close encounter. Usually, I reported, one sudden movement or a quick touch frightens every cattle, bull or cow. He looked down to me appraisingly and gulped, "Yes, usually."

After a chat about their protégés, I decided to stay here since it was already later in the afternoon. For the rest of the day, I watched them working. One hand around my cup of coffee, the other poked in a bag of dried fruits; this came close to watching one of the good old Western movies.

07/09   FLYING DIAMOND J RANCH, 17 MILES

When I woke up, I looked into a hundred cow's eyes. Most of the herd had gathered around my campsite, nosing at my things and closely watching what I would do next. I must have been a pretty view, or maybe it was a familiar smell. With the sound of the sleeping bag zipper, they stampeded in all four winds, as if the earth had opened up releasing the satanic butcher from a sleeping bag. All were dispersed, all of them but one. The black bull I already had the pleasure meeting before seemed to be making a point. It was clear that a simple flip wouldn't do it anymore. This time I crawled backwards behind a tree pulling my sleeping bag with me to make sure I would not have to assert my claims to it.

Finally, the cows plucked up their courage and came back trampling down the last clean spot of the creek. At least the bull was distracted now by so many lady cows, only casually stealing a disapproving glance at me, and I enjoyed a breakfast of couscous and canned sardines under ruminating supervision.

From the northern side of the Diamond Mountains, some 6,000 feet high, I could see Honey Lake Valley but not much left of a lake. The huge basin around the lake reminded me that spring was definitely past. Instead of filling up the lake, the creeks had sacrificed their waters to the sun.

Being one of the larger Californian lakes on the map, until summer most of its shallow body is evaporated. In dry and hot years, the lake looses nine tenth of its water with a congruent concentration of minerals. A walk to what was left would have been another four or five miles to probably not really clear water but a cloudy alkaline solution.

Coming down from the mountain range at a place called Milford, I was longing for fresh water or a soda, for something to drink with a taste different from chlorine purified water. The value of a chilled coke was not quantifiable in dollars anymore and increasing with every mile of the day. I had mentioned my recurring quest of the red canned elixir to a fellow hiker I met around Tahoe. He said I shouldn't be such a sissy, the pioneers didn't have cokes either. Well, let's put him into context, he was on a weekend trip with one overnight stay. In terms of the pioneers, they didn't have chlorine either.

Indeed, they had to have some awareness, too, not that the waters were strongly contaminated in those days but there weren't many doctors around. The pioneers knew about the giardia parasites, as did the trappers and emigrants. There are accounts containing their share of references in dealing with water sources, in some of which you find reports of travelers suffering from severe indisposition with Montezuma's revenge being the milder one.

Today, if it is treated, you would – after having relieved yourself constantly over a week or two – get off lightly. Having no cure, though, it might be terminating not only a hike. The pioneers had called the severe disease 'beaver fever'. While it was often associated with beaver ponds, it was as well their own livestock as other mammals that carried the parasite in their intestines, thus spreading it to creeks and lakes alike.

CHAPTER TEN

But first of all, people in those days were more resistant, their immune systems not that spoiled and condemned to idleness as ours today. I doubt they raised their kids with sterile baby water, or that they constantly – quite paranoid – cleansed their hands with sterilizer, just as an example. If one had survived the devastating conditions in the cities where they came from, by comparison, the open country they entered was a natural sanitarium.

The Indians either seemed to be immune or they knew where to get the good water. True for both, Natives and early emigrants, before colonization and industrialization, there were far less contaminants in the waters. Only later, with the massive contamination from all kinds of sources, there were enough catalysts for giardia's conquest of the wild.

As for bad water, I usually applied the cup-bottom test, taking a cupful of water from the source, a creek, river, pond, or a lake. If the water was just a little cloudy and the bottom still visible, like English tea, I let it rest for a while and slowly poured off only the first two thirds, added one drop of chlorine per quart and let it boil for some minutes. If the bottom was hardly visible anymore, like black tea, I did the same only longer and with two drops of chlorine. If it was already as dark as coffee, I applied the black tea rule adding a prayer.

In most areas however, it was as clear as desert or mountain water should be, then I applied only one of the two measures, preferably mere boiling when I was at camp and chlorination while walking.

There were occasions, however, when I came to such places where no one has ever been, where mountain walls shielded bad thoughts and the rippling cold water flowed right out of the green. There, I succumbed to its charm betimes and to my urge alike, and I drank it like the pioneers did it 150 years ago, and I wouldn't have traded it for pink champagne on ice.

Only later I learned that studies of Sierra waters found that the remoteness is not at all an indication for its purity. Some creeks close to campgrounds were almost virgin pure whereas others in exactly these pristine, unvisited places had a high concentration of contaminants. However, after three months traveling with no problem, I had apparently outdistanced Montezuma at the Mexican border. I concluded that getting water was – as most cases – also a matter of the mind and of common sense. Generally, running water was better than standing and the closer to a spring the better. Trying not to stir the sediments up seemed to be as important as not thinking about the tiny little bastards with every sip.

The valleys and meadows throughout the Diamond Mountains were grazing land, beautiful land yet with muddy waters – since too thin to plow, too thick to drink – strongly suggesting the prayer version. I had to admit, even after delivering a prayer, it tasted different here, somehow even the obtrusive chlorine taste was not noticeable anymore. So, coming down into civilization, I would have traded my soul for a coke.

But Milford was dry, had no store, not even a gas station or a soda android. It was just a name in my mapped second life, a line of storages and garages for farming equipment and machinery. A couple of miles later, I passed a farmhouse with luring sprinklers in the front garden. All doors were open but no one replied. After a while I took the sprinklers off, refilled my sacks, and bypassed the lake through salt-crusted sage.

All through California, sage has been one of the most common plants, sometimes spotty, sometimes covering larger slopes, dwarf-like in the mountains but in some valleys growing tall that even a jackrabbit could hide his ears behind it. From now on, it was more a state of being – *I was in sage*. Between the Diamond and the Warner Mountains, there was nothing but an ocean of sage.

Now I understood why Colin did not write much about this stretch. Unless you try a romantic approach for monotonousness, there isn't much to say. Over there in the east lay the Great Basin of Nevada, the largest sage community in the U.S. But also here in northern California, it became the framework for every mountain, every forest or lake, like an excessive baroque frame around a tiny engraving of nature.

If for no other reason, just the commonness of the name sage should alert every hiker. Every two miles, there was a Sage something, Sage Creek, Sage Flats, Sage Valley, Sagehen Mountain, Fort Sage, or the Big Sage Reservoir, and all Indian names, I was sure, being synonyms for that one word. It certainly requires a good imagination to take a shine to this area. And believe it or not, in fact I saw books romanticizing about sage lands.

You might find more in its details, like in its unique smell, effusing from both the living plant as when it is used as firewood.

Mark Twain, for example, had taken a closer look at its details, too. In *Roughing it*, he remembered his travels along the California and Nevada border in the 1860s, where he looked into the abundant herb and wrote: "Imagine a gnarled and venerable live oak-tree reduced to a little shrub two feet high, with its rough bark, its foliage, its twisted boughs, all complete. It is an imposing monarch of the forest in exquisite miniature."

And the plant itself seems to enthuse other species as well, as Twain continued: "Sage-brush is very fair fuel, but as a vegetable it is a distinguished failure. Nothing can abide the taste of it but the jackass and his illegitimate child the mule. But their testimony to its nutritiousness is worth nothing, for they will eat pine knots, or anthracite coal, or brass filings, or lead pipe, or old bottles, or anything that comes handy, and then go off looking as grateful as if they had had oysters for dinner."

CHAPTER TEN

Farther north and closer to Nevada, there were three long lakes in a row. The monotonous landscape seemed to have encroached on the pioneers' spirit too, where, at the apex of imagination, they named them Upper Lake, Middle Lake, and Lower Lake.

Regarding the frequency of sage mentions on my map, only the eagle came close to that. Eagleville, Eagle Peak, Eagle Lake and so on, but today the landscape was too boring for him. Not until in the Warner Mountains did I see the first one.

07/10   HONEY LAKE, 20 MILES

Before I left the road to walk straight across the desert, I made the acquaintance of a remarkable group of veterans who were instrumental in moving the frontier, a corral full of wild horses. If this had not been the 'back-in-the-desert' tract amidst hot flickering sage, I could have stayed for hours watching the wranglers work with these most beautiful symbols of the Wild West.

The Litchfield Corrals are a wild horse and burro program operated by the BLM, where populations exceeding a tolerable level were roped, checked, and eventually made available to the public in an adopt-a-horse program.

07/11   SCHAFFER MOUNTAIN, 17 MILES

Fortunately, there were two springs between Schaffer and Snowstorm Mountain, one of them hosting a lot of flying wildlife along with a couple of hungry coyotes showing great excitement and interest for the feathered gathering.

On the northern side of Schaffer Mountain, I found wagon tracks, only discoverable by two paralleling ruts, carved in the desert gravel by the wagon wheels of recurring treks. Along with another route that passed Mr. Wiggin's Trading Post south of Honey Lake, these routes had actually been the easiest ways to the West. Both of them were already discovered in 1851, the northern one accidentally by prospector William Nobles while searching for gold, the southern by James Beckwourth, the first black mountain man I heard of so far. While Nobles continued to try his luck with gold, Beckwourth had recognized the need of the hour. In those days, all new cities, except the short-lived mining towns, were competing with each other for new emigrants. Beckwourth contracted with several city councils and picked up treks in the East to feed them over his trail to the cities. Along the way, he made a living with trade.

Although these easy routes were more frequently traveled trails in the 1850s, they were short-lived and never diverted the masses to them. Even at that time, this lower section between the Sierra ranges in the south and the Cascade Ranges toward Oregon was called Sierra *Valley*, suggesting a comparably less burdensome travel. However, *nomen est omen* didn't count. The greed for gold and the fear of arriving too late led the majority to choose the more direct trails to the assumed fields of wealth and hazard the consequences of passing the High Sierra.

In the end, many spent much more time on the trek than they planned and were equipped for, some even had to stay for months, like the Donner and Death Valley parties, if they ran too late in the year to cross the mountains or through miscalculation or disorientation.

Yet, I believe, the challenging, at times remorseless role nature played on most routes to the West has helped shaping the mentality of this people and their imagination of a new possible future, more than an easy-going travel would have done it. The fact that the last barriers that had to be crossed on their paths into a new life were also the most difficult, implicating hardships and deprivation, demanding self-reliance and self-sufficiency, placed both the state's riches they were out to discover and some of the most dramatic scenes of this chapter of American history in one and the same state. Therefore, a prompt and deep emotional connection to the physical performance and the achievements of both, individuals and the groups, was anchored in their minds, shaping a mentality that believed devoutly that one can reach the impossible dream if one is willing to move into uncertainty, take risks, and perform to one's greatest ability.

A relatively easy terrain like here in this Sierra Valley implicates the lack of diversion by stunning nature drama. Hence, when you wake up from your walking routine, it doesn't take long and you start looking around for something to twiddle with. So far, I never thought about a walking staff. Here, for the first time, though, I wished I had one. I looked for a bough that I could carve while walking, but around me lay nothing but barren rock, and it would have demanded great skill to make one out of sage.

Unlike Colin and although people from Moses to Luis Trenker swore by it, generally, I don't enjoy walking with a staff. I preferred hiking with both hands free, and anyway, I would have lost it on the first day or otherwise spent much time of the days trying to remember where I last put it. Although there were situations where a stick would have been of great help, like fording waters, testing snow depth, or disturbing a rattler's nest, I just didn't want to carry one the whole journey. Whenever I wanted, I looked for one lying around, or I carved one.

Initially, I had considered the other factor of a walking staff, its nostalgic character, investing it with a heavy social or communicative feature not to be sneezed at. You could as well come with a sign around your neck saying,

CHAPTER TEN

'I've come a long way!' It is a discreet offer that you have something to tell, initiating social contacts before you could say Jack Robinson or introduce yourself. But I already had the backpack, fulfilling the same function, among others.

To me, a totally different issue is the walking stick that usually comes in pairs, slowly conquering the world these days from hiking trails to city sidewalks. For some, it already seems to be accepted as a common walking aid. I never understood how millions of people could have been convinced that you needed them for walking, and I mean walking. Most people using these sticks don't actually move any faster with them, or farther. The sportier variant, I think, is called Nordic Walking, and, indeed, here it looks as if a skier had forgotten something.

Nevertheless, they became so common that people now use them in the country, in city parks, and on boardwalks alike. As for me, especially in a mountainous terrain I'd rather trust my senses than a stick. This of course demanded that your sense of balance is trained, what we habitually do all of our (walking) life. Future archaeologists may find petrified stick prints and conclude that it was at the turn of the 20th century when people lost the ability to walk on their feet without an aid. (Admitted, due to some other habits as well, like driving to one's neighbor.)

In fact, it is an unequaled sign of our time, since the whole thing developed from an economical crisis of a Scandinavian company producing skiers and winter sports equipment. After a major drop in sales numbers, the company considered modern innovation development methods. Board members and labor held a brainstorming meeting, eventually augmenting an old acquaintance called ski pole by simply diversifying its use. Eureka! The walking stick was found.

They began promoting Columbus' egg based on produced, dubious or semi-scientific facts corroborating the advantages of the new walking aid. How successful they were, everybody can see for himself, on a boardwalk in Malibu or on the Pacific Crest Trail. Economic scholars could use this phenomenon as a didactic play when discussing product marketing in narrow markets. I cannot think of a better one, maybe the ladyshave – as compared to a regular razor.

Yet many walking stick fans cite medicinal and fitness aspects. Seriously, I do believe that for the purpose of a rather ineffective training of our upper arms, which is what most fitness gurus argue with, in the long *run*, it is at the expense of a good sense of balance. The other often heard argument is that it helped with obesity. Well, eating less and healthier food would be an option. Beyond all sticks-and-staff contemplation, I agree with English historian George Macauley Trevelyan: "I have two doctors, my left leg and my right."

322

07/12   SNOWSTORM MOUNTAIN, 19 MILES

On this day, the shrub monotony would be interrupted by the town of Ravendale. From the size in my map, it did not promise much more than a lost site in sage, but still it was a spark of hope for getting a little variety for my house bar and some conversation after more than fifty wordless miles.

From afar, I saw a pink building on the right side of the street. Actually, it was the only building I could see on both sides of the street. An hour later, I arrived at it, the Mission Inn Motel, and I found it closed. Since it was already late afternoon, I decided to stay and wait for the owner. It was exactly the kind of American roadside motel I mentioned earlier, the vanishing kind where you expect an unordinary fellow and possibly an interesting stay.

I put my pack in front of the door and sat down on a chair, pulling my hat down to shade my face from the sun. Looking around the area, I now noticed a small farm building across the street, hidden behind a stand of cottonwood. Further down the road, on the other end of what might have been a town in former times, there was another building; if the old scratched signboard leaning to a power mast had not been blown here by the wind, this was the post office.

I pushed my hat back up and decided to check if anyone was there. Reaching the farmhouse, I saw an old man sitting on the porch, slurping a dark fluid with something in it that looked like plant parts, though, it could have been tobacco as well, or insects. I asked him, if I could get a glass of water; "just water," I echoed as a precaution. Instead I got a beer and was ordered to sit down. While the old man was stirring the contents of his jar, I emptied my can with one hearty draught. When he came back with a second can, he began telling me the town's history, why the post office was still open, "assumably serving coyotes", and that his family were the last citizens left, after two fires had almost completely destroyed the town. He was audibly breathing throughout his sentences, disregarding any intonation pattern. It gave his narration a certain choppiness, though, and when he for the first time rose his voice on the last word of a sentence, followed by a long prominent pause, I was almost excited what would come next: "there never was much worth of destroying, though."

The name of the only street crossing the highway was School Street; "You may now put two and two together and see that there had been a schoolhouse before. While this one isn't there anymore – if you turned your head around – you can still notice the bulldozer parked on the former schoolhouse site."

His strange intonation along with frequent pausing became as much an utterance as his words itself, underlining his personal attitude all the more. "Quite contrary to the bulldozer – the parked farming equipment – over there. I have no clue – what that is waiting for."

CHAPTER TEN

For at least a minute, he stared at the old multi-crop thresher parked on the field half a mile from us. Following his gaze, I wouldn't have been surprised if the mower had suddenly started moving, caused by psychic abilities or maybe the ingredients of his drink. Instead he said:

"One smart mind – mowed down a straight – line through the corn and – left – didn't tell anybody what it was for – never seen since."

I liked his dry and matter-of-fact delivery of the local history punch lines. A bit provokingly, I asked him if he was from here and if he knew the area around. After a long rhetorical pause that already equaled an eloquent answer, the old man's voice rasped, "I know one thing – ain't nothin' 'round."

In between we were watching the neighborhood and staring at the fields, sometimes the eternity of five minutes without saying anything, and I realized he was right, there was actually nothing to stare at. When he turned his head to look back into his jar, stabbing its contents with a steely knife as if he was trying to kill that beast, I felt he was ready for another statement. He pointed to the motel and chipped in, "Saw you loitering there."

He shook his head, paused, and continued, describing the guy across the street, who would try to run a motel in no man's land, "Simply – crazy."

After a while, he became more clear, "Who knows what he's doing there – must be broke – all the time. There's absolutely no business. He must have some money – though – being on the road all time."

To my question, if the crazy guy would come back some time soon, he shook his head again and stared at the hardening ground in his emptied jar as if he could find an answer there.

"He'll be back some time – any time." His grimace did not in the least match what he was saying and I started wondering if even he himself knew what he was drinking there.

A wordless while later, I saw a car coming on the highway; it stopped at the corner. I said goodbye to the old man and walked back to the motel, but the car drove off, while the driver was shaking his head with disapproval.

Traffic would be the wrong word for that part of U.S. 395. The next car came by only an hour later; this time it turned off the highway and stopped right by my side. The driver introduced himself as "Jim, somehow burgomaster, somehow sheriff" and – assuming I wouldn't want to walk into the night – "definitely your host for a night in Ravendale".

"Back to the forties and fifties, that's my style, because when I grew up, the world was still OK", said Jim when showing me the rooms, "when you could take someone at his word."

He had bought the place in 1999 to fulfill his dream, restoring an old roadside motel in its nostalgic style. Until 9/11, the world was OK for him, "I counted fifty tour busses a day, fifty trucks and 395 cars daily on U.S. 395."

I imagined him sitting on his porch and counting cars, what else was there to do. But he reassured that this stop once was a busy place. He even planned opening a fifties-diner and a star market, like the old Texaco Star Markets. However, the county seat in Susanville made life difficult for him. Here was a tree that mustn't be cut down, there was not enough space and, overall, his lot would be too small for that kind of business. If that didn't do it – I can hardly imagine that space availability could be an argument out here – they still had licenses and paperwork to put him off and dispirit him. Then there was the attack on the towers and traffic broke down. He said, people just did not travel anymore like they used to. Somehow bizarre, I thought, how things were connected these days, al-Qaeda – New York – Ravendale.

Today you only see chips trucks, transporting woodchips to the incinerator and ashes back. He said, since September 2001, I was the first international guest in his house.

A moment later, Jim's friend Garret came by, a former rodeo cowboy now running a horse ranch north of Ravendale. Working with animals is in his blood since his dad had already been a famous stuntman and wild animals trainer for Hollywood. While he started the grill and threw in a tri tip, a cross-country bicyclist rolled by on the highway. He was heading for Alaska and asked if he could take a rest here. With a Jim-of-all-trades and his stories from the fifties, a rancher talking about his rodeo life, and comparing the thousand-mile summer with long-distance cycling from the Carolinas to Alaska, we made up quite an unorthodox round of people. The evening was saved.

The whole scene was so unreal, the rendezvous' characters so incoherent, it felt like one of those dreams where totally far-fetched scenes string together, making a plot as long as you sleep but vanish irretrievably as soon as you wake up.

Indeed, I did receive more reasons to believe my assumption was right. Walking to the bathroom, I passed one of the motel rooms and saw it furnished like a little church room with candles burning on a small altar. Jim explained, he reserved this room for service since he also was the pastor of the town.

Furthermore, he was able to see ghosts. By now, anything else would have surprised me. As a young boy he was a chaplain on a Navy ship, some of which are haunted, he said. One day, when going to the bathroom, he had seen an officer who was shaving, and by chance, in passing him, he recognized that he could grab through him. Another time he went to the nearer ladies' bathroom since the ship was completely disembarked and no one left aboard.

CHAPTER TEN

The mere thought, to be left alone on an ocean liner, would be frightening somehow, or unearthly. Just about when he wanted to sit down, he heard a woman's voice saying, "Can't we be alone somewhere."

He later researched the two incidents and found out that a certain Navy general had just passed away who always wanted to be relocated to that ship but never was, at least in his lifetime. The woman was a former Marine who loved the casino on that ship. Unfortunately, she had been overrun on a crosswalk in her hometown a short time ago. Apparently, both of them had decided to charter again and spend their afterlife there.

Garret had whipped up a gourmet dinner in four courses, salad, chili, steaks, and a cocktail of all fruits California had to offer. From a duct-taped set of loudspeakers in one of the rooms, the spirit of Woodstock sounded, nourishing Jim's good-ole-days nostalgia, "We haven't had that spirit here since nineteen sixty-nine..."

When the meat was grilled, two guys who build irrigation systems in the valley joined us chipping in soda and beer, and right after dinner the iceman zoomed past the motel. Without visible effort, with a single click of his fingers, Jim called him off the highway. I did not notice the driver looking to us; it might have been telepathy or just between soul mates.

As far as I could tell, Jim was the only living soul in the motel, but he did a fantastic job assimilating and impersonating a whole lot of characters who would elsewhere make up a smaller city. With all the stories, it became a small world in itself, and I wished him that no bad character would ever put up at his motel, only good souls attending Mass with the pastor, barbecue with the horse trainer, and spending an evening with the shaving general and a sitting marine.

When I asked him when he wanted me to check out next morning, he said, "Relax, you can check out any time you like," and I already knew what he was going to say, and that he was right, "but you can never leave." My soul would now remain, too.

All around Ravendale, there were open hills and open range. In the evening not only the coyotes came down from the hills but wild horses too. Although the landscape had not become more pleasant here, thanks to this chummy evening, it suggested again a feeling of the *Last Old West*, or quoting the regional Modoc Magazine: "Where the West still lives."

07/13   RAVENDALE, 20 MILES

This morning, Jim's daughters from Marine County came over for a two-week visit. In order to meet them, Jim drove up with flashing red lights, his recently acquired '85 ambulance car. Probably another job he had just taken over.

With the firm resolution to come back next year, I hit the road for my last adventure, the Warner Mountains, before, at their northern end, I would put one foot on Oregon ground.

Walking toward the town of Madeline, I wondered why I thought of that name as belonging to a little girl and what might have happened to her. Was it just the sonorous name, or did I start having visions too? The town consisted of some farmhouses and a general store, where I asked about it and learned that it was indeed a settlers' young child who had been killed by Indians, shortly after they arrived here.

Leaving Madeline behind, I was ascending the foothills of the Southern Warner Wilderness. Long ago, these plains were grassland with ranches all over. After a series of dry years, the ranchers had built dams to regulate the water to be prepared for future droughts. The result was that the grass dried up in many areas thus vacating the land for more frugal sage emigrating from Nevada.

Coming to a creek, I took my shoes off to wade through it. A minute later, I was in the water taking a bath; it was 80 F. First I thought there must be hot springs somewhere close, but when I later reached a shallow lake I knew better. The creek was an outlet of a huge puddle of alkaline water, which was heated by the sun. Sitting in that hot whirlpool, I felt how I regained the happiness and the high-flying feelings I had before the herald train woke me up in Truckee. I was back on my journey and walked without any pressure, without sorrows. As a matter of fact, besides my holidays along Walker River, only in the very beginning in the desert did I feel that free, whereas there it was a naïve unknowing freedom since I didn't reckon what lay ahead. From when I entered real desert in the Mojave, through Death Valley and even more in the snowy Sierra, there always was this *what-if* feeling.

In spite of all these natural reasons, I wasn't too sure if the major one was the inability to throw off our modern habit of hurry. As Colin mentioned, he couldn't unlearn it for long, how much more difficult must it be fifty years later, half a century faster, in a time when value is determined by bits and speed, and importance by the ability to outrun time. However, now and with the certitude that I almost made it, I gained that serenity and rose to the same elation again.

Here, suddenly, all became clear. I made it that far and was sure nothing challenging could happen anymore. The nights were warm now, some creeks even acceptable for taking a bath. The path has been covered; the finale was imminent. Now I could take it easy, rest my mind, and enjoy what I experienced to the fullest. It might sound strange, why would you do it then for four months instead of just going two weeks? But one only comes with the other. Without the uncertainty, the peradventure in the beginning, it would never become an adventure in the end.

CHAPTER TEN

Arriving at the shallow waters of Moon Lake, I camped at a large dry inlet. The meltwaters had run dry, leaving a green carpet with yellow flowers rolled out to the shore. At the edge of the forest, on the other side of the inlet, stood a group of wild horses, turning their heads for a last time before they disappeared behind the trees. A detachment of cattle had left the lakeshore and strode down the blooming carpet in a single line, obviously going to whatever they called home. Alone with the moon, I prepared dinner, heating a can of chicken noodle stew and metabolizing cloudy lake water into tea. Campfire musing kept me awake until late into the night; meanwhile the moon seemed to take a rest in the middle of the lake, until jumping fish broke its reflection into ripples. The real one was dolling up at the horizon for a finale grandiose. It was his fifth and last time accompanying me through the wilderness and shining bright for a good week.

07/14   MOON LAKE, 10 MILES

The sun was already waiting behind the hills, ready to take curtain calls, when I woke up from a squadron of wild geese flying over the lake. I sat up and felt that the atmosphere was full of anticipation, of speculation. Still, everything was quiet but an occasional flapping of a straggling bird hastening to catch up with the group. Deep inside, I heard the slowly rising sun as she took possession of the faraway mountains, then of the surrounding hills, and eventually of the tree tops and me.

When she touched the lake, the silence was broken. The hitherto restrained geese came back honking and circling above the lake. The group of cows came trotting out of the forest again, their two calves visibly capering for joy, almost stumbling over their own legs. I spent all morning there watching the buzz of activity, and it seemed that the closer I came to the end the more nature was enthusing me. Or I just learned to see more and experience those things that elude a passerby.

Most of the trails here were long overgrown; in places and only from afar, one could notice little variances of the colors or in the height of the plants, which would indicate a former path. Two miles later, I had to use my compass, the trails on my map had long been history. Sometimes names did really help. In a network of canyons, I was looking for a *Deep Canyon*. Looking down from a rim into the second one, I was convinced. With a depth that makes you shrink back first and, when you have a second guess, pulls you with an eerie gravity, I knew, this must be it. Later I should turn north after passing a *Cedar Creek*. There were two creeks and a runlet, the first two flowing through grassland, the latter bordered by cedar trees.

Between the trees, I found an old cabin completely overgrown. There were empty cans, kitchenware, and preserving jars lying around, some of them with contents, probably sugar, salt, and spices. Although I was running low on sugar for coffee and tea, I left the jars closed. One glass contained a moldering paste that vividly tried to escape its container, maybe a pioneer's sourdough.

Not far from the house was a drawbar trailer to a stagecoach. An assortment of wooden boxes, looking like sluice boxes, had fallen from it. Aside, between two trees, lay a larger chest with an iron lock at the top cover. It was so rusted that it fell off when I touched it. Cautiously, I lifted the cover to peer into the chest's past. When I had it high enough to let some light inside, I saw something moving, but at that same time the handle broke off the brittle cover with a loud crack. I couldn't tell if I was more frightened from the noise of the cracking handle or the movement inside. Probably it was the coincidence that made me think something inside had pulled the cover back down. That *something* would have been quite substantial.

Instinctively you think of a snake, but didn't I see fur? I picked up a stick and pushed the top slowly back up again until I could lean it to a tree behind. Bending down, I looked into eight intimidated eyes, a young family of mice sitting behind each other, frightened as if I was the snake.

I stepped back to watch them in their modest estate. Every once in a while they looked up to me as if I had caught them flat-footed. But from the coy and longing look in their eyes, I understood their wish, if only these jars would open somehow. Eventually, I couldn't resist their prayer any longer. Finally, after so many mice generations, the spices, the sugar, and that something else were set free. As soon as I stepped back, they gathered for the feast.

For two miles, I could follow the creek upstream. Then it turned off to its springs while I had to go east walking out of Cedar Canyon. I passed other cabins here and there, climbed over fences and No-Trespassing signs, and scared groups of wild or runaway cattle causing a stampede through the forest.

One of the cabins was more of a house, built of logs and metal sheets and parts of a truck. It seemed to be abandoned for years. Behind the building was a corral, but the horses were long gone, and high grass overgrew the remains of a pick up truck and a trailer falling apart. I could not figure how anyone would have got a car with a trailer into this wayless area. Then again, another fence with a plate warning: 'Absolutely No Trespassing'. But the sign was so old and rusty, I was sure it was no skin of anyone's nose crossing a property that nature had already repossessed.

After having climbed a heavily wooded slope, I could finally see the West Valley Reservoir in the northwest and below me the smaller Blue Lake, my next stop for the night. Up here, the forest just ended. The only sign that there ever was one were fallen, blackened logs and limbless tree stumps standing high above the fireweed, the first colonizer on burned lands after a

CHAPTER TEN

forest fire. Here, in 2001, the so-called Blue Fire had destroyed thousands of acres between this hill and the lake.

I estimate that from Devils Postpile, where the Rainbow fire had raged, to the southern Warner Mountains, about one third of the woods I walked through fell victim to fires in the course of the last thirty years; totally or at least the understory, caused either naturally, by arson, or carelessness. The year of my journey emerged to become one of the worst with some 1,000 fires burning throughout California simultaneously, and it became clear that the increasing number of fires each year surpassed nature's ability to recover. Some more years like that and our kids will live to see a treeless state. With subsequent soil erosion and surface drainage, my follower in fifty years might well walk through one thousand miles of desert.

On my run down to the lake, I passed a few ospreys' nests, decoratively built on the highest totem trees, but the ospreys had to wait; in my mind was only the lake. With clothes on, I jumped into the deep blue, a small, beautiful lake surrounded by a few white firs and ponderosas that were close enough to the water to be unscathed.

It was not as warm as the Moon Lake, but instead a wonderful refreshment after the fired atmosphere. I made a cup of coffee and sat down on a rock in the lake to watch the sunset while my clothes were drying.

It was only instant powder and none of the more expensive kind, but it tasted as delicious as a cup of Jamaican Blue Mountain, when on a beautiful morning turned into coffee with water and sugar. The crowning glory, however, always was enjoying a cup after a long walking day when settling down on a spot like that.

07/15   BLUE LAKE, 14 MILES

Before I left the lake, I walked to the nearby campground to ask some visitors for information about the summit trail, water sources, and fires. They said, they were familiar with the area and they would strongly advise to take the East Fork trail, just seven miles from here. It had more creeks along the way, and yes, there were faucets on the trailhead campground with drinking water. Good news to me, that meant easy walking with less than a gallon on my pack.

On South Warner Road, I ascended the first foothills of the Warner Mountains, walking along a valley of tall-growing, rangy mule's ears, when suddenly, I thought hearing bells from far away. Or was it a purling creek? But it became louder and clearer. I stopped again and again to prick up my ears, it came from the valley to my left, where Parship Creek must flow somewhere beneath mule's ears and cabbage. The bells mingled with soft cries, almost like babies cry. I wondered if again I was fooled by a trick played on me by the wind until, between a stand of birch trees, I detected the first sheep. It was the sound of sheep bells in the wind, and there came more and more, not a few, not hundreds, it had to be thousands. Apparently, I had eliminated any possibility of repeating this one of Colin's surprises so much that I realized the sheep only when I saw them. In my reality, I had excluded a sound that was quite familiar to me from home; hence I was caught by surprise and as delighted as he was fifty years ago. I would finally see my own Basque sheepherder, and when I thought about it, everything else would have disappointed me but meeting him about where Colin did.

I left my pack on the roadside and walked down to the creek, where the endless line of baaing sheep processed by. Three dogs acting as sheepboys were running back and forth several times, but only half an hour later did I see the leader, here, at the end of the procession, with a walking staff and a straw hat. There he was, my personal Basque sheepherder, his name was Gamaniel and he was from Peru.

Since he did not know a word in English, I had to dig my little Spanish to learn that he lived about a mile up the creek. He was watching over a flock of 2,000 sheep, 1,000 adults and some 1,200 lambs. I failed in an attempt to explain him the coincidence, but I could ask him, if he, too, would carve stories in aspen trees. He showed me his aspen grove on my map, from where he used to send his letters to Peru. When he talked about home, I didn't get much of it, but by looking into his eyes, I saw they were friendly smiling in a happy melancholia and I couldn't wait to read his stories.

I asked him to pose for some pictures for me, and we did sheepherder with sheep, sheepherder with dogs, and sheepherder with me. When I took my hat to leave, he rummaged around in his pack, signifying that he wanted to give me something. But his hands came out empty. I rummaged my pack to find a pen and a paper as he wrote something in the air. While he was stating that I was the first man he talked to this year, he wrote down his telephone number in Peru saying, should I make it that far, I must greet his family there.

When I was back on the trail, I turned around again to wave him goodbye. It seemed as if 2,000 sheep were waiting, apprehensively baaing at him, until the shepherd joined his flock again. As they disappeared behind the cabbage, I felt the urge to tell Colin about my encounter, and before the last *baa* had faded, I found me an aspen tree and carved my story into its bark:

Andreas
&
Sheepherder
15 July 2008

Four miles later, I stopped at another small creek, Mosquito Creek, which fortunately did not flow up to its name. With my feet on a bed of water daisies, I actually enjoyed the only fly-free hour of that day. With more and more flowers around, mainly sunflowers and lupines, droves of flies and bees have been accompanying me since I left the Blue Lake.

I was wondering what had happened here to the pioneer, had he been attacked by mosquitoes like me in the Sierra, and why then did he stay here? You would not name a creek if you just passed it, like I did. Otherwise I would rename it Nobuzz Creek. While we are at it, the mosquitoes weren't really that bad at all. With the exception of the depraved sub-species of Fish Valley, in general you were able to sort of communicate with them, to find something like an agreement, a mutual understanding. Using a repellent would mean, I do not like to be bothered. Let me alone. And it would work, as small as their brain might be, eventually they would understand and accept. Compared to some other species a remarkable performance of the brain. The common yet abundant fly is much worse and a real pain in the neck. Flies buzz around your head until they sit in your nose, your ear, or on your eyelashes. Heavy fidgeting with your hands, sudden movements like jerkily turning your head, ducking down or even a short sprint pretending you would run off – all of that is useless, they ignore any form of body language. If you try to swat it, first, 99.9% you miss them, second, they don't even take it personal. If you missed one by a whisker – your hand might even have slapped it – before you hit yourself – it sits right back at exactly the same spot just a split second later. Then, since your skin is still hot from the slap, you don't even feel it. Whatever cream or spray you apply, it would only attract the flies and make them curious for that funny odor. Eventually, you start yelling, going through all verb compositions ending with 'off'. Pointless.

As soon as you move, mosquitoes leave you alone, assumed you reached a certain speed. When flies detect you wandering, they come with supersonic speed – that is, you don't hear them coming until after they already landed on you. When you chase them away, they enter a flexible orbit, flying around you in horizontal to almost vertical circles at increasing speed, starting at your feet and moving up with every circle, a tactic obviously aiming at confusing the victim. Despite their high-velocity air acrobatics, they have the ability to precalculate a) where I would be after my next step and their next circle, b) where my hand would hit my skin and c) external factors like wind and rain. Now how are we to call that, zero intelligence? Or is it a higher form of intelligence, athletic endurance or credit where credit's due for perseverance?

And then, there is the uncrowned evil queen among flies, the horsefly. They not only hurt badly, they are also more persistent and keep stinging even when you hit them.

The farther I walked into this garden of flowering colors the worse they got. On slopes that were filled with paintbrush, sunflowers, and lupines, I had to fuel my campfires with fresh greens in order to produce thick smoke that would keep them at bay. Only recently, a scientist identified the gene factor that is responsible for powering drosophila's flight muscles through as many as 1,000 oscillations per second. Perhaps that allows a spark of hope for our mankind.

Understandably, you become conditioned to any buzzing noise getting closer to your ears. It causes you to look around hectically, which can in fact, with a heavy pack and after a long day, give you a muscle ache at your neck. The most frightening sound, however, was a buzz as if a monster fly was approaching. They fooled me several times and caused me to duck down, until I saw the cute little hummingbird, nodding its head in front of my face.

Arriving at the trailhead campground, I faced more surprises. The fact that it had been ten miles from the lake and not seven was unremarkable. But finding out that all camping faucets were turned off was remarkably unpleasant; worst case I would have to walk back down to Mosquito Creek. On the wooden board, where Park Services display trail maps and introduce you to the rules of outdoor camping, there was a sign warning hikers to stay away from the East Fork trail. After the last wildfire the trail had been totally overgrown.

Anyway, I wanted to take the Summit trail as Colin did, traversing the highest portions of the wilderness. Checking the empty campground to look for water, I found another sign that was more revealing.

CAUTION!

– Blackened trees, weakened to the point of falling

– Stumpholes and root tunnels could cause foot or leg injury

– Widow makers: fallen trees or branches hung up in other trees

And it continued:

– ENJOY THE WARNER MOUNTAINS.

An exclamation mark would have made it ironic, the mere period resembled the administrative soberness you would expect from an authority.

Fortunately, there was one tiny water flow across the site, the last remains of a snowmelt creek. It took me twenty minutes to fill a one-gallon sack.

The forest floor around was so dry that every step caused a crackling sound as if I had already lightened up the ground. From here, I became overcautious with fire. Everywhere stood tall wooden memorials moaning a note of warning. In order to cook my last canned stew, I built a sound fire pit with a stonewall around it, twice as high as usual.

Today's hiking fuel was called 'Homemade Chunky Grilled Chicken & Sausage Gumbo', the last can I bought in Madeline. Had the name been a little longer, they would have to wind the label twice around the can. As the name tried to attract everybody's taste buds, the content actually failed at it.

After lunch, I resumed the search for the summit trailhead. There was a wooden arrow to it behind the campground, but the path disappeared after one hundred yards. I walked back and checked it again. The only other trail I found lead to the East Fork. Again I stood at the Summit Trail arrow, and I understood that the trail was overgrown, too, from the start, and that it would be a challenge to spot it under a cover of two-foot-high sunflowers. Here, the forest had not burned down totally. The larger trees had survived, yet between them existed a chaos of fallen logs, others soon to fall, and probably a lot of hidden widow makers hovering above. When the forest finally opened up to scrub, I noticed the color variations in the blooming fields again. In a mix of mountain paintbrush, lupines, and sunflowers you could guess the trail under a vague line of lupines.

Reaching the Emerson Lake cut-off, I followed an eastbound trail for a mile to get a view of that lake. Lying several hundred feet below in a dark and chilly hollow, it was anything but inviting. I decided to move on, hoping that one of the many westbound creek beds flowing from the summits would carry water.

Lush yellow slopes opened up in front of me, enrobing the mountain's shoulders in a gown of sunflowers. The noble raiment was spotted with green groves of cabbage and birches, where small creeks found a way like hidden seams. One creek had its source right behind such a copse of birches. The eldest tree had Basque carvings, and it was Gamaniel's log.

I had just enough time to touch the adnate letters, before the sun sank into the vent of Mount Shasta. With me, a million flowers had turned their heads west, watching the spectacle of the Warner Mountains.

07/16   NORTH EMERSON LAKE, POISON CREEK, 11 MILES

Since I fell asleep at the creek, everything was wet from morning dew. I had to have a couple of coffees while waiting for the sun to dry my sleeping bag.

As I passed two more springs, each was so nice and inviting that I stopped for another one. The higher I got the more pine forest prevailed adorning the rim, while the flowers withdrew to creeks and springs. In fact, every water source was a little nature fiesta. Opulent fields of skunk cabbage followed the creeks along the slopes until you lost sight of them far down in the valleys. Besides the three main tenants, many more yellow and white flowers populated the stretches along the water. The queen of flowers, though, was the red and yellow blooming crimson columbine, growing two to three feet tall on the banks of each creek with its flowers dangling above the flowing water like crown-shaped lanterns.

Here and there, I discovered a new peculiar species, every single one worth stopping and closer examination. Among the most extravagant were the following three, each with its own fascinating story. In former life, the Brown's peony was a student of Asclepius, the Greek god of medicine, according to mythology. When the teacher became jealous of his student's wisdom, as a precaution Zeus turned Paeon into a flower to save him from Asclepius' rage. Today he grows in fleshy, bluish-green leaves and reddish-brown, ball-shaped flowers with yellow pistils and green, pea-like seeds, and indeed, the Native Americans have been using the plant as a medicinal tea and to heal respiratory diseases.

Then there were these lovely patches of pussy paws, an odd-looking plant growing flower-clusters of soft pink cushions. Depending upon daytime, their thin stems stretch to raise the flowers above the heated ground or crush to nestle up against the warmer ground when the air gets cool at night.

With purplish-pink flowers and fir-like leaves, the freckled milkvetch surprised me on higher elevations. The really interesting parts, though, are its inflated pods the size of a fingertip. When you press them between your fingers or wait until late summer when they dry to tout, papery balloons, they will catapult away the small seeds.

In summary, as unspectacular as they may seem in comparison to the higher Sierra, a walk through the flora of the Warner Mountains offers enough inspiration to compete with an imaginary fantasy story setting.

When I reached the last long rim leading to the peak, I was back in high alpine terrain, and the vegetation changed out of the blue. Hitherto most flowers were growing tall competing for the sun, from here, all were small and clinging to the soil, to gravel, and loose rocks to make sure they would not lose their footing with the strong winds blowing over the rim.

The range of the Warner Mountains was a massive uplift of lava flows, towering high above the alkali lakes in the east and Goose Lake in the west.

Despite being some 200 feet shorter than its neighbor Eagle Peak, with its massive cliffs rising dramatically from the rim, Warren Peak was the mightiest summit in the range. As the whole range, its western slope looked smooth and harmless, while the eastern side was the equivalent to the coastal cliffs of the West Coast in northern California.

CHAPTER TEN

With almost 9,000 feet, Warren Peak was also the last high mountain for me. Lingering in crevices around the summit, small patches of snow were trying to hold the rocky fort. Only the fish in the summit lake blabbered out that I was not the first one here. In fact Patterson Lake must have been visited regularly by anglers, since the fish knew exactly what I was out for. While I was watching the floater, a hover of trout gathered around gawping at my hook. Despite a relatively strong current to the outlet stream, they seemed to be nailed in the water. Occasional bubbles reaching the surface revealed their Homeric laughter. After a while, I gave up. Even throwing little pebbles of frustration on the water surface did not make these stubborn fish move. With the setting sun, a strong breeze came blowing around the summit, too cold to stay without building the tent. Just a little farther lay the smaller Cottonwood Lake protected by trees on one side and steep rising cliffs on the other. Here I found a quiet place for the night, away from the wind, away from their laughter.

07/17   WARREN PEAK, PATTERSON LAKE, 16 MILES

High, remote, and lonely, the Warner Mountains turned out to be one of the most isolated and beautiful places in California, a hardly traveled but wild and spectacular range with vast wildflower displays on wide open slopes and perfect views along the summit rim to both valleys east and west.

Descending from the last peak, I walked down to the valley in order to replenish for a last time, before I would cross the range again through the Highgrade mining district. There, in an area full of gold mines, I hoped to find my nugget in reaching the Oregon border. From now on it was only days away and I could not imagine how I would feel.

While the view from White Mountain resembled the median between desert and mountains, a temporal point of contemplation about two months traveled and two more to go, the rim up here allowed now only one view into the present. The future of four months walking had shrunk to only a couple of days and my mind was preoccupied with only one question: what will I find at the end or inside of me, how can I compensate the certainty that there will be a changing horizon, a new adventure, and another strike of nature's beauty, each day I woke up in the wild.

To know that we often cannot perceive the full impact of something too beautiful when we see it, but only later when we look back in nostalgia, was a little comfort now. Yet, I did not know of Wordsworth's promise, the bliss of solitude that would keep flashing upon my inward eye, long after I will have returned from this voyage.

As I left the rim trail descending through Granger Creek Canyon, I met forest ranger Mike, as a matter of fact the first hiking ranger. He was clearing the trail from fallen trees with four helping hands, Andrew and Chris. Talking to them about my journey in general and the remaining route in particular, my last doubt was dispelled. Here, Colin had to replenish too, and I knew that he was going west to a medium-sized town called Alturas, whereas I gravitated toward the valley in the east, another forgotten corner of California I had never heard of before. I understood that Colin's choice would offer just another supply town that would come up with no more than stores, motels, and gas stations. Furthermore, Alturas is located on the western gentler curb of the mountains, whereas the other side was more exciting with steep mountain cliffs. Perhaps it was just the promising name that hooked me – a secret valley called Surprise. Mike confirmed my idea; so I thought, I would complete my last leg with a both historically and geologically more interesting side-trip and replenish in Cedarville, reflecting Alturas in the rim line and located on the dramatic side of the range.

Cutting sharply into the geological history of California's northeast, the canyon is in fact a dramatic prelude to the peaceful valley below. Bounded by a mixed forest of pine trees, aspen, and cottonwood, the steep and rugged ravine snakes through several layers of lava, outcropped by the prehistoric uplift. While skyscraping forests covered the high mountain edges, the serrated volcanic outcrops on the steep cliffs allowed only cacti and thistles to consort with them, some of which were six feet tall. To the contrary, the rift valley below is the smoothest surprise one could imagine after the rugged peaks and jagged rims behind.

Historically, the early settlers had come from the other side, baptizing it after having traveled through the hot sagebrush desert of Nevada. The contrast they were facing must have been comparably surprising.

I walked into an agricultural oasis secluded between mountains and desert, and, by now, I wouldn't have been surprised if all farming equipment were horse-drawn and the people spoke an old Dutch dialect. After taking a shower from a wheel move irrigating alfalfa, I sat down on the field to dry. On a country road nearby, a tractor was slowly coming my way. The driver's singing, however, was less Dutch than Spanish, and the tractor was not drawn by a horse but driven by a young Latino – I couldn't believe it, Gamaniel, the reputed Basque, was sitting up there. I jumped up to meet him – I had sworn to myself he looked all the same and had the same whimsical smile – but he just twinkled, said a nice *"Buenas"*, and drove past.

Surprise Valley is split between California and Nevada, not only geomorphic but also historically. When the two tradesmen Bonner and Cressler founded the first settlement here in the 1870s, it was yet Nevada territory, until Bonner built the first road crossing the Warner Mountains, eventually applying for California legislation and forming Modoc County.

CHAPTER TEN

As I walked down the country roads to the town of Cedarville, I passed beautiful farmhouses and huge barns telling of a long farming tradition. Tall cottonwood giants of one hundred feet stood in front of the houses, and in every garden, along with kennels and stables, there were tall windmills reaching up to the tree tops. For vita contemplativa, most gardens came with a porch swing or a hammock.

Coming closer to town, the impressive monument-like trees began forming an alley, bestowing a processional character on my entry. I did not just walk into town, I strode. Nestled in the forgotten northeastern corner of California, the little community had the most peaceful atmosphere, an Amish ambiance, as if it had never been bothered by whatever turned the wheel of the outside world.

As I paraded down the cottonwood alley into Cedarville, it seemed that I was actually announced. Everybody on the street stopped to say hello. I was asked if I needed help so often, that at first I thought I must look pretty run-down until I understood it was the local way of greeting a newcomer. Cars slowed down, windows opened with hands waving out of them. In fact it felt as if I was on the home stretch.

I sat down at a café watching people come and go. On every car's passenger seat, there was a dog, sometimes two or more, and sometimes on the driver's seat. Somehow dogs must think it's a privilege to sit there; as soon as the driver had parked the car and got out, the dog would move to the driver's seat, like a child that was told to stay in the car, while mom and dad did grocery shopping.

It wasn't long and I got company, an old lady asked if I would mind – of course I didn't. She sat down and said she had to have her coffee outside to keep an eye on her friends, pointing to the truck parked on the other side of the street. There, five dogs were about to seize a 1950s Chevy pick-up, one behind the steering wheel, one on the passenger seat, and three left in the back, constantly barking at the lady next to me, which probably meant, "Now it's my turn, mom, me too!" When the waitress came out to take orders, the lady said: "Please, one large coffee and a piece of your best cake, for my pretty friend." The waitress twinkled and bent down to me, articulately whispering: "You better be careful with this lady, she got a lot of pretty, pretty boys she calls friends." I felt flattered and thanked. During our further conversation, I had two sentences to tell her what I was doing. Then she took over, and I received her report about Cedarville.

Overall, I had the feeling that people here were very proud of their valley and its historical towns and that they enjoyed talking about it. Most of the people were into farming or horse breeding, but a good many were retirees who found their little paradise off the beaten track and occupied their time volunteering it.

Jim from the JnR Hotel, where I would stay for the night, took me by the hand to show me a garage that was home to ten coaches and other horse drawn vehicles. From there, I was sent to the fairgrounds to check out the site of Louieville, a collection of historical buildings brought together for preservation and to keep them from decaying somewhere in the wilderness. When I was halfway to the site, a man caught up with me, saying he heard that I wanted to see Louieville, and he thought he could give me a little tour.

The place was named for its patron, Louis Vermillion, the patron of Louieville. In his truck-driving career, delivering to farms and ranches throughout the valley, the respected citizen had noticed an abundance of decaying machines, coaches, and buildings. Having restored the first buggy some fifteen years ago, he found his mission, restoring historical equipment and collecting the history of Surprise Valley.

The whole town looked like it had been preserved, painted over with a magical, invisible color about one hundred years ago to keep it from aging. Here, I sat on the porch of the 1865 Cressler-Bonner building, behind it was their trading post, which, at that time, had turned the small wagon train camp called 'Deep Creek' into the town of Cedarville. There were private homes dating back to the 19th century and the church building from 1880. All later buildings somehow matched older styles and fit into the town's historic charm. Bald eagles circling over the cottonwood trees were just the icing on the cake.

I wished they would make modern traffic stop at city limits and get Louis' conveyances out of the garage.

07/18   CEDARVILLE, 19 MILES

Leaving Cedarville behind, I passed the farms and ranches of its citizens. Along the highway, nosy horses and cattle came trotting to the fences. Then they stood in formation as if they were proudly presenting their pasture estates, some of which reached a mile or two from the edge of the mountains to the band of alkali lakes in the middle of the valley. Behind the lakes lay Nevada, from where another emigrant trail led into California, the Applegate-Lassen Route, crossing the mountains right where I stopped for the night, awaiting the trek on Fandango Pass.

07/19   FANDANGO PASS, 19 MILES

I was often wondering what kind of people these emigrants were, let alone the pioneers and pathfinders, whereas I am sure, pioneering alone or in small groups had been a breeze compared to guiding a group of a hundred settlers.

CHAPTER TEN

No sissy-minded person could have walked even a day through the heat of an unknown desert or hauled responsibility for goods and family over these rugged mountains.

There were people who gave up everything they had in the East, jobs, businesses, or farms, leaving home and sentiment behind for an uncertain, hopefully better future. Some were farmers looking for lush green lands, some prospectors hoping to strike it rich. There were business or craftsmen, religious people in search of God's own land where a life could be lived according to His rules or, sometimes, to their own rules. Others tried to abscond from their last judgment, outrunning the arm of the law, which was not that long in those days. But most of all and for all, it was an open land of freedoms where all was fair, all was viable, a land without rules but the ones nature set and those had to be broken first, before implementing their own. These people were not following any flag, they brought the flag and their rules with them.

Most emigrants did not give up a life in a modern city. They left already chaotic circumstances in developing towns or poor rural lives conditioned by diseases, nature hazards, and an ever-growing population of whom not everybody turned out to be a friendly neighbor. Many of them seemed to have established an all-or-nothing mentality, giving up everything and setting out on a voyage where most did not know what to expect. Driven by hope or by love of adventurousness, it was for a leap in the dark of an unknown land, though, of which they had not heard more than rumors between milk and honey on one side and ferocious beasts and savages on the other. Some had stuffed their belongings in a sack, others had tied their life up on an ox-drawn wagon, dragging horses, cattle, goats, or pigs behind. Life-threatening dangers were pervasive from sickness, lack of food and water to however nature could thwart them, by weather, impassable obstacles, or predators. Encountering Indians had become Russian roulette, because one could never know, what might have put them into rage or aggravated preconceptions right before one came. In most cases it was ones' forerunners.

With the hardships, the permanent danger, and the emigrants being on the edge in every respect, many weren't prepared to travel at the tip of the frontier, and for quite a few, the way out West had turned into something right out of purgatory.

Comparing the old emigrant routes with current maps, I sometimes thought they took wrong turns, detours that weren't necessary, and I wondered why they chose to roll through certain areas whereas other ways not far away would have been much easier. At places like Donner Pass or in Death Valley, where these most dramatic events of emigration took place, I thought, why didn't they just leave their households behind and make sure they would have crossed the mountains before winter.

It takes some time until one realizes that, even if geography had not altered, even if three dimensions still dictated the same hardships horizontally and vertically, two things had dramatically changed, that is our sense of time and our geographical knowledge in the form of cartography.

Looking on my fifty-year-old maps, I remembered how often I had to amend and consider how half a century might have altered the course of creeks or washes, how vegetation might have changed, blocking former ways or opening up a new one. And still I had maps where river or canyon, mountain or butte, highway or – sometimes – trails, were marked. Everything these first travelers had were vague drawings where a straight line marked a trail, a meandering line a river, and a zigzag line a mountain range. If they were lucky, they had guides, even more when those were trustful and talented with a sense of orientation.

Just by looking on a map, it was impossible to tell why the emigrants took one way instead of another or why a loop was made. Longer stretches of salt crusts, lava fields, or rocky slopes could have made wheeling impossible, compelling them to take large detours. An Indian camp or an attack might have caused a change maneuver, or sometimes just a guide's bad memory.

It is almost impossible for us to reconstruct their endeavor and understand what it meant to a life, accordingly, how that journey was sensed timely and how it determined their lives. Besides our modern knowledge of almost every detail of the terrain, the change we experienced only in the last century regarding our sense of time is even more relevant to our inability to conceive their voyage. Used to our more or less planned lives, with all its instant possibilities and accompanying transportation and communication tools, it took almost a one thousand-mile walk to understand that time elapses different when one leaves modern amenities behind.

While they were in a never-ending war with nature in the need to survive, in general, I enjoyed the luxury of voluntarily facing nature's challenges, often having an emergency exit. While my uncertainty lay in reaching the next town, which on average I did after one to two weeks, theirs was a matter of survival or, since so many prevailed, more a matter of hope.

They had no supermarket to replenish, no motel to rest, but they had to calculate their supplies to the end. I knew what to expect when I arrived, they didn't. While my escape routes would have lead me to the closest highway or town, in the case of illness, injury, or loss of equipment, they had to hang on, or die.

Reading reports of contemporary witnesses tells us about the dreadful hardships they had to suffer, but also how they experienced the wondrous, hitherto unknown nature. There are numerous accounts of travelers writing about arduous journeys, about starvation and freezing to death, and in the same breath adoring the almost unbearable beauty of nature. One hazards the guess that extreme or near-death experiences fire the imagination, transmogrifying the personal perception to a point where prose is written in verses.

Only on the few occasions, where I had no such exit strategy, no escape or emergency plan and no other option, where I came to experience my personal limits and maybe also subliminally, due to the permanent possibility of a wrong step or a fatal encounter, only then I could slightly retrace for short moments what it must have meant to be a pioneer or on an emigrants' train, and still see the beauty within the beast. "I can tell you no thing of the beauty and grandeur of the scenery – I could not speak, my breath was all gone, no person can give any idea of it."[*]

As highlighted earlier, the roots for the so-called West Coast mentality can be found in this history. From this most difficult part of the American frontier, many new Californians had inherited a mentality somewhere between the willingness to pull all stops and a credo in success. This might well have contributed to the state's many booms and its rapid growth.

American West historian Bernard de Voto once said: "The Yield of a hard country is a love deeper than a fat and easy land inspires … " Looking at California's explosive development and the aura it achieved, the word *hard* can hardly suffice to explain this last frontier's yield. There is a reason why the history of the American West became one of the most portrayed stages of the history of modern man, as de Voto continues: "… that throughout the arid West the Americans have found a secret treasure."[†]

Like here on Fandango Pass, I had often crossed their trails. Sometimes when I stood still in evoking silence, the sound of creaking wheels, snorting oxen, and cursing people arose from the trail. When I moved on, the noises seemed to be gone. But it was only my own steps that swallowed theirs, when, for a while, I had become the trek. At camp, when is was silent again, they would come back to my fireplace, play their fiddles and dance, scrunching their sorrows in the sand for as short as that night. Some danced to remember, some danced to forget, while their sparkling eyes were telling of hopes and dreams they had to suspend for another sunrise.

---

[*] Laura Hall Park, member of the 1861 Carleton Watkins expedition into the Yosemite wilderness.

[†] Bernard de Voto (1897–1955) was a social historian and literary critic who specialized on the impact of the frontier on American thinking. Awarded the Pulitzer Prize for history in 1948, his work *Across the Wide Missouri* (1947) was part two of a trilogy examining the country's modern genesis (pt.1, *The Year of Decision: 1846* (1943); pt.2, *The Course of Empire* (1952)). As a literary critic he became an authority on Mark Twain (*Mark Twain's America* (1932)) and Thomas Wolfe (*Genius is not Enough* (1936)). Famous novels include *The Crooked Mile* (1924), *We Accept With Pleasure* (1934), *and Mountain Time* (1947).

The Applegate-Lassen route was the northernmost trail into California, established in the late 1840s. Having hauled everything up Fandango Pass, the Applegate party then turned north into Oregon, the Lassen part headed to the goldfields in the south.

After a tragic incident during Joseph Walker's 1833 crossing, where the emigrants felt threatened, overreacted, and killed forty Natives, future emigrant trains constantly had to suffer the consequence of the ill-fated actions. Word got around quickly, and soon most tribes had agreed that the newcomers were a threat to their lives – which in fact they were. As a people that existed in complete equilibrium with a harsh environment and sparse resources, the sudden influx of people unbalanced their world to a degree, where either emigration or action was indicated. Understandably, communication between the two was not likely.

The settlers had to reach the Sierra before winter and consequently pass the deserts during the best hunting season. There, they decimated animal stocks to secure their own supplies and drove their cattle over the last remaining field of grass, thus depriving the Indians of potential winter supplies. They, in return, were forced to steal the settlers' stock.

Piute chief Tro-Kay, who was maybe the last Indian chief who had initially befriended and helped the white newcomers, could stand on a mountain and look on helplessly how their fragile equilibrium was shot or trampled down into oblivion. The inexorable cycle of misunderstandings and hostilities took its course.

Close to the last Californian city, right before you either get to Nevada or Oregon, I entered a Piute Indian Reservation. With a population of one hundred people scattered throughout the reservation, Fort Bidwell came across almost as a ghost town. By the time it was founded in the mid 1860s, John Bidwell had gotten ahead making a political career. After running for California Governor three times, he was nominated candidate for president for the Prohibition Party in 1892. On that I had to share a beer with three Piute teenagers who had tracked me down and besieged me on friendly terms with questions. After having addressed their main concern, why someone would do what I did, they took me for a tour through town and into the corners of their families' history.

Having been an active combat post for half a century, Fort Bidwell was eventually left to the Piutes. After passing the old post, the left vault of the bank, and the old general store, we stopped at the boarding schoolhouse, where they paused for a moment. Here their grandparents were sent to school, learning to forget their roots, their language and their tradition, they reported with a reflective pitch. When they dropped me at old Bidwell Creek Road, I was just checking my backpack and pulling all straps tight, the younger one asked me again, "Why would someone do that?" I replied, "Why wouldn't someone?" and I told them some of my experiences in the wilderness and also in meeting other Natives. I asked them why so many native people throughout the country, who have been claiming forever a close relationship with nature, seemed to have lost touch with it. Instead many were living a life they have condemned as long, while for the condemned it has been coming into fashion to revive a nostalgia that should be their heritage. "Deracinated," was the elder's answer, "We are all deracinated, and somehow homeless, there is no place for muse then." And I realized he was right, it now was a struggle for basics, less for survival; in many places they had become emigrants of history.

The state of this reservation town reflected a bit of many Natives' *tristesse* and their existence at the social outskirts of society, at the edge of the nation. Driving through town, the ambivalence was literally staged, historical melancholy displayed in the backyard of society.

Coming to places like that reservation, I always experienced both great skepticism and great hospitality, mostly along with a good awareness of history. Without further discussing American history and colonization here or plausible reasons for the state of the Nations, I think, it could be one of their best-selling services and the most wonderful gift to cultivate, share, and pass on what their grandfathers had told them. At least much more than the millionth dreamcatcher, malachite necklace, or a warrior chief doll.

*

After a couple of miles, I left the dirt road to follow the remaining sections of an old wagon trail. It followed the creek, and, here and there, I could recognize the roadbed. However, along most of the way, nature had stood up to history. Bushwhacking through the crisscross pattern of trees and brush, I ended up collecting a lot of wood in my clothes.

I noticed that I was not the only one here. Every now and then, the sound of breaking brushwood ahead of me suggested that a larger animal had chosen the same trail. What I mistook for a black bear first, turned out to be a huge black cow, no less substantial than a bear. Reaching a clearance along the creek, I had obviously disturbed her midday nap, and from that spot, I kept drifting her unintentionally. It became a malodorous affair. That lady was so scared that she was constantly marking the trail, dispersing the droppings with her wagging tail. When I stood still, she paused, turning her head around and waiting. When I did one step, she waited, two, three, she waited. Only when I came close enough that it was worth running, she started her tail dispenser and ran. I gave her several chances to return, I even walked off the trail into the woods to let her comfortably bypass me. She waited again. Somewhere in the Highgrade mining area, I lost sight of her. Hopefully, she had not fallen into an old shaft.

The creek turned away and with it the last signs of the old trail. An elder couple ensconcing themselves in the woods impersonated early settlers on their way across the Sierra. Judging from the firewood they piled on their campsite, they had no plans crossing the mountains before the coming winter.

Climbing a slope toward Mount Bidwell, I found myself back in mule's ears. I had hoped to find the forest road that would lead to some six mines around. However, it was too late. Bounded by thick pine forest, I had no idea how far I got. I just dropped the pack and started trampling a body-size space in the field of flowers.

When I paused my tossing and turning, I heard a soft plashing not far from me. Dusk left enough light to explore the environment, and only 300 yards from my site, I found a small spring spitting drops of water on the bank of the forest road. Knowing where I was now, I ran back to my site and crammed everything in my backpack. I thought, with the road, I should be able to find the Klondyke mines, they couldn't be farther than a mile or two, and what might be my last campfire should be honoring the species of prospectors and their share in California's history.

07/20   KLONDYKE MINES, 6 MILES

With the first daylight, I was up to walk around the mining area. Besides an old steam boiler and collapsed buildings, for a layman there was not much to see. Everything that looked like a shaft, a tunnel or a gallery, was blocked up and filled with debris and rocks. I wished one of the old miners would still be here and take me for a tour.

I had five more miles to walk to the border and another five out of the mountains into New Pine Creek, a small town on state line. But I wanted to find the place, where Colin put his foot on Oregon ground. I did not know how long it would take me to detect the side road he took, so I left the fields of gold postponing a more profound field trip to a later date.

Back on the forest road, I passed many more remnants of the mining boom in the Highgrade District, some well preserved, some less. One cabin was in pretty good shape, I could have moved in on the spot, only the roof was missing. Maybe these miners were as lucky as I was, hence omitting the roof. Since I left the Mexican border it never rained – both in Southern and Northern California – while I was hiking. I sat down at the building taking some pictures, when suddenly two pick up trucks drove by followed by a beautiful German shepherd. Either his masters were driving to fast for him or I was more interesting. In any case, the dog stayed with me and apparently enjoyed being photographed with me by self-timer. I recognized, the car had actually moved on, ten minutes later I was still alone with my new company.

CHAPTER TEN

Since there were many cut-offs and sideways to other mining areas, I stayed at the cabin, thinking they would drive back to where they came from as soon as they missed the dog. Before long they were back. I jumped up and waved for them with the dog by my side. They thanked and headed off saying they were late and had to check one of the mines. But the shepherd had already accomplished his mission, my last serendipity, which would open up for me after I had settled mine.

During the last two days, I had celebrated every ordinary action as a last time event. The last mountain, the last dinner, the last night, and some other last things. For my last lunch I picked Lily Lake, a small remote lake in a hidden, forested depression. I would not have thought of casting my rod, but since the fishes were jumping between yellow pond lilies, fairly screaming for it, I couldn't resist. The last time I fished. While I indulged myself into rice vermicelli with Spanish paella sauce and grilled trout, a family of deer dared to sneak out of the woods promenading down the lakefront.

After lunch, I had three last coffees, just because it tasted so good and because I couldn't let go. And I had work to do. Digging out Colin's book and two maps from the area, I tried to find the exact spot, where he set foot on Oregon ground. I read his paragraph again and again, a dozen sentences that could unveil the secret, assumed I was able to translate them geographically and temporally on my maps. The dirt road he was walking, where he saw a yellow, smoke-billowing scarred timber truck, could only be the Highgrade forest road.

He hurried on and a little before noon, he cut north into the woods toward the boundary. My map showed three thin, dashed lines cutting off north and higher onto the range, probably forest log roads. I was sure he took one of them, since he had marked all three with a big circle. The first branch came too early to be reached only by noon. A couple of miles later, the Highgrade main road bent farther north closer to the border, but the second was too much of a maintained road. The route Colin chose sounded more like an overgrown, maybe long abandoned tow way, "I climbed a slope, threading my way through thin trees."

The third must be it; the junction was less than a mile away from the dash-and-dot line marking the boundary. A road was hardly visible, long recaptured by large trees and ever-weathering foliage. With his open book in my hands, we climbed the slope together, threading our way through thick trees, until we finally crossed an open space with a grove of aspen trees in its center – it was exactly as he described it. Behind the clearing was the wire fence and on it a sign that said NATIONAL FOREST BOUNDARY. "I walked up to the fence and put one foot under its lowest strand." And so did I, onto the ground beyond. Both our walks were over.

Not all trees looked the same, how could they, half a century later. But the overall picture matched the photo I had glued on the last page of my diary. I saw grown trees where he saw thin ones, some trees and stumps matched those on the photo, and there was the open space right before the old wire fence, of which only smaller segments seemed to have been replaced in fifty years. But all of that did not matter anymore, as soon as I sat down, leaning to a fence post with both feet back in California.

The place where I was stood in sharp contrast to its personal meaning to me and to the actual occasion. It was just forest. And a fence. I was waiting for something to happen.

For four months and some days, I was hiking through California in the footsteps of the *Walker*. From early planning stage to my last days in the Warner Mountains, I thought that touching the border would be THE moment of a lifetime. Each night at the campfire I got excited about the feelings I would have. It was July 20th, 127 days after I started. I made it, but nothing happened. I caught myself watching me and the nature around. I was waiting for a big thunder, an outbreak of feelings, or just a little sign from Him. Nothing.

Arriving at the finish line meant nothing compared to the months before, the things I saw, the nature I experienced, the signs I had already received and the excitement of every evening's campfire when I thought about the following day.

American author Edward Abbey once wrote: "Every good hike brings you eventually back home."[*] Here for the first time, quite contrary, it felt as if I was about to enter foreign land, and in that moment, I wished I would see the hustle and bustle of Algodones with one foot on Mexican and the other on Californian ground.

When I left the little forest clearing, I asked myself, "And now, Walker II., can his walk be repeated?" and it fell into place that it is less a question of the environment or of the expanding civilization, nor of the struggle between the two.

---

[*] American author and environmental activist Edward Abbey (1927–1989) was known as the Thoreau of the American West. Leaving university with a master degree in philosophy, he worked for several years as seasonal park ranger at different places throughout the Southwest. Abbey considered wilderness to be the intrinsic backdrop for human nature and he saw this threatened by the developments of civilization. In his writing, his main motive was to become a voice for personal liberty in opposition to a state- and industry-controlled alienation from man's origin. Both through his literature and activism, he constantly provoked by advocating – at times extreme – means or positions for the sake of nature. Best known are his narrative *Desert Solitaire* (1968), regarded as one of the finest works of American nature writing, and the novel *The Monkey Wrench Gang* (1975), in which he portrays the struggle of a group of eco-terrorists and their feats.

CHAPTER TEN

Of course, many things have changed since Colin woke up at three o'clock in the morning, fifty years ago. Many things, among which there were some nature-threatening developments, and true, our life has become faster, louder, and more superficial. However, whether the walk could be repeated or, in other words, whether wilderness was still wild and capable of enchanting and striking us with awe, depends less on these circumstances but simply on you.

Whether you do it or not, and how you do it, from how you pack your things to how you walk into the wild, from how you meet the people to how you meet yourself.

If you're open for nature, for people, and for whatever you may find out about yourself, you may well repeat the Walk and maybe even write a journal about your observations, too. One may cut it down to, whether the Walk can be repeated merely depends on whether one does it or not.

*

The story would end here, had there not been the German shepherd. Late in the afternoon, I came down from the fence, torn between elation and sadness. I walked down straight through the forest to meet the Highgrade Road farther west. When I stepped out of the woods, I heard a car from behind; it was one of the guys I had met earlier with the dog. I accepted the ride out of the wild, as if I had made arrangements to be picked up as soon as I arrived at the finish line. His name was David, a geologist reinvestigating and analyzing the gold mines of the Highgrade Mining District. With an invitation to accompany him into the mines the following day, my life after the voyage began. Serendipity had me once again.

I have seen almost more beauty than I can bear.

EVERETT RUESS

Delete almost.

ANDREAS M. COHRS

*I wandered lonely as a cloud
That floats on high o'er vales and hills,
When all at once I saw a crowd,
A host of golden daffodils;
Beside the lake, beneath the trees,
Fluttering and dancing in the breeze.*

*Continuous as the stars that shine
and twinkle on the Milky Way,
They stretched in never-ending line
along the margin of a bay:
Ten thousand saw I at a glance,
tossing their heads in sprightly dance.*

*The waves beside them danced; but they
Out-did the sparkling waves in glee:
A poet could not but be gay,
in such a jocund company:
I gazed – and gazed – but little thought
what wealth the show to me had brought:*

*For oft, when on my couch I lie
In vacant or in pensive mood,
They flash upon that inward eye
Which is the bliss of solitude;
And then my heart with pleasure fills,
And dances with the daffodils.*

WILLIAM WORDSWORTH, *THE DAFFODILS*,
ENGLISH ROMANTIC POET, 1770–1850

CHAPTER TEN

LAST NOTE ABOUT GOFFS

Here in Goffs, I brought my travel notes and ideas together in spring of 2009, writing the first draft of the second Thousand-Mile Summer.

I came back in summer, fall, and winter and stayed most of 2010. I could not have imagined a better place than Goffs, both for inspiration and peace of mind. For occasional diversion, places to explore were numerous and right in my backyard, roughly 1.6 million acres of wilderness. Actually, I visited some places in the Mojave Preserve several times, yet experiencing something totally different, like snow-capped ranges in winter, the gaudy costumes of cacti and flowers in spring, or the infamous 'up-to'-extremes when all life comes to a standstill during the days of midsummer.

The Goffians' invitation to move into the most exceptional writer's residence, an old but furnished Santa Fe caboose, earns special thanks, likewise for their hospitality and their interest in my voyage.

A big, butte-high THANK YOU.

*

From someone who knows Goffs quite well, Phil's daughter Kristy, I received the following words that are likely to describe this outlying, yet outstanding, little community best:

"Goffs is an experience beyond belief. It is a tight-knit community of strangers that becomes a family who would do anything for each other and yet open their arms to a passerby. For those who frequent it, it is many things: it is home to some, an educational experience, an escape from the woes of life back home, it is a home away from home, a vacation spot, a resting spot on a long journey, a place of historic significance, a Zen place and an inspiring and peaceful place for an aspiring writer. But for those who never stopped, who whizzed by at 55 mph, it is just another ghost town in barren desert land, forlorn and foreign."

Thus, I end where I began, *Goffs*.

Five o'clock under the Green Tree: Dennis Casebier, Hugh Brown, John "Shady" Lightburn, Jackie and Harry Ridge, Carol Brown, Phil Motz, Jo Ann Casebier, Sharon and Danny Smith, Andreas M. Cohrs.

ADDENDA & ACCOLADES

Most important conversion tables 352
Equipment 353
    Tent or, to pitch or not to pitch. 355
    Down Bags 356
    Shoes 358
    Backpack 360
Photography, Cartography, Bibliography 362
    People & History 363
    Country & Nature 366
    Travel & Insight 367
    More Insight 368
    The Mojave Desert Heritage & Cultural Association 370
    Colin Fletcher, Chip Rawlins 371
Credits 372
Photos 375

temperature		weight & volume		length/distance	
Fahrenheit	*Celsius*	*Ounce, oz*	*Gram, g*	*Inch, "*	*Centimeter, cm*
"up to"	höllischheiß	1	28.4	1	2.54
134	57	2	56.8	6	15.24
100	38	9	255	12	30.48 = 1 ft
90	32	16	454 = 1 lb	36	91.44 = 1 yd
80	27	*Pound, lb*		*Foot, ft*	
70	21	1	454	1	30.48
60	16	*Kilo, kg*		3	91.44 = 1 yd
50	10	2	0.91	*Meter, m*	
40	4	30	13.61	-282	-86
32	0	60	27.22	14,243	4341
20	-7	90	40.82	*Yard, yd*	
10	-12			1	0.91
0	-18				
-10	-23			*Mile, m*	
-20	-29			1	1609
-30	-34	*Gallon, gal*	*Liter, l*		
-40	-40	1	3.79	*Kilometer, km*	
		2	7.57	1,000	1609
		4	15.14	1,272	2047

Boiling temperature: at sea level: 212°F/100°C; at 14,000 ft: 187°F/ 86°C

A FEW WORDS ABOUT OUTDOOR EQUIPMENT:

Since the idea of a wilderness hike had burst at Colin at 3 o'clock on a 1958 morning, like many other leisure industries, the recreational equipment sector became subject to constant change and development, amounting to an evolution from fulfilling basic needs for holiday campers to particular needs for survivalists and to the current vanity fair rather targeting catwalks than trails. In addition to the general dilution through fashion trends, tons of more or less useful gadgets labeled as *essential* have been blowing up sales catalogs to Sears size. Today, a preparatory visit to a modern outdoor warehouse can easily turn into a full-day program, no less amusing than a day in an entertainment park, though.

To me, the question never was, what else could I need, but how much do I want to carry, and how far can I rough it, that is, what can I leave out. Colin put it as the 'Law of Inverse Appreciation' stating: "The less there is between you and the environment, the more you appreciate that environment."

Going into the wilderness, I think, you should be prepared to become part of it. If you take up with nature, you will be rewarded with encounters of the stunning kind. However, that demands both readiness for self-effacement and some other qualities you will not find at a store such as closeness, flexibility, and the ability to extemporize. Quite the contrary, the less you take the more likely you gain these qualities.

Closeness implies Colin's law, meaning for example to leave the tent unpacked where possible and find oneself a cozy spot from where one can watch the panorama or the nightlife on a field, on a clearing, or in the meadows. It means, if you bring the outdoor version of every item you're using at home, spend all nights in a hermetic tent protecting your sleep from nocturnal sounds and movements, and – to top it all – leave navigation and orientation completely to GPS, chances for *closeness* aren't very high. It's not easy to understand why someone going into the wilderness, which somehow is the ultimate or the purest form of personal responsibility, would do that externally controlled, guided by extra-terrestrial science, a satellite crammed with cutting-edge technology and linked with a high-tech facility somewhere in Redmond, Cupertino, or Mountain View. I too am succumbed to modern technology's charms, especially iProducts and the new world of applications. But let me say it this way, when I enter God's own refuge, I'd rather come with my own senses, or sensors, and leave everything dispensable at home that would distract me from *closeness*.

Flexibility means both the ability to schlep your pack to wherever you feel attracted and to set up camp wherever it feels homey. If you brought too many 'survival items', there won't be much room left for *flexibility*, not to speak of the load you would have to carry.

As mentioned before, the essence lies not so much in the item but in renouncing it and in finding means to help yourself, that is, *learning to extemporize*, from making a walking staff to building a cook place with a tripod or a shelter to hold out during heavy rain. I wouldn't go as far as to leaving matches, compass, or a good-sized rope at home, although one could start a fire like caveman did, navigate with the sun, stars, or trees, and make a rope out of plant fibers. However, this sort of MacGyverism might not always work, or for everyone. In order to avoid a real survival situation, I use to balance an item's weight with the additional time or effort needed if you do it yourself, this, of course, in due consideration of manual skills and the respective availability of natural objects and tools.

Without a doubt, equipment manufacturers today are very imaginative, and many items really are fun to have, even for domestic use. However, as long as I am not accompanied by a herd of pack goats, I rather leave the store of plenty with not much more than Colin had in 1958. The depth of one's pocket might have a stake in it too. Hence, when I get endorphined by the pleasant anticipation of an adventure, before I enter a recreational equipment warehouse, I sit down and make a list of what I want while balancing the benefit of every item with its weight. This usually immunizes me against all bargains and alleged must-haves. Besides the bare essentials plus a lean, basic equipment (clothes, cooking utensils, food, navigation tools), most comforts aren't worth the discomfort of a heavier load.

There are quite a few brilliant manufacturers to choose from and one will hardly find anything like a *best brand*. It seems that the smaller an item is, the more replaceable it gets with other models. If there are some five manufacturers for tents and backpacks I would trust, there are about ten for sleeping bags, but surely twenties, thirties, and more for clothes and gadgets. Dwelling on those would go beyond the scope of this book and be, in my opinion, a waste of time. With his masterwork, *The Complete Walker*, Colin Fletcher has amply discussed and explored the world of outdoor gear, every aspect of what to use outdoors, how to use it or why not to use it, including all imaginable anecdotes about living outdoors.

Therefore, I want to cover only those bare essentials, without which a several-months hike into the wild could actually turn into a survival trip: tent, sleeping bag, shoes, and, to hold all that, the backpack.

I was very happy with the brands I used on this journey and after many wilderness trips and having used a great variety of models before, I am sure that the following products range among the best. However, there is a tendency to fall for the model you once made good experiences with, the one that helped you weathering the storm. Then stick to it, why spend useful time with studying catalogs to find marginal improvements, unless you totally change your playground like from a dry to a wet climate, or the travel time from summer to winter.

TENT – SLEEPING BAG – SHOES – BACKPACK

TENT (or, to pitch or not to pitch ...)

As stated earlier, I leave the tent in my pack wherever possible. On this trip that meant, I pitched it during most of the 500 desert miles and never did again from when I had crossed the last range of the Panamints above Deep Springs (or maybe once or twice to gain some intimacy where civilization was too close). The reason for using it in the desert was simply quiet sleep, to sleep undisturbed by invertebrates that assiduously conquer the night floor, from formidably sized ants to wind scorpions and giant hairy scorpions, all kinds of spidermen and some more aggravating -women. Also, the rattler was said to enjoy a well-tempered nest after a successful prowl. The only other reason for a tent should be bad weather; rainfall or snow or severe storm, though, if the storm is too heavy, one might rather find a hidden spot and hang in there instead of risking to lose the tent. I was lucky to have experienced that, despite all warnings that it pours, Albert Hammonds song held true for Northern California as well. In other regions, Mosquitoes might drive you into a tent. Here, it was sufficient to just move away from their breeding source, a creek or a lake. Even though strong winds and night temperatures below freezing point were quite common in both the desert and the Sierra, except that one night under the Bristlecone pine, just nestling in the sleeping bag was good enough for the months from March to July. This way I could enjoy unfettered listening to the staccato of freezing nature, and the morning allegro when the sun brought her back to live.

In order to cope with the broad spectrum of possible weather conditions on this journey and factoring in weight and my personal requirements (meaning if one considers spending more time in a shelter than from falling asleep to waking up, this would definitely be too small), I chose a lightweight from *Wechsel Tents* called *Pathfinder*, a geodetic, three-pole construction with the third pole creating a vestibule or, as I saw it, a small front garden. Yet, for an ultra-light it surprises with an extra long inner space, enough for an average-sized basketball player, a backpack-pillow, and for taking in shoes and clothes to keep them uninhabited. In a pinch, it has room for two persons, given that you have no fear of close contact. The self-supporting construction with pole sleeves and clips on the inner tent offers a very high stability and ventilation between inner and outer tent. The outer tent can be fixed at the pole ends and needs no additional pegs, rocks, or trees. It is free standing and can be moved or turned around (for cleaning) when set up. As for this trip, I used the outer only for wrapping and protecting the inner tent when stored in the pack. Leaving the pegs at home reduced the weight to less than 4 lbs (1.8kg).

The inner tent consists of a patchwork of No-See-Um mosquito netting and Ripstop nylon. Though a bit greasy, you can still enjoy the Milky Way from inside. All material is durable and tear resistant, even insistent thicket or accidentally touching thorns did not rip the fabrics. All in all, the handling is so easy that it is pitched in a few minutes, watched with incredulous amazement by fellow travelers.

Since I couldn't say anything about its practicability in less Californian weather, I later took the *Pathfinder* on a tour through the Bavarian Alps. It rained three days, the only dry place within a radius of sixty miles was the tent, thanks to the water-repellent seams and zippers and a one-foot ditch I dug around the tent on the second day. The integral floor material and lower tent wall is seamed well above the ground to protect from moisture and rain.

www.wechsel-tents.de/en/home

DOWN BAGS

More than for all other equipment, as to the sleeping bag I had to compromise or find the one piece that is good for three seasons and all weathers, robust, comfortable, and still a lightweight. According to statistics, night temperatures in the months from March to July, between low desert and White Mountain, could vary from the lower 70s (20°C) to well below zero (-20°C), regardless of the wind-chill. Since I was traveling through mostly dry climate, I wanted a down filling for its optimum warmth-to-weight ratio and superior compression.

After having slept around in most Scandinavian and North American brands, a German independent manufacturer named *Yeti* called my attention. Both the down quality and the workmanship sounded promising. Another thing I liked about their down products was that, according to their *Ethical Code*, the donor birds are not plucked in living condition, a painful process since it is rarely carried out at molt time. The animals they use are raised for meat production and plucked only after their death. Furthermore, immature down feathers, gained during the molt of young animals, would be smaller but with quills sharp enough to separate the fabric weave and work their way out.

Yeti's Crystal Downs reach the highest possible loft or bulking power of 900 cubic inches, measured by laboratories which are under control of the International Down and Feather Laboratory (IDFL) in Salt Lake City, USA. To measure its quality, an ounce of goose down is placed in a cylinder and loaded with a standard weight. The volume maintained by the downs under this pressure is measured in cubic inch. The higher the volume, the higher the loft and the warmth-to-weight ratio. In the last two years, the young company has perfected its product lines with state-of-the-art models for various areas of operations. With regards to the temperature rating, I needed (comfort zone around freezing point, coldest nights around 10 F (-12°C) and minimum 0 F (-18°C), the new portfolio comes up with a variety of products for all needs. There is the comfort model called *Sunrizer*, for the Paul Bunyans among us, body-wise, or for those who put sleeping comfort above size, weight reduction, or robustness. Then there is the Porsche among sleeping bags, the *Passion* line, for the prestige-oriented, where only the highest possible standard (also cost-wise) of down and fabrics has been processed to a 1 lb 11 oz (690g) wonder bag with a 97:3, 900 cu.in. fill, however, at the expense of resistance or suitability for rough country.

For real wilderness adventure between the Desert and High Sierra, one has two choices and sure a hard time to make up one's mind. Both the *VIB* and the *Fusion* combine every aspect of outdoor sleeping and range among the best all-terrain bags out there. While the *VIB* model is more weight-oriented (2 lbs 13 oz (1290g), with a 800+ cu.in. fill), the *Fusion* comes as the rough-terrain expert with a more hard-wearing cover (3 lbs 5 oz (1500g), with a 700+ cu.in. fill). If I was spared the late winter revival, I would suggest the respective lighter models with less down filling, the *VIB 600* or *Fusion 750*. This would save another 7 to 10 oz and cut the weight down to 2 lbs 14 oz (1320g) for the *Fusion* and 2 lbs 3 oz (1000g) for the *VIB*, respectively. As for me, for another Thousand-Mile Summer I'd choose the *VIB 800*.

Despite their extreme performance, both the *VIB* and the *Fusion* can be compressed down to 6" x 6" x 14". *Yeti*'s bags have down filled collars that seal in body heat markedly when the cold air snaps at it. The feet area and the hood have extra down fill to protect the more sensitive areas. Easily adjustable with a one-hand pull-cord, the contoured hood perfectly protects head and face. The comfort temperature zone of both the *VIB 800* and the *Fusion 900* goes down to 20 F (-7°C), that's where I already kept my shirt and socks on. At 10 F (-12°C) I used additional clothes like thermal underwear and only at 0 F (-17°C) I started counting the hours until the sun would rise. The manufacturer sets the survival range at around -30 F (-34°C), however, in California one has to take into account frequent strong winds and the chill factor.

www.yetiworld.com/en

YETI	Fusion 750	VIB 600	Fusion 900	VIB 800
weight (size L)	2 lbs 14 oz 1320g	2 lbs 3 oz 1000g	3 lbs 5 oz 1500g	2 lbs 13 oz 1290g
fill (cu.in.) (down : feather)	760 90 : 10	870 95 : 5	760 90 : 10	870 95 : 5
fill weight	27 oz 750g	21 oz 600g	32 oz 900g	28 oz 800g
stuff sack size	6.5 x 6.5 x 14" 16,5 x 16,5 x 36cm	6 x 6 x 12.5" 15 x 15 x 32cm	6.5 x 6.5 x 14" 16,5 x 16,5 x 36cm	6.5 x 6.5 x 14" 16,5 x 16,5 x 36cm
temp.range comfort/limit/extreme	27 / 16 / -17F -3 / -9 / -27C	30 / 21 / -9F -1 / -6 / -23C	21 / 9 / -26F -6 / -13 / -32C	19 / 7 / -27F -7 / -14 / -33C
lining	MicroMiniCell Pol. Mini RipStop	SupCell RipStop Nylon	MicroMiniCell Pol. Mini RipStop	SupCell RipStop Nylon

according to manufacturer's data

As with all – even 1st class – sleeping bags, the crucial point is the zipper. Here too, the *Yeti* surprises with snag-free use of its ankle-length two-way zipper column. If you open or close it easy, it works smooth and without swearing. Yet, I am happy my life never depended on if I made it fast enough out of the bag. As soon as you get hectic, the best zipper technology will fail and get jammed. I never found one that allows a really fast prison break if necessary, and I am afraid, worst case I would helplessly have to watch the bear tossing me around or the flash flood washing me away. Maybe manufacturers should consider an emergency rip-the-bag exit. At least, the *Yeti*'s zipper column fabric allows a quick and easy reverse pull if it's jammed; it could be the crucial split second.

More down: Covering down gear, I cannot leave the other goose fellow unmentioned. To the first depot, I had sent a down parka to be prepared for the summit climb. Its name alone was convincing, *Mountain Hardwear Sub Zero™ Parka*, and the sales person had done his best to assure me of its price-performance ratio; no easy job since you could get a no-name product for one quarter of its price. He said, it is designed for cold weather climbing and mountaineering. I thought I would use it only for a couple of days around White Mountain summit. However, in hiking routine, it proved to be beyond price, the most comfortable fellow on many evenings in the Sierra, where I used it as a second skin with just a t-shirt under it or, thanks to its ample pockets, for side excursions away from camp.

The *Sub Zero™ Parka* is insulated with lofty and warm 650-fill goose down. It has abrasion-resistant panels on the shoulders and arms, so you can really use it outdoors, lie down in it, or prowl through thicket and trees. With its six pockets, inside and outside, you can use it for a day excursion into winter wonderland without additional packs. Listening to the sales person with one eye on the price tag, I was convinced for good when I saw the space suit-like parka being stuffed into its sack where it contented itself with half the size of my sleeping bag. It weighs 1 lb 13 oz (825g), worth every down.

www.mountainhardwear.com

SHOES

When I assembled my gear in Los Angeles, I saw all kinds of special shoes for all types of terrain, some of which I didn't even know we needed shoes for. There were walking shoes, hiking shoes, trekking shoes, and approaching shoes; there were sandals for either walking, or hiking, or trekking, plus those for canyoning or walking on beaches. If you cannot change your chaussure while leaning to the trunk of your car, you have to compromise; one pair for everything between wet meadows, snowfields, and climbing – in shoe science that's a BC – and another one for walking around your camp and longer stretches on level surface, that is, a pair of running shoes, preferably the pair one is used to. With regards to hiking boots, here again, I needed an all-rounder, an all-terrain pair of boots that would be on one side elastic enough for long stretches on gravel or sand, on the other good for tough going, stiff and robust to keep my ankles from twisting on uneven surface when climbing rocks and debris in canyons or on scree slopes (i.e. lateral and longitudinal rigidity). The soles should allow me to tackle more tricky ascents and descents. The material had to be breathable, allowing moisture to leave the inner part especially on a hot day in the desert, but also waterproof for walking in morning dew, rain, or snow.

Here I trusted in a pair that shod my feet when I hiked along the Yukon River, to the same degree an all-terrain adventure, the *Meindl Borneo MFS*. Years ago, when I first looked it up, I read the manufacturer's description ensuring an invigorating hiking experience with minimal foot discomfort. I liked that, simply because everyone else seemed to promise an incredible carefree package, dry, warm, and well-protected feet, smoothness and comfort. One could almost see smiling feet. However, on a months-long hike with a load on your back, the feet are likely to be the ones who suffer most and indeed, it is all about getting used to the unusual, additional weight they have to carry and easing this particular discomfort.

According to a common classification system from A to D (from trail running shoes, light to heavy hiking boots, to mountaineering boots), the *Borneo* comes as a B; I'd credit it with a strong C-tendency, meaning it is suitable for demanding hikes and trekking from low-level mountains to transition zones.

The upper leather is oiled nubuck, the best you can get, and extremely resistant. The tongues are connected to the upper material with gussets, keeping dirt, snow, or water out of the bootleg. It has replaceable insoles, which I exchanged every 300 miles. The hooks are really stable; I remember having all kinds of shoe damage from scratching rocks before I was converted to this model: bended hooks, torn-out hooks that tear apart the leather skin, or just lost hooks. Mine still have all thirty teeth. The high rubber rand protects the most exposed part of the shoe and keeps your feet dry.

Directed by the heat generated by your feet, the smooth leather lining and padding interior does its best to adjust to the individual foot while breaking in the boots; this is what the *MFS* stands for, *Memory Foam System*. Breaking-in is mandatory, and it is the major problem with identifying the right pair of boots. You can never tell if a boot fits perfectly or causes minimal foot discomfort, unless you accomplished a first commendable hike. Since most retailers wouldn't accept a return after such a test, I will stick to the *Borneo* and hope that *Meindl* will continue to keep its Mercedes of trekking chaussure in their product line. One pair size 10 is 3 lbs 8 oz (1600g).

www.meindl.de/english

ADDENDA & ACCOLADES

BACKPACK

As for the house on my back, I was directed by Colin. In his notes from the eighties and nineties, I found that he had an affinity for the *Osprey* brand, a smaller and independent Colorado-based designer and innovator of outdoor packs. Colin later visited the company and happened to pick up on a sales meeting held out of backpacks in a remote canyon. He liked this combination of back-to-the-roots and a high-tech designing and development process, where the founder was as much involved as the workers, so in *The Walker* he summarized: "The crucial distinction to other brands would be that one has become a global enterprise while the other is still a maker of packs." (For the time being, this applies to all of the above selection of brands.)

If the following added to their quality remains to be verified: according to unauthenticated rumors, the *Osprey Packs* founder and chief designer had been abandoned as a newborn in Roswell, New Mexico, along with sample patterns and an odd assortment of buckles in his hand.

Howsoever, studying their catalog, I found what I was looking for, the *Aether 85*, a lighter than average internal-frame pack shaped like a squashed cylinder without any projecting side bags or bumps. The frame system with a single aluminum stay and peripheral stabilizer rods ensures stability and protects your back from bulky items. It has just two compartments, a top-bag and the main packbag.

The lower sleeping bag compartment is interiorly separated from the upper by just a drop-down divider. For easier access it has its own dual zipper. Thanks to the small stuffsack size of my sleeping bag, I could add spare pants, a pair of socks, and the thermal underwear.

Osprey now added another zipper alongside the pack for faster access to packed gear in the upper compartment. The top pocket served as my stuff bag for smaller or often used items, mainly everything that would get lost in the depths of the main bag. It can easily be detached from the pack and with an extra hip belt be used for shorter trips away from base camp. Extra straps and buckles on the front and sides allow you to compress the pack according to the load or serve to keep external items tight and fastened. Stretch woven exterior front and side pockets offer space for water bottles, a tripod, or clothes.

The lightwire frame flexes, bringing the load in close against the back so it can ride close to the body. A major argument is the ventilated ribbed foam back panel with grip mesh, which allows your back to be ventilated, thus ensuring a rather comfortable carrying or, to be more realistic, easing the discomfort of carrying a heavy load at best. The custom-moldable hip belt can easily be adjusted as loosening and tightening of all belts and straps goes easy and smooth.

The L version holds 5,400 cu.in. (88 liters), a maximum pack weight of 55-65 lbs (30kg), and weighs 5 lbs 3 oz (2.3kg).

As per manufacturer's specifications, I mildly overloaded the backpack when carrying up to four gallons of water. However, as my contact at *Osprey Packs* later stated, I had no chance once I was out there. Likewise the backpack didn't, and anyway, it still did a tremendous job. Despite the occasional overload of up to 25 pounds, it proved to be extremely durable. The little wear it sustained is absolutely tolerable and caused by just this having casually overstrained its capacity over four months. After more than 1,000 miles, the only part I might have to exchange is a strap or two, while all buckles are still good.

Summarized, the *Osprey* captivated by its simplicity. The ventilated back panel really is a plus, especially when climbing on steep slopes where I had to tighten the pack close to the body or also on long hot days. And as reported earlier in the text, if all straps are tight, one may even swim through a spring-swollen creek.

www.ospreypacks.com

For all items, I stick to the adapt-to-the-environment rule and try to become a mimesis. I dislike fashionable bright colors that call every living being's attention, preferentially chasing off those you want to see and luring the species you don't. Therefore, the choice of colors always is a criterion, as for me preferably camouflaging green and brown tones or unobtrusive shades of grey. As the *mimic*, I try to fit into the environment as an inconspicuous and inedible object that is of no interest to another individual or a population, like a highwayman or a swarm of mosquitoes, respectively.

Some of the smaller items that found a loophole into my pack though, were a candlelight for romanticism, a good knife for everything from opening blisters to carving wood to gutting and filleting fish (cleaned in between), and a rope for hauling the pack into a tree, bear-safe, to rappel it down a canyon, or just to lasso high-hanging dead branches for firewood. Also very useful was a dark-green fishing vest. Although the maker had labeled it "successful angling guaranteed", I used it more for half-day exploring tours. Its ten pockets filled with a water bottle and food, camera and lenses, map and compass, spare socks, matches, and my journal, I could leave the backpack behind and dare, fleet of foot, some adventurous side trips.

Besides the right equipment and a reasonable competence in using it, a tolerable degree of physical fitness helps – one will grow into the superman on the way – and a clear understanding of one's limitations, though. Last not least, what helps best to get along with odd challenges is a good pinch of faith; faith in what you set out to do, your mission, faith in your capabilities, and faith in God or, if you will, good luck.

PHOTOGRAPHY

All photos (photo pages and chapter headers) by the author, except as indicated otherwise.

Chapter headers:
PROLOG Wooden gate to Goffs
I	Wild burros along the Colorado
II	Goffs Butte and BNSF line
III	Evaporated soul of a cattle
IV	Waving the Colors on White Mountain summit
V	Engelmann's prickly pear cactus in Lemoigne Canyon
VI	Melt water creek in the Sierra
VII	Mono Lake tufas
VIII	Under the canopy of the forest
IX	Malibluish beach at South Lake Tahoe
X	(Not really a) Basque sheepherder

More photos from the route, of flora and fauna and people, are posted on the author's website, www.1000milesummer.com, some of which are available as postcards or prints on canvas on www.colinfletcher.com

CARTOGRAPHY

All maps were designed by David Lindroth, based on the author's data and specifications.
David Lindroth Inc. – Custom Cartography. www.lindrothmaps.com

BIBLIOGRAPHY

Sources for inspiration, quoted or leaned on, or just read with wonder. To me, it is interesting when a book was originally written; therefore, and for first-edition aficionados, I give original publication information where found. In most cases though, there are more current or revised editions available, which are easy to find at the local bookstore. The best places to indulge yourself in old books still are libraries and museums, second-hand stores or online auctions.

Listed literature includes a short description where book title is not sufficiently self-explanatory.

PEOPLE & HISTORY

The American Heritage Dictionary of Indo-European Roots – Calvert Watkins; Houghton Mifflin Co., 2000.

Noticias de la California – Miguel Venegas; Viuda de M. Fernández, 1757.

Native Americans of California and Nevada – Jack D. Forbes; Naturegraph Publishers, 1982. (History of local tribes and their relations with the emigrants.)

Medieval Iberia: An Encyclopedia – E. Michael Gerli; Routledge, 2003. (History of Iberian kingdoms and empire.)

Las Sergas de Esplandián – García Ordóñez de Montalvo. Published in Sevilla in 1510. Translated by Edward Everett Hale for the Antiquarian Society, Atlantic Monthly, 1864.

De l'Amadís de Gaule et de son influence sur les moeurs et la littérature au XVIe et au XVIIe siècle – Eugène Baret; Auguste Durand, 1873. (History of Amadís de Gaule and his influence on literature.)

The Three Princes of Serendip – Elizabeth Jamison Hodges; Atheneum, 1964.

Serendipity and the Three Princes, from the Peregrinaggio of 1557 – Theodore G. Remer; University of Oklahoma Press, 1965.

The New Country: A Social History of the American Frontier 1776 – 1890 – Richard A. Bartlett; Oxford University Press, 1975 (History of the westward movement and everyday life in the 18th and 19th century.)

Memoirs of My Life – John Charles Frémont; Belford, Clarke & Co., 1887. (reprinted as:)

Narratives of Exploration and Adventure by John Charles Frémont – Allan Nevins; Longmans, Green & Co., 1956. (Reprint of the expeditionary text.)

The Expeditions of John Charles Frémont: Travels from 1838 to 1844 – Donald Jackson and Mary Lee Spence, University of Illinois Press, 1970. (Reprint of the first two expeditions.)

Kit Carson and the Wild Frontier – Ralph Moody; Random House, 1955.

The Pioneers Go West: To California by Covered Wagon – George Rippey Stewart; Random House, 1954. (Eyewitness child story of an emigrant trek.)

Great Surveys of the American West – Richard A. Bartlett; University of Oklahoma Press, 1962. (History of exploration and mapping the West.)

Emigrant Trails: The Long Road into California – Marshall Fey, Joe King, Jack Lepisto; Editor Stanley W. Paher, Western Trails Research Association, 2008. (History of emigrant routes into California; excerpts from participants' journals.)

Ghost Trails to California – Thomas H. Hunt; American West Publishing Company, 1974. (History of emigrant routes to California and background.)

The Old Trails West – Ralph Moody; T. Y. Crowell Co., 1963. (Portrayals of early pioneers and their trails.)

Trail of the First Wagons over the High Sierra – Charles Graydon; The Patrice Press, 1986. (Trail details and history of the Donner Party.)

Patty Reed's Doll: The Story of the Donner Party – Rachel Kelly Laurgaard; Tomato Enterprises, 1989. (Eyewitness report of the Donner Trek, as told by a child's doll.)

Ordeal by Hunger – George R. Stewart; Henry Holt & Co., 1936. (History and accounts of the Donner trek.)

Pilgrims in the Desert: The Early History of the East Mojave Desert and the Baker, California Area – Le Hayes; Mojave River Valley Historical Ass., 2005.

What I Saw in California, Being the Journal of a Tour, by the Emigrant Route and South Pass of the Rocky Mountains, across the Continent of North America, the Great Desert Basin, and through California, in the Years 1846, 1847 – Edwin Bryant; D. Appleton & Co., 1848. (Journal of an emigrant trek.)

Trail to California: The Overland Journal of Vincent Geiger & Wakeman Bryarly – Yale University Press, 1945. (In 1849, Vincent Geiger & Dr. Wakeman Bryarly joined an organized emigrant group to the California gold fields.)

California As It Is, and As It May Be; or, A Guide to the Gold Region – Felix Paul Wierzbicki; Washington Bartlett, 1849. (One of the first published factual reports on California, its history, mining advices, and general situation.)

Three Years in California – John David Borthwick; William Blackwood and Sons, 1857. (Personal account of the early gold rush era.)

Afoot and Alone: A Walk from Sea to Sea by the Southern Route. Adventures and Observations in Southern California, New Mexico, Arizona, Texas, etc. – Stephen Powers; Columbian Book Co., 1872. (One of the last excursions on foot before the railroad connected the two sides.)

BIBLIOGRAPHY

Roughin It – Mark Twain; American Publishing Co., 1872. (Semi-autobiographical report on Twain's travels through the Wild West 1861-1867.)

Death Valley in '49 – William Lewis Manly; Pacific Tree and Wine Co., 1894. (Autobiography incl. eyewitness report of the Death Valley drama.)

Death Valley & the Amargosa: A Land of Illusion – Richard E. Lingenfelter; University of California Press, 1986. (Account of the history of Death Valley, real characters and legends.)

The World Rushed in: The California Gold Rush Experience – J.S. Holliday; Simon and Schuster, 1981. (Comprehensive story about the California gold rush, based on stampeders' journals and letters.)

Mines of the Eastern Sierra: The Pioneers, Their Mines & Stories – Mary DeDecker; La Siesta Press, 1966.

Mines of the Mojave – Ronald D. and Peggy J. Miller; Siesta Press, 1976. (History of mining in the Mojave Desert.)

Picacho: Life and Death of a Great Gold Mining Camp – Peter Odens; Peter Odens Publ., 1973.

The Story of Bodie – Ella M. Cain; Fearon Publishers, 1956.

Small Town America: A Narrative History, 1620 to the Present – Richard Lingeman; Putnam, 1980. (History of America told through the developments of its small towns.)

Historic Spots in California – Mildred B. Hoover; Stanford University Press, 1966. (Comprehensive guide to the state's historic sites incl. local museums.)

An American Idea, The Making of the National Parks – Kim Heacox; National Geographic Society, 2001. (The development of wilderness conscience and the formation of the National Park idea.)

Beyond the Hundredth Meridian: John Wesley Powell and the Second Opening of the West – Wallace Stegner; University of Nebraska Press, 1954. (Exciting chronicle of Powell's 1869 exploration of the Grand Canyon, describing his dramatic encounters and scientific insights into the challenges confronting the Western United States.)

Desert: The American Southwest – Ruth Kirk; Houghton Mifflin, 1973. (Human and natural history in the Southwest.)

Desert Passages – Patricia Nelson Limerick; University of New Mexico Press, 1985. (The role of the desert in American history; exploring our changing relations and attitudes, interpreting contemporaries from Frémont to Abbey.)

Shavetails & Bell Sharps, The History of the U.S. Army Mule – Emmett M. Essin; University of Nebraska Press, 1997.

ADDENDA & ACCOLADES

Land of Little Rain – Mary Austin; 1903. (Poetic essay on ranch life between the Sierras and the deserts.)

Sheep Rock – George Rippey Stewart; Random House, 1951. (Western desert novel.)

The Voice of the Desert – Joseph Wood Krutch; William Sloane Associates, 1955. (A naturalist's view on life in the desert.)

Desert Solitaire – Edward Abbey; Dutton, 1977. (Humorous collection of essays on life in the desert from the eyes of a seasonal park ranger.)

All the Pretty Horses – Cormac McCarthy; Alfred A. Knopf, 1992. (Cowboy-life novel, pt. 1. of the Border Trilogy.)

The Crossing – Cormac McCarthy; Alfred A. Knopf, 1994. (pt. 2)

Cities of the Plain – Cormac McCarthy; Alfred A. Knopf, 1998. (pt. 3)

COUNTRY & NATURE

A Natural History of California – Allan A. Schoenherr; University of California Press, 1992. (Comprehensive guide to the state's ecological regions and landforms.)

An Island Called California – Elna Bakker; University of California Press, 1971. (Ecological introduction to the state's natural communities.)

The Sierra Club Guide to the Natural Areas of California – John Perry and Jane Greverus; Sierra Club Books, 1983.

An Introduction to California Plant Life – Robert Ornduff; University of California Press, 1974.

A Field Guide to Pacific States Wildflowers – Theodore F. Niehaus; Houghton Mifflin, 1976.

A Field Guide to the Insects of America North of Mexico – Donald J. Borror and Richard E. White, Houghton Mifflin, 1970.

Adventuring in the California Desert – Lynne Foster; Sierra Club Books, 1987. (Guide to the deserts of the Southwest.)

The California Deserts – Edmund C. Jaeger; Stanford University Press, 1965. (Guide to natural history, flora, fauna, and history of economic utilization.)

Gathering the Desert – Gary Paul Nabhan; The Arizona Board of Regents, 1985. (Human ecology and ethnobotany in the deserts of the Southwest.)

Wildlife of the Southwest Deserts – Jim Cornett; Nature Trails Press, 1975. (Guide to animal wildlife in the Southwest.)

Conversations with a Pocket Gopher and Other Outspoken Neighbors – Jack Schaefer; Capra Press, 1978. (Schaefer turned his interest from fictional characters (Shane, Monte Walsh) to a real hero, the Old West's hardest worker, the gopher snake, depicting the animals decisive role in the West.)

Desert Wild Flowers – Edmund C. Jaeger; Stanford University Press, 1979.

Death Valley – Charles B. Hunt; University of California Press, 1975. (Local geology, geography, ecology and archeology.)

Deepest Valley: Guide to Owens Valley and its Mountains, Lakes, Roadsides and Trails – Genny Schumacher; Wilderness Press, 1969.

Ecological Relationships of Bristlecone Pine – R.S. Beasley and J.O. Klemmedson; American Midland Naturalist, 1980.

A Sierra Club Naturalist's Guide to the Sierra Nevada – Stephen Whitney; Sierra Club Books, 1979.

Andrew H. Grayson: The Audubon of the Pacific – Juliette Mouron Hood; Lancaster, PA, 1933.

Mono Lake Guide Book – David Gaines and the Mono Lake Committee; Kutsavi Books, 1981.

An Ecological Study of Mono Lake, California – David W. Winkler; University of California Press, 1977.

The Tahoe Sierra: A Natural History Guide to 100 Hikes in the Northern Sierra – Jeffrey P. Schaffer; Wilderness Press, 1975.

The Sagebrush Ocean – Stephen Trimble; University of Nevada Press, 1989. (Natural history and accounts of the Great Basin Desert.)

TRAVEL & INSIGHT

Walden; or, Life in the Woods – Henry David Thoreau; Ticknor and Fields, 1854. (Account of Thoreau's social ego-experience, retreating to a cabin in the woods for two years in order to separate from civilization; criticizing consumerism and emphasizing the importance of contact with nature, solitude and contemplation.) (see also footnote p.23)

Travels with a Donkey in the Cévennes – Robert Luis Stevenson; Roberts Brothers, 1879. (Hiking account of Stevenson's travel through the French Cévennes in 1878.)

Steep Trails – John Muir; Houghton Mifflin, 1918. (Collection of Muir's letters about travels in the West.)

Everett Ruess, A Vagabond for Beauty – W.L. Rusho; Gibbs Smith Publ., 1983.

(Biography of a teenage solitary hiker and poet, who was exploring the deserts and the High Sierra while pursuing his dream of oneness with nature.)

Look Homeward, Angel – Thomas Wolfe; Scribner, 1929. (Novel about life and wanderlust.)

Of Time and The River – Thomas Wolfe; Scribner, 1935. (Sequel to *Look Homeward, Angel*.)

Hourglass in the Mojave – Ruth Forbes Sherry; Wagon & Star, 1941. (Desert poetry.)

On the Road – John Kerouac; Viking Press, 1957. (Beat generation road trip across America.)

Travels with Charley: In Search of America – John Steinbeck; Viking Press, 1962. (What-are-Americans-like travelogue.)

Desert Notes: Reflections on the Eyes of a Raven – Barry Holstun Lopez; Andrews and McMeel Publ., 1976. (Short essays on Lopez' trip into the desert and its inspirational power.)

Blue Highways: A Journey into America – William Least Heat-Moon; Little, Brown & Co., 1982. (Autobiographical soul-searching road trip through small-town America.)

Teaching a Stone to Talk – Annie Dillard; Harper & Row, 1982. (Collection of essays on human-nature encounters and personal reflection.)

Into The Wild – Jon Krakauer; Villard Books, 1996. (Biography of Chris McCandless', aka Alexander Supertramp, disputable ego-trip into the wilderness and his fate.)

Anatomy of Restlessness – Bruce Chatwin; Jonathan Cape Publ., 1997. (Collection of essays depicting Chatwin's nomadic life; advocating that nature tells us to keep in motion.)

A Walk in the Woods – Bill Bryson; Broadway Books, 1998. (Humorous hiking report of the Appalachian Trail and its surrounding sociology and ecology.)

Eat, Pray, Love – Elizabeth Gilbert; Penguin, 2006. (Memoir about her travels around the world, encounters with fellow human beings and personal discoveries.)

MORE INSIGHT

Man: An Autobiography – George Rippey Stewart; Random House, 1946. (Novel about the story of humanity.)

A Sand County Almanac – Aldo Leopold; Oxford University Press, 1949.

(Collection of semi-philosophical essays developing the idea of a land ethic; substantiating the importance of wilderness experiences.)

Man in the Landscape, A Historic View of the Esthetics of Nature – Paul Shepard; Knopf Publishing, 1967. (Exploring reasons and the roots for our attitudes towards nature; America's identity and its special relation to wilderness.)

Wilderness and the American Mind – Roderick Frazier Nash; Yale University Press, 1967. (Study of America's attitudes towards wilderness and reflection on society.)

Dreamtime, Concerning the Boundary between Wilderness and Civilization – Hans-Peter Duerr; Blackwell Publishers, 1985. (Ethnological/ecopsychological approach to the relationship between humans and wilderness.)

The Idea of Wilderness: From Prehistory to the Age of Ecology – Max Oelschlaeger; Yale University Press, 1991. (History of the evolution of wilderness in the human mind, based on Thoreau, Muir, Leopold, Snyder, and Jeffers.)

Sight & Sensibility, The Ecopsychology of Perception – Laura Sewell; Tarcher and Putnam, 1999. (about the importance of our relationship with nature in order to reawake sensitivity, attention, and imagination.)

The Voice of the Earth – Theodore Roszak; Phanes Press, 2001. (Eco-Psychology classic; Holistic approach to the relationship between humans and the earth, criticizing the devaluation of the natural world; nature therapy; teleological reasoning.)

*

For background entertainment while writing, the online-stream of The Coast KOZT-FM turned out to be the *californiest* possible diversion.

An inestimable source of both historical and current information has been the local NPR radio program (National Public Radio).

Both stations are available as online streams, *www.kozt.com, www.npr.com.*

ADDENDA & ACCOLADES

PUBLICATIONS FROM THE
MOJAVE DESERT HISTORICAL AND CULTURAL ASSOCIATION, GOFFS

Mojave Road Guide – An Adventure Through Time – Dennis G. Casebier; Tales of the Mojave Road Publ. Co., 1986.

Guide to the East Mojave Heritage Trail (4 editions) – Dennis G. Casebier; Tales of the Mojave Road Publ. Co., 1987.

Goffs & its Schoolhouse – Dennis G. Casebier; Tales of the Mojave Road Publ. Co., 1995.

For more literature or information on how to support the work of the association or participate in its heritage and land conservation program, contact:

MDHCA
37198 Lanfair Road, G-15
Essex, CA 92332

or visit www.mdhca.org

You will receive a complimentary issue of the Mojave Road Report.

COLIN FLETCHER BIBLIOGRAPHY

The Thousand-Mile Summer, In Desert and High Sierra; Howell-North, 1964.

The Man Who Walked Through Time; Knopf, 1967.

The Complete Walker; Knopf, 1968.

The Winds of Mara; Random, 1973.

The New Complete Walker; Knopf, 1974.

The Man from the Cave; Knopf, 1981.

The Complete Walker III; Knopf, 1984.

The Secret Worlds of Colin Fletcher; Knopf, 1989.

River, One Man's Journey Down the Colorado, Source to Sea; Knopf, 1997.

The Complete Walker IV, co-written by Chip Rawlins; Knopf, 2002.

Walking Man, The Secret Life of Colin Fletcher – Robert Wehrman
(Colin Fletcher biography; projected publishing date IV 2012.)

MORE BOOKS BY CHIP RAWLINS

A Ceremony on Bare Ground; Utah State University Press, 1985.

Sky's Witness: A year in The Wind River Range; Henry Holt, 1993.

Broken Country: Mountains and Memory; Henry Holt, 1996.

In Gravity National Park; University of Nevada, 1998.

THANK YOU

Although I walked most of these miles alone, besides Mother Nature who kept me in good health and who opened my senses to let me appreciate what I saw, heard, smelled, and felt, many other people helped making this journey possible or contributed to the voyage and enriched it with content, *nolens volens*, making this extraordinary experience tangible. I want to say,

thank you to you all.

NAMED IN THE TEXT IN ORDER OF APPEARANCE:*

Nathan *Tankum* Hall; Mr. Sears; visionary and MDHCA founder Dennis Casebier & his wife Jo Ann (in this case, someone who made his vision come true); Red Brooke; MDHCA vice president and Mojave support crew Phil Motz and his daughter Kristy; MDHCA caretaker Hugh Brown & his wife Carol; MDHCA director Chris Ervin; collector of antiques and memories Holly Henson and Zen; Ms. *"Wunderbar"* Angie Luna; Colin's friend and accountant J. Breck Tostevin; rangers Marian Brown and Lily; Picacho fishermen Ralph Bosse, Dale, Ronda & Devin; arachnologist Rick Vetter and ornithologists Willemina & Jim Hutch; the Colorado River Heach Clan, Benton & Linda, Jessica & Andrew and Isa; my first travel companion Roland Weber who almost sacrificed his feet joining me; Nipton architects Roxanne & Jerry Freeman; good soul and coffee enthusiast Jim; William "Bill" Sarbello, whose heavenly gourmet burgers were lifted to new heights, may God rest his soul; inexhaustible source for highway stories, Harold; my American soulmate Lyon Bell and brothers Christian Bernard and Dennis; desert angel Cécile Blanchard; desert rats Jay and David; president of Deep Springs College David Neidorf; artist Carroll Thomas who left us shortly after his 100th birthday – may he paint in peace – & his wonderful wife Helen; the haute cuisine of Rossi's and piano player Steve; artists from the heart Victoria & Robert Sutliff who found a new home in (the town of) Paradise, CA; Brian J. Keithley who had culinary pity on me; my second travel companion Sonja Kandels for being the nightingale who sang to cheer my solitude; body-sculpturing Utta and her open house; my back-into-civilization driver Bisser Stoyanov; Giovanni; media supporters Diane Eagle, Patti Cole, and Susan Morning from the Mammoth Times; campground resident Ken Gustavson; café and Mono Motel Kelly-of-all-trades; carpenter *Filthy* Pete Jones; postmaster of the year Margaret Daniels; heart and soul of the J. Marklee Toll Station Sandy Matlock; pack goats raiser Gary Coyan; Markleeville historians Jim Long and Dick Edwards; gourmet chef and friend Randy Fisher and the adorable Emma; Paul & Mary; Paul and Terry Dyer; PCT resident and walker George "Billy Goat" Woodard; the magnificent six: Lucius, Scott, Dan, Jim, Mike, and Bill; owners of the parrots cottage Bill & Joan; the Hall family and Linda Hopkins; trading post owner Mr. Wiggin; Mission Inn owner, burgomaster, pastor, and seer James

---

* (A handful of names have been changed to protect the identity of individuals.)

Jim Wallace; rodeo and horse breeder Garrett Maas; sheepherder Gamaniel; forest ranger Mike and assistants Andrew and Chris; collector of historical vehicles Louis Vermillion; geologist and prospector David Hembree, his wife Susan, and their son William; Don Henley, Glenn Frey, and Don Felder.

NOT NAMED IN THE TEXT BUT INTEGRAL TO THE STORY:

For support and advice on equipment, Kay Steinbach from Yeti World, Sam Mix from Osprey Packs, and outdoor gear specialist Heinz Balinger from Intersport Gruner in Konstanz, Germany.

Furthermore from the MDHCA board, Steve Mongrain, Russ Kaldenberg, Randy Kimball, John Fickewirth, John Terrill, Roger and Loris Mitchell. To all you guys from the association, you're the center of this project's universe.

Jim McGee, B.J. Donnelly, Lyle Trottier, and Cliff McDonald for introducing me to the wild world of guzzlers.

Colin Fletcher biographer Dr. Robert Wehrman, University of Hawaii, Honolulu, for frequent exchange about the protagonist.

For critique and editing of 150,000 words, for helping a pioneering German to write a book in English and get it published, Andrea Miller, Michael Gelzhiser, and again Lucius Sorrentino and Phil and Kristy Motz; for fine-tuning and finishing and both the most personal and professional attention, Thomas Lindemann & his wife Constanze and the team at Info Verlag.

Admiral Peter *"The Fox"* Bertsch and Christa Ulsamer for keeping the pioneer spirit alive. Helmut and Brigitte Cohrs for opening a world beyond rusty gates to us, Sylke and Susanne for sisterly support, Marion Frank for understanding the fires I burned as my struggle with the Devil and the tower, until the hermit stops the wheel of fortune and water flows from one cup into another. Niels Heinzinger for your support and friendship – one day, we'll do the Top-Of-The-World thing again.

The Hall Family, Ma Lili Mae and Pa Charles TJ, Diane and Henry, Betty and Floyd, Trent and Ed, James "Pete" and Hattie, Carolyn and Jay, Felecia and Steve, Al James, Cousin Benny, for being my American family.

Marcus "Cadillac" Sykes, Gloria Sapponaro, Berlinda Tolbert, Bill Kraus, travel writer Barbara Steinberg, publisher of the Scenic 395 Magazine Meta Cheryl White, Adelheid Gehringer and her Café Bilderbuch team; Svenja Galle for taking me to the Puig, Brenda Pierce and Maxine Weldon for taking care of *"The Kid"*, TJ Michel and Klaus Eppert for still being friends – despite a back-breaking adventure, Ray Montes for the best barber talk while looking at a drove of wild horses; Gloria Marley and Andrea Miller for continuously equipping me with Jamaican Blue Mountain coffee,

thank you and happy trails. Aye

NOTES

NOTES

Photos from left to right, top down: 1. Maps from 1958. Colin used to write departure and arrival times on his maps, he marked camps and also places where he met people or critters, e.g. "START Mar 8/58", "Triple Slash Ranch", "Tuttle", or "KILLED RATTLESNAKE". 2. Wild burros, frequent companions along the Colorado River 3. Overlooking the river from 'El Loco Mountain'

1. Gone swimming – first pool break at Blythe   2. The Devil's Elbow
3. The Needles and Chemehuevi Mountains forcing the Colorado into a narrow gorge
4. Desert night camp   5. Thunder and lightning over the Mojave Desert

1. The Dennis G. Casebier Memorial Library, a replica of the old railroad depot, is located at the Boulevard of Dreams in Goffs.   2. Long – long – short – long. There's a train a comin'.
3. Anonymous souls in the Mojave Desert   4. Man and barrel cactus   5. Sunset and cholla cactus
6. Phil Motz   7. Offense is the best defense, a gopher snake acting like its venomous look-alike.

Desert engineering – rebuilding desert artifacts
1. an old wind pump and
2. the Stotts two-stamp mill.
3. The story of the Mojave camel. Drawing by Carl Faver, based on the anecdote about frightened mules when seeing Edward F. Beale's exotic pack animals. (Courtesy of Dennis G. Casebier, Mojave Desert Archives, Mojave Desert Heritage & Cultural Association, Goffs, California).
4. Guzzler team, Jim, Lyle and B. J., cleaning and refilling an underground water tank for desert wildlife.

1. Landmark of the West – Mojave wind pump, "rhythmically sighing with the wind".
(Photo by Dennis Casebier)   2. Goffs' neighbors, Tim Henshaw, Mike Blair, Cody Blair, and Rob Blair
Following pages: 1. Burlington Northern Santa Fe skyline   2. Sending letters to the loved ones

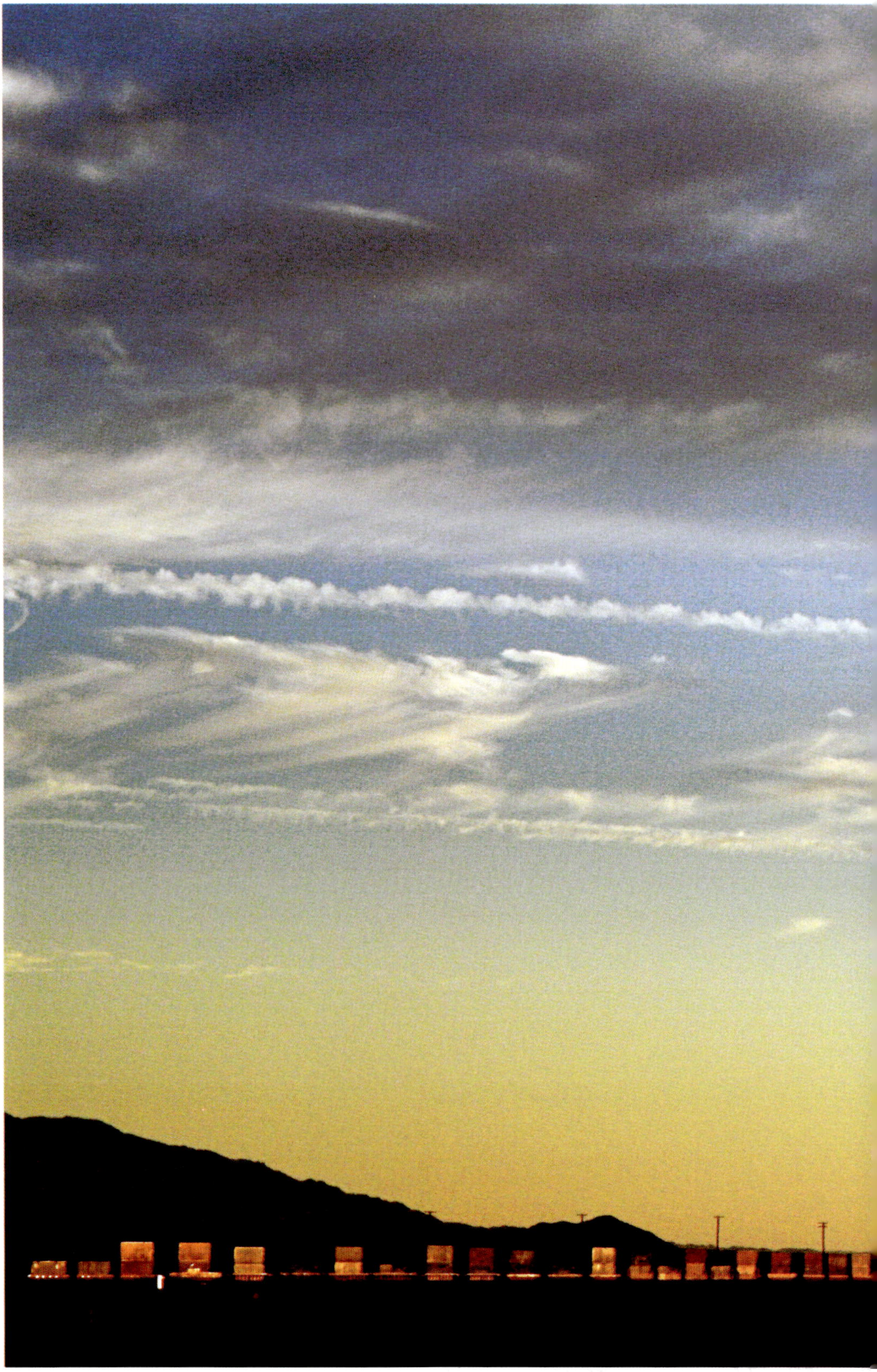

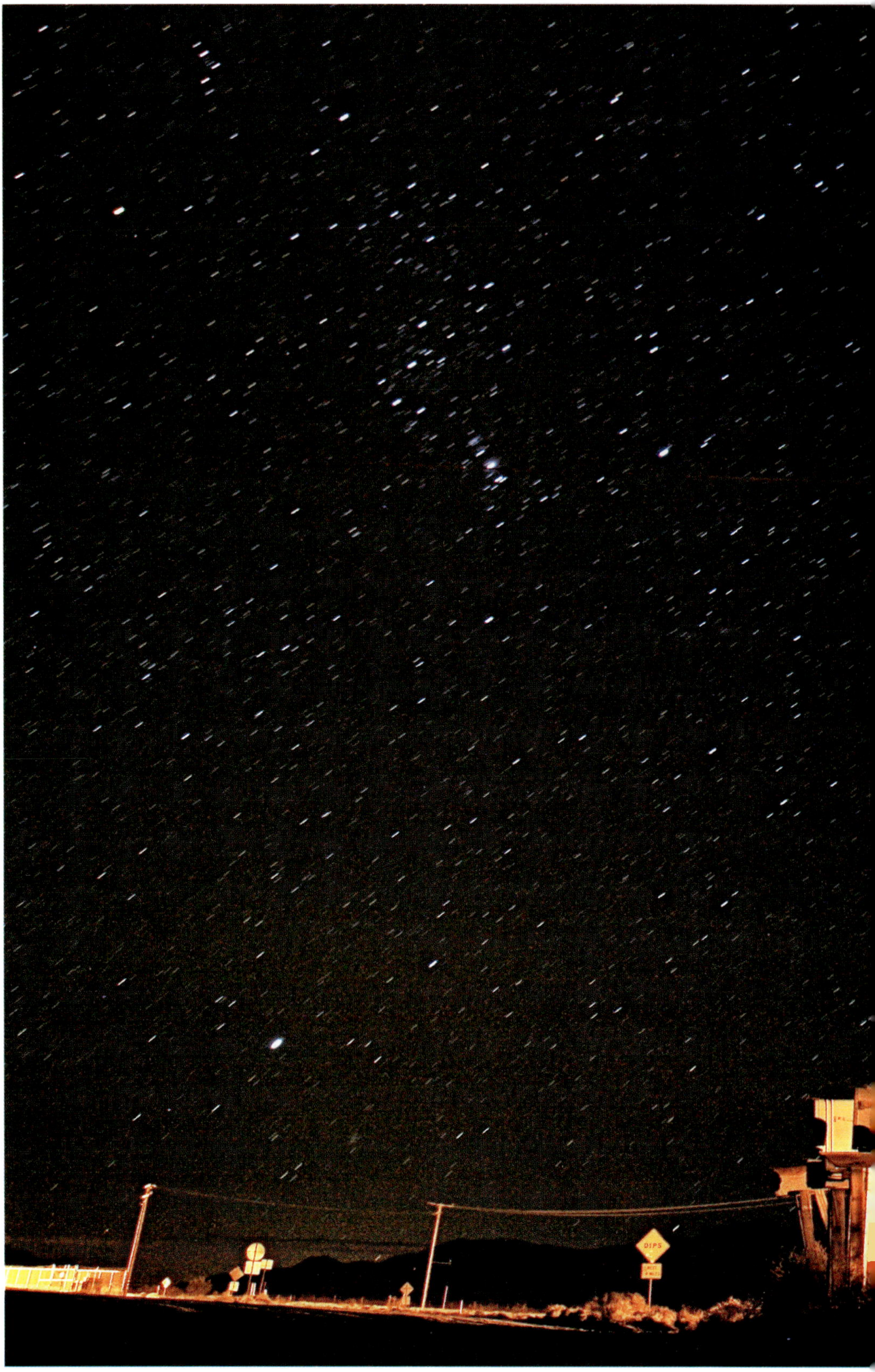
DIPS

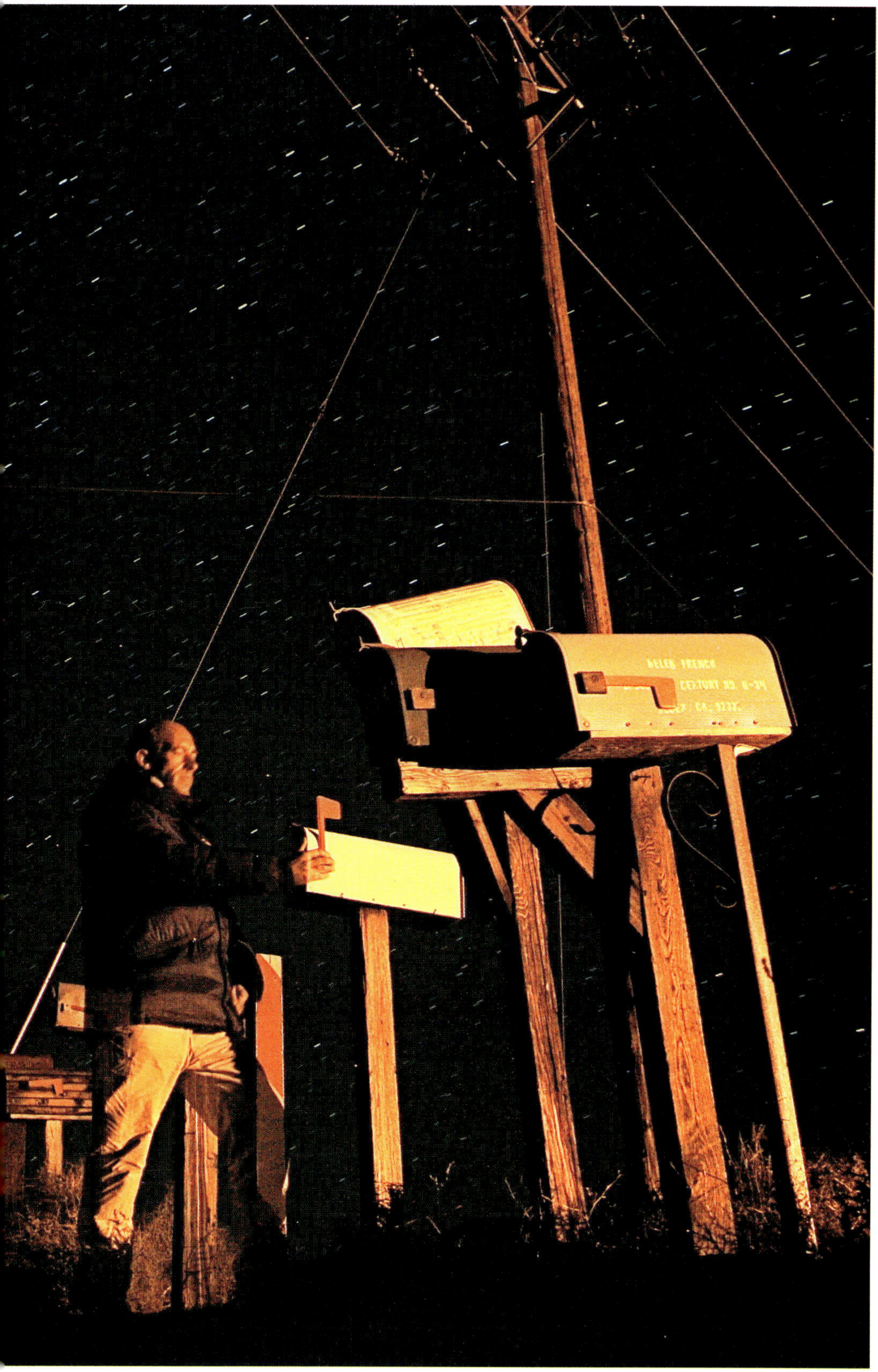
HELEN FRENCH

1. A tent in the desert,
   and a few good reasons for using it:
2. Black widow,
   note the red hourglass on its belly,
3. Tarantula,
4. Sun spider or wind scorpion,
5. Giant hairy scorpion.
6. Look into a scorpion's mouth

Opposite page: *Less harmful critters:*

1. An antelope ground squirrel climbing a barrel cactus to reach for the fruits of a beavertail. It could never climb the beavertail's pads, which contain numerous barbed bristles. The long and thick spines of the barrel, though, form an excellent climbing scaffold   2. Young cottontail rabbit found a safe nest.

3. Greater roadrunner and 4. one of its favorite tidbits, a desert iguana.
5. Wingspan 70". Early in the morning, turkey vultures are often seen standing in a spread-winged stance. As soon as the sun's intensity reaches a certain level, they strike this horaltic pose in order to raise their body temperature, which they lower at night to save energy.

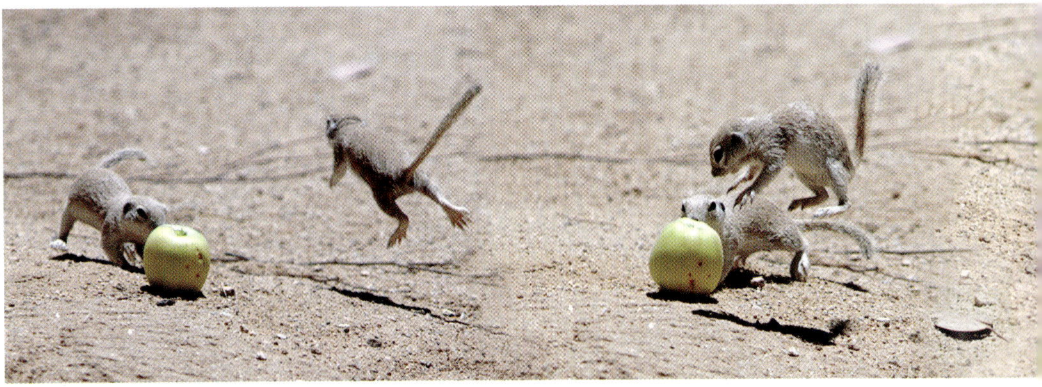

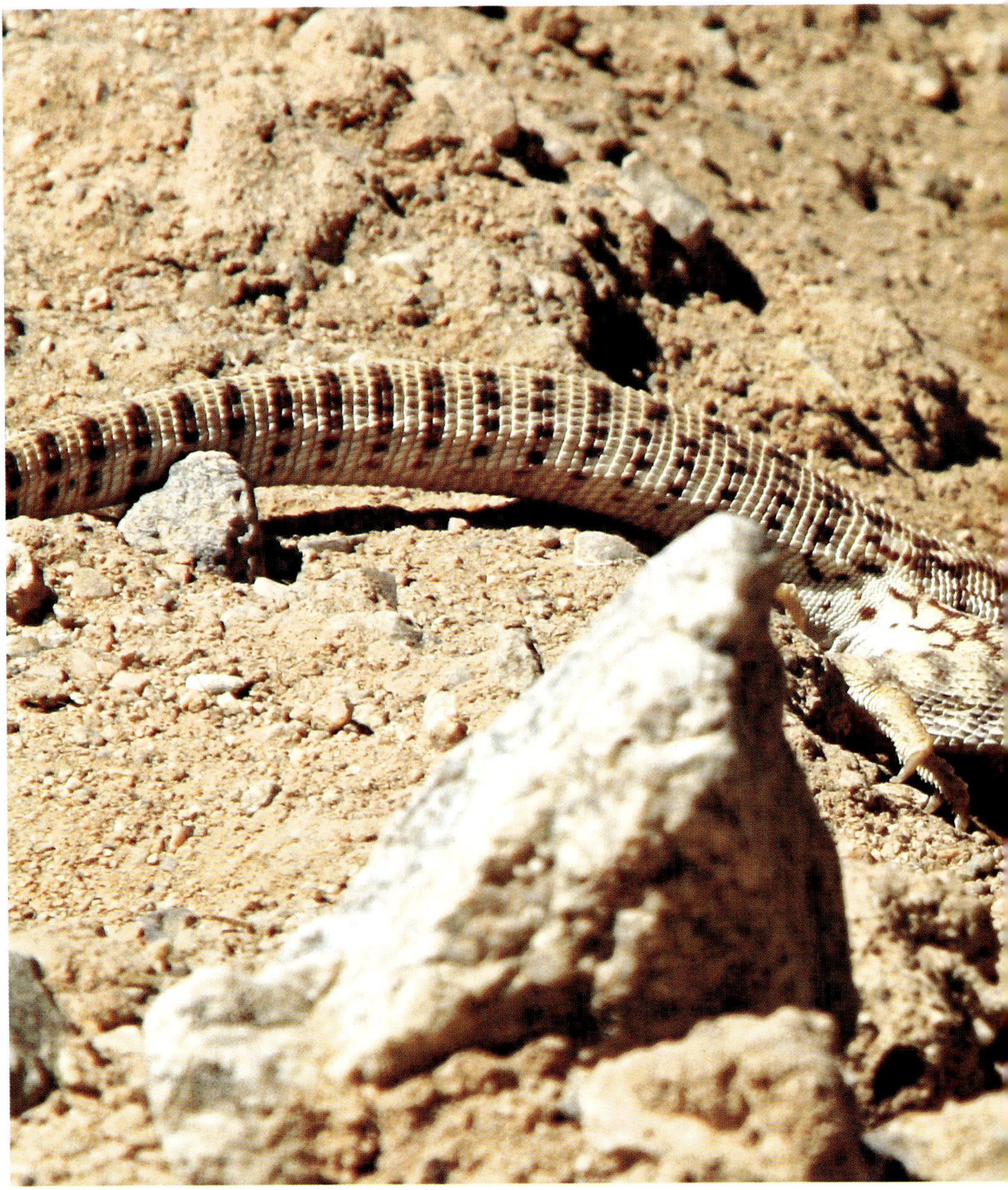

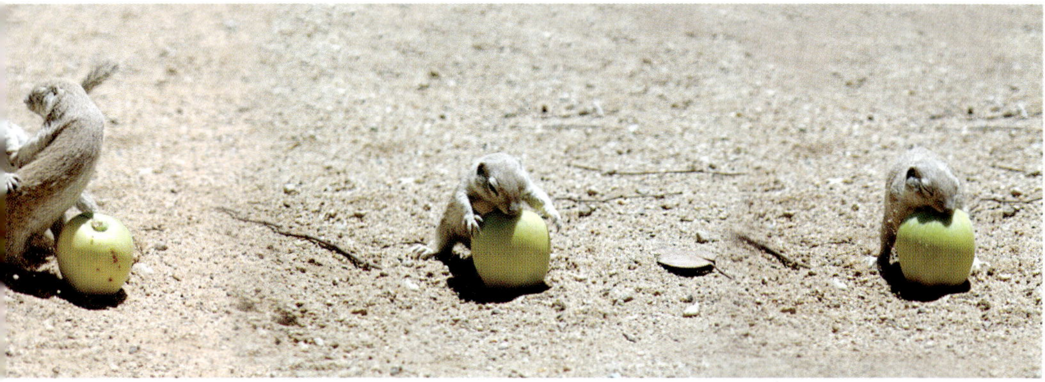

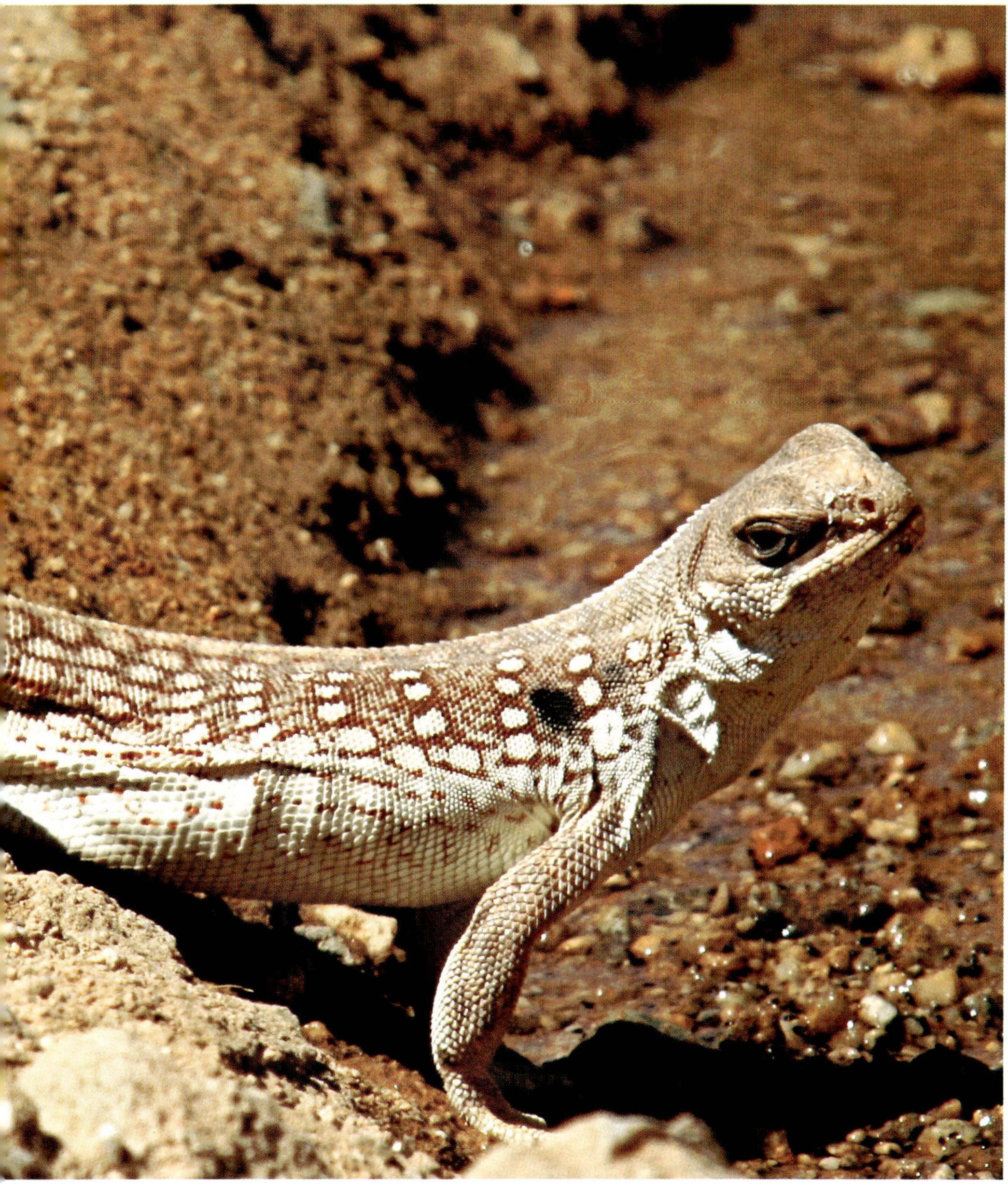

Preceding pages:
1. Series of photos: round-tailed ground squirrels arguing over a rare fruit
2. A desert iguana left its burrow for a drink

1. *Crotalus scutulatus*, the Mojave green rattlesnake. "This snake should be avoided!"
(Photo by Dennis Casebier)
2. Coyote

Desert flora:
1. Desert five-spot
2. Brown-eyed evening primrose
3. Bruneau mariposa lily
4. Desert mariposa lily
5. Desert globemallow or apricot mallow
6. Desert Canterbury bell
7. Two ladybirds on a sunflower
8. The trumpet flowers of the sacred datura grow up to 8" long; aka Devil's trumpet, Jimson weed, thorn apple, moonflower, locoweed or hell's bells - yes, it is poisonous.

1. *"With red-tipped tentacles like a sun-worshipping octopus"*, the ocotillo grows to a height of 30 feet. Though not a member of the cactus family, its stems have a similar texture and come with long spines. It is also known as Jacob's staff, vine cactus, desert coral, or coachwhip.

Desert cacti:

2. Beavertail cactus
3. Engelmann's prickly pear or cow's tongue cactus
4. Buckhorn cholla

Opposite page:
1. Mojave mound cactus
2. Cane cholla
3. Easter lily cactus
4. Hedgehog cactus
5. Plains prickly pear
6. Silver cholla
7. Cottontop cactus
8. Barrel cactus

393

394

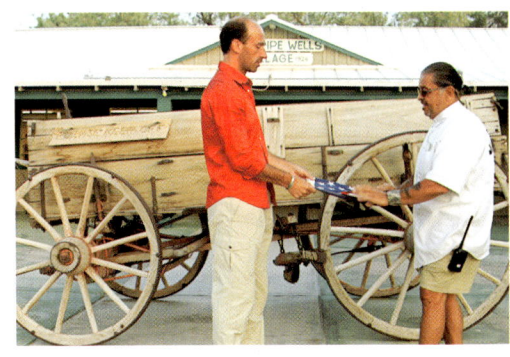

This page:
1. Cottonwood springs in the Panamint Range   2. Chasing me out of my tent, a Northern Mojave rattlesnake   3. Coffee time at Hunter's cabin   4. First sight of the High Sierra from Marble Canyon
5. The ocotillo flowers are a major food source for hummingbirds on their northward migration. Bees and these little birds are the plant's most important pollinators.

Opposite page:
1. The Saratoga Springs; "attending a phenomenal concert by the Saratoga Philharmonic Orchestra, composed for four ducks and one hundred frogs".   2. "Creosote milepost 44"   3. Devil's Golf Course
4. Mesquite Flat Dunes in northern Death Valley   5. Death Valley's varied past comes to light at the eroded badlands of Zabriskie Point.   6. The Flag Ceremony at Stovepipe Wells

1. Soldier Pass, "If only she could speak and tell her story".
2. One of many haunted houses in the desert

1. Friendly reception committee at Deep Springs College   2. "Highest outhouse in the West", the walk along the rim of the White Mountain Range is stuffed with great views.   3. Wondering what would expect me in 300 FT.   4. White Mountain summit 11,246'   5. "A picture out of The NeverEnding Story; had I been able to touch it, I was sure, it would have grown a straight, spiraled horn on its forehead."

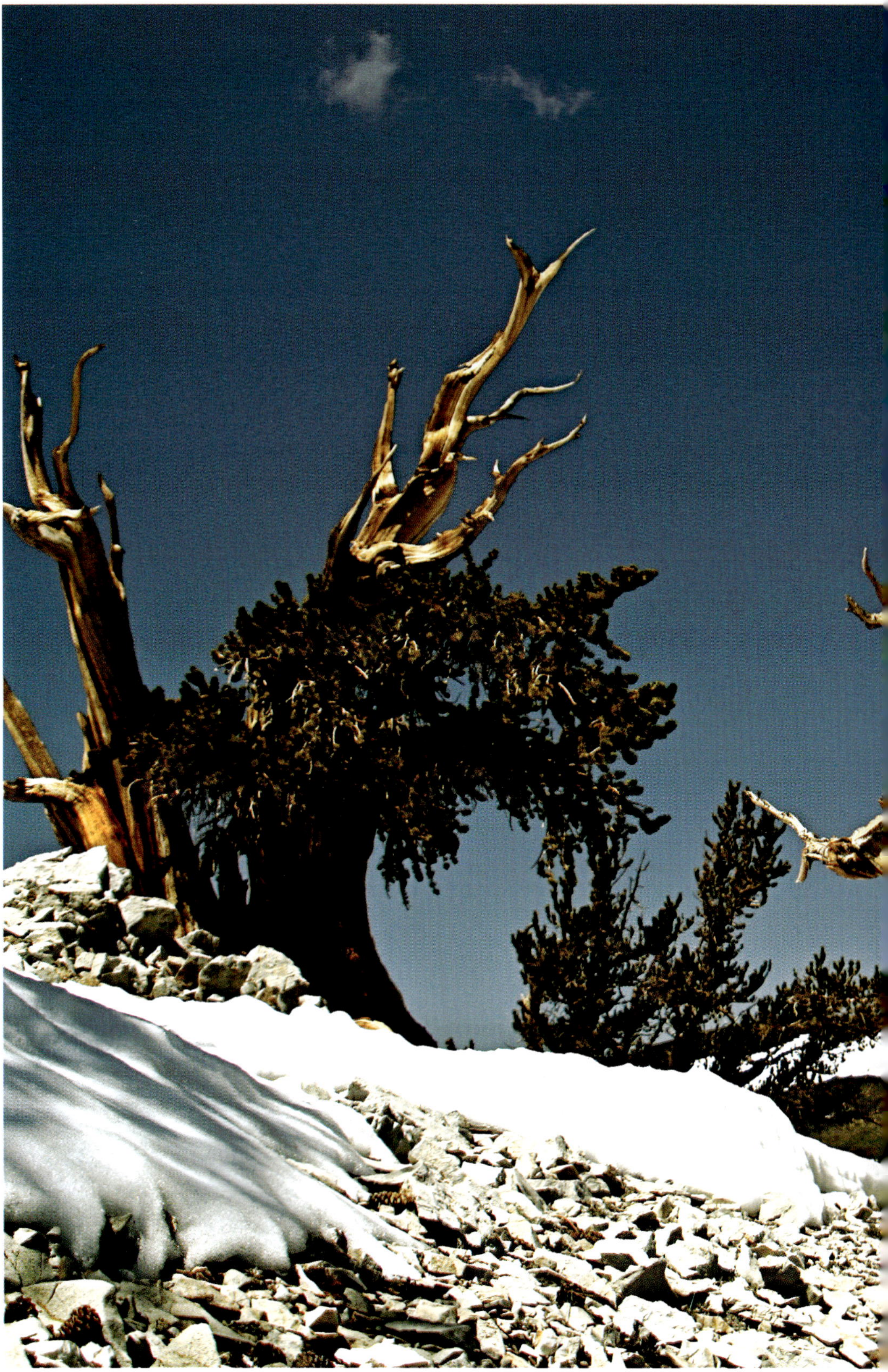

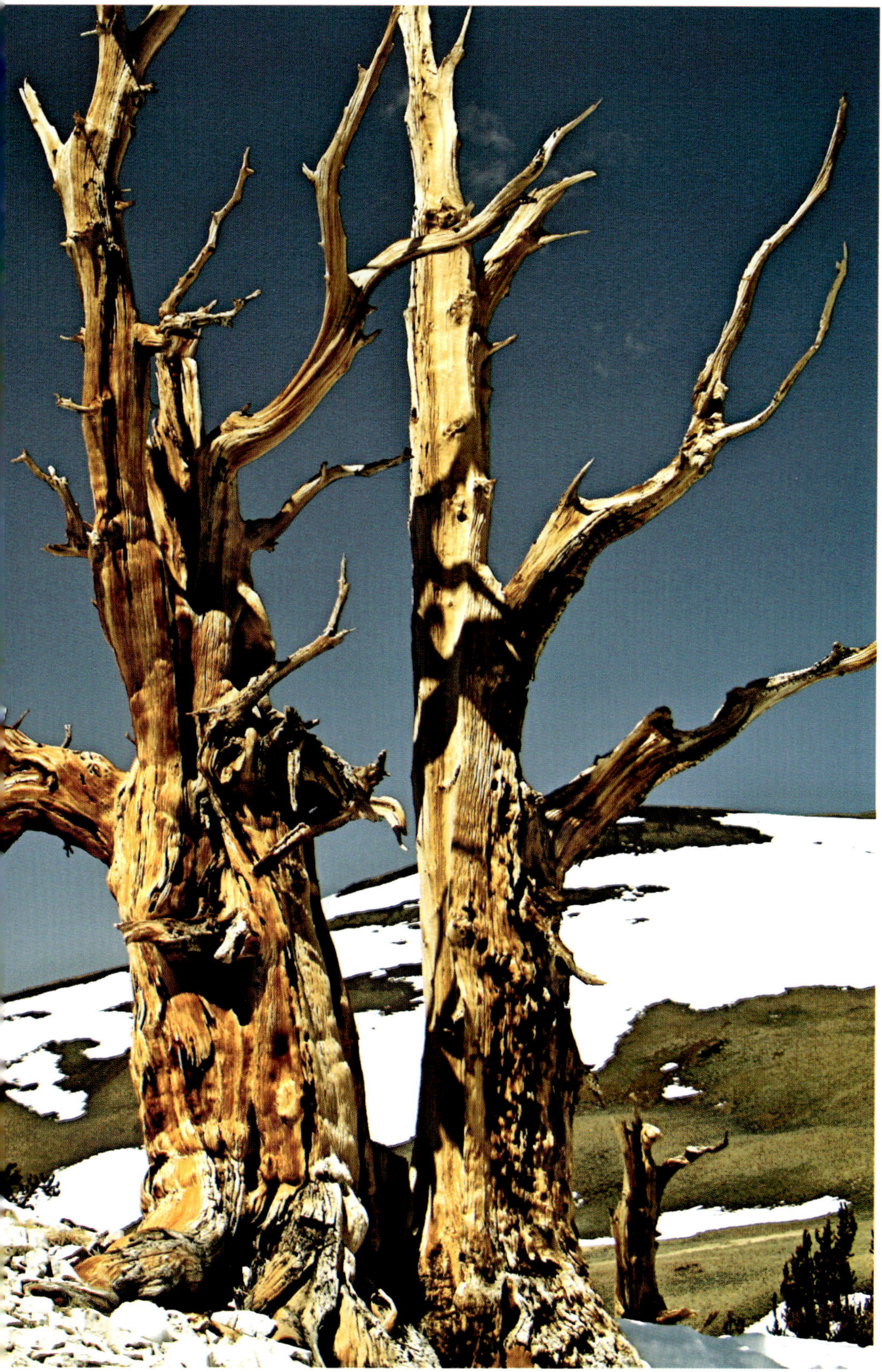

400

Preceding pages:
1. *Ancient Bristlecone Pines in the White Mountains*

Opposite page:
1. *'Death Valley Symphony'* and
2. *'Rainbow Falls' on canvas by Carroll Thomas*

This page:
1. *Carroll Thomas presenting one of his most famous works:*
2. *'Bristlecone Pine' on canvas by Carroll Thomas*

401

1. The Arts of the Heart Gallery, Big Pine. Victorina and Robert
2. White Mountain, seen from the opposing Sierra

1. Entering the Sierra, I was surprised by a late winter revival   2. North Lake   3. Ascending Piute Pass
4. Roaring melt water creeks daunting the most lion-hearted hiker   5. Piute Pass 11,423 ft

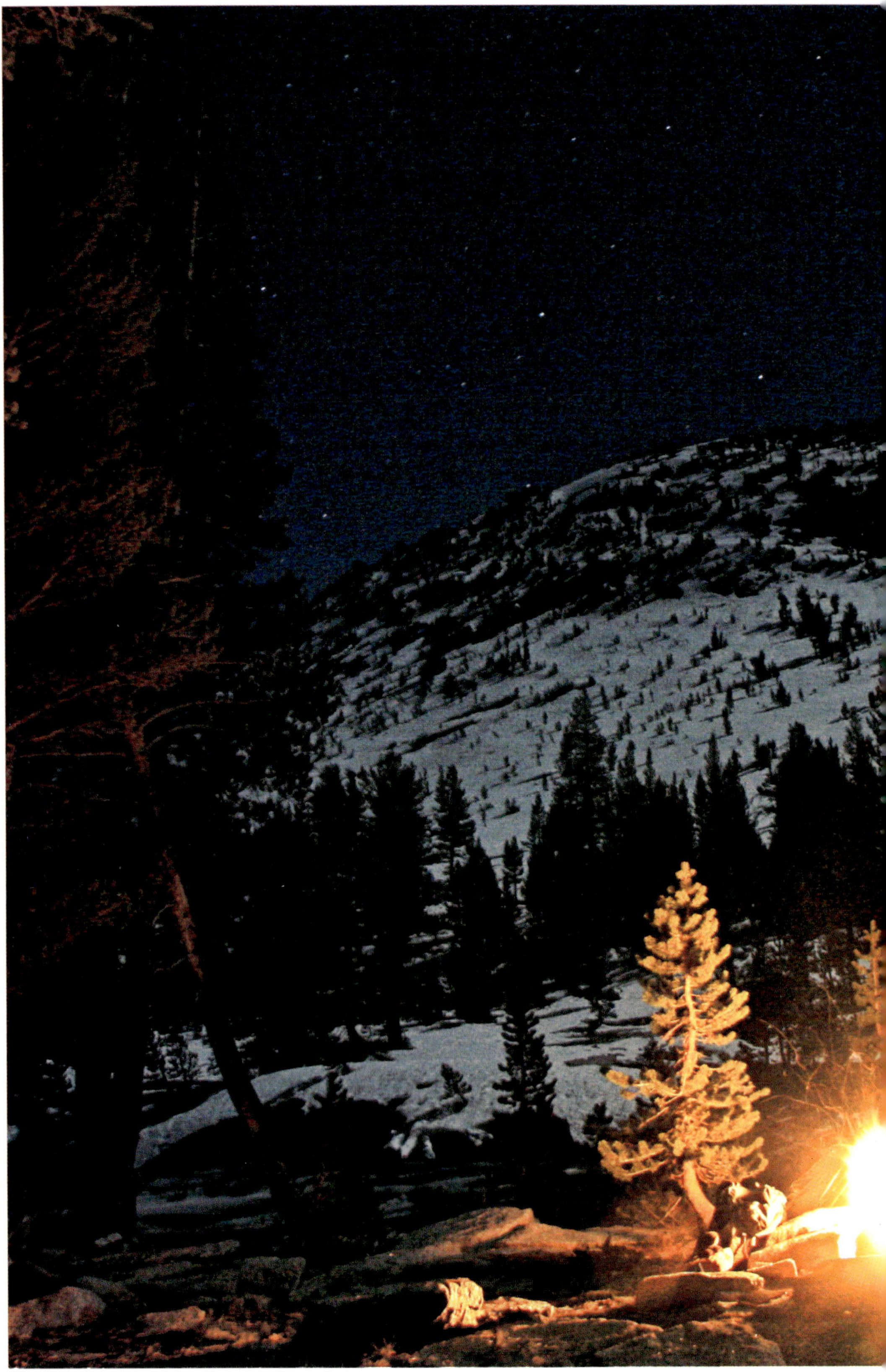

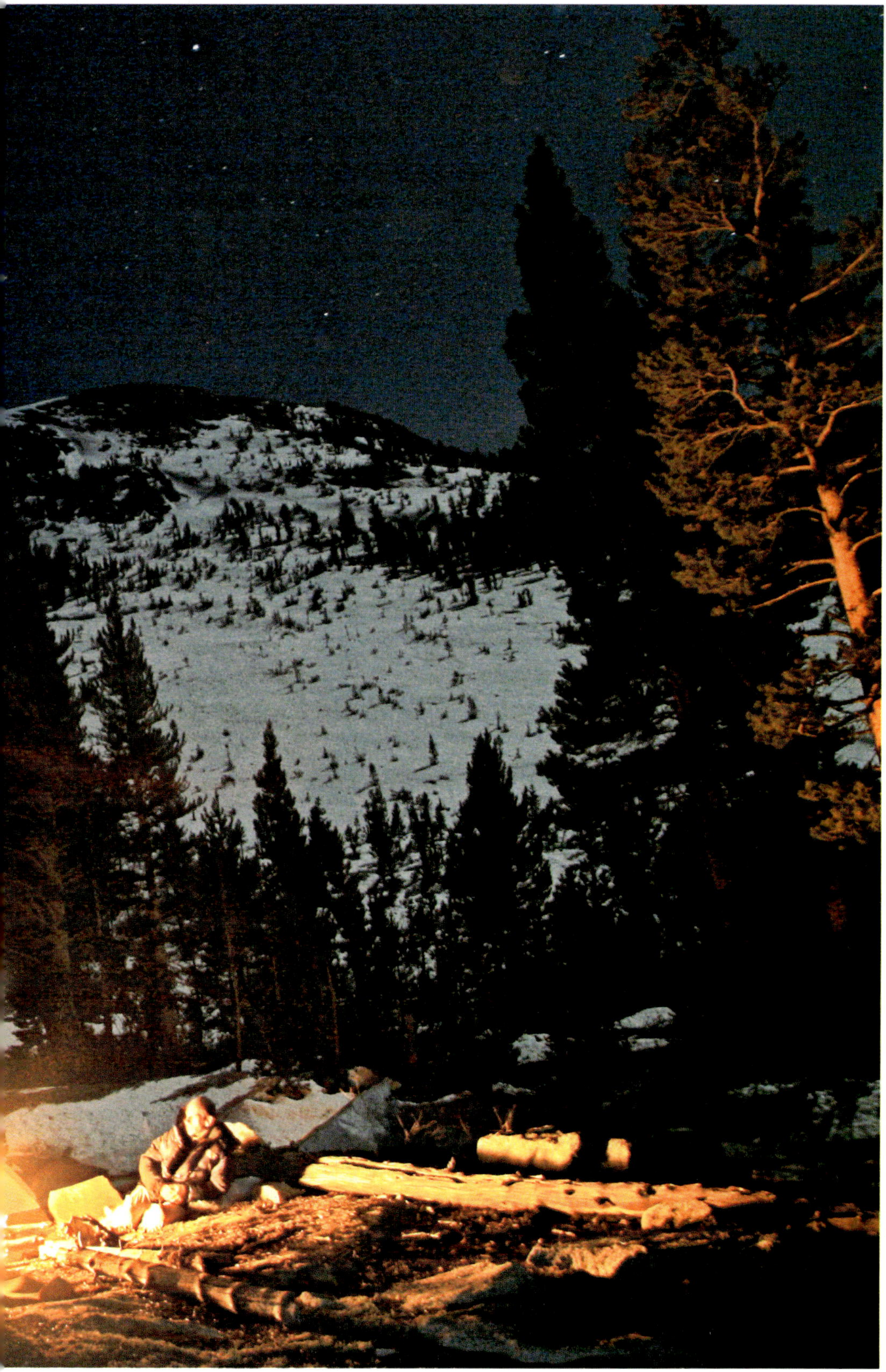

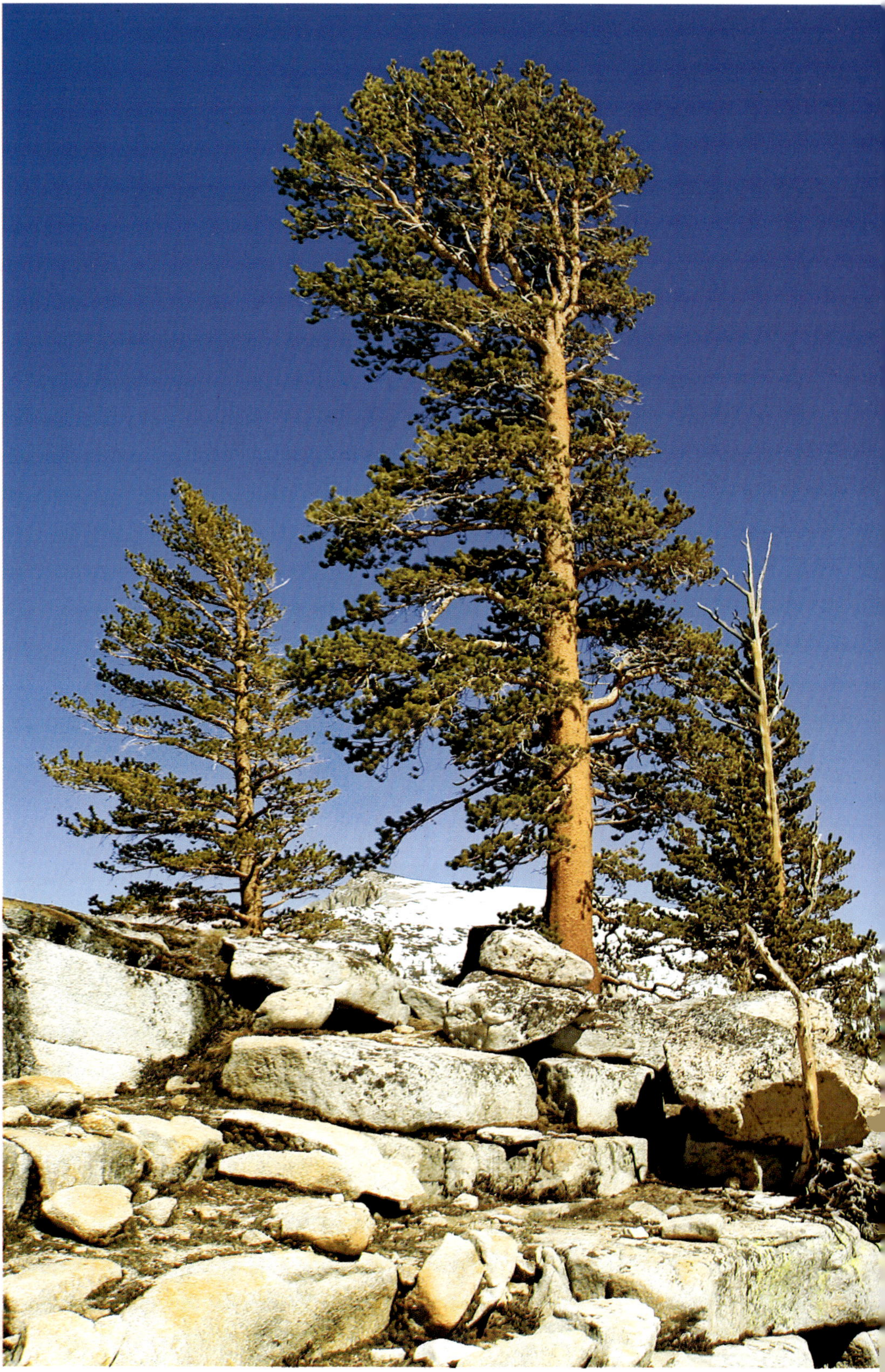

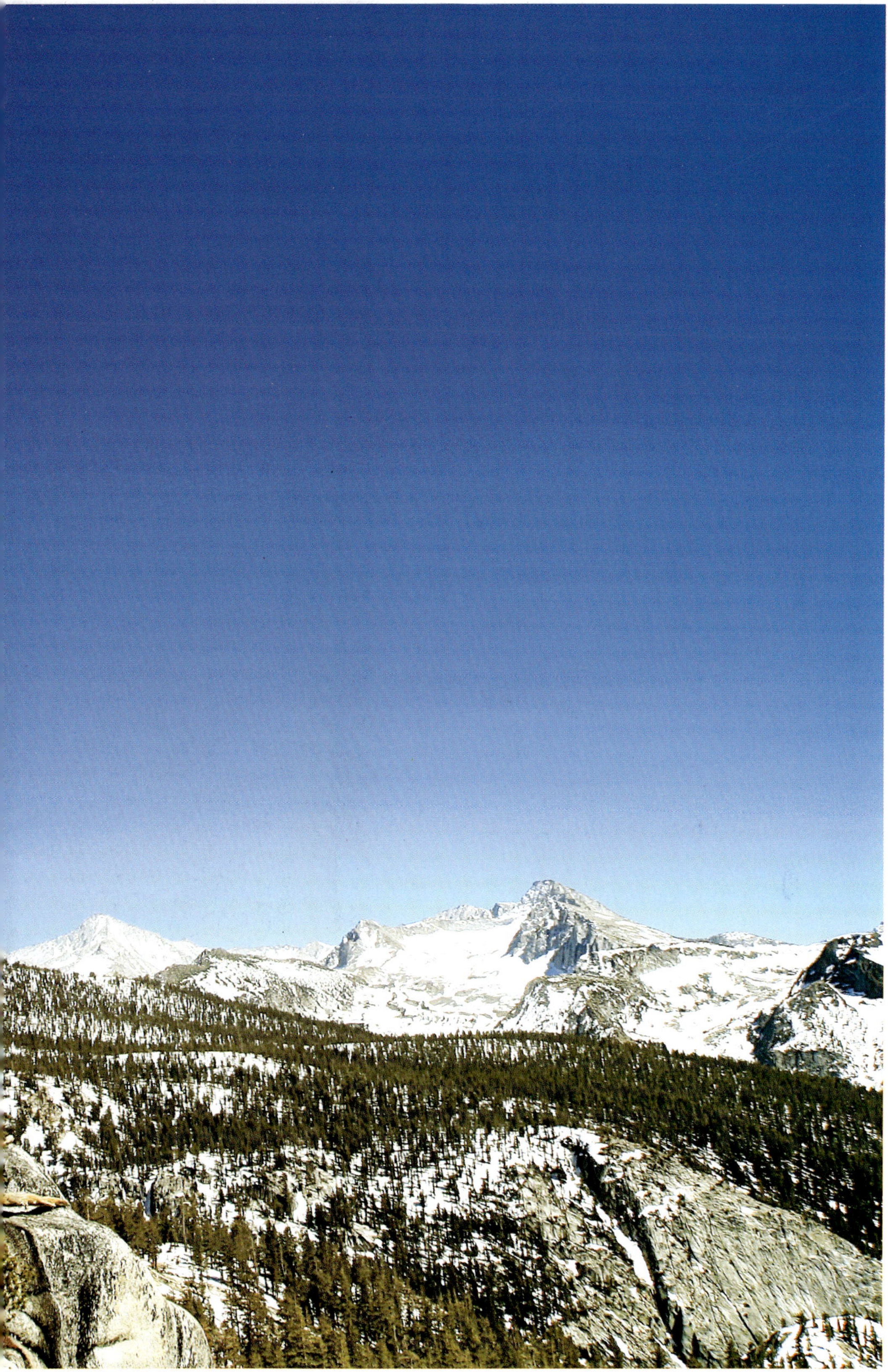

Preceding pages:
Camp at Hutchinson Meadow
Singing trees

This page:
1. *San Joaquin South Fork*
2. *Sallie Keyes Lake*

1. View from Selden Pass 10,860 ft
2. Bear Creek
3. Simply – exhausted.
4. Chief Lake
   below Silver Pass 10,895 ft
5. Grizzly bear at Fish Creek –
   travel companion Klondyke
6. Breakfast at Rainbow Falls
7. Entering Ansel Adams'
   monochrome world

1. Ken Gustavson and campground host – talking fish
2. Inyo Crater
3. Leaving the Sierra behind – entering the Crater Flats
4. Floating on Mono Lake

Opposite page:
Methodist church in Bodie

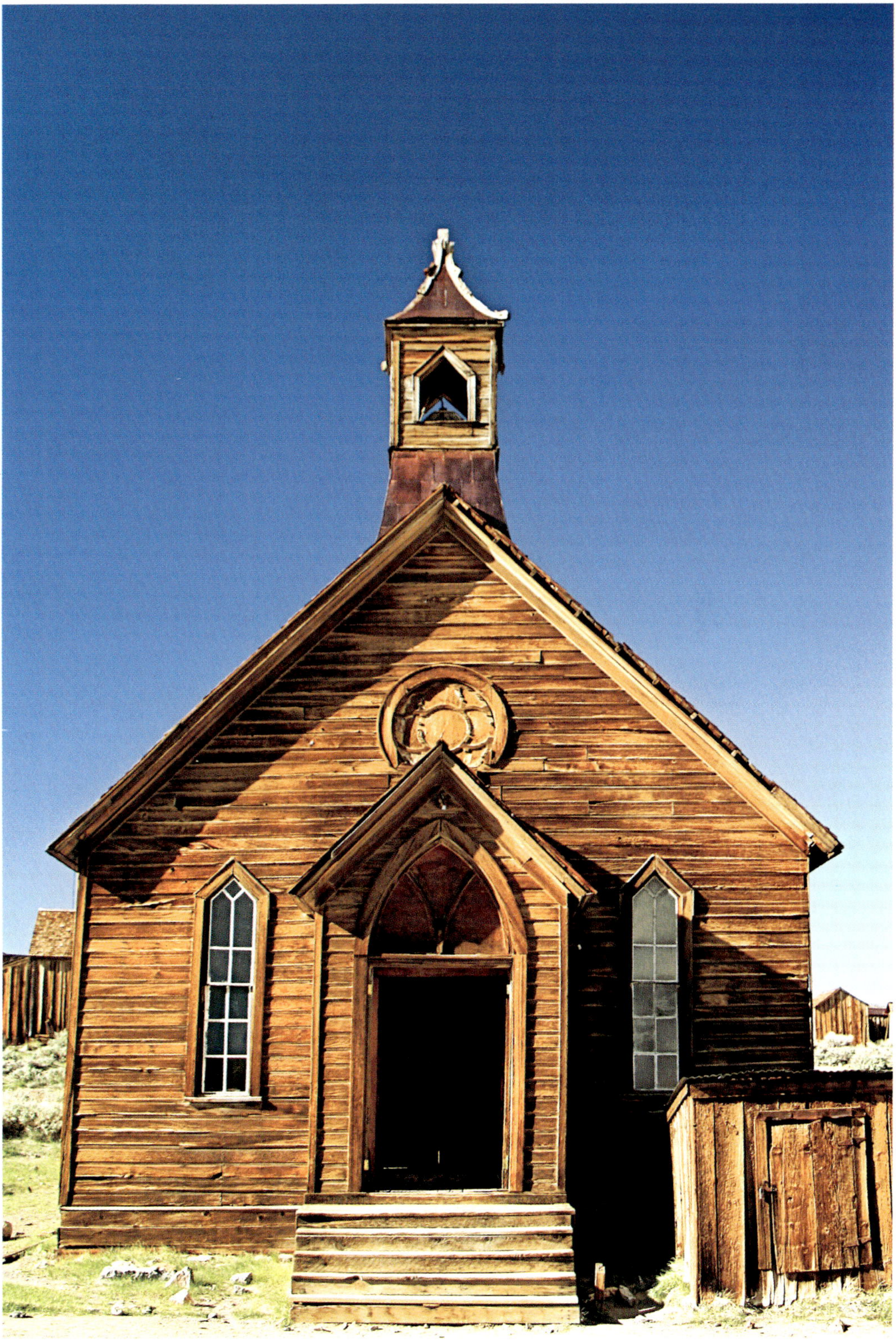

412

Opposite page: *1. Swazey Hotel, Bodie   2. Once upon a time in the West, …   3. … there was a walker …
4. 'Tentrise' over Bridgeport Valley, Buckeye Ridge   5. East Walker River, Big Meadows*

This page: *1. Crossing the 'Big Meadows' – entering the Northern Sierra   2. Grazing cattle along East Walker River   3. Capering at Piute Meadows   4. Lower Piute Meadows   5. West Walker River*

1. *Paintbrush at Leavitt Meadows*
2. *Markleeville, Wolf Creek Restaurant & Bar (left) and J Marklee Toll Station (right)*

1. *"Who, me?"*   2. *Carson River*   3. *Emerald Bay and Fanette Island, Lake Tahoe*
4. *Chefs Randy and Emma preparing dinner*   5. *Pier at Tahoe City*

1. *The good soul of the trail; Billy Goat knows where the bear shits in the buckwheats.*
2. *Donner Lake, view from Donner Pass*   3. *The 'Wild Bunch' of Truckee, Lucius and Scott and four brothers Dan, Jim, Mike, and Bill*   4. *Firefighters in Tahoe National Forest*   5. *Farmhouse in Sierra Valley*

1. Flying Diamond J rancher and his protégés; Last Chance Creek
2. The land of many ranches, Madeline Plains   3. Cedar Creek, water temperature 80 F
4. Wildflowers in the Warner Mts., mule's ears and lupines   5. Climbing the summit range

Mountain flora:
1. Freckled milkvetch
2. No one knew this little beauty's name, I called it Dancing Ballerina
3. Baby blue eyes or wild geranium
4. California poppy

Opposite page:
1. Snow plant forest
2. Brown's or wild peony
3. Crimson Columbine
4. Pussy paws

419

1. Warner Mountains Rim Trail,
   Greeting a friendly cedar
2. Photo session with my travel companion;
   Highgrade Mining district,
   near Klondike Mines
3. Inside the gold mine,
   exploring an old shaft
   with geologist David Hembree

Opposite page: *Equipment for 1,000 miles*
Next page: *Surprise Valley, Nevada horizon*

YETI: *VIB 800*

Osprey Packs: *Aether 85*

Wechsel Tents: *Pathfinder*

Meindl: *Borneo MFS*

Mountain Hardwear: *Sub Zero Parka*

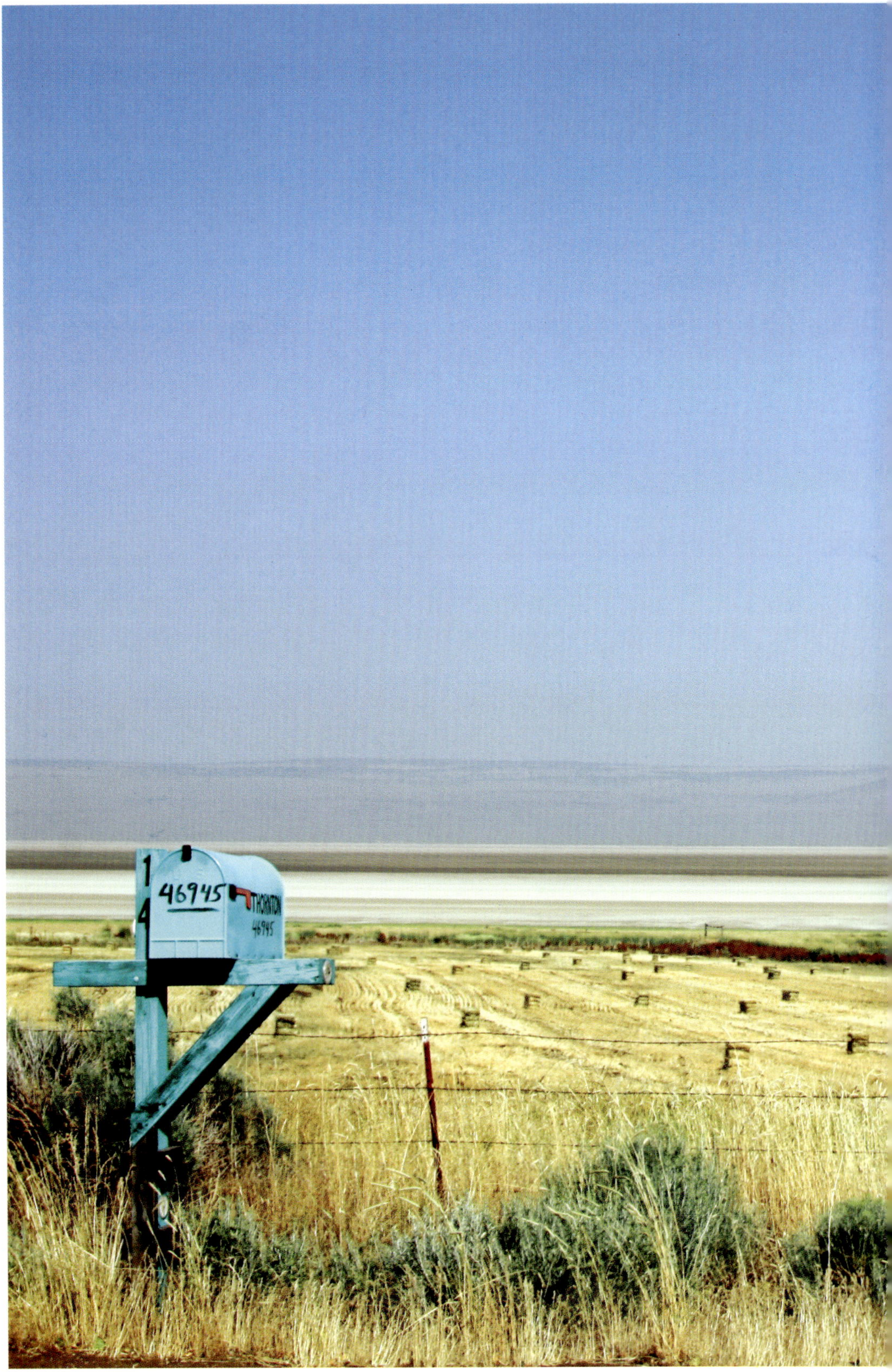
14
46945
THORNTON
46945

The Walker, Acrylic on paper by Sergej